James Robinson Graves is an impressive and important treatment of the life, thought, and seemingly nonstop activities of one of the most controversial Baptist leaders of all time. Not only is this first-rate volume a valuable analysis of J. R. Graves, but it is also an informative look at nineteenth-century Baptist life. I congratulate Prof. Patterson on this fine accomplishment.

David S. Dockery
president, Union University

The author's copious, original-source research is evident throughout. James Patterson's lucid and detailed chronicle of J. R. Graves' colorful ecclesiastical contributions to the fabric of formative nineteenth-century Baptist life in the North American South constitutes a rewarding and definitive study by a leading Southern Baptist historian.

C. Berry Driver
dean of Libraries and associate professor of Systematic Theology
Southwestern Baptist Theological Seminary

J. R. Graves continues to cast a long and often controversial shadow over Southern Baptist history. Graves was an influential denominational editor, a Baptist institution-builder, a gifted debater, a widely read author, a tireless provocateur, and most importantly, the key popularizer of Landmark theology in the SBC. He was also arguably one of the half dozen most important Southern Baptists in the denomination's first century of history. Though numerous dissertations and essays have been devoted to Graves, before now no one has attempted a scholarly biography of the Landmark patriarch. How fortunate we are that Jim Patterson has finally gone where angels fear to tread. Patterson is a respected historian and devoted Baptist churchman who teaches at an institution greatly shaped by Graves during the nineteenth century. Patterson's biography is critical but even-handed—a welcomed contribution to the fields of Baptist studies and Southern religious history. Scholars interested in studying Graves, Landmarkism, or the early years of Southern Baptist history will do well to begin with this fine biography.

Nathan A. Finn
associate professor of Historical Theology and Baptist Studies
Southeastern Baptist Theological Seminary

D1104191

Jim Patterson is one of our ablest historians, and he has given us a superb biography of the indomitable J. R. Graves, the South's most influential Baptist in the nineteenth century. The legacy of Graves still lingers on in various ways and this is presented here with nuance and critical appreciation. A great read!

Timothy George
founding dean, Beeson Divinity School
general editor, the Reformation Commentary on Scripture

J. R. Graves's lingering influence on Southern Baptist life is indisputable, but he has remained largely inaccessible until now. James Patterson's biography offers considerable insight and clarity on one of nineteenth-century America's most colorful and controversial ministers.

Keith Harper
professor of Church History
Southeastern Baptist Theological Seminary

Here is Baptist history at its best. Jim Patterson's clear, careful, even-handed, and masterful portrait of J. R. Graves reveals not only much insight into the person, context, culture, and ideology of Graves, but also church life, theology, missions, and relations among denominations. Historians and theologians will esteem its precision; pastors and church leaders will welcome its relevance.

Christopher W. Morgan,
dean and professor of Theology
California Baptist University

James R. Graves was perhaps the most influential, and certainly the most controversial, individual in Baptist history in America. Patterson offers the most thorough examination of Graves to date, and does so with balanced historical judgment. He explains convincingly that Graves, the man with the sharpest elbows in the denomination, attained his extensive and enduring popularity by constructing his Landmark version of Baptist identity as a combination of mainstream Baptist ideas and the American political principles of individualism and freedom. Based on painstaking research, this important book books fills an extraordinary hole in Baptist scholarship.

Gregory A. Wills
professor of Church History
Southern Baptist Theological Seminary

James Robinson Graves

STAKING THE BOUNDARIES OF BAPTIST IDENTITY

James Robinson Graves

STAKING THE BOUNDARIES OF BAPTIST IDENTITY

BY

JAMES A. PATTERSON

STUDIES IN BAPTIST LIFE AND THOUGHT

MICHAEL A. G. HAYKIN, SERIES EDITOR

ACADEMIC

NASHVILLE, TENNESSEE

ISBN: 978-1-4336-7166-1

Published by B&H Publishing Group
Nashville, Tennessee

Dewey Decimal Classification: 286.092
Subject Heading: GRAVES, JAMES ROBINSON \ LANDMARKISM \
BAPTISTS—DOCTRINES

Scripture quotations marked NIV are taken from the *Holy Bible, New International Version*, copyright © 1973, 1978, 1984 by Biblica. Used by permission of Zondervan Bible Publishers.

Printed in the United States of America

1 2 3 4 5 6 7 8 9 10 11 12 • 17 16 15 14 13 12
VP

Dedication

*To my beloved wife, Donna, in honor of our
40th wedding anniversary (1971–2011)*

Contents

List of Abbreviations

ABA	American Baptist Association
ABSC	Arkansas Baptist State Convention
BFM	Baptist Faith and Message
BGCT	Baptist General Convention of Texas
BMAA	Baptist Missionary Association of America
FBC	First Baptist Church (Nashville and Memphis)
FMB	Foreign Mission Board
GCR	Great Commission Resurgence
HMB	Home Mission Board
IMB	International Mission Board
NABA	North American Baptist Association
SBC	Southern Baptist Convention
SBHLA	Southern Baptist Historical Library and Archives
SBPS	Southern Baptist Publication Society
SBSSU	Southern Baptist Sunday School Union
SBTS	The Southern Baptist Theological Seminary
SWBTS	Southwestern Baptist Theological Seminary
TBPS	Tennessee Baptist Publication Society

Preface

Autobiography often influences the topics and direction of a scholar's research. In August of 1989 I joined the faculty of Mid-America Baptist Theological Seminary, which was then in midtown Memphis, Tennessee, and participated in the annual Founders' Day services that launched each new academic year. One of the speakers at the second evening session abruptly roused my curiosity when he departed from his assigned theme—"The Holy Spirit in Revival"—to offer a litany of rhetorical questions aimed at ridiculing a particular ecclesiological concept. Although I did not take detailed notes, this is a paraphrase of that Southern Baptist preacher's pertinent queries: "Who teaches Sunday school in the universal church? Who are the deacons in the universal church? Who is the pastor of the universal church? When are worship services in the universal church?"

I soon discerned from some colleagues that this series of questions reflected a Landmarkist view of the church that was an integral part of the theological legacy of James Robinson Graves (1820–93). This prominent Southern Baptist journalist, preacher, and controversialist held distinctive ideas about Baptist doctrine and practice that apparently enjoyed enthusiastic support among some of the Mid-America Seminary constituency. My 30 years in the Northeast and 12 years in Georgia, however, had failed to give me an adequate context for immediately understanding what I heard on that humid summer evening in West Tennessee. Earlier in Toccoa, Georgia, I occasionally passed a small independent church whose sign identified it as "Landmark Baptist," but I never investigated what that name meant. In addition, a deacon at First Baptist Church in Toccoa gave me a 1956 printing of English Baptist historian G. H. Orchard's *Concise History of Baptists from the Time of Christ Their Founder to the 18th Century*, which included an introductory essay by Graves.[1] The deacon said he wanted me to have it, but he did not indicate whether he agreed with the book and never followed up with me to see if I had read it. Besides, I did little with the Orchard volume before moving to

---

[1] G. H. Orchard, *A Concise History of Baptists from the Time of Christ Their Founder to the 18th Century* (Lexington, KY: Ashland Avenue Baptist Church, 1956). This book was originally published as *A Concise History of Foreign Baptists* (London: George Wightman, 1838). The essay by Graves appeared in the 13th edition (Nashville: Graves & Marks, 1855).

Memphis, when I discovered that successionist history was also part of the Landmark heritage. I eventually detected evidence of residual successionism in the sporadic avowals from some mid-South pulpits that Baptists were not Protestants because they had never been part of the Roman Catholic Church.

Through many years of teaching Baptist history at both Mid-America Baptist Theological Seminary and Union University, I came to a fuller appreciation of the significant, albeit disputed, role that the Landmark tradition played in shaping Southern Baptist life and thought. In fact, at Union's Founders' Day chapel in 2001, I discovered just how much the university had been permeated by Landmarkism in the nineteenth century. Timothy George, church historian and dean at Beeson Divinity School, regaled his audience on that occasion with interesting vignettes about Landmarkers like Graves, J. M. Pendleton, T. T. Eaton, and T. P. Crawford, all of whom had close ties to Union University.[2] Then, in the process of preparing my first article on Graves, I learned more details about his service to Union University as trustee chair (1885–92), utilized the special Graves Collection in the Union library, and came across information about a room on the old campus that he funded for the J. R. Graves Society for Religious Inquiry. From a prior naiveté about Landmarkism, my career clearly has taken me to places where I have encountered both the lingering vestiges and historical memories of a once potent, if regional, movement.

While I have found as much to differ with as to endorse in Graves's theology and practices, I am inclined to affirm Baptist historian Walter Shurden's assessment in 1972 that the venerable Landmarker "may well have had more lasting influence on Southern Baptists than any other single individual in our 125 year history."[3] The mere quantity and scope of Graves's words found in periodicals, books, and sermons challenge the resolve of even the most ambitious researcher who dares to read them all. J. R. Graves was easily one of the most dominant, energetic, and polemical personalities in nineteenth-century Baptist life.

---

[2] T. George, "The Legacy of Landmarkism and Union University." See a report by S. Horn, "Union Dedicates History Book; Traces Roots," *Baptist & Reflector*, February 21, 2001, 4. At the same chapel service, President David S. Dockery dedicated the 175-year history of Union. See J. A. Baggett, *So Great a Cloud of Witnesses: Union University 1823–2000* (Jackson, TN: Union University Press, 2000). This volume explains the sometimes complicated history of Union in the nineteenth century, including the several feeder institutions (e.g., Union University in Murfreesboro, Tennessee, where Graves was first involved as a supporter and trustee).
[3] W. B. Shurden, *Not a Silent People: Controversies That Have Shaped Southern Baptists* (Nashville: Broadman, 1972), 24.

Many journal articles, chapters in books, encyclopedia entries, and dissertations from the last several decades testify to a resilient scholarly interest in Graves. All the same, no published volume devoted to Graves has appeared since 1929, when the Landmark patriarch's son-in-law, O. L. Hailey, released a nondescript "biography" of a little over 100 pages.[4] Hence, this current monograph attempts to fill the curious gap between Graves's historical standing among Baptists and the lack of a published study in a book.

One of the obstacles in researching J. R. Graves is the absence of an archival collection or even a set of personal papers. Apart from a few items at the Southern Baptist Historical Library and Archives in Nashville, Tennessee, there are no private diaries, letters, or other types of historical memorabilia that would contribute to a richer biographical portrait. No modern scholar or librarian seems to know what might have happened to such material; given his customary reticence about his private life, Graves himself may have thwarted the preservation of such items. At any rate, many of the events and activities of his first 25 years lack sufficient documentation in accessible sources. This volume, then, should not be read as a traditional biography; instead, it is weighted more toward Graves's thought than his life. Nonetheless, the Landmarker's ideas cannot be fully grasped apart from the historical settings and conflicts that helped to shape them. Graves, moreover, acquired a reputation among his contemporaries more as a religious periodical editor than as a systematic theologian. Thus the book seeks to blend biographical insight with a more thematic approach that focuses principally on his controversial beliefs about ecclesiology, Baptist history, and eschatology.

Chapters 4 and 5 of this volume represent revised and expanded versions of previously published articles. The former originally appeared as "The J. R. Graves Synthesis: American Individualism and Landmarkist Ecclesiology" (*Tennessee Baptist History* 7 [Fall 2005]: 9–18) and is used with the permission of the Tennessee Baptist Historical Society (8072 Sunrise Cir., Nashville, TN). The latter ran as "James Robinson Graves: History in the Service of Ecclesiology" (*Baptist History & Heritage* 44 [Winter 2009]: 72–83) and is used with the permission of the Baptist History and Heritage Society (3001 Mercer University Dr., Atlanta, GA). The consent of these journals' respective

---

[4] O. L. Hailey, *J. R. Graves: Life, Times and Teachings* (Nashville: by the author, 1929). Hailey's book betrayed a heavy dependence on S. H. Ford's 12 articles, "Life, Times and Teachings of J. R. Graves," *Ford's Christian Repository and Home Circle*, October 1899, 606–16; November 1899, 670–79; December 1899, 741–49; January 1900, 39–48; February 1900, 100–105; March 1900, 162–69; April 1900, 225–33; May 1900, 287–90; June 1900, 349–55; July 1900, 425–27; August 1900, 487–93; and September 1900, 556–59.

editors, James E. Taulman and Pamela R. Durso, to use these materials here is gratefully acknowledged.

The majority of research for this project was conducted during a faculty research leave in the spring semester of 2008 that was graciously granted to me by the Union University administration and trustees. I especially recognize Dean Gregory Thornbury of the School of Theology and Missions, Provost Carla Sanderson, and President David Dockery for their assistance in making my sabbatical possible. I also thankfully acknowledge professional development funds from the dean and provost that facilitated my travel to other libraries during the research leave, as well as a reduced teaching load during the fall semesters of 2008 and 2010 that added to my writing time.

I am deeply indebted to several librarians for their expert service and cooperation. Steve Baker, former director of the Emma Waters Summar Library at Union University, went out of his way to ensure my ready access to Graves's books in special collections and to the microfilm collection of Graves's newspaper, the *Tennessee Baptist*. Paul Sorrell, Creative Projects coordinator, expeditiously arranged for interlibrary loan material and also assisted with microfilm retrieval. Ian Crawford, a former Union University student, assisted with some of the early research that went into the *Tennessee Baptist History* article.

Nashville, an important venue for J. R. Graves's early career, proved to be indispensable for my research. I deeply appreciate the good work of Director Bill Sumners and his staff at the Southern Baptist Historical Library and Archives. Three separate visits during my sabbatical only increased my respect for this valuable collection. I am also thankful for the SBHLA's award of a Lynn E. May Jr. Study Grant, which helped to defray some of the costs of my trips to Nashville. During one of my stays in the Tennessee capital, I spent an afternoon in the Lila D. Bunch Library at Belmont University, where Reference Librarian Judy Williams kindly arranged for me to use materials from the Tennessee Baptist Collection, which is now housed at the Tennessee Baptist Convention headquarters in Brentwood, Tennessee. I also benefited from telephone conversations with Harold Smith and Albert Wardin in the Nashville area.

Additionally, I profited from my time at two seminary libraries. First, Archives and Special Collections Librarian Jason Fowler and his assistant, Chris DeWease, aided my archival research in the T. T. Eaton Papers at the James P. Boyce Centennial Library of the Southern Baptist Theological Seminary in Louisville, Kentucky. Second, Dean of Libraries Berry Driver and his staff at the A. Webb Roberts Library of Southwestern Baptist Theological Seminary in Fort Worth, Texas, rendered invaluable assistance during my visit there. They quickly retrieved items that I needed and set me up in a special area where I could peruse hard copies of the *Tennessee Baptist* (which had been given to the seminary by O. L. Hailey). Dr. Driver and his wife Kathy also cordially provided hospitality in their home during my week in Fort Worth.

I am so grateful to the editors and staff at B&H Academic in Nashville. In particular, Jim Baird, Chris Cowan, and Dean Richardson provided stellar support as they expedited the publishing process.

Finally, I owe my wife Donna a profound debt of gratitude for her love, support, and encouragement, even as she experienced the death of her father during the early days of my research leave. She was able to accompany me on a trip to Louisville and on my third trip to Nashville. Her patience through this entire project has been commendable.

Soli Deo Gloria.

James A. Patterson
Jackson, Tennessee

Introduction

I n 1974 the civil parish of Cholesbury-cum-St. Leonards in Buckinghamshire, England, revived a curious, ancient ceremony known as the "Beating of the Bounds." In a celebratory mood, people of the parish proceeded around its outer limits and stopped at various markers such as trees, walls, roads, or hedges. At each boundary indicator, they performed a little ritual and then beat it with sticks. These observances vividly reminded the residents of the geographical extent of the parish. In addition, they helped to fortify the identity of the parish and perhaps instill a more robust sense of community. Beating events have been repeated in Cholesbury at least three times since 1974, as well as being widely copied across the United Kingdom in both rural areas and urban sites like the Tower of London.[1]

The practice of boundary beating actually traces back to pagan Britain more than 2,000 years ago. First the Celts and later the Romans often incorporated the inspection of boundaries with superstitious ceremonies of blessing for crops or animals. For instance, the Roman god Terminus was the deity assigned to boundaries and landmarks; one Roman festival in his honor included a procession in which participants marched around their fields and then anointed young maidens to ensure the fertility of the land. During the Anglo-Saxon period, ceremonial processions included the tradition of holding young boys upside down and forcefully bumping their heads on boundary stones so that the location of the marker would be better remembered! Later, under Christian influence, boundary marking became associated with the feast of Rogantide, which was in the fifth week after Easter. In a typical medieval parish, the priest directed a colorful procession by chanting biblical texts, praying for the land to be productive, and staking stone crosses at the intersections with other parishes.[2] Ritual, whether pagan or Christian, consequently functioned to help maintain the integrity of historic boundary lines.

While these time-honored rites may seem quaint or even bizarre to the average American living in a bustling city or suburb, they point to the basic human need for

---

[1] "Beating the Cholesbury Bounds," accessed April 14, 2008, http://www.cholesbury.com/beatbounds.htm.

[2] "Beating the Bounds," accessed April 14, 2008, http://www.bbc.co.uk/dna/h2g2/A805871. Cf. "Parish Maps: The Parish Boundary," accessed April 14, 2008, http://www.england-in-particular.info/parishmaps /m–boundary.html.

a sense of place that is delineated by well-defined borders. Moreover, social scientists recognize that the concept of boundary marking transcends the literal drawing of lines between two or more territories. Their theories suggest that boundaries often operate at a metaphorical or symbolic level for individuals, groups, and societies as identity signs that make them unique. Sociologists and social psychologists, therefore, speak of "boundary maintenance" as a necessary and legitimate function of every human group, be it a religious organization, political party, labor union, or civic club. Group cohesion, solidarity, and identity all suffer in the absence of meaningful boundary markers. The late Dean Hoge, former professor of sociology at the Catholic University of America, put it this way in reference to religious groups:

> All religious communities need boundaries. Boundaries show clearly which persons are members and which are not, they define good members, and they strengthen collective identity. They "contain" commitments. . . . Any group without boundaries will find that its members are troubled by questions about how they are different from outsiders and whether the existence of a group really matters.[3]

In other words, appropriate boundaries are an essential component of group life and failure to maintain them might well produce blurred or forgotten memories of group distinctives.

As sociologist Zygmunt Bauman explained in his "us and them" analysis, boundary maintenance commonly surfaces in seasons of conflict when enemies are identified and calls to vigilance are sounded. In perilous times, he contended, boundaries must be precisely drawn and maintained so that the in-group's unity and identity over against the out-group is upheld. At the same time, heretics, renegades, or traitors from within the ranks pose perhaps even greater dangers. Bauman's analysis thus tends to underscore some of the more negative functions of boundary maintenance, particularly when he discussed issues like in-group prejudice and conformity.[4]

---

[3] Dean Hoge, "Who Is a Good Catholic? Boundaries of Catholicism," first draft of a paper, accessed February 4, 2008, http://hirr.hartsem.edu/bookshelf/CathHartford.doc. I was also helped by Hoge, email to author, March 24, 2008. On boundaries and group solidarity, see M. A. Hogg, *The Social Psychology of Group Cohesiveness: From Attraction to Social Identity* (New York: University Press, 1992).

[4] Zygmunt Bauman, *Thinking Sociologically* (Oxford: Blackwell, 1990), 46–47, 58–59. For applications of sociological insights about boundary maintenance by church historians, see M. Kahlos, *Debate and Dialogue: Christian and Pagan Cultures c. 360–430* (Burlington, VT: Ashgate Publishing, 2007); and C. Shepardson, "Defining the Boundaries of Orthodoxy: Eunomius in the Anti-Jewish Polemic of His Cappadocian

Recent studies of conservative Protestantism in modern America bear out the role of conflict in helping to clarify group boundaries. Jon R. Stone, for example, applied boundary theory to twentieth-century evangelicalism and concluded that "the intensity with which boundaries are defended is equal to the intensity of the boundary threat members perceive."[5] In a similar vein, sociologist Christian Smith argued that contemporary evangelicalism actually *"thrives* on distinction, engagement, tension, conflict, and threat. Without these, evangelicalism would lose its identity and purpose and grow languid and aimless." One of his propositions in support of this thesis contends that conflict between groups in a pluralistic setting "typically strengthens in-group identity, solidarity, resources mobilization, and membership retention." One implication of this research is that a religious movement, particularly one that seeks to preserve traditional beliefs, can be simultaneously "embattled and thriving."[6] The findings of Stone and Smith, albeit with a fairly specific focus, nonetheless point to a wider relevance in the analysis of both past and present groups engaged in ecclesiastical or theological clashes.

Indeed, both boundary-beating rituals and boundary-maintenance theories suggest some intriguing applications for interpreting the life and legacy of J. R. Graves. Accordingly, this book portrays him primarily as one who beat the boundaries of Baptist belief and practice in the still essentially frontier culture of the nineteenth-century mid-South. There, where several denominations aggressively competed for adherents in a pluralistic setting, he brazenly staked out the lines that separated Baptists from their rivals. In response to what he perceived as threats to historic Baptist principles, Graves likewise took on those in the Baptist fellowship who—from his standpoint—had muddled the boundaries or conceded too much ground to the enemy troops. Since warfare is often over territory, Graves could also be depicted as a military officer ready for battle, rallying his troops to keep the borders intact and hence safeguard Baptist identity. For that reason, Southern Baptist historian W. W. Barnes referred to the Landmark leader as a "warrior."[7]

Opponents," *Church History: Studies in Christianity and Culture* 76 (December 2007): 699–723. In current mission debates, advocates of traditional apologetics ministries defend the validity of boundary maintenance against "emerging church" enthusiasts, who are generally less confrontational. See "Boundary Maintenance!" accessed June 3, 2008, http://midwestoutreach.org/blogs/72/boundary–maintenance.

[5] Jon R. Stone, *On the Boundaries of American Evangelicalism: The Postwar Evangelical Coalition* (New York: St. Martin's, 1997), 48.

[6] See Christian Smith, *American Evangelicalism: Embattled and Thriving* (Chicago: University of Chicago Press, 1998), 89, 113. The use of italics in the first quotation is Smith's.

[7] W. W. Barnes, *The Southern Baptist Convention, 1845–1953* (Nashville: Broadman, 1954), 103.

Ultimately, Graves revealed his concern for boundaries in the very name of his movement as he urged faithful Baptists to defend the "ancient landmarks," a term that originally denoted the stone markers in Old Testament times. What is more, he did not hesitate to extend that analogy when describing his mission. In a conversation with J. J. Burnett—who was then serving as a supply pastor in Memphis while on a break from seminary—Graves referred to a "Jacob staff" as one of his tools. He then offered the younger minister pointers on "theological surveying, running boundary and divisional lines, giving metes and bounds, establishing corners, setting up landmarks, etc., that in future generations no 'true Israelite might ever lose his inheritance.'"[8] Although Graves did not know the boundary maintenance jargon used by social scientists today, he did seem keenly conscious that he was marking and guarding borders for his beloved Baptist flock. He may even have understood the benefits of conflict for the success of his Landmark movement.

While Graves certainly was a complex individual whose interests and endeavors ranged widely, boundary setting may well represent his most significant contribution to Baptist life and thought. In this role, he vigorously strove to define core Baptist doctrines and practices that he tracked to the first-century church. Mere definition, however, was not enough for proper boundary maintenance. Authentic Baptists, according to Graves, also needed to be alert to beliefs and traditions that fell outside of their boundaries. Only then could they effectively defend themselves against challenges to or assaults on their borders.

Graves apparently sensed a pressing need for the Baptists of his time to have secure boundaries. He genuinely believed that this task of defending the Baptist cause was necessary and that he had staked the correct markers for belief and practice. Furthermore, he understood that weak or confused boundaries would eventually erode any meaningful denominational identity. In light of both a theological and sociological rationale for boundary maintenance, Graves can hardly be faulted for engaging in it. As this volume seeks to demonstrate, he can be criticized for the choice of boundaries that he chose to establish and the murky historical memories on which he constructed his somewhat idiosyncratic version of Baptist identity.

The elucidation of Graves as a boundary setter is offered in part to offset some of the more egregious interpretations of him in modern scholarship. The late James Tull,

---

[8] J. J. Burnett, "J. R. Graves," in *Tennessee's Pioneer Baptist Preachers* (Nashville: Marshall & Bruce Company, 1919), 196. For the "landmarks" passages, see Job 24:2; Prov. 22:28; 23:10 (KJV). On the importance of boundary marking in the ancient world, see J. F. Drinkard Jr., "Boundary Markers," *Biblical Illustrator* 34 (Summer 2008): 47–49.

for example, unmercifully pressed a caricature of the pioneer of Landmarkism as an ecclesiological innovator whose dispensationalism exposed him as "the greatest heretic ever produced by Southern Baptists."[9] More recently, Belmont University professor Marty Bell—in an otherwise insightful study—has explained Graves's appeal in the nineteenth-century South as largely a product of his populist demagogy and exaggerated rhetoric.[10] Such historiographical renderings do not serve Southern Baptists in the early twenty-first century, many of whom still wrestle with issues of denominational identity. The Graves legacy may well be both uncomfortable and problematic; nevertheless, it deserves to be recounted in a just and fair manner. As a matter of fact, the story of how one Baptist forebear defined boundaries in a distant nineteenth-century context—when the Southern Baptist Convention was in its formative years—might shed some light on similar undertakings today.

---

[9] James E. Tull, "A Study of Southern Baptist Landmarkism in Light of Historical Baptist Ecclesiology" (Ph.D. diss., Columbia University, 1960), 520. Tull specifically targeted J. R. Graves, *The Work of Christ in the Covenant of Redemption; Developed in Seven Dispensations* (1883; repr., Texarkana, AR: Baptist Sunday School Committee, 1928 and 1963).

[10] Marty G. Bell, "James Robinson Graves and the Rhetoric of Demagogy: Primitivism and Democracy in Old Landmarkism" (Ph.D. diss., Vanderbilt University, 1990), 24, 240–43.

Chapter 1

Graves and the Separate Baptist Ecclesiological Tradition

The Early Years (1820–45)

ROOTS IN THE GREEN MOUNTAIN STATE

J. R. Graves's life commenced on April 10, 1820, in the small town of Chester, Vermont, which is in the southeastern region of the state not far from the Connecticut River. Settlement first began in the area in 1764; in 1766 the royal governor of New York granted a charter under the name "Chester" 25 years before Vermont became a state in 1791. Chester was located at the juncture of two major stage coach lines, which might help to explain its general prosperity around the time of Graves's birth. The town's most scenic attraction, the Stone Village, was built in 1834 when he was a young teen.[1]

Young Graves was the third and last child born to Lois Schnell and Zuinglius Calvin Graves. In light of his later conviction that Baptists were not Protestants, it is ironic that his father's name was not uncommon in the family; in fact, the elder Graves inherited "Zuinglius" from his father and in turn passed on "Zuinglius Calvin" to J. R.'s

---

[1] "History of Chester," PDF format, accessed March 18, 2008, http://www.chester.govoffice.com. Chester had almost 2,500 people in 1820. Current population is about 3,000. Basic biographical material on Graves can be found in J. H. Borum, "J. R. Graves, LL.D.," in *Biographical Sketches of Tennessee Baptist Ministers* (Memphis: Rogers & Company, 1880), 282–89; J. J. Burnett, "J. R. Graves," in *Tennessee's Pioneer Baptist Preachers* (Nashville: Marshall & Bruce Company, 1919), 184–200; W. Cathcart, ed., *The Baptist Encyclopedia: A Dictionary*, rev. ed. (Philadelphia: Louis H. Everts, 1883), s.v. "Graves, J. R., LL.D."; H. L. Grice, "Graves, James Robinson," in *Encyclopedia of Southern Baptists* (Nashville: Broadman, 1958), 1:576–78; O. L. Hailey, *J. R. Graves: Life, Times and Teaching* (Nashville: By the author, 1929); and *Dictionary of American Biography*, s.v. "Graves, James Robinson." The most carefully researched and accurate account of Graves's life can be found in H. S. Smith, "A Critical Analysis of the Theology of J. R. Graves" (Th.D. diss., Southern Baptist Theological Seminary, 1966), 2–53.

older brother, who later served for many years as president of Mary Sharpe College in Winchester, Tennessee. In addition, an uncle in the family bore the name Luther Graves.[2]

J. R. Graves never said or wrote much about his family background or Yankee origins, perhaps because as an adult in antebellum Tennessee he found himself responding to allegations that he opposed slavery or was a secret northern sympathizer.[3] On one of the rare occasions when he reflected on his genealogy, Graves traced his father's family to some Huguenots who fled persecution in France and immigrated to America via England. His paternal grandfather and great-uncle ultimately settled near Boston and became merchants. In the same discussion, Graves vaguely noted that his mother "descended from an ancient and titled family."[4]

Both of Graves's grandfathers fought in the American Revolution. With noticeable pride, he wrote of how the experiences of his ancestors inspired an intense devotion to religious and political freedom at a young age:

> I may add here, my deep-seated and uncontrollable hatred of monarchy, despotism, hierarchy, and oppression, is doubtless owing to my Huguenot blood, and to the early impressions especially made upon my young mind, when listening, as I did during my whole youthhood, to the recitals of the persecutions of the Reformers—to my grand father's [*sic*] fightings, sufferings, and the tyrannical acts of King George—to the battle tales of the revolution—how the soldiers of the revolution fought—how my *mother's* father fought at Lexington, but especially at Bunker's Hill, and his bloody marches and snowy beds, for it was at her side and from her lips I heard it—until my young nature was all on fire and glowed with patriotic indignation.[5]

---

[2] On the prevalence of Reformers' names in the family, see J. R. Graves, ed., *The Little Iron Wheel: A Declaration of Christian Rights and Articles, Showing the Despotism of Episcopal Methodism* (Nashville: South-Western Publishing House; Graves, Marks & Company, 1856), 256. Graves's sister, Louisa Maria, married W. P. Marks, and they both became professors at Mary Sharpe College. See Hailey, *J. R. Graves*, 12.

[3] For example, see J. R. Graves, "The Last Charge of the S.W. Baptist. Has He Proved It?" *Tennessee Baptist*, June 12, 1858, [3]. "He" was Samuel Henderson, editor of the *South Western Baptist* of Alabama, with whom Graves had a running dispute in the 1850s. See W. T. Martin, "Samuel Henderson and His Responses to J. R. Graves and Landmarkism through *South Western Baptist*, 1857–1859" (M.A. thesis, Samford University, 1977).

[4] Graves, *The Little Iron Wheel*, 256.

[5] Ibid., 257–58. In the same context, he commented that his grandfather's long gun was still a family heirloom. At the end of this recollection, Graves requested pardon from his readers: "I never wrote so much of my family before, and never expect to write so much again." Unless otherwise noted, any italics in quotations from primary sources throughout this monograph are in the original texts.

Eventually this ardent patriotism, steeped as it was in the rhetoric of revolutionary New England, would fuse with Graves's doctrine of the church. His subsequent hostility to ecclesiastical tyranny began to be cultivated well before he moved away from Vermont.

Notwithstanding this honorable family lineage, tragedy struck when Graves's father unexpectedly died before little J. R. was a month old. Although the senior Graves co-owned a successful mercantile business, his unscrupulous partner extorted most of the money that should have gone to a grieving widow, who was now forced to raise three children with meager resources. Lois Graves, nonetheless, wanted her offspring to be suitably nurtured; she taught them some of the educational basics in the home and also instilled basic virtues like independence, a work ethic, and a resolve to persevere through adversity. The educational picture beyond the home, however, is a bit cloudy. T. A. Patterson claimed in his 1944 dissertation that Mrs. Graves successively enrolled her two sons in public school, the Chester Academy, and the Baptist Normal School in nearby Ludlow. While this schooling history apparently matches Z. C. Graves's résumé—at least according to biographical sketches by Burnett and Cathcart—it is not so clear that his younger brother followed the same course of study. J. R., in fact, recalled that his mother instructed the children at home "until they reached an age to be able to educate themselves, which we have done thus far *without the least assistance from any source*."[6] Z. C. Graves somehow may have found the means to attend private schools, but it appears that J. R.'s formal education was more limited.

On the religious front, Lois Graves attended the Congregational church in Chester and reared her children in that tradition. After her death from yellow fever in 1867, a writer for J. R. Graves's *Baptist* depicted her as a Calvinist who enjoyed reading the "metaphysical speculations" of Jonathan Edwards, the famous colonial American theologian and pastor. Nevertheless, her Congregationalist pastor, Dr. Burnap, immersed her as a believer about a decade after her husband's death; her study of the Bible evidently led her to reject infant baptism.[7]

---

[6] Ibid., 258. Cf. T. A. Patterson, "The Theology of J. R. Graves and Its Influence on Southern Baptist Life" (Th.D. diss., Southwestern Baptist Theological Seminary, 1944), 3. For summaries of Z. C. Graves's education, see Burnett, "Z. C. Graves," in *Tennessee's Pioneer Baptist Preachers*, 200; and Cathcart, ed., *The Baptist Encyclopedia*, s.v. "Graves, Z. C., LL.D."

[7] T. (J. Tovell), "Death of Mrs. Lois Graves," *Baptist*, November 2, 1867, 4. Her younger son eventually questioned the validity of her immersion, which he witnessed, by a "Pedobaptist" minister. See Graves, *Old Landmarkism: What Is It?*, 2nd ed. (Memphis: Baptist Book House; Graves, Mahaffy & Company, 1881), ix. Tovell noted that Mrs. Graves was rebaptized by J. M. Pendleton at First Baptist Church, Nashville, in 1855.

Graves deeply loved and admired his mother, especially for her sincere piety and her courage in difficult circumstances. Since she never remarried, her younger son took her in to live with his family for the last 20 years or so of her life. In regard to her presence in his home, Graves commended her as "the mainspring of all our untiring exertions."[8] As a man who never knew his father, J. R. clearly sustained a close relationship with his mother from which he drew inspiration for his own career.

Lois Graves's example may also have motivated her son's denominational pilgrimage since her immersion preceded his conversion and baptism in 1834 at North Springfield Baptist Church, also in Vermont. Furthermore, his older brother had affiliated with the same church through profession of faith and baptism a year or two earlier.[9] As questions no doubt surfaced in his mind about Congregationalism, J. R. likewise carried some vague sense of guilt about his behavior. In one of the few later comments about his adolescence, he confessed: "That I was a lively and jocose youth— and too much so—I admit, and it is still my constitutional failing. This I regret."[10] Unfortunately, the fullest account of Graves's ensuing step of faith is found in a secondary source written 65 years after the event. Baptist editor S. H. Ford duly testified that J. R.'s "conviction was deep, his struggle was intense, and his surrender and trust in the atoning work of Christ was full and joyful."[11] While he obviously had much to learn about Baptist beliefs and principles, Graves appeared to experience a life-changing conversion that helped to prepare him for a calling that he would gradually embrace over the next several years.

---

[8] Graves, "Shadow of Death," *Baptist*, November 16, 1867, 4.

[9] Burnett, "Z. C. Graves," *Tennessee's Pioneer Baptist Preachers,* 200.

[10] Graves, "Reaction of Injury," *Tennessee Baptist*, July 10, 1858, [2].

[11] S. H. Ford, "Life, Times, and Teachings of J. R. Graves: Chapter 1," *Ford's Christian Repository and Home Circle*, October 1899, 606–7. This was repeated almost verbatim in Hailey, *J. R. Graves*, 16. Graves's own report of his baptism and membership was regrettably brief. He did mention he was baptized by Cyrus Hodges, pastor of the North Springfield church at that time. See Graves, "Reaction of Injury," 2. In the context of his aforementioned controversy with Samuel Henderson, Graves verified the exact date of his baptism as November 9, 1834. See Graves, "The South Western Baptist," August 14, 1858, [2]. This was validated in 1965 by the clerk of the North Springfield church. See Smith, "A Critical Analysis of the Theology of J. R. Graves," 5, n11. Thus both Ford and Hailey incorrectly gave Graves's age at baptism as 15, perhaps misinterpreting his "Reaction of Injury" reference to being in his "15th year."

THE BACKGROUND AND IMPACT OF THE
SEPARATE BAPTIST MOVEMENT

When J. R. Graves joined the North Springfield Baptist Church in 1834, its history as a distinct congregation stretched only a little over 30 years. As early as 1788, some residents of Springfield, Vermont, had covenanted to start a Baptist "society" to be organized in the town. Their efforts, however, came to naught and the North Springfield church in due course traced its roots to the Baptist church in Chester, Graves's hometown. The Chester congregation began in 1786 with a group of about 15 believers—none of whom were Baptists—who asked Aaron Leland (1761–1833) to come and preach to them. This young minister, a distant relative of the more famous John Leland (1754–1841), had previously been ordained at a Separate Baptist church in Bellingham, Massachusetts. He accepted the call, moved to Chester, and helped to organize a new Baptist congregation within three years. Following a decade of slow growth, a noteworthy revival in 1799 brought the church a surge of new members, many of whom lived in neighboring towns; within four years, 186 people were added by baptism. The developments in Chester and its environs in many ways represented a microcosm of overall Baptist success in Vermont during the late eighteenth and early nineteenth centuries. Leland, moreover, exercised considerable clout as an ecclesiastical leader in the region.[12]

As a result of the Chester church's prosperity, several branch churches were established in surrounding towns. By 1803 four of these branches became independent sister churches, including the North Springfield congregation. The original 59 members, many of whom lived in Weathersfield and Baltimore, soon voted to request admission to the Woodstock Baptist Association, and this was quickly granted. North Springfield Baptist Church's articles of faith, which were revised a year after Graves's birth, revealed a Calvinistic theology and an approach to the ordinances that restricted the Lord's Supper to those who had been immersed as believers. The church proudly dedicated a new brick sanctuary at the end of 1835, a little over a year after Graves's baptism. In the mid-1830s, in fact, the church seemed to flourish under the pastoral

---

[12] For Baptist history in southeastern Vermont at this time, see H. Crocker, *History of the Baptists in Vermont* (Bellows Falls, VT: P. H. Gobie Press, 1913), 182–250; C. C. Goen, *Revivalism and Separatism in New England, 1740–1800: Strict Congregationalists and Separate Baptists in the Great Awakening* (New Haven: Yale University Press, 1962), 251–55; and W. G. McLoughlin, *New England Dissent, 1630–1883; The Baptists and the Separation of Church and State* (Cambridge: Harvard University Press, 1971), 2:791–812.

leadership of Cyrus W. Hodges, who ministered there from 1833 to 1837 and baptized 89 during his tenure.[13]

Although the North Springfield church experienced the usual ebbs and flows that typify most congregations, it remained rural and hence relatively modest in size. At the same time, an occasional intriguing episode intervened to keep things from getting too dull. For instance, Pastor M. D. Miller, who arrived in North Springfield in April of 1837, recounted that William Miller had spoken at the church a few months earlier. The latter Miller, who predicted that Christ would return in 1843, delivered lectures on that controversial topic. According to Miller the pastor, the future Adventist "made a deep impression, but gained few converts."[14] While Graves still remained in Vermont in 1837, there is no evidence to prove whether or not he actually attended Miller's lectures. In reality, church records indicate that he was granted a letter of dismissal in March of 1836, although he evidently did not move to Ohio for three more years.[15] Graves, moreover, recalled more than 20 years later that he had "opposed Miller to his face"—either at the church or in some other setting. Hence, James Tull likely pressed the evidence too far when he suggested that Graves's subsequent views on eschatology were influenced by Millerism. Indeed, just before the Civil War Graves himself categorically repudiated "the madness and folly of the Millerites" because they only served to discredit the study of prophecy.[16] Although Graves lived in New England at a time when Miller itinerated through it and gained some followers, about the most that can be inferred from this is that Graves's initial interest in prophecy was possibly sparked by his awareness of the

---

[13] For an interesting, sometimes humorous historical account of this church, see R. G. Johnson, *Historical Sketch of the North Springfield Baptist Church* (Ludlow, VT: Warner & Hyde, 1880), accessed March 18, 2008, http://www.geocities.com/baptist_documents/vrmt.no.spgfld.hist.1.html. Johnson was pastor when the church celebrated its seventy-fifth anniversary (1878). Graves returned to North Springfield in 1856 and administered the Lord's Supper. See Graves, "Reaction of Injury," 2.

[14] Johnson, *Historical Sketch of the North Springfield Baptist Church.* For background on William Miller, see D. L. Rowe, *God's Strange Work: William Miller and the End of the World* (Grand Rapids: Eerdmans, 2008). Apparently these two Millers were not related.

[15] See Smith, "A Critical Analysis of the Theology of J. R. Graves," 7, n19. As Smith remarked, a mystery surrounds Graves's biography for the period 1836–39.

[16] See Graves, "The Examination. Elder J. R. Graves' Defence before the Church and Council," *Tennessee Baptist,* April 16, 1859, [4]; and Graves's editorial introduction to "Napoleon III—The Man of Prophecy," *Southern Baptist Review* 7 (March 1861): 24–25. The Napoleon article itself, apparently written by a "Mr. Faber," carried no byline. For Tull's attempt to link Graves to Miller, see "A Study of Southern Baptist Landmarkism in the Light of Historical Baptist Ecclesiology" (Ph.D. diss., Columbia University, 1960), 245–46. He did concede that "direct sources of influence here are not easily discernible."

Millerite phenomenon. At the same time, Graves always responded negatively to Miller's specific teachings.

The real significance of the North Springfield church for Graves is that he undoubtedly imbibed the distinctive character of Baptist life in Vermont in the early nineteenth century. Although the historic divisions between Separate and Regular Baptists had begun to diminish in some parts of the United States, the Separate Baptist legacy had marked New England to such a degree—especially in the small towns and rural areas— that it could not be readily eradicated. Virtually all sources agree, moreover, that southern Vermont in particular was home for many Separate Baptist congregations.[17]

The Separate Baptist tradition first emerged in colonial America around the middle of the eighteenth century during the First Great Awakening. In New England, the revival unsettled the Congregational establishment as Separate or "New Light" Congregationalists—who enthusiastically supported traveling evangelists such as Gilbert Tennent and George Whitefield—and concluded that the old order was hopelessly stuck in spiritual lethargy. As the Separates organized new congregations to promote revival, many of them started to question the practice of infant baptism, which they could not harmonize either with Scripture or with their stated principle of regenerate church membership. Consequently, a sizeable number of Separate Congregationalists became Separate Baptists, thus launching a new and distinctly American brand of Baptists. These Separates quickly acquired an identity as sectarian dissenters who openly challenged the state churches in the New England colonies. In so doing, they drew on some of the more radical elements of the Puritan tradition that had been expressed by seventeenth-century activists like Roger Williams and John Clarke.[18]

In contrast to the already established Regular Baptists, the Separates were less educated, more rural, more apprehensive of doctrinal statements like the Philadelphia Confession of 1742, more suspicious about strong associations, and more prone to endorse loud and emotional preaching. Unlike the General Baptists, who originated in England, Separate Baptists rejected Arminian theology. Most important, Separates vigorously championed the full independence of each local church. As a minority move-

---

[17] For example, see Goen, *Revivalism and Separatism in New England*, 282, n51, where he identified the Woodstock Association, which included North Springfield Baptist, as having "large numbers of Separate or New Light Baptist churches."

[18] See ibid., 107–257, for background on Separate Congregationalists and Baptists.

ment that faced discrimination and even overt persecution, they treasured freedom and localism.[19]

For half a century, the most dominant personality among Separate Baptists in New England was Isaac Backus (1724–1806). A convert in the Great Awakening, he identified for a number of years with Separate Congregationalism. After embracing believers' baptism, he attempted to lead a "mixed" congregation in Middleborough, Massachusetts. By 1756 he saw the need to organize a Separate Baptist church in that locale. He stayed on as pastor until his death 50 years later. Through his itinerant preaching, writings, associational activities, and efforts on behalf of religious liberty, he became legendary in and beyond Massachusetts. He is rightfully credited with helping to undermine the established church in his state, even though it was not officially terminated until 1833. An evangelical Calvinist, Backus combined the doctrines of grace with a fervent proclamation of the gospel and an acute sense of what it meant to be a Baptist.[20]

Backus stamped the Separate Baptist movement with several enduring characteristics. First, the Massachusetts preacher steadfastly put forward perhaps more effectively than any other Separate Baptist what has been variously dubbed as "local church ecclesiology" or "local church protectionism."[21] His perspective on this issue lined up closely with that of nineteenth-century Landmarkism; well before Graves, Backus argued that Jesus instituted only "particular" churches. Backus's ecclesiology, therefore, allowed no room for either a visible or invisible universal church. Each local congregation, moreover, possessed the sole authority to call and ordain its officers, as well as to govern and discipline its members.[22] His own wearisome experiences with the Congregational

---

[19] Ibid., 288–95, and L. B. Hogue, "A Study of the Antecedents of Landmarkism" (Th.D. diss., Southwestern Baptist Theological Seminary, 1966), 114–23.

[20] On his remarkable career, see S. J. Grenz, *Isaac Backus—Puritan and Baptist: His Place in History, His Thought, and Their Implications for Modern Baptist Theology* (Macon, GA.: Mercer University Press, 1983); and William G. McLoughlin, *Isaac Backus and the American Pietistic Tradition* (Boston: Little, Brown, 1967).

[21] See respectively Goen, *Revivalism and Separatism in New England*, 288; and W. H. Brackney, *Historical Dictionary of the Baptists* (Lanham, MD: Scarecrow Press, 1999), s.v. "Landmarkism." For a more extended treatment of Backus's ecclesiology, see D. J. Boyles, "Isaac Backus and His Ecclesial Thought" (Ph.D. diss., Southwestern Baptist Theological Seminary, 2002).

[22] I. Backus, *A Discourse, Concerning the Materials, the Manner of Building, and Power of Organizing the Church of Christ* (Boston: John Boyles, 1773), 145; and Backus, *A History of New England: With Particular Reference to the Denomination of Christians Called Baptists*, 2nd ed. (Newton, MA: Backus Historical Society, 1871), 2:231–33. In the latter work, Backus ascribed convictions about local church prerogatives to all Baptists in New England, not just Separates.

Standing Order in New England, which he labeled as an ecclesiastical and political tyranny, merely underscored for him the value of local church autonomy.

Second, Backus helped to shape Separate Baptist traditions regarding the ordinances of the church. Rather early in his ministry in Middleborough, for example, he decided that open communion was both unworkable and deceitful. Because he insisted on the immersion of believers as the only legitimate mode of baptism, he presently concluded that this practice was both absolutely foundational for a true church and a requirement for admission to the Lord's Supper. Eventually most Baptist congregations in New England adopted Backus's strict or closed communion policies, including Graves's North Springfield church.[23]

Third, Backus's heightened sense of denominational identity in the years after the Great Awakening meant that he and his Separate Baptist successors in New England would set clear boundaries of faith and order. Beginning in 1756, he plainly delineated his differences with Congregationalism and "pedobaptism" in general. Later on, the energetic Baptist spokesman turned his guns on other enemies that he deemed even more sinister. As William McLoughlin observed, "Backus was positively vitriolic in his tracts attacking Universalists, Shakers, and Methodists, all of whom he considered as dangerous heretics to a Christian commonwealth as the Puritans had considered the Munsterite Anabaptists to be."[24] Thus Backus unknowingly anticipated the combative boundary marking that characterized J. R. Graves many decades later.

Finally, Backus—without endorsing Baptist successionism—pointed to the footprints of faithful witnesses who struggled against oppression and injustice in earlier historical eras. In his preface to *A History of New England*, he cited Petrobrusians, Waldensians, Wicklifites, and Hussites as examples of those who endured the tyranny of the medieval Roman Church.[25] Although Backus did not identify these forebears of liberty as Baptists, he at least suggested a broad outline for those who later would take just that step. His keynote themes of freedom, dissent, and anti-Catholicism subsequently filtered into future accounts of the Baptist heritage that highlighted a "trail of blood."

The impact of Backus continued to be felt by Baptists in New England for a long time. In more localized settings, Separate leaders like Aaron Leland sounded many of

---

[23] Backus, *A History of New England*, 2:487. For Backus's influence on later strict communion practices, see Goen, *Revivalism and Separatism in New England*, 259–60; and Hogue, "A Study of the Antecedents of Landmarkism," 118–20.

[24] William McLoughlin, *Soul Liberty: The Baptists' Struggle in New England, 1630–1833* (Hanover, NH: University Press of New England, for Brown University Press, 1991), 256.

[25] Backus, *A History of New England*, 2:vi–vii.

the same notes as Backus. The "bishop" of southeastern Vermont, who had a direct hand in planting the North Springfield church, entered politics as a member of the Vermont legislature. As Speaker of the House in 1807 he led a successful fight against the hated certificate system, which granted dissenters exemptions from the mandatory church tax that supported Congregationalism. The demise of the certificate requirement in effect ended the state church in Vermont. Along with his governmental duties, Leland continued to shepherd his congregation in Chester until his death in 1833, which meant that Separate Baptist perspectives still had influential supporters in northern New England well into the nineteenth century.[26]

In Massachusetts, the Vermont pastor-politician's better known relative John Leland stood as a prominent, if somewhat unconventional, Separate Baptist leader. A native New Englander, Leland preached in Virginia from around 1777 until 1791, when he returned to Massachusetts. While known primarily as a staunch opponent of the state churches in both places, he also heartily affirmed the Separate Baptist ecclesiology that stressed the complete autonomy of the local church. His lively rhetoric incorporated both localism and the republican spirit of post-revolutionary America:

[A]s far as church government on earth is the government of Christ, it is of democratical genius. Church government is congregational, not parochial, diocesan, nor national. Each congregated church disclaims the power of Popes, kings, bishops, kirks, or presbyteries, and claims the right and power to govern itself according to the laws of Christ. And it must be confessed, that the spirit and rule by which the subjects of Christ's kingdom are to live one among another, greatly resemble the genius of a republic. . . . By a Christocracy I mean nothing more than a government of which Christ is law-giver, king, and judge, and yet so arranged, that each congregational church is a complete republic of itself, not to be controlled by civil government or hierarchy. . . . [Churches are] little republics which form the empire of Christ.[27]

---

[26] McLoughlin, *New England Dissent*, 2:810. Leland additionally served a six-year term (1822–28) as lieutenant governor of Vermont. On broader trends in the region, see S. M. Balik, "The Religious Frontier: Church, State, and Settlement in Northern England, 1780–1830" (Ph.D. diss., University of Wisconsin, 2006). Balik distinguished between the "townchurch" model of the establishment Congregationalists and the "itinerant" model of dissenting groups.

[27] J. Leland, "The Government of Christ a Christocracy," in *Writings of the Late Elder John Leland*, ed. Louise F. Greene (New York: G. W. Wood, 1845), 275–78. This was a sermon preached in 1804.

For Leland, then, an authentically biblical ecclesiology resisted centralization, hierarchy, and anything else that would interfere with the inalienable rights of a local congregation.

While Separate Baptists in New England—including Backus—had long demonstrated a marked individualism, Leland definitely intensified this impulse. As Samford educator Brad Creed has shown, Leland's heavy emphasis on the believer's personal relationship with Christ caused him to lose interest in the corporate church or the denomination. In fact, he wrote much less on the nature of the church than on baptism. Furthermore, he increasingly discounted the importance of the Lord's Supper, even refusing to celebrate it in his Cheshire, Massachusetts, congregation for 20 years.[28] Leland's individualism, moreover, probably contributed to his (1) contempt for the mission activities of benevolent societies; (2) opposition to ministerial training; (3) skepticism about ordination; and (4) resistance to the Sunday school movement. At any rate, historians have been quick to link this iconoclasm to both the primitivism and anti-missionism that spread on the nineteenth-century American frontier.[29] In addition, as chap. 4 suggests, some of Leland's emphases surfaced in the work of J. R. Graves. Even though it is difficult to discern how much Graves may have read of Leland's writings, the budding Landmarker was an adult by the time the Massachusetts preacher died in 1841. It is hard to imagine that Graves, with his New England roots, was oblivious to Leland's role in helping to fashion the Separate Baptist tradition.

At the same time, Graves's doctrine of the church was more explicitly indebted to J. Newton Brown (1803–68), another New Englander who so well exemplified the Separate Baptist character. Brown, who was best known for his service as editorial secretary of the American Baptist Publication Society, earlier boosted local church ecclesiology as the principal author of the New Hampshire Confession of 1833. That statement omitted any reference to the invisible or universal church as it defined a visible church as "a congregation of baptized believers, associated by covenant in the faith and fellowship of the gospel; observing the ordinances of Christ; governed by his laws; and exercising the gifts, rights, and privileges invested in them by His Word." In the following section, the Confession identified baptism as "the immersion of a believer"

---

[28] J. B. Creed, "John Leland, American Prophet of Individualism" (Ph.D. diss., Southwestern Baptist Theological Seminary, 1986), 157–60. Cf. Goen, *Revivalism and Separatism in New England*, 288–89. On the 20-year communion hiatus, see McLoughlin, *New England Dissent*, 2:930.

[29] See Creed, "John Leland," 174–97; M. A. Dain, "The Development of the Primitive Impulse in American Baptist Life, 1707–1842" (Ph.D. diss., Southwestern Baptist Theological Seminary, 2001), 62–72; and B. C. Lambert, "The Rise of the Anti-mission Baptists: Sources and Leaders, 1800–1840 (A Study in Religious Individualism)" (Ph.D. diss., University of Chicago, 1957), 116–52.

and called it a "prerequisite" to church membership and the Lord's Supper. It also at least implied that communion was for "the members of the church," although the exact implications of that clause remain unclear.[30] The publication of this document in a neighboring state just a year before Graves's baptism codified an ecclesiological stance that had marked the Separate Baptists in New England since the mid-1750s. In turn, the Confession would display a resiliency of its own as it proved attractive in a variety of Landmark and other settings.[31]

When Graves birthed the Landmark movement in the 1850s, for instance, he found the localism of the New Hampshire Confession well suited to his developing ecclesiology. In addition, as James Tull first detected in his massive study of Landmarkism, Brown's 1846 circular letter to the Central Union Baptist Association of Pennsylvania virtually equated "the church" (i.e., the aggregate of local churches) with "the visible kingdom of Christ on earth."[32]

Furthermore, just as Brown's understanding of the kingdom influenced Graves's thinking about the church, the former's approach to Baptist history contributed to the latter's successionism. In two 1855 articles, Graves approvingly cited Brown to justify the need for a rewriting of church history and to propose that a revisionist tack demanded a special focus on faithful believers through the ages who had suffered at the hands of ecclesiastical tyrants. In particular, Graves responded most favorably to Brown's *Memorials*, which mixed history with glowing martyrology. Like Backus before him, Brown laid out a trail of witnesses, although several of them were more obscure than those invoked by his Separate Baptist predecessor. Brown, moreover, went beyond Backus by presenting the martyrs in his historical survey as Baptists. For his part, Graves recognized the relevance of the *Memorials* for dissenters like himself: "[T]hose who in the face of bitter scorn and the fires of the inquisition of public opinion, hold

---

[30] "The New Hampshire Confession (1833)," in J. A. Broadus, *Baptist Confessions, Covenants, and Catechisms*, ed. T. and D. George (Nashville: B&H, 1996), 134.

[31] Goen traced this impact in *Revivalism and Separatism in Separatism in New England*, 293–94. He noted the inclusion of the New Hampshire Confession in J. M. Pendleton's widely circulated *Church Manual, Designed for the Use of Baptist Churches* (Philadelphia: American Baptist Publication Society, 1867), 43–61. Yet Goen neglected the obvious correspondence between the New Hampshire Confession and the SBC's first Baptist Faith and Message (1925). Unlike the 1925 statement, the 1963 BFM asserted the universal church. For a side-by-side comparison of the 1925 and 1963 versions, see "The Baptist Faith and Message," in *A Sourcebook for Baptist Heritage*, ed. H. L. McBeth (Nashville: Broadman, 1990), 503–18.

[32] Tull, "A Study of Southern Baptist Landmarkism," 282–86. Since Tull interpreted Graves as an ecclesiological innovator or, at best, a theologian who pushed the New England tradition to an extreme, it is not surprising he classified Brown's doctrine of the church as a minority view in Baptist history.

forth the old time-worn, fire-scathed banner, inscribed with the motto of the martyrs."[33] For Graves and his Separate Baptist forebears, familiarity with the annals of persecution at the hands of state churches often fired zeal for local church protectionism. Indeed, the tradition of dissent in New England was forged in conflicts with intrusive religious establishments.[34]

During J. R. Graves's early career, the most prominent exponent of New England Baptist localism was Francis Wayland (1796–1865). Following a pastorate at First Baptist Church, Boston, and a short stint as a professor at Union College in Schenectady, New York, Wayland achieved his greatest fame while serving for 28 years as president of Brown University in Providence, Rhode Island. More than any other figure, he disposed Baptists in the North toward a decentralized polity that responded less than enthusiastically to grand denominational ventures. In a classic statement of his ecclesiology, the preacher-educator placed an almost exclusive emphasis on the local congregation:

> The Baptists have ever believed in the entire and absolute independence of the churches. By this, we mean that every church of Christ, that is, every company of believers united together according to the laws of Christ, is wholly independent of every other; that every church is perfectly capable of self-government; and that, therefore, no one acknowledges any higher authority under Christ, than itself; that with the church all ecclesiastical action commences, and with it terminates, and hence, the ecclesiastical relations proper, of every member, are limited to the church to which he belongs.[35]

---

[33] Graves, "An Old Landmark," in *The Southern Baptist Almanac and Register, for the Year 1855*, ed. J. R. Graves (Nashville: Graves & Marks, 1855), 36. This comment followed long quotations from J. N. Brown, *Memorials of Baptist Martyrs: With a Preliminary Historical Essay* (Philadelphia: American Baptist Publication Society, 1854), passim. On the need for a new church history, see Graves, "Church History," *Southern Baptist Review and Eclectic* 1 (April and May 1855): 193–218. This article excerpted at length Brown's previously noted circular letter.

[34] Graves's interest in these themes is seen in a book he edited, *Trials and Sufferings for Religious Liberty in New England* (Nashville: South-Western Publishing House; Graves, Marks & Company, 1857). He neither specified the original author of this work nor clearly stated that he was simply the editor, which led to charges of plagiarism. See Graves, "Who Wrote the Historical Sketch Entitled 'Trials and Sufferings for Religious Liberty?'" *Tennessee Baptist*, May 1, 1858, [2].

[35] F. Wayland, *Notes on the Principles and Practices of Baptist Churches* (New York: Sheldon, Blakeman, & Company; and Boston: Gould & Lincoln, 1857), 177–78. This book collected a series of short papers originally published in the *Examiner*. For a full discussion of Wayland's ecclesiology, see G. T. Halbrooks, "Francis Wayland: Contributor to Baptist Concepts of Church Order" (Ph.D. diss., Emory University, 1971).

Like Backus, Leland, and the New Hampshire Confession before him, Wayland thus trumpeted the merits of full congregational autonomy as one of the highest expressions of Baptist identity. He similarly inherited from his Baptist ancestors the New England legacy that boosted Baptist democracy as the antidote to both political and ecclesiastical oppression. Furthermore, as church historian Norman Maring fittingly explained, Wayland's localism was a direct product of the individualism, moralism, and revivalistic piety that flowed through the nineteenth-century Baptist bloodstream.[36]

In many respects, President Wayland's ecclesiology represented the culmination of the Separate Baptist tradition in New England. In particular, his local church protectionism and individualistic ethos resonated in the thinking of J. R. Graves. True to his New England roots, Graves especially shared Wayland's concerns—which echoed John Leland's earlier worries—about the machinery of denominational mission agencies infringing on the prerogatives of local churches. At a time when Landmarkers rose to challenge the role of the Foreign Mission Board in the Southern Baptist Convention, Graves ran in his denominational paper a series drawn from a pamphlet by Wayland that seemed to question even the society model that had traditionally been the preference of Baptists in the North. Wayland, in fact, called for a more local church-based approach to missions as a counter to the "centralizing" tendencies of missionary organizations; he wanted missionaries to be supported by and accountable to a local congregation or, at most, a "combination of churches."[37] By invoking the authority of Wayland, Graves indicated the extent to which his New England Baptist heritage overrode the more pronounced denominationalism that characterized several of the SBC's initial architects.

Graves's affinities with the Separate Baptist tradition in New England intimate that he was not a radical innovator who was totally out of step with the beliefs and practices of his predecessors. LeRoy Hogue rightly expressed the significant continuities between a New England Baptist lineage beginning with Backus and the

---

[36] N. H. Maring, "The Individualism of Francis Wayland," in *Baptist Concepts of the Church: A Survey of the Historical and Theological Issues Which Have Produced Changes in Church Order*, ed. W. S. Hudson (Philadelphia: Judson Press, 1959), 136–38. Unfortunately, Maring (or his editor) contorted the Wayland statement cited above when he quoted the first sentence and replaced "ever" with "never" (154). For Wayland on Baptists versus tyranny, see *Notes on the Principles and Practices of Baptist Churches*, 132–47.

[37] Wayland, "Missions. Thoughts on the Missionary Organizations of the Baptist Denomination [Numbers I–III]," *Tennessee Baptist*, February 12, 1859, [3]; February 19, 1859, [2]; and February 26, 1859, [2]. Cf. Wayland, *Thoughts on the Missionary Organizations of the Baptist Denomination* (New York: Sheldon, Blakeman, & Company, 1859). On Wayland and societies, see *Notes on the Principles and Practices of Baptist Churches*, 183–95. Here he sharply distinguished between Baptist churches and benevolent associations set up and managed by individual Baptists.

Landmarkism of J. R. Graves, pointing out that well before the mid-1850s "there was a substantial part of the Baptist denomination in the United States that held to a strictly local ecclesiology, that maintained the independency and authority of every local church as a scriptural concept, and that insisted upon a strict observance of the ordinances in their relationship to the authority of the local church."[38] Although Graves often was not explicit about the precise sources of his ecclesiological beliefs and practices, his early nurture in a New England Baptist context suggests that he imbibed at least some of the ideas that gave the Separates a distinctive identity. In other words, he gained exposure in his formative years to a notable tradition of dissent that set out clear boundaries of Baptist faith and order. The borders that he eventually drew were not altogether identical with those of the Separate Baptists in New England, but his kinship with them is beyond dispute.

ON TO OTHER FRONTIERS

Both the Separate Baptist tradition and J. R. Graves ultimately moved beyond the confines of their New England birthplaces. Some Separate Baptists, in fact, began migrating southward even before the American Revolution. Localism, individualism, and a passion for religious liberty characterized most of their adherents in the rural South. Nonetheless, the Separate Baptist imprint on the southern frontier revealed some novel variations. Shubal Stearns, a New England native who founded the Sandy Creek Association in North Carolina, gravitated toward a more connectional church polity that differed from the decentralized pattern favored by John Leland in Virginia. For the most part, Stearns's approach was atypical of the Separate movement; indeed, C. C. Goen properly concluded that "the eventual triumph of a centralizing ecclesiology in the South is due not to Separate Baptist influence but to continued agitation by Philadelphia-oriented leaders in the East."[39] In other words, Leland's ecclesiological legacy remained

---

[38] Hogue, "A Study of the Antecedents of Landmarkism," 122–23. This stress on continuity indirectly weakens Tull's claim that Graves "embraced the views of the most extreme wing of the New England Baptists." See Tull, "A Study of Southern Baptist Landmarkism," 265.

[39] Goen, *Revivalism and Separatism in New England*, 299, n9. For other sources on the progress of Separate Baptists in the South, see W. L. Lumpkin, *Baptist Foundations in the South: Tracing through the Separates the Influence of the Great Awakening, 1754–1787* (Nashville: Broadman, 1961); and J. O. Renault, "The Development of Separate Baptist Ecclesiology in the South, 1755–1976" (Ph.D. diss., Southern Baptist Theological Seminary, 1978). On the relationship of frontier culture to church life, see T. S. Miyakawa,

vital in both New England and the South, even after the lines between Regulars and Separates became less distinct.[40] When Graves eventually unleashed Landmarkism in the mid-South, he benefited from the lingering remnants of the Separate Baptist heritage.

The relevance of the Separate Baptist impact beyond New England, nevertheless, is difficult to track for Graves's first major stopping point outside of Vermont. At the age of 19, Graves moved west in 1839 with his mother and sister to join brother Zuinglius in northeastern Ohio. The latter had opened a school in Ashtabula, a small town on the edge of Lake Erie, and he soon facilitated the appointment of his brother J. R. as principal of an academy in nearby Kingsville. The younger Graves's background and qualifications for this post remain unclear. At any rate, he worked tirelessly at this institution for about 18 months, at which point his health collapsed and he headed for the warmer climes of Kentucky.[41] Virtually nothing is known of his relationship to Baptist life during his first stay in the Buckeye State; for example, there is no surviving evidence of any local church affiliation, let alone any significant contact with heirs of the Separate Baptist tradition.

The biographical picture improves somewhat for Graves's years in Kentucky. In 1841 he arrived in a rural section of Jessamine County, Kentucky, near the towns of Nicholasville and Wilmore. This region of the Bluegrass State placed the transplanted northerner in fairly close proximity to the larger towns of Frankfort, the capital, and Lexington. He shortly assumed the office of principal at the Clear Creek Academy, which evidently prospered under his energetic leadership—he maintained his Kingsville work routines with long hours of preparation each night for the next day's classes.[42] At the age of 21, Graves appeared to be well ensconced in an educational career, despite his limited training.

Protestants and Pioneers: Individualism and Conformity on the American Frontier (Chicago: University of Chicago Press, 1964).

[40] On the nineteenth century fusing of Regular and Separate Baptists in the South, see J. L. Garrett Jr., "The Distinctive Identity of Southern Baptists vis-à-vis Other Baptists," *Baptist History and Heritage* 31 (October 1996): 7.

[41] On the first Kingsville period, see Hailey, *J. R. Graves*, 16; and Smith, "A Critical Analysis of the Theology of J. R. Graves," 7. These biographical sources record a two-year stint for Graves at the Kingsville Academy, whereas Graves himself remembered it as 18 months. The fact that he apparently departed for Kentucky in the middle of a school year favors the shorter span of time. See Graves, ed., *The Little Iron Wheel*, 258, where he also reported 18 as his age when he left Vermont—19 works better with known dates for his time in Ohio and Kentucky. Overall, these transitional years reveal many biographical gaps.

[42] Hailey, *J. R. Graves*, 16–17; and Smith, "A Critical Analysis of the Theology of J. R. Graves," 8. Graves also referred to a Clifton Academy (see *The Little Iron Wheel*, 258).

In due course, however, Graves's association with the nearby Mount Freedom Baptist Church helped to redirect his professional aspirations. Although several details concerning his relationship to the church are unknown, he initially joined during a revival that was led by Pastor Mason Owens and Elder Thomas Fisher in May of 1842. Graves quickly engaged himself in the life of the congregation; in the very year that he affiliated, he recorded minutes as clerk pro tempore and also served as a delegate to the Boone's Creek Association. More importantly, Mount Freedom licensed the young educator in 1842, apparently without his knowledge. The church's minutes for May of 1842 briefly logged his membership and licensure—with no explanation—as virtually simultaneous events. Son-in-law Hailey, on the other hand, portrayed Graves as a timid, reserved young man who needed to be tricked into filling the pulpit by the pastor's pretense of being ill. Graves then preached on the text, "Adam, where art thou?"; he evidently seized this opportunity to challenge pious chameleons who lacked the fortitude to stand for bedrock principles. The sermon impressed the congregation to the degree that Graves's licensing presently ensued.[43]

Ordination followed, probably in October of 1842; Graves's own pastor Owens and Ryland T. Dillard of the East Hickman Baptist Church were prominent members of the examining council, with the latter preaching the ordination sermon. By 1843 Graves was invited to preach at Mount Freedom once a month. Throughout this period, he continued to wrestle with his call to the ministry; in fact, biographer Hailey described a noteworthy spiritual crisis during which Graves "met God and joyfully surrendered to him, and God gave him his life message to his own generation." [44] Perhaps Graves's introverted

---

[43] Hailey, *J. R. Graves*, 17–18. Hailey's account raises questions of historical accuracy since he wrongly identified the Mount Freedom pastor as Ryland Dillard. Cf. Minutes of Mount Freedom Baptist Church, Wilmore, Kentucky, 3rd Saturday of May, 1842, in Church Records, 1832–1961, microfilm version, Southern Baptist Historical Library and Archives [hereafter SBHLA], Nashville, Tennessee. For a short summary of Graves's first sermon, see W. B. Shurden, *Not a Silent People: Controversies That Have Shaped Southern Baptists* (Nashville: Broadman, 1972), 68.

[44] Hailey, *J. R. Graves*, 19. Graves identified Dillard as his ordination preacher (see *The Little Iron Wheel*, 258). For a good overview of the chronological issues related to Graves's ordination, see Smith, "A Critical Analysis of the Theology of J. R. Graves," 9–12. Smith addressed the omission of Graves's ordination from the Mount Freedom minutes at the time that it took place. The issue was later raised in 1858 in the context of a controversy involving Graves, and the church inserted a retroactive entry placing the ordination in 1842. See Minutes of Mount Freedom Baptist Church, October 1858. This notation differed from Graves's own recollection of the date. See Graves, "The Positions of the 'Western Recorder' on the Administrator of Baptism," *Tennessee Baptist,* February 2, 1878, 150, where he gave 1844 (an unlikely date since he was no longer a member of Mount Freedom). Smith also provided evidence that Graves struggled with a call to preach as far back as his teen years in Vermont.

personality—along with a pronounced sense of his unworthiness to assume a ministerial role—triggered his hesitant response to what he finally determined was a divine calling.

In October of 1843, before returning to Ohio, Graves was granted a favorable letter of dismissal from the Mount Freedom church.[45] Nonetheless, his year and a half as a member contributed not only to his personal and professional growth but also to his general exposure to issues in Kentucky Baptist life. Both Regular and Separate Baptists—many from Virginia—settled in Kentucky before it became a state in 1792 and experienced steady growth. In a step parallel to what occurred earlier in Virginia, Regulars and Separates amicably merged in 1801. As Regular-Separate differences gradually receded, however, new contentions emerged during the first third of the nineteenth century involving the overlapping movements of Campbellism and anti-missionism. Alexander Campbell (1788–1866), a Scottish émigré and former Presbyterian, sojourned for about a decade with Baptists in western Pennsylvania, where he shared their views on believer's baptism by immersion and the autonomy of the local church. In spite of this common ground, it soon became apparent that his restorationist, "Reformed" agenda diverged significantly from other traditional Baptist positions, Regular or Separate. In 1832 this frontier preacher and polemicist joined with Barton Stone to organize the Disciples/Christian movement, which flourished in frontier states like Kentucky. Campbell tilted toward baptismal regeneration and, like some of the New England Separates, opposed any practices that could not be squared with the letter of the New Testament, including mission societies that functioned beyond the authority of local congregations. The anti-mission sentiment of those who repudiated Campbell and remained Baptist often was inspired by a hyper-Calvinism that opposed any organized human effort in the dissemination of the gospel; this perspective, of course, clashed with Campbell's Arminianism. All the same, many Baptist churches and associations in Kentucky had battled extensively over both Campbellism and anti-missionism in the years immediately preceding Graves's arrival in Jessamine County.[46]

---

[45] Minutes of Mount Freedom Baptist Church, October 21, 1843.

[46] On Baptist history in Kentucky during the late eighteenth and early nineteenth centuries, see L. T. Crismon, ed., *Baptists in Kentucky: A Bicentennial Volume* (Middletown, KY: Kentucky Baptist Convention, 1975), 12–16; F. M. Masters, *A History of Baptists in Kentucky* (Louisville: Kentucky Baptist Historical Society, 1953), 41–255; and J. H. Spencer, *A History of Kentucky Baptists* (Cincinnati: J. R. Baumes, 1885), 1:33–38, 581–643. On Campbell, particularly as a controversialist, see R. J. Cherok, *Debating for God: Alexander Campbell's Challenge to Skepticism in Antebellum America* (Abilene, TX: Abilene Christian University Press, 2008); and P. A. Verkruyse, *Prophet, Pastor, and Patriarch: The Rhetorical Leadership of Alexander Campbell* (Tuscaloosa: University of Alabama Press, 2005). On anti-missionism, see Lambert, "The Rise of Anti-mission Baptists"; and L. D. Smith, "The Historiography of Anti-missionism Examined in Light

Mount Freedom Baptist Church, which was originally constituted in 1832, fully embraced the articles of belief that had accompanied the Regular-Separate union three decades earlier. In addition, the church made it plain at its founding that it had no use for Campbellism: "Owing to many strange doctrines lately propagated among the Baptist denomination, and in order that society and the world may know our opinion, we do solemnly protest against the doctrines of the Rev. Alexander Campbell and all its adherents."[47] Further boundary marking followed in early 1838, just a few years before Graves affiliated with the church. On this occasion, the Mount Freedom congregation tackled the issues of the Lord's Supper and baptism, passing two resolutions from member Joseph Minter that were presented in a query/response format: (1) "Is it right that a member of this church should commune with any other church that is not of the same faith and order? Answer: No."; and (2) "Is it right for this church to receive a member's baptism [as] valid that was baptized by another society, that is not of the same faith and order with us? Answer: In the negative."[48] It is likely that both of these questions surfaced when they did—at least in part—because of the edgy relationships in Kentucky between Baptists and Campbell's followers. Moreover, matters that would later figure prominently in Graves's Landmark agenda came up for discussion and formal vote at Mount Freedom not long before he joined. While it is difficult to measure the exact impact of these actions on Graves's emerging views, his Kentucky experience likely fortified the ecclesiology that he had previously gained exposure to in Vermont.

Graves apparently knew little about Campbell's movement, however, until he spent time in Kentucky and discovered the disdain that his Baptist colleagues openly expressed toward it. In particular, the young teacher in due course imitated the aggressive stance of mentors like R. T. Dillard and John L. Waller, both of whom aimed their rhetorical barbs at Campbellism. Dillard, pastor of a neighboring church, evidently emboldened Graves to stand firm against Campbell's doctrines, at least according to biographer Hailey.[49] Waller (1809–54) was the son of Edmund Waller, who pastored the Mount Pleasant Baptist Church in Jessamine County during the time that Graves lived

---

of Kentucky Baptist History" (Ph.D. diss., Southern Baptist Theological Seminary, 1982). Tull provided an insightful account of both controversies in "A Study of Southern Baptist Landmarkism," 81–113.

[47] S. J. Conkwright, *History of the Churches of Boone's Creek Baptist Association of Kentucky with a Brief History of the Association* (Winchester, KY: Boone's Creek Baptist Association, 1923), accessed June 2, 2008, http://www.geocities.com/baptist_documents/KYjessamine.mt.freedm.bc.html.

[48] Ibid. Minter was elected deacon three months after presenting his motions.

[49] Hailey, *J. R. Graves*, 18, 21. Recall, though, that Hailey incorrectly placed Dillard in the Mount Freedom church.

there. The younger Waller gained his reputation as the editor of Baptist publications, first the *Baptist Banner and Pioneer*, and later the *Western Baptist Review* and the *Western Recorder*. He and Graves first met in 1841, and the young schoolmaster was well aware of Waller's published broadsides against Campbell and his followers.[50] Hence, Graves's developing ecclesiological posture in many ways combined the New England Separate Baptist stress on local church autonomy with the anti-Campbell polemics that he absorbed in Kentucky.

Despite the strong sentiment against Campbellism among Baptist leaders in the Bluegrass State and Graves's own subsequent writings against the movement, during his time in Nashville he faced allegations that he once professed sympathy for it. In the context of a dispute with some fellow Southern Baptists in 1858, his opponents produced a letter from W. G. Cogar of Jessamine County that called Graves "a wild, thoughtless man" who once plotted to turn the Mount Freedom church into a "reform" or Campbellite congregation. Cogar apparently surmised all this from comments Graves made while boarding in Cogar's home for about 18 months in the early 1840s. For his part, Graves published excerpts of a letter Cogar wrote to him in which the former landlord testified that his lodger was "a gentlemen of good moral character" and that he said nothing that would indicate a desire to convert Mount Freedom Baptist Church to Campbellism.[51] It is not clear why Cogar wrote two very different letters in a span of less than two weeks; indeed, the vindication of Graves in the second letter does not explain the serious charges that were leveled in the first one. Cogar might have had a faulty memory of events from several years prior, or perhaps one of the letters was a fake. At any rate, a later controversy fittingly revealed the extent to which worries about Campbellism gripped the minds of many Baptists on the Kentucky frontier during the time Graves took up residence there. Moreover, Graves became a setter of Baptist bound-

---

[50] See Graves, "Reaction of Injury," 2; Graves, ed., *The Little Iron Wheel*, 258; and A. H. Lanier Jr., "The Relationship of the Ecclesiology of John Lightfoot Waller to Early Landmarkism" (Th.M. thesis, Southeastern Baptist Theological Seminary, 1963), 12–37. Ironically, Graves took his first significant step as a Baptist controversialist in 1848 by attacking Waller's approval of alien immersion. See the next chapter.

[51] Graves, "Reaction of Injury," 2. Both the Cogar letter to Graves's foes (June 18, 1858) and the one to Graves (June 30, 1858) were cited in this *Tennessee Baptist* article. According to this piece, editor Samuel Henderson of the *South Western Baptist* initially made the first Cogar letter public. Graves felt compelled to bring up the Cogar correspondence again in "The Charges of the *South Western Baptist* Met by Mr. Henderson's Own Witnesses," *Tennessee Baptist,* September 4, 1858, [4]. On the disruptive effects of Restorationism on Baptist church life in Kentucky, see H. L. McBeth, *The Baptist Heritage: Four Centuries of Baptist Witness* (Nashville: Broadman, 1987), 377.

aries in part because he observed his fellow Baptists engaged in boundary staking at a formative time early in his career.

In 1843, Graves returned to Kingsville, Ohio, to be closer once again to his family. This seemingly innocuous transition, however, became additional fodder for his Baptist critics in the late 1850s when they attempted to use it as evidence that the *Tennessee Baptist* editor opposed slavery. In 1858, around the same time Graves had to defend himself against insinuations found in Cogar's first epistle, his antagonists dug up evidence pertaining to an alleged conversation in 1843 with J. L. Waller in which Graves shared his moral reservations about the peculiar institution. After Graves closed his academy in Jessamine County, Waller evidently advised him to relocate to a free state; a move back to Ohio soon followed. Graves later protested that his expressed concerns about the abuses of slavery did not make him an abolitionist and that he did not return to Ohio for that reason: "We left Kentucky on a visit North to our mother, and sister and brother, and, if it must be told, so deeply enlisted another heart in our own interest and the 'Sunny South,' that she [his mother] left all and made its fair skies her own, and she now sleeps beneath them with her babes."[52]

While Graves made it sound like he undertook a quick trip to Ohio to fetch his mother and take her to live in a southern state with him, in reality he appreciably telescoped the duration of his second stay in the Buckeye State, which turned out to be at least a year and a half.[53] During that period, the aspiring minister applied the already strict disciplines of his work ethic to focused study of the Bible, theology, and foreign languages, including Greek. Unfortunately, the books that he might have read other than the Scriptures remain unidentified. All the same, his eight-hour-a-day scholarly regimen, coupled with his earlier nocturnal efforts in Kentucky, likely approximated the requirements of a college degree in those days. Although the nineteenth-century American frontier offered few opportunities to pursue formal schooling, Graves ambitiously charted a vigorous program of self-study that prepared him adequately for a demanding career in religious journalism, preaching, and theological polemics.[54]

---

[52] Graves, "The Last Charge of the S.W. Baptist. Has He Proved It?" [2]. Cf. Martin, "Samuel Henderson and His Response to J. R. Graves," 15ff.; and Smith, "A Critical Analysis of the Theology of J. R. Graves," 13–14. On more than one occasion Graves reprinted a July 12, 1853, letter from Waller to M. W. Phillips of Mississippi that seemed to vindicate Graves of the charge of abolitionism. For example, see Graves, "Abolitionism and the S.W. Baptist," *Tennessee Baptist,* July 17, 1858, [2]. In this context, Graves openly acknowledged himself as a slaveholder.

[53] See the dates (late 1843 to mid-1845) in Smith, "A Critical Analysis of the Theology of J. R. Graves," 14–15. Graves's own misleading summary of this time frame can be found in *The Little Iron Wheel,* 258.

[54] On his self-education, see Hailey, *J. R. Graves,* 19.

While in the Kingsville area, Graves evidently affiliated with the First Baptist Church, although surviving church records do not confirm it and the level of his participation in congregational life is unknown. Nonetheless, biographer Hailey narrated a possibly embellished incident in which Graves triumphantly stood up to an infidel through both a moving prayer and a two-hour sermon and thereby fortified local Baptists in neighboring Ashtabula. Finally, Graves married Lua Ellen Spencer of Kingsville in June of 1845, just before moving to Nashville, Tennessee. The daughter of Dr. Daniel and Marian Spencer, the new bride was also the sister of brother Z. C.'s wife Adelia.[55] Although Graves said or wrote virtually nothing about how this romantic relationship blossomed, he obviously allowed for some diversion from his studies. Moreover, his courtship and marriage suggest that perhaps his second time of residence in Ohio was more settled than his subsequent reminiscences admitted.

By the age of 25, J. R. Graves had experienced Baptist life in three states. While a structured Baptist *denomination* did not truly exist in the United States before 1845, Baptist identity in the context of several institutions, movements, and traditions had been taking shape in New England, the mid-Atlantic region, the Southeast, and the trans-Appalachian frontier. Graves's Vermont roots alerted him to some key elements of the Separate Baptist ethos such as local church independence, relatively strict practices regarding church ordinances, and resistance to both ecclesiastical and political tyranny. This Separate Baptist legacy continued to influence Baptists in Kentucky, even after the 1801 union of Regulars and Separates. Apart from the controversy over Campbellism in Kentucky, what Graves learned about Baptist life and thought there was not appreciably different from what he was exposed to in Vermont.

In fact, Graves's ecclesiological lessons on the Kentucky frontier resonated quite well with the Separate Baptist tradition in New England. From John Waller, in particular, he gleaned far more than just anti-Campbellite polemics. The noted Kentucky editor reinforced for Graves the impression that Baptist identity included emphases on the (1) independence and sovereignty of local, visible congregations; (2) repudiation by true churches of any efforts to persecute those who differ with them, which accompanied the Baptist insistence on ecclesiastical and political freedom; and (3) restriction of the Lord's Supper to immersed believers—although Graves later would tighten this further by insisting that only members of a particular local church should be invited to communion.

---

[55] On these biographical items, see ibid., 20–21; and Smith, "A Critical Analysis of the Theology of J. R. Graves," 14–15. Smith, 15, n44, cited a 1965 letter from the pastor of First Baptist, Kingsville, that reported no reference to the name Graves in church records. Smith, however, went on to note that Graves joined First Baptist, Nashville, in 1845 on the basis of a letter from the Kingsville church.

Furthermore, Waller espoused a theory of true church perpetuity that provided—along with New Englander J. Newton Brown's similar views—fertile ground for Graves's developing ideas about Baptist church successionism. At the same time, Waller and Graves ultimately disagreed on the concept of the universal church, as well as on practices like pulpit exchanges by ministers of different denominations and the acceptance by Baptist churches of immersions performed in non-Baptist settings.[56] Graves's fierce opposition to both pulpit affiliation and alien immersion set him apart from Waller and contributed to a consequential debate between them that is unfolded in the next chapter.

The main point of these considerations is that when Graves headed for Nashville in the summer of 1845 as a newlywed, he stood as a fairly typical representative of Baptist beliefs and practices that he had encountered in Vermont, Ohio, and Kentucky; his thinking, particularly about the church, was not unusual or exceptional. He had lived, fellowshipped, and struggled with a call to preach among mainly rural or small-town Baptists who embodied many of the basic principles of the Separate Baptist tradition. In addition, he attentively spotted the distinctive markers that these Baptists had posted to ensure their identity would not be lost or compromised. He also found Baptists to be combative dissenters, whether against the oppressive state churches in New England or the problematic teachings of Campbell and his followers in Kentucky and Ohio. Although Graves subsequently took positions that were classified as extreme by some of his contemporaries, much of what came to be known as Landmarkism was not radically discontinuous from what he was tutored in as a teenager and young man. Moreover, the ecclesiological agenda that he eventually set forth in Nashville had deep roots in both the New England and "western" frontier habitats of his first 25 years.

---

[56] The best treatment of Waller's ideas about the church is Lanier, "The Relationship of the Ecclesiology of John Lightfoot Waller to Early Landmarkism," 71–124. Cf. Tull, "A Study of Southern Baptist Landmarkism," 299–302, 311–13, 394.

Chapter 2

The Formation of a Boundary Staker

The Nashville Years (1845–62), Part I

NASHVILLE IN TRANSITION

When J. R. and Lua Graves arrived in Nashville in July of 1845, they found a relatively small, bustling city of about 8,000 people on the banks of the Cumberland River in what is unofficially called "Middle" Tennessee.[1] From a primitive settlement that was established by James Robertson late in 1779, before the end of the Revolutionary War, the area at first boasted little more than a stockade that was constructed for protection against Native Americans. Under the authority of the North Carolina legislature, nonetheless, Nashville became incorporated as a town in 1784 even before Tennessee achieved statehood in 1796.

In the early nineteenth century, its strategic location propelled Nashville's growth as a notable commercial, political, and even cultural center. Banks, steamboats, railroads, and the slave labor that worked the corn, cotton, and tobacco fields outside of Nashville all eventually contributed to growth and prosperity, in spite of setbacks caused by the financial panics of 1819 and 1837. The choice of Nashville as Tennessee's permanent state capital in 1843 in many ways symbolized the city's overall progress since its pioneer days. Although its frontier character still lingered somewhat through the early decades of the nineteenth century, the urbanization process was unmistakably in place.

Meanwhile, Nashville's rising political importance reached a national level in the 1820s with the presidential campaigns of Andrew Jackson. "Old Hickory," a Carolinian

---

[1] The 1840 census listed a population of almost 7,000, which grew to a little over 10,000 by 1850. See the table in A. S. Goodstein, *Nashville 1780–1860: From Frontier to City* (Gainesville: University of Florida Press, 1989). In this section, I am indebted to her monograph for providing helpful information on Nashville's early history.

who moved into Tennessee before it was a state, bought the Hermitage plantation near Nashville in 1804 and also gained repute as a lawyer, judge, politician, and military officer. After an unsuccessful bid for the presidency in 1824, Jackson subsequently was elected to two terms in the White House (1829–37). He oversaw the transformation of the Jeffersonian Republicans into the Jacksonian Democrats; so dominant was his political role in the 1820s and 1830s that Pulitzer Prize winning historian Arthur Schlesinger Jr. dubbed this era "the Age of Jackson."[2]

Jacksonian ideology was generally populist, egalitarian, and anti-aristocratic; Jackson built a strong base of support with the common people and attacked powerful entities like the Bank of the United States, which he viewed as an elitist institution that worked against the interests of farmers and laborers. Oddly enough, his championing of the "little people" did not extend to the slaves that he owned, nor to the Cherokee Indians that he forced westward during his presidency. Despite the long shadow that Jackson cast over Middle Tennessee—even after his death in 1845—the rival Whig party enjoyed some success on his home turf of Nashville well into the 1850s by promoting economic development, social mobility, and moral improvement; the Whigs, however, offered no compelling alternative to the Democrats on the slavery question.[3] As a later chapter illustrates, J. R. Graves was not immune to the political rhetoric of his day; for example, he evidently imbibed some of the motifs of Jacksonian democracy, including its dubious defense of slavery.

As Nashville gradually evolved from a frontier outpost to a modestly sized urban area, the growth of religious organizations tended to lag behind political and economic advances. In the context of the Second Great Awakening, the "western" frontier certainly did not lack for spiritual enthusiasm; for instance, camp meeting revivals in Bourbon and Logan counties in Kentucky attracted much attention and stirred considerable controversy over some of the "exercises" that accompanied the open-air preaching and singing. Although the camp meetings originated under Presbyterian auspices, Methodists, Baptists, and the emerging "Christian" movement seemed better poised to exploit the new energies and methods that shaped these revivals.[4] Nevertheless, religious excitement in the hinterlands did not bring immediate or dramatic church growth to Nashville.

---

[2] A. M. Schlesinger Jr., *The Age of Jackson* (Boston: Little, Brown, 1945). See pp. 36–38 for a concise discussion of Jackson's achievements in Tennessee before moving to Washington.

[3] For how the Democrat versus Whig competition played out in Nashville politics, see Goodstein, *Nashville 1780–1860*, 93–135, 157–204.

[4] See P. Conkin, *Cane Ridge: America's Pentecost* (Madison: University of Wisconsin Press, 1990). For a contemporary account of the more unusual phenomena, see P. Cartwright, *Autobiography* (Nashville:

Methodists and Baptists; in fact, both focused their initial church-planting efforts in the rural areas of the Cumberland region.[5]

Methodists and Presbyterians showed the greatest progress in Nashville during the late eighteenth and early nineteenth centuries. The Methodists, who utilized the tireless ministries of circuit riders, appeared to have the first church house in the city, a small stone building that was purchased in 1790 but proved to be a temporary facility. In 1812 they put up another building near the edges of town at about the same time that the Presbyterians built a church in a more central location. In the long run, the Methodists surpassed the Presbyterians in numbers and overall popularity, ultimately making Nashville a vital hub for Methodism in the South. Methodists also represented the largest denominational grouping by the time that Graves and his wife came to Nashville. Indeed, Graves's biographer O. L. Hailey claimed that Methodists in Nashville outnumbered Baptists five to one in the late 1840s.[6]

Moreover, Baptists seemed to avoid intentional work in Nashville for many years as they primarily relied on farmer-preachers to start churches in the rural communities that surrounded Nashville. The region's most vibrant Baptist congregation in the early nineteenth century was the Mill Creek church, which began in 1797 in a home about five miles from Nashville. It was led for many years by James Whitsitt, who simultaneously pastored other Baptist churches in the area and vigorously supported associational endeavors. This preacher was the grandfather of William Whitsitt (1841–1911), who grew up in the Mill Swamp church, knew J. R. Graves, but much later incurred the wrath of Landmarkers when he challenged their successionist view of Baptist history.[7]

The first Baptist congregation within Nashville proper essentially sprang from an 1820 revival preached by evangelist Jeremiah Vardeman in both a former Methodist building and the city courthouse. Whitsitt and his church closely cooperated with the revivalist, and many of the new converts were soon baptized and accepted into the membership of Mill Swamp Baptist. By July, 35 individuals brought letters of dismissal from Mill Swamp and duly constituted what became the First Baptist Church of Nashville.

Abingdon, 1956), 33–49. Cartwright was a Methodist circuit rider and frontier evangelist who originally published his memoirs in 1856.

[5] On the general range of early denominational activity in Middle Tennessee, with a major focus on Baptists, see L. E. May Jr., *The First Baptist Church of Nashville, Tennessee, 1820–1970* (Nashville: First Baptist Church, 1970), 14–21.

[6] O. L. Hailey, *J. R. Graves: Life, Times, and Teachings* (Nashville: By the author, 1929), 23. On Methodist and Presbyterian progress in Nashville, see Goodstein, *Nashville 1780–1860*, 15–16, 56–60.

[7] J. H. Slatton, *W. H. Whitsitt: The Man and the Controversy* (Macon, GA: Mercer University Press, 2009), 2. On Mill Creek, see May, *First Baptist Church*, 17–20.

Thus when J. R. and Lua Graves moved to Nashville and joined this church, it had been in existence for just 25 years. Furthermore, the church almost died in the 1820s when its second pastor, Philip Fall, successfully persuaded most of the members to embrace the Restorationist principles of Alexander Campbell. Since only a tiny remnant of five resisted Fall—and, in the process lost their meeting house on what was then Spring Street—First Baptist's very survival seemed uncertain until 1834, when the by then 105-member congregation called R. B. C. Howell (1801–68) of Virginia as its fourth pastor. This distinguished Baptist statesman, who engaged Graves in a monumental fracas in the late 1850s, assumed his duties in Nashville in early 1835.[8]

J. R. Graves lived and worked in the burgeoning river town of Nashville for almost 17 years; he was 25 when he came and 42 when he fled the city during the Civil War. It was arguably the most critical period of his long career; after all, in Nashville he emerged as a major voice in Baptist journalism, launched a publishing empire, fathered one of the most influential movements in nineteenth-century Southern Baptist life, and engaged in the most heated controversies of his life. The reputation that he acquired during the Nashville years basically defined the man for years in the minds of both his friends and enemies. In addition, the ways in which he is remembered today have been largely molded by what he did, said, and wrote in the Tennessee capital.

For Graves, the Nashville setting helped to crystallize what he brought to the city from prior experiences in Vermont and Kentucky. In a context of denominational pluralism, the Baptists of Nashville were an embattled species. Methodists, Presbyterians, and the followers of Alexander Campbell all seemed stronger and posed a threat to the still fragile Baptist identity. His roots in the Separate Baptist tradition suggested an ecclesiological path that might strengthen the Baptist cause and delineate its fundamental distinctives. Baptist clashes with Campbellites for control of local churches that Graves undoubtedly heard about when he arrived in Nashville surely reinforced the antagonism toward the Disciples movement that he had begun to cultivate in Kentucky. Hence, it was in Nashville that Graves commenced to stake Baptist boundaries in earnest.

FAMILY AND WORK

Although the precise reasons for the newlyweds' choice of Nashville remain murky, an announcement in R. B. C. Howell's *Baptist* pointed to their coming: "The Rev. J. R.

---

[8] Ibid., 21–53.

GRAVES, of Lexington, Ky., has arrived in Nashville, and wishes to conduct a Classical School the next Session. He may be found at the City Hotel."[9] Probably because of his prior experience with educational academies in Ohio and Kentucky, Graves soon opened the Vine Street Classical and Mathematical Academy in rented facilities. Unfortunately, historical records reveal very little about the school; no available source, for example, even indicates how long it was in operation.[10] In the bigger picture of Graves's Nashville years, whatever services that he rendered at the Vine Street academy appear to be inconsequential.

In less than two weeks after settling in Nashville, the young Graves couple became members of First Baptist Church, J. R. by transfer of letter from the Kingsville, Ohio, church and Lua by "application."[11] The Nashville congregation now boasted more than 330 members and a stately, four-year-old building on what was then Summer Street; it had clearly recovered from a rocky first decade and was progressing nicely under the pastoral leadership of Howell, who was marking 10 years of service. In addition to his local ministry, Howell contributed to the Baptist cause as editor of a denominational paper, supporter of cooperative mission ventures in the state, and an early leader of the newly created Southern Baptist Convention. He became a strong proponent of this new body after being elected—*in absentia*—as a vice president at the May 1845 organizational meeting in Augusta, Georgia.[12]

Although more than a decade later Graves and Howell would be the central protagonists in an intense conflict at First Baptist, the two appeared to have a constructive relationship in the mid-1840s. First, editor Howell invited his new member to write

---

[9] *Baptist*, June 28, 1845, 720. The capital letters were in the original. Presumably editor Howell, who started the denominational paper shortly after assuming the pulpit at First Baptist Nashville in 1835, inserted the announcement—perhaps at Graves's request. The references to Lexington and the timing of the move are puzzling, since Graves had most recently resided in Ohio and came to Nashville with his wife in early July (not late June). On the confusion surrounding the relocation, including whether or not John Waller of Kentucky had a role in it, see H. S. Smith, "A Critical Analysis of the Theology of J. R. Graves" (Th.D. diss., Southern Baptist Theological Seminary, 1966), 16, n48 and n49.

[10] The brief discussion in Smith, "A Critical Analysis of the Theology of J. R. Graves," 16–17, is typical of how the secondary sources treat this episode in Graves's career.

[11] Ibid., 17.

[12] Secondary literature on Howell includes J. W. Burton, *Road to Augusta: R. B. C. Howell and the Formation of the Southern Baptist Convention* (Nashville: Broadman, 1976); J. E. Hilton, "Robert Boyté Howell's Contribution to Baptist Ecclesiology: Nineteenth Century Baptist Ecclesiology in Controversy" (Ph.D. diss., Southeastern Baptist Theological Seminary, 2005); L. T. Horne, "A Study of the Life and Work of R. B. C. Howell" (Th.D. diss., Southern Baptist Theological Seminary, 1958); and R. B. Spain, "R. B. C. Howell, Tennessee Baptist (1801–1868)" (M.A. thesis, Vanderbilt University, 1948).

occasional pieces for the *Baptist*, including a series in which Graves pleaded for Baptists in Tennessee to support organized mission and benevolence activities designed to reach American Indians in the West. These articles revealed a frank uneasiness about white mistreatment of Native Americans, as well as a genuine desire to reach them with the gospel. Moreover, they suggested that Graves did not align himself with the anti-mission Baptists who had caused division in several Tennessee churches—including First Baptist—by opposing any intentional or structured evangelistic and missionary endeavors; on the contrary, he promoted agencies like the Indian Mission Association almost from the beginning of his time in Nashville.[13]

Second, Howell apparently paved the way for Graves to become pastor of Second Baptist Church, Nashville, later in 1845. Under Howell's leadership, this Cherry Street congregation was established as a mission church on the city's College Hill district in early 1844, with Thomas Haynes serving as first pastor. It is not clear why Haynes left, but the church had suffered membership losses, many of which were attributable to a Campbellite schism. At Graves's installation in November of 1845, Howell gave the prayer as well as charges to the church and the new pastor. Soon after, Howell applauded Graves in the *Baptist*: "The Pastor, who is lately of Kentucky, although quite young, is thoroughly educated, exemplary in his piety, ardently devoted to his work, and not without some ministerial experience."[14] Howell continued to provide encouraging updates on Second Baptist in his paper, including a poignant account of Graves's first

---

[13] J. R. Graves, "Indian Missions. A Parable.—No. 1," *Baptist*, August 30, 1845, 20–22; "Appeal for Indian Missions. No. II," *Baptist*, September 6, 1845, 39–40; "The Indians. No. III," *Baptist*, September 13, 1845, 53–55. On the anti-mission movement among Baptists in Tennessee, see A. Wardin, *Tennessee Baptists: A Comprehensive History, 1799–1999* (Brentwood, TN: Executive Board of the Tennessee Baptist Convention, 1999), 137–57. Two historians have suggested that the anti-mission crusade helped "to provide a favorable milieu for the dramatic spread of Landmarkism." See R. T. Hughes and C. L. Allen, *Illusions of Innocence: Protestant Primitivism in America, 1630–1875* (Chicago: University of Chicago Press, 1988), 92. Although Graves eventually raised alarms about mission boards beyond the control of local churches, he specifically repudiated anti-missionism, calling it "an unscriptural sect and apostate from the faith and practice of the Apostolic Baptists." See Graves, *Trilemma: All Human Churches without Baptism, or Death by Three Horns*, 2nd ed. (Memphis: Graves, Mahaffy & Co., 1881; repr., Memphis: J. R. Graves & Son, 1890), 198. The original edition was published in 1860 (Nashville: Graves, Marks, & Co.), when the anti-mission controversy could still arouse a passionate response. Graves's very first published offering in Howell's paper likewise showed his support for denominational causes, namely the Baptist weekly itself. See Graves, "Our Paper," *Baptist*, August 30, 1845, 19.

[14] R. B. C. Howell, "Installation," *Baptist* (November 8, 1845): 178. On the origins of Second Baptist, see May, *The First Baptist Church of Nashville*, 70–71.

communion service in early 1846 at which his long-widowed mother Lois, a former Congregationalist, was admitted to membership:

> The fact of her reception, the affectionate address of her son—choked with weeping—and her own streaming eyes, filled the whole house with tears. She has the appearance of almost youth. She remarked, that she had, she confessed it, always been a Baptist at heart, that from her sons, she had given TWO MINISTERS to the Baptist Church, and that she could not, in conscience, any longer withhold *herself.*[15]

These encouraging comments thus seemed to infer that Graves's first months at Second Baptist were proceeding acceptably under the tutelage of First Baptist and her pastor.

While the written accounts from Howell's editorial pen contain no hint of any friction with Graves, the occasion of Lois Graves joining Second Baptist possibly touched off some questions in her son's mind about the validity of her immersion by a Congregationalist minister in 1832. Many years later, well after his infamous row with Howell at First Baptist in the late 1850s, Graves even claimed that as a 12-year-old he entertained reservations about his mother's baptism. Apparently when she presented herself for membership at Second Baptist in 1846, Graves turned to Howell for advice; the older pastor evidently communicated at least a tacit approval of "pedobaptist" immersion—i.e., done by someone who would normally sprinkle infants. Graves, however, later recounted that the whole affair caused him to examine carefully the issue of who could legitimately administer baptism.[16] Since Graves's memories in his later years were not always accurate—including his recollection of the time frame between his mother's immersion in Vermont and her affiliation with his church in Nashville—he might have been projecting future concerns backward to early 1846. At the same time, Graves openly solicited questions about acceptable baptismal boundaries less than two years after his mother was received at Second Baptist. Hence, some connection likely

---

[15] Howell, "Nashville Second Church," *Baptist,* January 10, 1846, 306. Capitals and italics are both in original. Available sources do not indicate the exact time of Lois Graves's arrival in Nashville.

[16] Graves, *Old Landmarkism: What Is It?* 2nd ed. (Memphis: Baptist Book House; Graves, Mahaffy & Company, 1881), ix–xi. On Howell's alleged acceptance of alien immersions at First Baptist, see Graves, "Reaction of Injury," *Tennessee Baptist,* July 10, 1858, [2].

existed between that event and his impending rejection of "alien" immersion, although it was almost a decade before his mother was baptized by a Baptist administrator.[17]

At any rate, Graves stayed at Second Baptist for almost four years, even though many biographical sources erroneously report it as a one-year pastorate.[18] At times his ministry there suffered from distractions, such as travel in support of his growing journalistic and publication interests, the loss of an infant son Zuinglius, and his wife's serious illness.[19] Nevertheless, active membership tripled in his first year; in addition, debt was liquidated and a building program launched in the second year. By 1848 Graves noted that a total of 123 members had been received by letter and baptism during his first three years at the church. His pressing duties with the *Tennessee Baptist* and his publishing firm finally led to his resignation in September of 1849, when he and Lua reunited with First Baptist Church.[20] Although he preached on numerous occasions after this, he did not serve as the regular pastor of a local church until he led the Spring Street congregation following the schism at First Baptist in 1858.

Third, Howell had a distinct role in helping to put his younger protégé in an editorial post at the *Baptist* that in due course would necessitate Graves's departure from Second Baptist. Late in 1846, when the newspaper functioned under the Tennessee Baptist Education Society's Committee of Publication, Graves was appointed as assistant editor while Howell continued as editor-in-chief. Even though Graves had shown an obvious interest in the paper and had contributed some articles, he seemingly possessed minimal qualifications for editorial responsibilities. Nonetheless, Howell introduced the

---

[17] See Graves, "Ecclesiastical Questions," *Tennessee Baptist,* August 1847, [2]. On his mother's eventual rebaptism, see previous chapter, n7. Graves telescoped the time between the 1847 piece and his mother's 1855 baptism in *Old Landmarkism,* xi.

[18] The original source of this misinformation appears to be S. H. Ford, "Life, Times and Teachings of J. R. Graves," *Ford's Christian Repository and Home Circle,* October 1899, 606ff. It has been repeated several times; e.g., H. L. Grice, "Graves, James Robinson," in *Encyclopedia of Southern Baptists* (Nashville: Broadman, 1958), 1:576.

[19] On his travel, see "Nashville Second Church," *Baptist,* November 21, 1846, 193. On the death of his son, see the note "DIED," *Baptist,* September 12, 1846, 47 (capitalization in original). On Lua's illness, see Howell, "To the Second Church, and Others in Nashville," *Tennessee Baptist,* July 10, 1847, [2].

[20] On statistical and financial progress at Second Baptist, see "Nashville Second Church," 193; Howell, "Second Church, Nashville," *Baptist,* February 20, 1847, 401 or 409 (pagination discrepancy); "Second Baptist Church," *Tennessee Baptist,* September 4, 1847, [2]; and Graves, "Extract from the Anniversary Sermon of 1848," *Tennessee Baptist,* February 8, 1849, [3]. On Graves's resignation from Second Baptist, see "Resignation," *Tennessee Baptist,* September 20, 1849, [2]; and Graves, ed., *The Little Iron Wheel: A Declaration of Christian Rights and Articles, Showing the Despotism of Episcopal Methodism* (Nashville: South-Western Publishing House; Graves, Marks & Co., 1856), 260.

new name on the masthead as "our beloved brother J. R. Graves, the indefatigable and successful pastor of the Second Church in this city. Brother Graves is already favorably known to many of you as an eloquent speaker, and a very handsome writer."[21] A change in the business side of the *Baptist* quickly followed the new editorial appointment; the publication, printing, and debts of the newspaper passed to Graves and A. B. Shankland, who had recently become partners in a Nashville bookstore, while the Education Society still owned the list of about 1,000 subscribers.

By May of 1847 the periodical assumed a new name, the *Tennessee Baptist*, and a wider format that allowed more columns per page. In the fall of 1847 Graves organized the Tennessee Baptist Publication Society; this led the Education Society—which now operated under the Baptist General Association of Tennessee—to shift all interests in the paper to Graves's new entity. In light of all these changes, it is hardly surprising that Howell relinquished his editorship in June of 1848; by this time the TBPS had been duly chartered, with Graves listed as corresponding secretary. Graves was now in full control of the newspaper and continued in that capacity for four decades. For his part, Howell departed Nashville in 1850 to shepherd Second Baptist Church of Richmond, Virginia; he returned to Nashville in 1857, when he would engage with Graves in an intense conflict at First Baptist that would eventually affect the entire Southern Baptist Convention.[22]

The career opportunity in religious journalism that J. R. Graves stepped into beginning in 1846 proved to be momentous. While he was manifestly a man of many talents such as preaching and public debate, he commanded his greatest audiences through his writing, editing, and publishing. He gained considerable renown—as well as notoriety—

---

[21] Howell, "An Assistant," *Baptist,* November 21, 1846, 193. On the apparently unknown origin of Graves's interest in religious journalism, see Smith, "A Critical Analysis of the Theology of J. R. Graves," 17, n53. Later, in a more contentious time, Howell specifically labeled Graves's pastorate as "unsuccessful." See Howell, "Charges against Rev. J. R. Graves," Robert Boyté Crawford Howell Collection, AR. 595, vol. 1 (2), SBHLA, Nashville, Tennessee. Howell's additional comments in this same context revealed a different understanding of the new appointment than Graves himself entertained. Cf. Graves, ed., *The Little Iron Wheel,* 261; and "Personal History," *Tennessee Baptist,* March 12, 1859, [4].

[22] The changes with the paper can be tracked through several of its issues; e.g., Graves, "The Baptist" and "The Baptist Depository," *Baptist,* November 28, 1846, 212; Title Page, *Tennessee Baptist,* May 1, 1847, [1]; and Masthead, *Tennessee Baptist,* June 29, 1848, [1], which omitted Howell's name. Howell later aired his objections to Graves's "style and spirit" as an editor. See "Charges against Rev. J. R. Graves," Howell Collection, vol. 1 (2). A useful summary of the sometimes confusing developments of 1846–48 can be found in Wardin, *Tennessee Baptists,* 159–64. For an overview of the editorial leadership of Howell and Graves, see W. F. Allen, *Telling the Truth in Love: A Brief History of the "Baptist and Reflector" from 1835,* ed. L. Wilkey (Nashville: Fields Publishing, 2005), 17–35.

through the *Tennessee Baptist* as it became the primary vehicle for his attempts to define Baptist distinctives and shape denominational identity.

At the same time, his editorial efforts drew support from the sizable publishing network that he ambitiously launched in Nashville. Although the Tennessee Baptist Publication Society stumbled into oblivion when Graves and Shankland terminated their partnership in 1854, Graves and his brother-in-law W. P. Marks joined together the following year in a publishing venture that took the trade name of South-Western Publishing House. Eventually, Graves's publishing empire faced financial distress and controversy within Southern Baptist circles. Nonetheless, it allowed him to crank out a steady stream of books and pamphlets, some of which originated as series in the newspaper. It likewise made possible additional periodical literature like the *Southern Baptist Almanac and Annual Register*, begun in 1848 when he was still allied with Shankland, and the *Southern Baptist Review and Eclectic*, a journal of thought and opinion that was published between 1855 and 1861 by Graves, Marks, and Company.[23] What became known as Landmarkism in the 1850s was integrally related to all these publications; the movement would not have been as widely and effectively promoted without them.

The *Tennessee Baptist*, of course, predictably remained the strategic nerve center of Graves's Nashville enterprise, if only because he built up its circulation to around 13,000 in Tennessee and surrounding states by the late 1850s.[24] From this platform, the Landmark patriarch exhibited remarkable print media skills for someone who was not formally trained in journalism. As Barry Jones put it in his assessment, Graves's "understanding and use of the communication tools at his disposal gave him wide influence in his denomination."[25] In an era when a denominational press was in its infancy, he easily surpassed Howell and most of his contemporaries as an innovative, albeit idiosyncratic religious journalist.

---

[23] For a helpful overview of Graves's publishing endeavors, see H. L. Grice, "Graves (James Robinson) Publication Organizations," in *Encyclopedia of Southern Baptists* (Nashville: Broadman, 1958), 1:578–80. On the almanac and theological journal, see Smith, "A Critical Analysis of the Theology of J. R. Graves," 63–65.

[24] Graves, "The Year and Its Close," *Tennessee Baptist,* December 25, 1858, [3]; and Graves, "The Goal Won at Last," *Tennessee Baptist,* January 8, 1859, [2]. In the latter he claimed that his paper was the largest Baptist weekly in the world, and he was probably right. According to Graves, "Editorial Telegrams," *Tennessee Baptist,* March 12, 1860, [2], the number of subscribers hit 14,500.

[25] B. W. Jones, "James R. Graves, Baptist Newspaper Editor: Catalyst for Religious Controversy, 1846–1893" (Ph.D. diss., Ohio University, 1994), 158. Jones's degree is from the College of Communication at Ohio University; therefore, his focus is more on journalism than theology.

While Graves's ideological face was displayed most prominently in the pages of the *Tennessee Baptist*, his more personal side occasionally surfaced. In fact, the paucity of unpublished sources from Graves himself puts even more of a premium on what the newspaper revealed about matters like marriage and family. In early 1851, for example, the editor experienced another tragic loss when his wife Lua, to whom he had been married about five and a half years, died while delivering a baby daughter, Luella.[26] Graves, who tended to be quite reserved about such things, did not comment much on his first wife's death until the almost 10-year-old Luella passed away from croup and scarlet fever in the fall of 1860. In the intervening time, he had married Louise Jane Snider in 1856; they subsequently brought five children into the world before her death in 1867. All the same, as Graves noted in a sad newspaper column right after Luella's death, she was "the last sweet link that connected us to our former family." Continuing his use of the editorial first person plural, he then clarified this obvious reference to his first wife: "Child after child we were called to give up until the last one was taken; then the wife of our youth left us, the night she bade farewell for Heaven, and placed this almost perfect image of herself in our arms and gave it her name—the only living memento of our love. How much the labor of our life has been influenced by her." The grieving father concluded with a poetic tribute to the "lovely flower" who was with the Lord in "bright angelic form."[27] While Graves earned a deserved reputation as a hard-edged polemicist, he was fully capable of bringing a measure of pathos into his paper.

The sprightly editor also used his periodical to report on some of his own physical problems. His frequent preaching and speaking engagements apparently placed a severe strain on his larynx to the degree that one doctor advised him in 1853 to suspend such activities for a year. Graves expressed palpable frustration in that he had just returned from a two-month trip to the East Coast to seek relief: "We return with the disease

---

[26] S. E. S, "Obituaries," *Tennessee Baptist,* January 18, 1851, [3]; and Adelia C. Graves, "Lament for My Lost Ones," *Tennessee Baptist,* February 22, 1851, [4]. The latter was a poem written by Lua's sister (and J. R.'s brother's wife).

[27] Graves, "The Dark Cloud," *Tennessee Baptist,* November 10, 1860, [2]. The loss also was noted in T., "Death of Luella Kells Graves," *Tennessee Baptist,* November 3, 1860, [2]. The "labor of our life" that Graves referred to included his careerlong interest in strengthening female education. On his second marriage and family, see Smith, "A Critical Analysis of the Theology of J. R. Graves," 42–43. Neither Smith nor any other biographical source, however, supplies the date of the wedding. I discovered through Internet surfing that it occurred in Madison County, Tennessee, and called the county clerk's office to learn that it was July 31, 1856. The more than five-year gap between the death of his first wife and his marriage to Louise suggests that Graves, who was frequently away from home, relied on his mother for much of the care of young Luella during that time.

greatly aggravated. We have never suffered more at any previous time."[28] He later rued the abuse that he had inflicted on his voice as a young preacher; he even published in the *Tennessee Baptist* a series of practical talks that he had given to ministers, urging them to avoid such things as speaking in a monotone, wearing stiff collars, or using tobacco.[29]

One additional nugget of advice that Graves offered his ministerial audience was a bit hairy; he recommended that they let their beards "grow upon the glands."[30] His promotion of beards actually reflected a strict biblicist hermeneutic that sometimes showed in his writings, particularly those that addressed Christian practice or church order. His six-part series on beards, which appeared in his newspaper during the early period of the Civil War, began by proof texting Lev 19:27, "Do not cut the hair at the sides of your head or clip off the edges of your beard" (NIV), and also citing Ps 133:1–2, which compares brothers living together in unity with precious oil running down Aaron's beard.[31] For Graves, the Bible was clear that men should proudly cultivate beards. As the series proceeded, he blamed the Roman Catholic Church for the tiresome routine of shaving; furthermore, he classified the razor as "a heathenish and barbarous tool."[32] Toward the end of this set of articles, he invoked more than a touch of male chauvinism by extolling the beard as "one of the distinguishing characteristics of the ruling sex."[33] In his cultural context, Graves's spirited defense of long beards probably raised few eyebrows. On the other hand, to run a protracted series on the subject in wartime may indicate that he was running short on material to publish, or that he could be obsessive on some issues.

A MODE OF MILITANCY

Despite intermittent diversions on adiaphorous matters like beards, the father of Landmarkism manifestly intended that the *Tennessee Baptist* be principally devoted to the beliefs and practices that made Baptists a distinctive people. News, advertisements, poetry, sermons, and travel reports certainly had their place in the denominational paper;

---

[28] Graves, "Personal," *Tennessee Baptist,* July 16, 1853, [2].

[29] Graves, "To Ministers about the Voice [in four parts]," *Tennessee Baptist,* March 30–April 14, 1860, all on [2].

[30] Graves, "To Ministers about the Voice. Talk No. 4," *Tennessee Baptist,* April 14, 1860, [2].

[31] Graves, "The Beard—History and Uses of," *Tennessee Baptist,* December 7, 1861, [2].

[32] Graves, "The Beard—Its History and Uses. No. 3," *Tennessee Baptist,* December 21, 1861, [2]. Monastic practices may have been behind his charge against Catholicism.

[33] Graves, "The Beard—Its History and Uses. No. 5," *Tennessee Baptist,* January 11, 1862, [2]. See Smith, "A Critical Analysis of the Theology of J. R. Graves," 209–10, for a discussion of Graves and beards.

Graves, however, typically subordinated such items to what he sensed as a divine mission—standing firm for the historic Baptist truths. Chad Hall has captured this dimension of Graves as well as any modern researcher:

> Graves drew from a deep well of confidence that was divinely supplied. His task was godly. His aim was clear. His efforts were focused. Such were the traits of a man motivated by what he perceived to be God's calling. Graves believed that God had named him for a special task. . . . Graves saw himself as God's appointed gardener, charged with removing the ecclesiological weeds from the American frontier.[34]

As an editor, Graves held some extraordinary reins of influence that greatly facilitated his fulfillment of that call.

Not long after R. B. C. Howell yielded his already ebbing editorial responsibilities at the *Tennessee Baptist*, it became evident that Graves anticipated a robustly controversial role for the newspaper. By this time, brewing conflict over baptismal questions was undoubtedly weighing on the young editor. Reminiscent of an Old Testament prophet (Ezek 3:17ff.), he saw himself as a watchman on the wall who, in the face of danger, had the solemn duty "to sound the alarm, else blood will be found on us." In almost the same breath, he turned to the New Testament, where he found a Paul "who was a great agitator, and controversialist."[35]

Several months later, in the context of a general attack on the Protestantism of his day, Graves doggedly allowed no room for neutrality or compromise in religion as he called for Christian soldiers "not only to *entrench against error*, but to carry war into its very strong holds."[36] He implored the true church—i.e., Baptists—to be both vigilant and militant like "an army in active operation, waging a war of extermination upon sin and error in every shape and guise." Moreover, Graves hammered home the point that Baptists were "a distinct people" who should refuse to cooperate with non-Baptists, even in the enterprise of world evangelization. In conclusion, the editor appealed to his

---

[34] C. W. Hall, "When Orphans Become Heirs: J. R. Graves and the Landmark Baptists," *Baptist History and Heritage* 38 (Winter 2002): 122. For an overview of Graves as a controversialist, see Smith, "A Critical Analysis of the Theology of J. R. Graves," 81ff. One historian has suggested that Graves stirred controversy not only out of conviction but also as one way of attracting new subscribers. See W. M. Patterson, "The Southern Baptist Theologian as Controversialist: A Contrast," *Baptist History and Heritage* 15 (July 1980): 9–10.

[35] Graves, "A Chapter on Controversy," *Tennessee Baptist,* February 8, 1849, [2].

[36] Graves, "Volume Sixth," *Tennessee Baptist,* September 6, 1849, [2].

denominational colleagues to remember past oppression and to remain steadfast in current battles:

> We advise Baptists to stand "firm as the surge repelling rock," upon the ground that has so oft been made the altar upon which our fathers have been offered in sacrifice by even protestants, because they would not bow the knee to the great idol they have set up. Though we feel it our duty to oppose their principles, let us do it in love, and in the spirit of religion.[37]

Graves did not explain exactly how militancy would mix with the more positive virtues that he evoked at the end of his editorial. In terms of the tone that was conveyed in his published writings, the former plainly trumped the latter. At times, however, observers detected a softer, more charitable demeanor in his public addresses and debates.[38]

Throughout the Nashville years, Graves stood constantly ready and willing to engage in combat against the enemy. In early 1857, before his epic struggle with Howell and First Baptist Church, he had the threats posed by those outside the Baptist fold more in mind when he once again employed martial images to motivate the troops: "Christ Jesus wants Christian soldiers of just such nerve and moral heroism."[39] His frequent allusions to spiritual and ecclesiastical warfare disclosed an aggressive temperament that probably caused his opponents to characterize him as obnoxious or angry. His style of attack and defense could not have been accidental or impromptu; after all, the setting of well-defined boundaries between Baptists and other Christian groups ultimately benefited from an approach that highlighted differences, and avoided ambiguity or compromise. The problem that Graves discovered rather early in his editorial career was that not all his fellow Baptists were ready to demarcate border lines as tightly or narrowly as he did. In fact, the period 1847–51 proved to be especially formative for Graves as a boundary staker. During that time he attempted to put distance between Baptists and other denominations, only to find that some of his Baptist brethren openly resisted his efforts.[40]

---

[37] Ibid.

[38] See "J. R. Graves in Mississippi," *Tennessee Baptist,* October 13, 1860, [3], which was an account of a Graves discourse that originally appeared in the *Eastern Clarion* of Paulding, Mississippi.

[39] Graves, "Stand Firm," *Tennessee Baptist,* February 28, 1857, [2].

[40] See P. W. Stripling, "Attitudes Reflected in the Editorials of J. R. Graves, 1848–1851" (Th.M. thesis, Southwestern Baptist Theological Seminary, 1965), 103. He argued that Graves's "later ideals and all their ramifications can be found in embryonic stages in this period. . . . These few years can serve as a modified

THE CONFLICT WITH JOHN WALLER

As early as 1847 Graves came to realize that not all Baptists agreed with him on some basic issues relating to church life. In that year he initiated a column called "Ecclesiastical Questions" in which he responded to inquiries from readers. In June of that year John A. Wheelock of Eastport, Mississippi, wrote and asked Graves the following question: "Is it scriptural to receive members from a Paedobaptist denomination, who have been immersed by a Pedobaptist denomination, without re-baptizing them?" The *Tennessee Baptist* editor responded in the August 14 issue by first rewording the query to read, "Ought a person, immersed by a Paedobaptist, to be received into our communion without baptism?" This rewording actually anticipated his answer by implying that pedobaptist immersion was not true baptism. Graves went on to insist that the kingdom of Christ had explicit laws that needed to be followed when it came to ecclesiastical order, particularly those regarding the requirements for the administrator of any valid baptism. Graves then drew what was for him an inescapable conclusion:

> Therefore, no one is amenable to church membership who has not been
> immersed by an administrator, *who is himself an immersed believer.* If you are
> a Baptist, this must be your decision. . . . To admit a person immersed by an
> unimmersed administrator, would be to admit into your church an unbaptized
> person, and this would be in violation both of the Scripture and the usage of
> our church—consequently schismatic. It would be surrendering one of the great
> doctrines of our church.[41]

The young editor thus appeared to be driving a boundary stake concerning Baptist practice that he did not follow himself when admitting his mother to Second Baptist only a little over a year and a half earlier. He later reported he had changed his mind on this issue due to inquiries like Wheelock's, although his mother was not scripturally baptized—according to his standards—for another eight years.[42]

---

gauge of the total spectrum of Graves' attitudes." Stripling could have strengthened his case by beginning in 1847.

[41] The material in this paragraph is drawn from Graves, "Ecclesiastical Questions," *Tennessee Baptist,* August 14, 1847, [2]. Eastport was spelled incorrectly as "Easport," and the state was abbreviated as "Mi." The assumption here is that Mississippi was intended, since there is no evidence that the newspaper circulated as far away as Michigan in 1847.

[42] See Graves, *Old Landmarkism*, x–xi, where he explained how he came to reject alien immersion.

In the context of answering Brother Wheelock, Graves also maintained on similar grounds that "we as Baptists cannot invite our Paedobaptist brethren to our communion table. We can find no authority in the Bible to invite any to the Lord's table, except such as have been properly baptized, nor can we partake with them."[43] This second point, however, was clearly overshadowed by the baptismal question for several years, as Graves admitted much later in his career.[44] Indeed, the dispute with John Waller from Kentucky, his friend since 1841, focused primarily on the issue of alien immersion.

In 1848 Waller, editor of the *Western Baptist Review*, defended the practice of Baptist churches accepting Pedobaptist immersions in his reply to an inquiry from Richard B. Burleson, a pastor in the Muscle Shoals Association of Alabama.[45] Shortly thereafter, the pseudonyms of "Fidus" and "Veritas" as signatories to a series of letters in the *Tennessee Baptist* came to dominate the discussion of this issue, with Fidus attacking alien immersion and Veritas defending Waller's position. Although the identities of these two contributors have not been convincingly established, Graves's son-in-law O. L. Hailey penciled in "OLH. 7/27/91—is J. R. Graves" by the name "Mr. Fidus" in a hard copy of the *Tennessee Baptist* that he later donated to Southwestern Baptist Theological Seminary.[46] If Graves indeed was Fidus, he sustained a considerable work of fiction for some time, because Fidus was consistently portrayed in the paper as a correspondent from the abovementioned Muscle Shoals who was actively involved in the associational discussions that had led to Burleson's contact with Waller. At one point, moreover, Graves outwardly directed this editorial exhortation to both Fidus and Veritas: "Brethren, write kindly and affectionately, and you will be heard."[47] At any rate, readers

---

[43] Graves, "Ecclesiastical Questions," [2].

[44] Graves, *Intercommunion Inconsistent, Unscriptural and Productive of Evil* (Memphis: Baptist Book House; Graves, Mahaffy, 1881), 14. He wrote some on the Lord's Supper in 1848 defending restricted communion, but soon after this became absorbed in the controversy with John Waller. See Graves, "The Lord's Supper," *Tennessee Baptist,* May 11, 1848, [1]; "The Lord's Supper, No. II," *Tennessee Baptist,* May 18, 1848, [3]; and "The Lord[']s Supper, No. III, *Tennessee Baptist,* May 25, 1848, [3]. Cf. Graves, "Plain Answers to Plain Questions," *Tennessee Baptist,* November 16, 1848, [2], where he defined the Lord's Supper as a church ordinance and rejected communing with Pedobaptists. At this point he did not appear to limit communion exclusively to members of a local congregation.

[45] J. L. Waller, "The Validity of Baptism by Pedobaptist Ministers," *Western Baptist Review* 3 (March 1848): 267–72.

[46] The note can be found in the margin of SWBTS's copy of the *Tennessee Baptist,* June 29, 1848, [2]. A bound set of the newspapers is housed in the Roberts Library on the seminary campus, Fort Worth, Texas.

[47] Graves, "To Our Correspondents Fidus and Veritas," *Tennessee Baptist,* July 20, 1848, [2]. For scholarly skepticism about the identification of Graves as Fidus, see C. W. Sumerlin, "A History of Southern Baptist State Newspapers" (Ph.D. diss., University of Missouri, 1968), 338. By 1849 A. B. Gilbert of Mississippi

certainly understood the nature and scope of the debate, whatever literary ruses might have been utilized; they also would have recognized a close proximity between the views of Graves and Fidus.

A letter from Fidus first appeared in the May 25, 1848, issue of the *Tennessee Baptist*, not long after Graves had returned to Nashville after preaching a three-week revival in Shelbyville, Tennessee. Speaking on behalf of the Muscle Shoals Association, as well as ministers in northern Alabama and Middle Tennessee, this new correspondent challenged Waller's by now widely known piece in defense of alien immersion, including the *"spirit"* that motivated it.[48] On the very same page Graves ran an editorial calling attention both to Waller's earlier article and Fidus's letter; he then dismissed Waller's argument with the sweeping assertion that "we do not know of one church in Tennessee or Alabama that would vote the affirmative of the question discussed by Bro. W." He likewise asserted that Waller could help the "cause" and his *Western Baptist Review* by giving "all the arguments in favor of the re-immersion of such subjects."[49]

Graves's not so subtle attempt to enlist Waller in a campaign to uphold strict Baptist principles fell on deaf ears. Even though the two editors shared some ecclesiological viewpoints, as noted in the previous chapter, this particular quarrel turned out to be intractable. As the rhetoric heated up on both sides, it sometimes moved beyond substantive exchange to a more *ad hominem* level. For instance, Fidus sarcastically repudiated what he referred to as "Wallerism": "It appears to me that a more monstrous and absurd doctrine was never promulgated in the Baptist Denomination than that an administrator is not necessary to christian baptism!! Surely, Bro. Waller must have written this article in some dream, when reason *rested* and fancy *raved*."[50]

On the other side, Veritas sent letters in defense of Waller and contended that Fidus had placed the association as a court of appeal over the decisions of local, independent churches.[51] Waller used his own journal to issue a forceful attack on Fidus, arguing that the latter's position on the validity of baptism required "an unbroken chain of proper administrators" going all the way back to the New Testament church, which he knew

---

raised questions about Fidus's anonymity, insinuating that his "productions, which have been attributed to bro. Graves and his standing as an editor, injured thereby with some readers of the Tennessee Baptist." See Gilbert's letter in *Tennessee Baptist*, March 15, 1849, [3].

[48] "'Fidus,' Muscle Shoal [*sic*], May 16, 1848—Letter [No. 1]," *Tennessee Baptist*, May 25, 1848, [2].

[49] Graves, "The Western Review," *Tennessee Baptist*, May 25, 1848, [2].

[50] "'Fidus,' Muscle Shoal [*sic*], May 24, 1848—'No. 2,'" *Tennessee Baptist*, June 1, 1848, [2].

[51] E.g., see the letter from Veritas in *Tennessee Baptist*, June 22, 1848, [2]. On this point, Fidus later charged that Waller held to "church infallibility." See "'Fidus,' Muscle Shoals, Feb. 10, 1849—'No. XI,'" *Tennessee Baptist*, February 22, 1849, [2].

was impossible to trace.[52] Fidus's understanding of church succession—i.e., a trail of true Baptist churches through the ages—encompassed baptismal succession; on the other hand, Waller understood ministers who performed baptisms as servants of the kingdom of Christ, which went beyond their pastoral duties in a local church. Hence, an unimmersed preacher could still administer a legitimate baptism, in part because it was a kingdom ordinance more than a church ordinance.[53] At the same time, the Kentucky editor acknowledged Baptist perpetuity; even during his dispute with Graves he provided a series of articles for the *Tennessee Baptist* that attempted to give a historical rationale for a less rigid brand of successionism.[54]

Graves and Waller in reality shared much in common, but alien immersion was the central point of their rift. The Landmark founder set a boundary between Baptists and other denominations that Waller obviously spurned. While Waller certainly respected Baptist teachings and distinctives, his ideas of the kingdom and the church universal helped to shape his conviction that tolerance of immersion by non-Baptists would not automatically lead to a weakening of Baptist identity or compromise on other ecclesiological matters. On the other hand, Graves feared that even the slightest recognition of Pedobaptist practice implied that their churches possessed some measure of authenticity.

By November of 1848 Fidus reported that the Muscle Shoals Association had decisively rejected Waller's position and adopted what would later be the Landmarkist policy on baptismal administrators: "It was resolved to adhere to that article in our constitution, that requires every member received into its fellowship to be immersed by an authorized

---

[52] Waller, "The Administrator of Baptism," *Western Baptist Review* 3 (August 1848): 473–74. Graves complained about the spirit and language of this article as "not worthy of our Bro. Waller"; at the same time, he endorsed much of what Fidus had written. See his "The Western Review," *Tennessee Baptist,* October 19, 1848, [2].

[53] Waller, "Important Questions," *Western Baptist Review* 4 (September 1848): 31–32. For a helpful explanation of this, see J. E. Tull, "A Study of Southern Baptist Landmarkism in the Light of Historical Baptist Ecclesiology" (Ph.D. diss., Columbia University, 1960), 359ff. Cf. A. H. Lanier Jr., "The Relationship of the Ecclesiology of John Lightfoot Waller to Early Landmarkism" (Th.M. thesis, Southeastern Baptist Theological Seminary, 1963), 94–103.

[54] E.g., see Waller, "Were the Waldenses Baptists or Pedo–Baptists?" *Tennessee Baptist,* May [10], 1849, [1]. This concluded a seven-part series reprinted from the *Western Baptist Review.* Graves also reprinted a series from the same source that Waller had done on infant baptism. See the concluding piece in *Tennessee Baptist,* September 28, 1848, [1]. After Waller's death, Graves's publishing house put out a supposedly coauthored volume, Waller and G. H. Orchard, *Baptists but the "Two Witnesses"* (Nashville: South-Western Publishing House; Graves, Marks, & Co., 1857), which clearly linked Waller to a theory of perpetuity. The book actually was drawn from separate articles by the two writers that had appeared in the *Southern Baptist Review and Eclectic.*

Bap. minister."[55] He continued to post opinions in Graves's paper into 1849, but by the middle of that year the Graves-Waller skirmish showed real signs of abating.

The two combative journalists continued to respect each other, despite their divergent views on alien immersion. In the early 1850s Waller, for instance, marveled at Graves's frequent jousts with Pedobaptists and judged that the Nashville editor got the better of them. He even enjoyed lunch with Graves when the younger man was preaching a revival in Kentucky in 1853, after which Waller penned this tribute for the *Western Recorder*: "We have known Brother Graves long and intimately, and a kinder and bolder heart throbs not in the breast of any man. He combines the meekness of a lamb with the boldness of a lion. He is yet young, but he has done great good. May he live long to bless the cause of truth with his labors."[56] Graves reciprocated the good will when he commented on Waller's sudden death in 1854, noting that their differences had been chiefly focused on "one subject."[57] Nonetheless, their heated controversy underlined one of the "landmarks" that would come to characterize Graves's by now emerging movement.

THE COTTON GROVE MEETING

J. R. Graves's adverse reaction to Waller's endorsement of alien immersion lends support to historian Bill Leonard's observation that Landmarkism "began over a question of Baptist relationships with other denominations."[58] Early in his editorial career, Graves felt compelled to deal with Waller and his allies on baptismal issues before drawing up well-defined borders against those he habitually referred to as Pedobaptists and Campbellites. As scholar Joe Early Jr. has perhaps overstated, the *Tennessee Baptist* editor faced the initial challenge of "solidifying his Baptist base and defeating those in his own denomination who disagreed with his ecclesiological assumptions before he would be able to take on an outside foe."[59] Graves's strict standards for acceptable baptisms, which were at best muted before he became a religious journalist, virtually guaranteed an antagonistic posture toward other denominational traditions. The aggressive and confrontational approach that he displayed to his denominational kin only intensified when directed toward those beyond the peripheries of Baptist life. At the same time, Graves

---

[55] "Letter from Fidus," *Tennessee Baptist,* November 16, 1848, [1].

[56] Waller, quoted in Hailey, *J. R. Graves*, 41–42.

[57] Graves, "John L. Waller," *Tennessee Baptist,* October 28, 1854, [2].

[58] B. J. Leonard, *Baptists in America* (New York: Columbia University Press, 2005), 144.

[59] J. Early Jr., "The Cotton Grove Resolutions," *Tennessee Baptist History* 7 (Fall 2005): 46.

never slackened in his opposition to those in the Baptist ranks who did not share his perspective and had survived the early skirmishes.

By 1850 Graves appeared ready to take up arms in earnest against external enemies. As he described a scene of tense religious rivalries in his part of the world, he seemed to welcome the unique pressures of the age:

> Truly, truly, we have fallen upon singular times. A period in Tennessee and the Southwest, unequalled by any, since the persecution of Anabaptists in the 15th [*sic*] century. This section of the Union is being convulsed with religious discussion—the claims of the different sects upon the support of the public are being subjected to the fiery ordeal of truth. . . . Controversy, discussion, agitation and intense excitement are the consequents. . . . There is nothing in all this to be regretted.[60]

In the same editorial comments, he did not allow the urgent nature of denominational warfare to draw him into the kind of polemics that would question the faith of his enemies, at least at this stage: "We regard the large mass of Pedobaptists as pious, godly, and devoted, and as such, we extend to them *Christian* fellowship and brotherly love, but we at the same time most conscientiously believe them deceived."[61] To be sure, the deceptions to which Graves alluded were serious enough that genuine believers found in non-Baptist movements belonged to organizations or societies that did not qualify as true churches.

In the months following his first wife's death, Graves relied primarily on his paper to aim several critical remarks at Pedobaptists; some of these were written in response to their journalistic disparagement of him. Then in his editorial column of June 14, 1851, he noted that a debate had been scheduled in rural Madison County, Tennessee, between the preacher at the Baptist church in nearby Jackson and a representative of the Methodist Episcopal Church. Perhaps because such public events often attracted decent-sized crowds, the editor announced plans for a "*mass meeting*" on June 24 at the same location, the two-year-old building of the Cotton Grove Baptist Church, which was in a small community less than 10 miles east of Jackson. As Graves conceived it, this gathering would function to rally the Baptist troops to stand against the attacks "now making upon

---

[60] Graves, "Remarks on the Above," *Tennessee Baptist,* May 11, 1850, [2]. This was the editor's response to a letter from L. D. Massengale of Lawrence County, Alabama.
[61] Ibid.

our doctrines, principles and history." He proceeded to declare the specific purpose of the assembly: "The main question to be discussed is, What is the true policy for Baptists to pursue to meet, most successfully the exigencies of the present time—the united assaults of all the Pedobaptist sects, 0 and Protestants, and to bring a correct knowledge of our principles more directly and generally before the public mind."[62] While the sources do not indicate how many came to Cotton Grove, what transpired there had all the markings of an exercise in boundary setting for those in attendance.

Less than a month after the Cotton Grove meeting, Graves published the formal results in the *Tennessee Baptist*. After he had addressed the gathering, he put forward to his audience a set of basically rhetorical questions that became the substance of the Cotton Grove Resolutions:

> 1st. Can Baptists, consistently with their principles or the Scriptures, recognize those societies not organized according to the pattern of the Jerusalem Church, but possessing different *governments*, different *officers*, a different class of *members*, different *ordinances*, *doctrines* and *practices*, as churches of Christ?
>
> 2d. Ought they to be called gospel churches, or churches in a religious sense?
>
> 3d. Can we consistently recognize the ministers of such irregular and unscriptural bodies as gospel ministers?
>
> 4th. Is it not virtually recognizing them as official ministers to invite them into our pulpits, or *by any other act that would or could be* construed into such a recognition?
>
> 5th. Can we consistently address as *brethren* those professing Christianity, who not only have not the doctrine of Christ and walk not according to his commandments, but are arrayed in direct and bitter opposition to them?[63]

---

[62] The direct citations in this paragraph are all from Graves, "Another Debate," *Tennessee Baptist,* June 14, 1851, [2]. On the popularity of religious debates in the nineteenth century, see E. B. Holifield, "Theology as Entertainment," *Church History* 67 (September 1998): 499–520. He briefly treats Graves. On the Cotton Grove church, see Early, "The Cotton Grove Resolutions," 41, 48–50. Early confuses some of the chronology and wrongly identifies J. L. Phillips, a member of the church, as Graves's brother.

[63] For texts of the Resolutions, see "Communications: Mass Meeting at Cotton Grove, June 24, 1851," *Tennessee Baptist,* July 19, 1851, [2]; "Communications: Mass Meeting at Cotton Grove, July 24, 1851," *Tennessee Baptist,* September 20, 1851, [2]; and Graves, *Old Landmarkism,* xi–xii. In his book (p. xii) Graves reported that all the questions "were unanimously answered in the negative," which overlooks the fact that the intended answer to number four was affirmative.

In essence, the Cotton Grove Resolutions called into question both the authority and legitimacy of non-Baptist churches and their ministers. Although they did not directly tackle the issues of baptism and the Lord's Supper—other than can be inferred from the reference to ordinances, doctrines, and practices—the queries from the meeting seemed to tighten up on positions that Graves had taken earlier. First, the fourth question was a clear attack on the practice of pulpit affiliation, where a Baptist preacher might exchange pulpits with a pastor from another denomination. Second, the last inquiry implied that there might be something seriously defective about the faith of people in non-Baptist "societies." Three years prior, the Baptist editor drew a hard line against the baptismal modes of sprinkling and pouring, yet showed more charity in observing that Baptists "will exchange pulpits—mingle in the social and prayer circle; they will rejoice in the prosperity of the cause of Christ in Pedobaptist churches."[64] Either Graves did not include himself as part of the subject in this statement from 1848, or the passionate nature of his clashes with Methodists and others caused him to change his mind.

The proceedings at Cotton Grove constituted a defining moment for Graves's as yet unnamed movement. Historian Early has aptly summarized the significance of the event in rustic western Tennessee this way: "At this meeting, the tenets of Landmarkism were first defined, the organization of the Landmark movement began, and J. R. Graves was elevated from Baptist editor to denominational spokesman and champion."[65] Thus, at the age of 31, the ardent journalist and Baptist apologist became the acknowledged leader of a burgeoning crusade that would soon become a powerful bloc within the relatively youthful Southern Baptist Convention.

In the early 1850s the ideology that emanated from Cotton Grove gained confirmation from other Baptists in the mid-South region. As a follow up to the Madison County gathering, a rally was held in conjunction with the Big Hatchie Association's annual

---

[64] Graves, "The Lord['s] Supper, No. III," *Tennessee Baptist,* May 25, 1848, [3]. Graves usually recognized that non-Baptist "societies" contained genuine Christians in their ranks. E.g., in *Trilemma* (p. 116) he averred that "there are many precious Christians in the Pedobaptist sects, *though in great error.*" Bruce Gourley wrongly attributed to Landmarkers the attitude "that only persons immersed in Baptist churches were truly saved." See *A Capsule History of Baptists* (Atlanta: Baptist History and Heritage Society, 2010), 58.

[65] Early, "The Cotton Grove Resolutions," 41. Years later, Graves credited the Cotton Grove gathering with sparking a renewed interest in education—particularly female education—among Baptists in the "Southwest." See Graves, "Our Schools," *Baptist,* June 25, 1870, [4]. Confirmation of the fact that education was on the agenda at Cotton Grove can be found in Graves, "The Mass Meeting Resolutions: Why Baptists Have Been Recommended to Patronize Their Own Schools," *Tennessee Baptist,* September 20, 1851, [2]. Although this aspect of Cotton Grove was understandably overshadowed, a strict position on Baptist identity would naturally lead to support of distinctly Baptist institutions.

meeting at Bolivar, Tennessee, in late July of 1851, where the Cotton Grove Resolutions were formally approved. Other associations in Arkansas, Alabama, Tennessee, and Texas likewise followed suit, creating what Early has dubbed "a strong grassroots movement."[66] In response to perceived threats from non-Baptist denominations, Graves and his followers had hammered out an ecclesiological framework that was designed to protect Baptist principles and simultaneously denigrate their religious competitors. Although his confident use of the print media and demonstrable oratorical skills allowed Graves to function as the principal point man in staking out the acceptable boundaries of Baptist faith and practice, he would subsequently recruit two key allies to aid the cause. As a result, Landmarkism would acquire a name as well as a more clearly defined sense of identity and direction.

PENDLETON AND DAYTON ENLIST FOR COMBAT

J. R. Graves, James Madison Pendleton (1811–91), and Amos Cooper Dayton (1813–65) are often branded as the "Great Triumvirate" of the Landmark movement. The late W. W. Barnes, onetime professor at Southwestern Baptist Theological Seminary, used that expression and also gave each man a distinct role: "Pendleton was the prophet, Graves the warrior, and Dayton the sword-bearer in the new campaign."[67] Although these leaders did not always convey unanimity on all points of doctrine or practice, their physical presence in the Nashville area and editorial duties with the *Tennessee Baptist* for a fairly short span of time in the 1850s served to provide Landmarkism with its most visible platform. For various reasons, their alliance ultimately failed to survive the Civil War; nevertheless, Pendleton and Dayton supplied Graves with a sizable amount of ammunition for Landmarkism's early battles.

Pendleton contributed to Graves's paper at least as early as 1850, when he was pastor of the First Baptist Church of Bowling Green, Kentucky, about 60 miles north

---

[66] Early, "The Cotton Grove Resolutions," 50. He incorrectly dated the Big Hatchie meeting in 1854. Cf. "Communications: Mass Meeting at Cotton Grove, June 24, 1851," *Tennessee Baptist,* July 19, 1851, [2], which referred to the Big Hatchie meeting; and Graves, *Old Landmarkism*, xii, where he claimed that "multitudes all over the South, indorsed [*sic*] the decision." Many years later, Graves suggested that he had a major role in helping to sway the Big Hatchie Association, pointing out that when it was organized in 1828 it accepted alien immersion and pulpit affiliation. See Graves, "Jubilee Sermon Preached before the Big Hatchie Association on Its Fiftieth Anniversary," *Baptist,* August 17, 1878, 577–79.

[67] W. W. Barnes, *The Southern Baptist Convention, 1845–1953* (Nashville: Broadman, 1954), 103.

of Nashville.[68] His relationship with Graves essentially blossomed in 1852, when the *Tennessee Baptist* editor took part in a four-week protracted meeting in Pendleton's church. The revival yielded a good number of converts, including Pendleton's 13-year-old daughter. It also aroused the ire of some Pedobaptist ministers, apparently because Graves delivered stinging indictments of their ecclesiastical traditions. Pendleton likely alluded to this when he recounted that his guest preacher "presents the doctrinal, the experimental, and the practical topics of the Gospel in suitable proportions. . . . Baptism is very judiciously *sprinkled* into his discourses."[69] Graves's admiration for Pendleton was communicated in an editorial in which the Kentucky pastor was depicted as "a man who has few superiors as a writer and reviewer, a ripe scholar and in deep and ardent piety,—he is eminently a man of God—too little known to be appreciated as he deserves."[70]

The two preachers, however, remembered some other aspects of the 1852 services and their aftermath quite differently. First, Graves later recalled that while he was in Bowling Green he persuaded Pendleton to turn away from accepting alien immersion.[71] On the other hand, Pendleton disavowed in an 1877 letter that he had recognized alien immersion before the 1852 revival. He added a comment that implied it was a different issue, giving credence to S. H. Ford's explanation in his later biographical articles on Graves: "I never denied that I was a pulpit affiliationist before I examined the subject." Furthermore, the venerable Baptist theologian raised questions about his then former colleague's ability to recall certain details: "It rather amused me to see how confident Bro. Graves is in the accuracy of his recollections when I know how his memory deceives him."[72]

---

[68] Graves reprinted a piece that Pendleton had written for the *Baptist Banner* of Kentucky. See P., "Tennessee Correspondence," *Tennessee Baptist,* June 29, 1850, [2], where Pendleton lauded Graves as a preacher. "P." became the primary byline for Pendleton's articles in Graves's newspaper.

[69] Letter from Pendleton, reprinted from the *Western Recorder,* in *Tennessee Baptist,* March 27, 1852, [2].

[70] Graves, "Ferguson, McFerrin & Co.," *Tennessee Baptist,* March 27, 1852, [2]. Ferguson was a follower of Alexander Campbell and a pastor in Nashville, while McFerrin was editor of the Methodist paper, the *Christian Advocate.* Graves had exchanged barbs with both of them.

[71] The account from Graves's perspective can be found in Hailey, *J. R. Graves,* 73. This was one of the few instances where Hailey made a substantive change from the articles of S. H. Ford, who reported that Graves influenced Pendleton on relationships with Pedobaptist ministers, which connected more with the issue of pulpit affiliation. See Ford, "Life, Times and Teachings of J. R. Graves," *Ford's Christian Repository and Home Circle,* December 1899, 741ff. Scholars who accept Hailey's version include J. E. Hill, "James Madison Pendleton's Theology of Baptism" (Th.M. thesis, Southern Baptist Theological Seminary, 1958), 48; and K. E. Eitel, "James Madison Pendleton," in *Baptist Theologians,* ed. Timothy George and David S. Dockery (Nashville: Broadman, 1990), 191.

[72] J. M. Pendleton to Brother Dobbs, July 5, 1877, in W. C. Huddleston, "James Madison Pendleton: A Critical Biography" (Th.M. thesis, Southern Baptist Theological Seminary, 1962), Appendix A. Huddleston was granted access to the letter by Pendleton's grandniece, Virginia Evans of Bowling Green, Kentucky.

Second, Pendleton likewise disputed Graves's sense of timing on his request to the Kentucky preacher for a series of articles dealing with the third and fourth questions from Cotton Grove about Pedobaptist clergy. While Graves recalled asking for the pieces "a few weeks" after the protracted meeting in Bowling Green, Pendleton remembered it as occurring more than two years later.[73] At any rate, the pastor from the Bluegrass State penned a series that appeared in the *Tennessee Baptist* late in 1854; Graves soon published them in pamphlet form under the title *An Old Landmark Re-set*, which attracted thousands of readers and supplied the name for his movement.[74] Against the Pedobaptists, Pendleton asserted that their societies were not true biblical churches and their ministers could not be regarded as genuine gospel preachers: "If Pedobaptists fail to exemplify the precepts of the New Testament in reference to the subjects and the action of baptism, they have no churches of Christ among them."[75] Echoing some of Graves's concerns, Pendleton used his classic broadside to repudiate pulpit affiliation and other fraternal practices that might blur the differences between Baptists and other denominations. What is more, like Graves he quickly discovered that there were other Baptists who did not exactly appreciate his boundary setting.[76]

Three years after the publication of his tract, Pendleton accepted a position as theology professor at Union University in Murfreesboro, Tennessee, a school that

[73] Ibid. Cf. Hailey, *J. R. Graves*, 74.

[74] Pendleton, "Ought Baptists to Recognize Pedobaptist Preachers As Gospel Ministers," *Tennessee Baptist* (1854), passim; and Pendleton, *An Old Landmark Re-set* (Nashville: Graves & Marks, 1854). See Graves's editorial column, "An Old Landmark," *Tennessee Baptist,* November 4, 1854, [3]. The term "landmark" was in the air even before 1854. See W. R., "Let Every Baptist Read and Think," *Tennessee Baptist,* January [25], 1849, [2], where the author complained that Baptists in the North were "pulling down the 'old *landmarks'*" by rejecting the doctrine of perseverance, and accepting alien immersion and open communion. Landmarkers usually cited two Old Testament uses of the term—Job 24:2, "Some remove the landmarks . . ."; and Prov 22:28, "Remove not the ancient landmark, which thy fathers have set" (both KJV). The NIV renders it "boundary stone(s)."

[75] Pendleton, "Ought Baptists to Recognize Pedobaptist Preachers As Gospel Ministers?" in *The Southern Baptist Almanac and Register, for the year 1855*, ed. J. R. Graves (Nashville: Graves & Marks, 1855), 9.

[76] E.g., see W. W. Everts, "The Old Landmark Discovered," *Christian Repository and Literary Review* 4 (January 1855): 20–34. The author, pastor of the Walnut Street Baptist Church in Louisville, opined on the last page of his article that Pendleton and his supporters were not restoring old landmarks but rather driving "a new stake, which can be set down and maintained only in sectarian arrogance." *An Old Landmark Reset* evidently had an impact on the 1855 Southern Baptist Convention meeting in Montgomery, Alabama, where a typical resolution to invite ministers of other denominations to sit in the sessions was withdrawn to avoid a floor fight. See J. A. Broadus, *Memoir of James Petrigu Boyce* (New York: A. C. Armstrong and Son, 1893), 98–99.

Graves served as a trustee and helped to influence in a Landmark direction. In addition, Pendleton assumed the pulpit at the First Baptist Church of Murfreesboro. Already a regular contributor to the *Tennessee Baptist*, he also became a joint editor for a short period beginning in 1858. By the eve of the Civil War, he sensed a clear divide with Graves over slavery and secession; he did not support the Confederacy, prompting his decision to leave Tennessee and relocate to Ohio in 1862. Moreover, his espousal of a universal church and more skeptical posture toward Baptist successionism meant that he was not always on the same page with Graves regarding what was essential to Landmark ecclesiology.[77] Nonetheless, Pendleton worked alongside of Graves during a critical period of Landmarkism's history. The Landmark patriarch, moreover, recognized his debt to the movement's most noteworthy and accomplished theologian when Pendleton died in 1891. Minimizing their manifest differences, Graves utilized a characteristically military image to commend his late comrade: "Side by side in closest touch we fought upon the high places of the field for Christ and his truth, and never during all those years did our enemies boast of having taken a color from us."[78]

A. C. Dayton, another important collaborator with Graves, became best known for a work of fiction that he contributed to the cause. A transplanted Yankee like Graves, Dayton held various positions with the Bible Board, the Southern Baptist Sunday School Union, and the *Tennessee Baptist* in Nashville during Landmarkism's formative decade of the 1850s. Indeed, his employment with the Bible Board caused him to be a key flash point in Graves's clash with R. B. C. Howell, which is covered in a later chapter. His novel, *Theodosia Ernest*, was first serialized in Graves's newspaper in 1855 and appeared in book form the following year. The heroine of the story was a young Presbyterian girl who became a Baptist after deciding that she had found the "true church"; in this respect, she mirrored the author's own pilgrimage. Dayton's melodra

---

[77] On the Murfreesboro years, see J. H. Davis, "Union University: Over 175 Years of Christian Education: Part 1," *Tennessee Baptist History* 4 (Fall 2002): 53–54. On the more notable divergences between Pendleton and Graves, see Eitel, "James Madison Pendleton," 198; and T. White, "James Madison Pendleton and His Contributions to Baptist Ecclesiology" (Ph.D. diss., Southeastern Baptist Theological Seminary, 2005), 12–13, 37, 193. After serving in Hamilton, Ohio, Pendleton ultimately took a pastorate in Upland, Pennsylvania. At the time of his death as many as 60,000 copies of *An Old Landmark Reset* had been printed. See R. G. Torbet, "Landmarkism," in *Baptist Concepts of the Church: A Survey of the Historical and Theological Issues Which Have Produced Changes in Church Order*, ed. W. S. Hudson (Philadelphia: Judson Press, 1959), 182.

[78] Graves, "Rev. J. M. Pendleton," *Baptist and Reflector,* March 26, 1891, 7.

matic flair ostensibly appealed to some who were not directly convinced by the more straightforward polemics of Graves or Pendleton.[79]

At the same time, Dayton revealed a marked skill in doctrinal disputation. Whereas Pendleton was known for his critique of pulpit exchanges, Dayton's best ecclesiological writings were his unfavorable appraisals of Baptist leaders who defended alien immersion, including John Waller. In 1858 Graves's publishing firm collected several of Dayton's contributions to the *Southern Baptist Review and Eclectic* and released them under the title of *Pedobaptist and Campbellite Immersions*. Graves prepared a nine-page introduction in which he attempted to link together various concepts of Landmark ideology in a logical chain. He warned, for example, that the acceptance of immersions by non-Baptists would lead directly to open communion and other compromises of Baptist identity. Graves believed, however, that Dayton had dealt a decisive blow against the inconsistent ecclesiology that some Baptist divines had set forth:

> Baptists, then, must admit that this question is settled by the Scriptures. If this is granted, all Baptists must admit that christian baptism can only be Scripturally administered by a duly baptized administrator who is a member of a true visible Church and acting under the authority of such Church. If Baptists recognize the *immersions* of Pedobaptists and Campbellite Societies, they thereby recognize such Societies as truly Scriptural and Evangelical Churches?[80]

Since the debate over this question had been smoldering for a decade, Graves undoubtedly appreciated Dayton's capable assistance in marshaling arguments against a practice

---

[79] See A. C. Dayton, "Theodosia Ernest," *Tennessee Baptist,* September 1, 1855, [3] for the first installment of the novel; and Dayton, *Theodosia Ernest: Or, The Heroine of Faith* (Nashville: Graves & Marks, 1856). Dayton eventually completed a trilogy, which included *Theodosia Ernest: Ten Days Travel in Search of the Church* (Nashville: Graves & Marks, 1857); and *Emma Livingston, the Infidel's Daughter* (Nashville: Graves & Marks, 1859). On Graves's recruitment of him to write the novel, see Hailey, *J. R. Graves,* 76–77. For scholarly analysis of Dayton, see J. E. Taulman, "Amos Cooper Dayton: A Critical Biography" (Th.M. thesis, Southern Baptist Theological Seminary, 1965); and Taulman, "The Life and Writings of Amos Cooper Dayton (1813–1865)," *Baptist History and Heritage* 10 (January 1975): 36–43. Taulman's master's thesis (pp. 31–35) challenges Hailey's account.

[80] Graves, "Introduction" to A. C. Dayton, *Pedobaptist and Campbellite Immersions: Being a Review of the Arguments of "Doctors" Waller, Fuller, Johnson, Wayland, Broadus, and Others* (Nashville: South-Western Publishing House, Graves, Marks, & Co., 1858; repr., Louisville: Baptist Book Concern, 1903), vi–vii. James Tull called Dayton's work "the most cogent attack upon 'alien immersion' which the Landmark movement produced." See Tull, "A Study of Southern Baptist Landmarkism," 135.

that—more than any other single issue—had really spawned the rise of the Landmark movement.

As things turned out, Pendleton and Dayton both ended their close association with Graves during the Civil War. As noted above, Pendleton moved to the North; Dayton took his family to Georgia early in 1863, where he pastored two churches and edited the *Baptist Banner*, which was known for a Landmark allegiance. His chronic lung problems flared up in 1864 and he died of pulmonary consumption in 1865.[81] In retrospect, Graves's relationships with both men appeared to be in decline even before they all left Middle Tennessee.

The denominational pluralism of Nashville, along with Graves's awareness that Baptists in his region lacked any substantive consensus on some basic ecclesiological matters, set the backdrop for much of what transpired during his time in the Tennessee capital. It was a truly amazing period of his life; among other things, he commenced what would be a lengthy career in journalism, clashed with fellow Baptists over issues like alien immersion and pulpit affiliation, laid the groundwork for a new movement in Southern Baptist life, and found two colleagues who stood as his most important reinforcements in the defense and expansion of Landmark ideology. Before, during, and after these developments Graves understood, of course, that Pedobaptists and Restorationists represented serious threats to the Baptist cause. After all, he became agitated with some of his Baptist brethren because he sensed that they had carelessly let down their guard. Moreover, the heated exchange with Waller, the legendary Cotton Grove meeting, and the literary support of Pendleton and Dayton all pushed Graves to persevere in what he saw as one of his imperative tasks. Indeed, J. R. Graves was a man driven to mark the proper boundaries of Baptist identity over against the menacing reality of other Christian traditions in his city and the wider region in which his newspaper circulated.

---

[81] J. Burch, "A Tennessee Baptist Returns to Georgia: The Latter Life of A. C. Dayton," *Tennessee Baptist History* 7 (Fall 2005): 19–28.

Chapter 3

Setting the Boundaries between Baptists and Other Denominations

The Nashville Years (1845–62), Part II

Despite his early roots in New England Congregationalism, J. R. Graves rarely showed any appreciation for non-Baptist denominations or movements. Since Congregationalists, Episcopalians, and Lutherans did not claim significant numbers of adherents in the mid-South, he wrote or said little about those traditions; however, they would have been included in his general caricature of Protestantism. According to his view of history, which is probed in a later chapter, Baptists were not Protestants; hence, he felt free to attack all of them for hierarchy, traditionalism, and the overall partial character of the Reformation.[1] Toward the end of his time in Nashville, he reaffirmed the key aims of his polemics: "to expose the monstrous assumptions upon which the Protestant and Reformed sects rest."[2] Nonetheless, his explicit campaigns focused predominantly on Restorationist followers of Alexander Campbell, who themselves were not quick to identify with Protestantism, Presbyterians, and Methodists; all of these boasted reasonably healthy constituencies in states like Tennessee and Kentucky. In addition, the *Tennessee Baptist* editor aimed his weapons at the Roman Catholic Church. In the mid-nineteenth century, Catholics hardly represented a major statistical threat in regions west of the Appalachians, except perhaps in New Orleans, yet Catholicism carried some of the same liabilities that could be found in Protestant groups, especially the

---

[1] See J. R. Graves, "Volume Sixth," *Tennessee Baptist,* September 6, 1849, [2]. In this context, he even advanced the notion that Protestantism was a more significant obstacle to the coming of the millennium than the papacy.

[2] Graves, "Protestantism. Tract No. II," *Tennessee Baptist,* September 22, 1860, [2].

practice of infant baptism. Even worse, as Graves viewed it, the Roman Church was the "Mother of Harlots" (Rev 17:5 KJV).[3]

A CATHOLIC CONSPIRACY?

One of the justifiable criticisms by more recent commentators is that the Landmark tradition fostered a harsh anti-Catholicism in Southern Baptist life.[4] At the same time, virtually all Baptists and other American Protestants in the middle of the nineteenth century expressed hostility toward the Roman Catholic Church. Graves undoubtedly absorbed some of his antagonistic attitudes toward Catholicism from his nurture in a New England environment; there the Puritan assessment of Romanism was openly negative and profoundly affected civic attitudes well into the nineteenth century. Furthermore, Graves was well aware of nineteenth-century Protestant alarms about a suspected Catholic subversion of American liberties. In 1834 Samuel Morse, the inventor of the telegraph, blamed European Catholic powers like Austria for designing despotic plots against the United States: "The serpent has already commenced his coil about our limbs, and the lethargy of his poison is creeping over us."[5]

Perhaps more to the point for Graves, especially after relocating from New England to venues like Kentucky and Tennessee, was the widely-held perception that the Catholic Church entertained notions of infiltrating and capturing the comparatively wide open American frontier. The well-known Congregationalist/Presbyterian preacher and revivalist, Lyman Beecher, echoed many of Morse's conspiratorial themes in his *Plea for the West*, which he issued in 1835—not long after he had moved from Boston to Cincinnati, Ohio. Beecher, who was the patriarch of a famous nineteenth-century American family, viewed the untamed West as the great battleground for an epic confrontation between the

[3] Graves, "Protestantism. Why Baptists Are Compelled to Oppose and Repudiate It. Tract No. 1," *Tennessee Baptist,* September 1, 1860, [2]. For a useful discussion of Graves's conflicts with Catholics, Campbellites, Presbyterians, and Methodists from the perspective of "republicanism versus despotism," see M. G. Bell, "James Robinson Graves and the Rhetoric of Demagogy: Primitivism and Democracy in Old Landmarkism" (Ph.D. diss., Vanderbilt University, 1990), 144–79. These themes are examined more thoroughly in the next chapter.
[4] For example, see T. George, "Southern Baptist Ghosts," *First Things* (May 1999): 24.
[5] S. F. B. Morse, "A Foreign Conspiracy against the Liberties of the United States," in *The Fear of Conspiracy: Images of Un-American Subversion from the Revolution to the Present*, ed. D. B. Davis (Ithaca, NY: Cornell University Press, 1971), 99.

children of darkness and the children of light. His most immediate worry centered on the alleged efforts of the Jesuit order, officially known as the Society of Jesus:

> An association of more moral and political power than was ever concentrated on earth—twice suppressed as too formidable for the crowned despotism of Europe, and an overmatch for his holiness himself—and twice restored as indispensable to the waning power of the holy see. And now with the advantages of its past mistakes and experience, this order is in full organization, silent, systematized, unwatched, and unresisted action among us, to try the dexterity of its movements, and the potency of its power upon unsuspecting, charitable, credulous republicans.[6]

In Beecher's apocalyptic imagination, Protestant America needed to rally its evangelistic forces in the West to defeat the villainous Jesuits and ensure the dawning of the millennial age.

The warnings that were sounded by respected Protestant leaders like Beecher surely helped to intensify feelings of hatred and distrust toward Catholicism in the period leading up to Graves's years in Nashville. The widespread use of anti-Catholic propaganda, mixed as it was with republican and Jacksonian rhetoric, meant that Graves could draw on ideas that were already woven into public discourse. Indeed, he seemed attracted to Beecher's stress on the strategic value of the American West. For his part, Graves focused in an 1853 sermon a bit more narrowly on the Mississippi Valley as the focal point of the inevitable battle between "true Christianity and popery."[7] The following year, the editor maintained—in language reminiscent of Morse and Beecher—that Roman Catholicism was inherently incompatible with American institutions: "The Catholic element in this country is dangerous to our republican government, and the direct tendency of it is to subvert our free institutions."[8] After the Civil War, Graves

---

[6] L. Beecher, "A Plea for the West," in Davis, *The Fear of Conspiracy*, 93. I have discussed Morse and Beecher in J. A. Patterson, "Changing Images of the Beast: Apocalyptic Conspiracy Theories in American History," *Journal of the Evangelical Theological Society* 31 (December 1988): 448–49. As evidence that some old conspiracy theories never die, see R. Cooke, *The Vatican-Jesuit-Global Conspiracy* (Hollidaysburg, PA: Manahath Press, 1985).

[7] Graves, "The Desire of All Nations: A Sermon" (Nashville: Graves & Shankland, 1853), 55–56. This was preached at the Big Hatchie Association in Bolivar, Tennessee. For a similar reference to the Mississippi Valley, see Graves, "The Watchman's Reply: A Sermon" (Nashville: Graves & Shankland, 1853), 60. He delivered this to the Mississippi Baptist Education Society in 1852.

[8] Graves, "Anti-Republican Religion," *Tennessee Baptist,* October 28, 1854, [2].

continued to fret about the malevolent designs of the Roman Church to triumph in America by attacking "our Common School System" and other cherished foundations of a free society. He also asserted that Baptists represented the only force that could stand up for "pure Christianity against the Catholic juggernaut."[9] Whereas Beecher had sought to mobilize Protestant evangelicals for mission in the West, Graves singled out Baptists to utilize the pulpit, press, and Sunday school to counteract anticipated Catholic aggression in the same territory.[10]

Graves's long-term antagonism toward the Roman Catholic Church sprang in part from his understanding of history. First, he was convinced that honest historical inquiry demonstrated conclusively that papal Rome had inflicted persecution and caused untold human suffering for centuries. In other words, the Church of Rome epitomized tyranny and the denial of freedom to those who did not conform to its dictates. While he aimed his *Trilemma* more at Protestants who had not sufficiently dissociated themselves from Catholic ways, Graves exploited his opportunities to deliver jabs against the ultimate source of religious oppression: "It is the spirit of the Papacy, whose power is the power of darkness, to repress free thought, and the liberty of speech and the press."[11] The Landmark patriarch could just as easily have said that Roman Catholicism was anti-American, and many of his contemporaries would have agreed with him.

Second, Graves connected Roman Catholic history very closely to what he called "traditionism." Over time, the Catholic Church had developed traditions such as infant baptism and other sacraments that Graves viewed as totally inconsistent with New Testament Christianity. In an attempt to define the essence of the Roman Church in a pithy manner, he posed one of his emblematic rhetorical questions: "What is Roman Catholicism but the development of tradition?"[12] After many years of expounding Landmark Baptist views on the ordinances of baptism and the Lord's Supper, Graves

---

[9] Graves, "Eighteen Hundred and Seventy-One Year More," *Baptist,* January 8, 1870, [4].

[10] Graves, "The Great West. An Address Delivered before the Southern Baptist Convention, Macon, GA, in Mass Meeting for S.S. Board," *Baptist,* January 29, 1870, [4]. Chapter 7 on the Memphis years shows that Graves had a personal stake in the SBC's Sunday school work.

[11] Graves, *Trilemma: All Human Churches without Baptism, or Death by Three Horns,* 2nd ed. (Memphis: Graves, Mahaffy & Co., 1881; repr., Memphis: J. R. Graves & Son, 1890), 11. The original edition was published in 1860 (Nashville: Graves, Marks, & Co.). For colorful images linking the Catholic Church to spiritual slavery and papal rule to "a vast prison," see Graves, "The Desire of All Nations," 16, 31. A convenient summary of the criticisms of Catholicism that Graves also applied to Protestantism can be found in J. E. Tull, "A Study of Southern Baptist Landmarkism in Light of Historical Baptist Ecclesiology" (Ph.D. diss., Columbia University, 1960), 237–39.

[12] Graves, "The Philosophy of Traditionism," *Tennessee Baptist,* March 29, 1851, [2].

eventually summed up his rationale for spurning the term "sacrament," which originated in Roman usage: "It has no place in our vocabulary. . . . We should carefully eschew the use of it. . . . The ordinances of the church are not means of grace to the sinner . . . nor the conductors of invisible grace to the soul, but simple emblems, monuments."[13] His disparaging treatment of tradition thus equipped Graves with another tool for distinguishing between Baptist and Catholic ecclesiology.

Third, the argumentative journalist employed successionist history to declare that the Baptist movement was of more ancient origin than Roman tradition. In his scheme of things, the earliest Christians were Baptists. By comparison, the papacy was a relative newcomer; in Graves's humble estimation, "popery" was established by "Hilderbrand" in the year 606.[14] Later in the same volume, Graves logically derived some implications from his concept of Baptist antiquity. His "trilemma" for Roman Catholics began by arguing that if they regarded Baptist baptisms as valid, they should therefore grant that Baptist churches were true ones and that Catholics "are schismatics and anti-Christian." He then moved to what he saw as his clinching point: "[I]f Catholics say that our baptisms and ordinances are *invalid* because we are not or were never true churches of Christ, then they are compelled to admit that they themselves have neither baptisms nor ordinations, or any just claims to be called a Christian Church, since they received all their baptisms and ordinations from the Baptists of the third and fourth centuries!!"[15] It is hard to conceive that many Catholics would have been persuaded by Graves's reasoning, even if they read his book. Moreover, Graves plainly sacrificed historical credibility on the altar of religious polemics.

Finally, the Baptist editor's perspective on history became intertwined with what in the 1850s was a still emerging fascination with biblical prophecy. In one of his earliest

---

[13] Graves, "Insensible Teachings—No. 6. The Sacraments," *Baptist,* May 15, 1875, 85. For typical critiques of Catholic—and Protestant—practice, see Graves, "The Evils of Infant Baptism" and "What Is, and What Is Not Christian Baptism," in *The Southern Baptist Almanac and Annual Register, for The Year of Our Lord 1850,* ed. J. R. Graves (Nashville: Graves & Shankland, 1850), 21–27, 41–47.

[14] Graves, *Trilemma,* 83. It is not exactly clear what Graves intended to say in this context. Pope Gregory VII, who reigned 1073–1085, was "Hildebrand" before assuming his throne name.

[15] Ibid., 186. This point was in *Trilemma,* Part II, which was not in the first edition. For an early expression of Graves's successionism, albeit from the pen of "Fidus," see "Re-Baptism. No. VII," *Tennessee Baptist,* December 7, 1848, [1]. This was a letter from Fidus "sent" to the paper November 27, 1848. In H. S. Smith, "A Critical Analysis of the Theology of J. R. Graves" (Th.D. diss., Southern Baptist Theological Seminary, 1966), 95, n3, the author commented that "this article marked the first time Graves revealed a definite interest in history, particularly a successionism." This assumes that Fidus and Graves were one and the same. Smith confused the dates of the letter from Fidus and the newspaper issue in which it was published.

journalistic ventures into this realm in 1853, Graves attempted to mark off the rule of the "papal hierarchy," which began when the pope was granted the 10 kingdoms of the western Roman Empire in the early Middle Ages: "A.D. 591 may be considered the earliest, and 606 the latest period, from which to date the supremacy of the Beast. His dominion then will cease in the year 1851 or 1866 [after 1260 years]. There is an image of the Beast to continue to exert a persecuting power for some years—and until the coming of Christ. . . . Truly we are in the last days!"[16] Furthermore, Graves brooked no ambiguity about the identity of Babylon in the Book of Revelation:

> The City Babylon is as clearly a representation of the Papacy including her daughters, the nationalized hierarchies of Europe. The people, multitudes and nations of the ten kingdoms are to their hierarchies, mystical Babylon, what the river Euphrates was to Babylon of old. The drying up of those waters can mean nothing else than the turning away of these people from the Papacy and dissolving the connection with the legalized ecclesiasties [*sic*] or Established Churches."[17]

The image of the papal beast that Graves invoked certainly had a long and storied lineage in Western Christianity, particularly since the time of the Reformation.[18] For him, it provided another means of reinforcing the borders between true churches and apostate ecclesiastical structures. After all, New Testament prophecy ensured that the false systems would collapse, and Graves used purportedly historical calculations to indicate when.

Graves's pronounced anti-Catholicism apparently provoked accusations that the *Tennessee Baptist* was sympathetic to the Know-Nothing movement, a nativist group that had some appeal in Nashville during the 1850s in response to a growing immi-

---

[16] Graves, "The Drying Up of the River Euphrates," *Tennessee Baptist,* October 1, 1853, [2]. The title of the editorial alludes to Rev 16:12 where the sixth angel poured out his bowl of judgment. Graves possibly based 1,260 years on references to 1,260 days in Rev 11:3; 12:6. As chap. 7 contends, during his years in Memphis Graves intensified his eschatological interest and developed it into a full-blown dispensationalism.

[17] Ibid. In the same column, Graves likewise depicted the Protestant establishments of Europe as "the daughters of the adulteress, and they with their mother have committed fornication with the kings of the earth," another indirect reference to Rev 17:5. Graves, however, did not identify the papacy with "the man of sin." See Graves, "Is Papal Rome the Man of Sin?" *Southern Baptist Review* 6 (September 1860): 375–88.

[18] See B. McGinn, *Antichrist: Two Thousand Years of the Human Fascination with Evil* (San Francisco: HarperSanFrancisco, 1994), 143–230. Note that not all interpreters of biblical prophecy equate the beast and the Antichrist. See preceding footnote.

grant presence. There is no evidence, however, that Catholics made up a large portion of the ethnic population, nor that Graves showed any higher level of animosity toward Catholics than other denominational editors in the city. Graves, in fact, rebuffed any connection to "Know nothingism": "We have never affiliated with it as a party. . . . We repudiate the idea of a secret political party in this Union, composed of whomsoever it may be, as we did at an early day the secrecy of this new party. We have no connection with secret organizations."[19] Graves may have unintentionally contributed to the nativist impulse, but his antipathy toward the Catholic Church far surpassed any real or imagined aversion he might have had toward foreigners who settled in America.

One of the ironies of Graves's fervent opposition to the Roman Church is that some modern interpreters of the Landmark tradition have found "Catholic" tendencies in its strict approach to Baptist principles. For instance, historian Leon McBeth made this provocative comparison:

> Perhaps the Landmark movement is best understood as a Baptist equivalent of nineteenth-century Roman Catholicism. The two groups show remarkable similarity in doctrine and spirit. For Landmark Baptists, the principle of church successionism plays the same role as apostolic succession for Catholics, validating their claims to be the only true church. Both claimed to have the only true ordinances or sacraments, and both embraced a doctrine of "high churchism."[20]

McBeth's criticism, leveled in the context of his attempt to marginalize the Landmarkers, tends to elevate some superficial similarities between Catholicism and Landmarkism while ignoring some substantial differences. Graves clearly displayed a *catholic* spirit in some of his ecclesiology; at the same time, his attacks on the Catholic Church were strongly motivated by his revulsion at what he perceived to be its tyrannical hierarchy.

---

[19] Graves, "Volume XII," *Tennessee Baptist,* September 1, 1855, [2]. On nativism and the Know-Nothing party in Nashville, see A. S. Goodstein, *Nashville 1780–1860: From Frontier to City* (Gainesville: University of Florida Press, 1989), 130–35, 178–80, 202–3. For a modern attempt to link Graves to nativism, see Tull, "A Study of Southern Baptist Landmarkism," 247–48.

[20] H. L. McBeth, *The Baptist Heritage: Four Centuries of Baptist Witness* (Nashville: Broadman, 1987), 459. The former Southwestern Seminary professor likely drew on the work of an earlier Southwestern educator for both the Catholic analogy and the "high churchism" characterization. See W. W. Barnes, *The Southern Baptist Convention: A Study in the Development of Ecclesiology* (Fort Worth: By the author, 1934), 61; and Barnes, *The Southern Baptist Convention, 1845–1953* (Nashville: Broadman, 1954), 100–108. As the next section of this chapter shows, a Presbyterian critic of Graves appeared to be the originator of the "high church" charge.

On matters of church polity, he radically distanced himself from the Roman Catholic tradition.

In the long run, Graves's harsh broadsides against Catholicism did not convey as much urgency as his battles with Protestant denominations. There is no evidence that he ever engaged in a public debate with a Roman Catholic, and he did not specifically name Catholic opponents in the *Tennessee Baptist*. In Nashville it is unlikely that he had much personal contact with Catholics; they were not a looming presence in the city, even though a bishop had been consecrated as early as 1838.[21] In many ways, his critique of Catholicism was a means to an end, giving him a launching pad for his attacks on those groups that could be traced directly or indirectly to the Protestant Reformation.

THE PRESBYTERIAN TRILEMMA

Although Presbyterians were not as numerous as Methodists in Nashville in the mid-nineteenth century, they earlier had constructed the first church building in the downtown area and—at least for a while—"held priority."[22] Of all the Protestant denominations, the Presbyterian churches perhaps bore the most family resemblance to Baptists, with notable exceptions in the areas of baptism and church government. One of the early Baptist groups in seventeenth-century England, after all, was called "Particular" because of its Calvinistic perspective on doctrinal issues like the atonement, election, and perseverance.[23] Graves himself received his earliest Christian nurture in Congregationalism, a denomination that essentially mirrored the Reformed theology of the New England Puritans well into the nineteenth century.

Graves, however, found none of those considerations to be especially relevant when he took up his pen against Presbyterianism. His attitude toward John Calvin, the Reformation founder of the Presbyterian tradition, was ambivalent. The Baptist editor was anything but a consistent Calvinist, despite the attempts of modern scholars to place him in that camp. James Tull, for example, labeled Graves a "high Calvinist," based largely on the Landmarker's apparent espousal of limited atonement in an

---

[21] Goodstein, *Nashville 1780–1860*, 134.

[22] Ibid., 57–58.

[23] See D. W. Bebbington, *Baptists through the Centuries: A History of a Global People* (Waco, TX: Baylor University Press, 2010), 43–63.

1883 volume that set forth his dispensational theology.[24] Southern Seminary historian Gregory Wills, pointing mainly to Graves's preparation for a debate with Methodist preacher Jacob Ditzler in 1875, contends that Graves "disavowed the label of Calvinism but nonetheless advocated traditional five-point Calvinism."[25] What Tull and Wills discovered in Graves's later publications may have indicated an unannounced shift in his theological views. Nevertheless, during the Nashville years the Baptist polemicist advocated what might be classified at most as a "soft" Calvinism. In early 1848 he printed a series in his paper based on a sermon that he had preached in two places the previous year; his theme was the compatibility of God's sovereignty with humanity's free moral agency. Graves clearly linked predestination to divine foreknowledge and also proposed that "God predestinates, raises up and elects certain persons, to perform certain parts in the drama of nations, and he irresistably [*sic*] inclines their wills or hearts to do his pleasure, in these respects, but in no wise compelling any to love or hate him, so as to be saved or lost."[26] His apparent refusal to link irresistible grace with soteriology became even more striking when he targeted the Geneva Reformer himself for reprimand: "The doctrine of eternal and unconditional election, and reprobation as taught by Calvin, and assented to by many professed christians [*sic*], we utterly repudiate—it finds no place in our faith and affections. It is as contrary to our reason as to our understanding of the Word of God."[27] Furthermore, the young journalist and preacher offered the confusing comment that limited and unlimited atonement were "extremes"; he understood it as unlimited for God and limited from the perspective of believers, because only they

---

[24] Tull, "A Study of Southern Baptist Landmarkism," 519–21. Cf. Graves, *The Work of Christ in the Covenant of Redemption; Developed in Seven Dispensations* (1883; repr., Texarkana, AR: Baptist Sunday School Committee, 1928 and 1963), 96.

[25] G. A. Wills, *Southern Baptist Theological Seminary, 1859–2009* (New York: Oxford University Press, 2009), 91. Wills relied heavily on a letter that Graves wrote to John A. Broadus before the debate, as well as the published account. See Graves and Jacob Ditzler, *The Graves-Ditzler: or, Great Carrollton Debate* (Memphis: Southern Baptist Publication Society, 1876), 26–42. On the other hand, see Myron James Houghton, "The Place of Baptism in the Theology of James Robinson Graves" (Th.D. diss., Dallas Theological Seminary, 1971), 63–64, where the author disputed the notion that Graves taught a limited atonement. Cf. H. Wamble, "Landmarkism: Doctrinaire Ecclesiology among Baptists," *Church History* 33 (December 1964): 430, where the Southern Baptist professor claimed that Graves "abhorred Calvinism."

[26] Graves, "The Sovereignty of God—Not Inconsistant [*sic*] with Free Moral Agency: Proposition II," *Tennessee Baptist,* February 3, 1848, [2]. Under the same title, "Proposition I," *Tennessee Baptist,* January 27, 1848, [1], he explicitly listed foreknowledge before predestination, decrees, election, and ordination.

[27] Graves, "The Sovereignty of God: Proposition III," *Tennessee Baptist*, February 17, 1848, [2].

ultimately benefit from it. Finally, he concluded his discourse by virtually equating Calvinism and fatalism.[28]

Graves was surely not a trained systematic theologian, so his bold ventures into this realm probably raised more questions than they answered. His unfavorable assessment of traditional Calvinist doctrine, however, seemed to predispose him to find additional faults that he could underscore in his disputes with Presbyterians, which overall were more limited than his encounters with Campbellites and Methodists. In one notable exchange with William H. Hill, editor of the *Presbyterian Herald* in Louisville, Kentucky, Graves found himself needing to answer a charge that the Landmark movement was guilty of "high churchism." In a foreshadowing of twentieth-century Baptist historian W. W. Barnes's description of Landmark ecclesiology, Hill indicted Graves and his colleague J. M. Pendleton for being "high church" because they made the mode of baptism an "essential element of a true church," and consequently "unchurched" those groups that did not properly immerse believers. He proceeded to compare this to "high-church" Episcopalians who mandated a particular form of ordination. Hill—citing the Westminster Confession of Faith—also drew a distinction between the church "invisible and visible," perhaps knowing that Graves rejected such a separation. In another implicit swipe at Graves's ecclesiology, Hill asserted that his own church was "a complete Church, according to the New Testament model, and that all others differing from it and yet holding the essentials of the gospel, are still true churches, but deformed or incomplete ones, just so far as they have departed from the Scripture model."[29] Thus the Presbyterian editor sought to take the higher ground, since Graves typically dismissed Pedobaptist and other non-Baptist denominations as "societies."

In response, Graves naturally defended a position on Presbyterians and others that had already been incorporated in the Cotton Grove Resolutions two years earlier. He

---

[28] Ibid. The sermon on the sovereignty of God was reprinted in Graves, *Satan Dethroned and Other Sermons*, ed. O. L. Hailey (New York: Fleming H. Revell, 1929), 36–57. See another negative reference to Calvinism in his editorial, Graves, "Election," *Tennessee Baptist*, June 21, 1851, [2].

[29] See the three installments of Graves, "High Churchism," *Tennessee Baptist*, August 27, 1853, [2]; September 3, 1853, [2]; and November 12, 1853 [2]. In the latter issue, Graves reproduced one of Hill's editorials on the subject. On Barnes's use of the "high church" moniker, see *The Southern Baptist Convention, 1845–1953*, 100–108. Barnes, 100, n5, found evidence in the *Western Recorder*, April 25, 1855, 2, that "Graves himself refers to the position opposed to his as 'low church practices,' thus indirectly calling his own position 'high church.'" There is no evidence, however, that Barnes was aware of Hill's use of the term in 1853 or Graves's reply to it. Pendleton responded to Hill in 1855 on a narrower issue in "Ought Baptists to Recognize Pedobaptist Preachers as Gospel Ministers?" in *The Southern Baptist Almanac and Register, for the Year 1855*, ed. J. R. Graves (Nashville: Graves & Marks, 1855), 23–31.

promptly disallowed Hill's designation of churchly status for the Presbyterian denomination, as well as for all other non-Baptists who made such claims: "They have adopted humanly contrived systems of government, with earthly heads, and legislation, either in persons or ecclesiastical bodies, and thus they set at naught the government of Christ, and frustrate the gracious and glorious design for which he gave it."[30] The two editors obviously entertained very disparate views on what constituted an authentic New Testament church.

Graves's rejoinder to the charge of "high churchism," however, remained somewhat ambiguous. After critiquing Hill's attempt to "fix the odium of 'high churchism' and bigotry upon us" for policies that the Presbyterians themselves followed, Graves subsequently arrived at a carefully nuanced acquiescence in his rival editor's allegation:

> Mr. Hill is welcome to use upon us the phrase of "high churchism," if the above principles [i.e., on baptism and church polity] render us obnoxious to the charge—and "exclusive," also, if he please. But we will remind him that the Church of Christ is one—he gave but one form of government—not a score of different and necessary [sic] antagonistic organizations; but one character of membership, but one form of church ordinances, and doctrine, and if strictly conforming to these in our churches exposes us to the odium of the world, the sneers of men, or the hatred of devils, we must suffer, if we would be accepted of Him.[31]

If Landmarkism was a "high church" movement, it was not because it promoted ritual or elaborate ceremony in worship. Graves may have halfheartedly permitted Hill to use the term in reference to what was undeniably a restricted concept of the true church. At the same time, Graves never fully embraced the idea that Landmark ecclesiology represented a "high-church" posture. Hill, nonetheless, readily perceived that his Baptist counterpart set tight denominational boundaries; he did not hesitate to dub this "high churchism."

In the late 1850s Graves engaged in correspondence with N. L. Rice, a Presbyterian minister in Cincinnati who had earlier debated publicly with Alexander Campbell over baptism. Some of the letters, which focused on a number of issues that divided Baptists and Presbyterians, appeared in the *Tennessee Baptist* from the summer of 1857 through

---

[30] Graves, "High Churchism," *Tennessee Baptist,* November 12, 1853, [2].
[31] Ibid.

early 1858. Several of the inquiries and replies dealt with historical matters relating to Graves's successionist view of Baptist origins. For instance, Rice asked whether the Donatists of the Patristic Era were really Baptists and called for some proof for that claim. Graves replied to the query but did not directly answer Rice's request.[32] The correspondence revealed that the two writers held highly divergent ideas about the antiquity of pedobaptism.

The letters also provided Graves with an opportunity to air his distinctive theory about the ministry and baptism of John the Baptist, which at times was incorporated into his apologetic against both Pedobaptists and Restorationists.[33] He built his interpretation of John principally on what James Tull depicted as a "radically sectarian" notion that the kingdom of God is made up of the aggregate of authentic (e.g., Baptist) churches; just as there was no place for an "invisible" kingdom or church in Graves's theology, there was also no real distinction between kingdom and church. As he put it in one of his more definitive expositions, the kingdom **"is constituted of the sum total of all his true visible churches as constituents, which churches are the sole judges and executives of the laws and ordinances of the Kingdom."**[34]

Graves's explication of John the Baptist grew out of his ecclesiology, which remained essentially unchanged from the early 1850s to the 1880s when he published his most systematic expressions of it. He contended that he differed from his Pedobaptist and Campbellite opponents by denoting John's ministry and baptism as specifically Christian. When he eventually gathered all his previous ideas about John and weaved them into his dispensational theology, he regretted that "the overwhelming majority of Pedobaptists believe that John's baptism belonged to the Jewish Dispensation, and that the act John administered to Christ was a washing of consecration appointed for the formal and legal induction of Christ into His office of High Priest."[35] For Graves, on the

---

[32] See "N. L. Rice's Reply.—No. 1;" and "N. L. Rice's Reply.—No. 2," *Tennessee Baptist,* July 25, 1857, [2]. Cf. Graves, "Reply to No. 1," *Tennessee Baptist,* July 25, 1857, [2]; and Graves, "Reply to N. L. Rice.—No. II," *Tennessee Baptist,* August 1, 1857, [2].

[33] See Graves, "Historical Discussion. Letters to N. L. Rice. Number II. Did John's Ministry Commence the Gospel Dispensation?" *Tennessee Baptist,* June 27, 1857, [2]; and Graves, "Historical Discussion. Letters to N. L. Rice. Number II. Objections to John's Baptism Considered," *Tennessee Baptist,* July 4, 1857, [2].

[34] Graves, *Intercommunion Inconsistent, Unscriptural, and Productive of Evil* (Memphis: Baptist Book House, 1881), 160. Bold face is in the original. Cf. Graves, *Old Landmarkism: What Is It?* 2nd ed. (Memphis: Baptist Book House; Graves, Mahaffy & Co., 1881), 29ff. For Tull's comment, see "A Study of Southern Baptist Landmarkism," 167.

[35] Graves, *John's Baptism: Was It from Moses or Christ? Jewish or Christian: Objections to Its Christian Character Answered* (Memphis: Southern Baptist Book House, 1891), 25. What he expressed in this volume

contrary, the ministry of John the Baptist actually resulted in a visible church that was functioning before the Day of Pentecost. By using Landmark ecclesiology to override sound biblical exegesis, Graves ended up with confusing and idiosyncratic conceptions of both John and the kingdom.[36]

Beyond Graves's more limited scuffles with Hill and Rice, his contentions in *Trilemma* best articulated his disagreements with Presbyterianism. This treatise, which was originally published in 1860, joined together his campaigns against Catholicism and Protestant Pedobaptists. In essence, the Landmark patriarch alleged that Presbyterians could not sufficiently distance themselves from their origins in the Church of Rome. After reviewing the discussions of Presbyterian general assemblies in the nineteenth century, Graves pointed out their inability to reach a decisive resolution on whether or not Roman Catholic baptisms were valid. Following his own ecclesiological principles and pushing his relentless logic, Graves averred that if Roman baptisms were classified as legitimate, then the Catholic Church would have to be accepted as a true church. This, however, created a thorny predicament: "[I]f Protestants admit this, they surrender their own claims to be true churches of Christ, because they, in separating from the true Church of Christ, become schismatics. But they were excluded and anathematized by the true Church, and therefore their ministers were deprived of all authority to baptize, or to administer Church ordinances."[37] In other words, if Roman Catholic sacraments ever possessed any validity, the divisions that occurred during the Reformation effectively severed Protestant ministers from any chain of authority that would have allowed them to perform bona fide baptisms. On the other hand, if Pedobaptists denied the legitimacy of Roman baptisms, they also removed any justification for their own: "[N]o Christian Pedobaptist has any other baptism than he received from the priests of Rome. . . . But if their baptisms are invalid, then their societies can not be considered churches in any sense, as there can be no church without baptism; and if not churches, Protestant ministers have no Scriptural right to preach the gospel, or baptize others into their societies."[38]

---

is consistent with the arguments in his letters to N. L. Rice many years earlier. Cf. Graves, "John's Baptism Shown to Be Christian," in Graves, ed., *Southern Baptist Almanac and Register for the Year of our Lord 1852* (Nashville: Graves and Shankland, 1852), 19–28. His classification of John's baptism as Christian required him to explain Acts 19:1–7, where John's followers were evidently rebaptized. Graves maintained that those individuals had been baptized by John's disciples 20 years after John's ministry had ceased. See *John's Baptism*, 39–47; and Graves, "Exegesis of Acts XIX," *Southern Baptist Review* 6 (September 1860): 389–95.

[36] Graves explicitly related ecclesiology to his assignment of John to the Christian dispensation. See *John's Baptism*, 80–83.

[37] Graves, *Trilemma*, 13.

[38] Ibid., 13–14.

Thus Graves triumphantly believed that he had nullified the ordinances of all Protestants, whether or not Catholic baptisms were valid. In reference to Presbyterian deliberations of his day, he posed that denomination's particular quandary: "The *Tri–lemma* [*sic*] is the middle horn: the confession of the General Assembly of its inability to decide whether its own ministers are baptized, or have authority to baptize, and, consequently, whether their societies are visible Churches of Christ!" [39] In short, Graves traced Presbyterians and other Protestants to a corrupt fountain in Rome, while avowing that Baptists remained untainted because they had never been part of the Catholic Church. Successionist history, a denial of the church universal, and a tendency to ascribe guilt by association all combined to shape Graves's apologetic for Baptist superiority to all other Christian groups. [40] Even though Presbyterians historically affirmed salvation by grace through faith, the supreme authority of Scripture, and other doctrines dear to Baptists, according to Graves's reckoning they were to be judged almost as harshly as Roman Catholics.

GRAVES AND ALEXANDER CAMPBELL: A PASSIONATE WAR OF WORDS

J. R. Graves's *Trilemma*, of course, was not limited to Catholicism or Presbyterianism. The contentious volume included a short section toward the end in which the author aimed a volley of abbreviated remonstrations against the followers of Alexander Campbell, even though they had not directly separated from papal Rome and did not practice infant baptism. In fact, Campbell had tried unsuccessfully to transcend denominationalism through a movement that he hoped would unite all Christians. Graves's disapproval of Campbell and his "Christian Church" in *Trilemma* seemed to be connected mainly to the unhappy history of Baptist-Campbellite relations since the early nineteenth century. First, he asserted that Campbell himself was not scripturally baptized. Since a Baptist preacher had administered immersion to Campbell in 1812, Graves must have been implying that the subject—Campbell—lacked truly biblical faith; indeed, Campbell later appeared to teach that regeneration by the Holy Spirit did not come prior to baptism. Second, Graves tagged the Restorationists as schismatics, likely due to his direct

---

[39] Ibid., 72.

[40] See ibid., 119–51, for Graves's appeal to Baptist perpetuity through the ages. See Tull's critical evaluation of *Trilemma* in "A Study of Southern Baptist Landmarkism," 237–42.

knowledge of Baptist churches that had been split by controversies over Campbellism in both Kentucky and Tennessee.[41] Nonetheless, the material in *Trilemma* represented only a small taste of the fervor that marked his unwavering campaign against this group. To the theologically untrained observer, Baptists looked like they shared some basic beliefs and practices with Campbellites. Nevertheless, Graves intently sought to disabuse his public audiences of reading too much into any superficial similarities.

While it would be a blatant exaggeration to posit that Landmarkism originated primarily as a reaction to Campbell's "reformation," the biographical, geographical, and ecclesiastical realities of Graves's career in the 1840s and 1850s ensured that Campbellism would receive a substantial share of attention when the pugnacious journalist sought to draw appropriate lines between Baptists and other denominations. Other than perhaps in his battles with Methodists, who had outpaced Baptists in Nashville by the time Graves arrived in 1845, his sense of urgency in religious warfare with Campbellites was unsurpassed. In presuming what Graves and fellow Landmarkers may have sensed in the middle of the nineteenth century, theologian Jeffrey Mask suggests that the Restorationist movement "seriously threatened not only Baptist identity, but Baptist survival in the South."[42] Although the manifest confidence that Graves normally displayed in polemical contexts may raise questions about Mask's analysis, the founder of Landmarkism knew that he faced a formidable foe. After all, Campbell's movement already had depleted Baptist ranks in some places very close to home. In addition, Graves's dispute with Waller in 1848 had largely centered on whether Campbellite immersions were valid. Finally, about a decade later Graves found himself fending off charges that he had once dabbled with the suspect movement's ideas as a young man in

---

[41] Graves, *Trilemma*, 190–97. These pages are in Part II, which was not in the first edition. For a useful summary of Campbell, particularly in reference to his period as a Baptist, see J. E. Tull, "Alexander Campbell: Advocate of Reformation," in *Shapers of Baptist Thought* (Valley Forge, PA: Judson Press, 1972), 101–27. On Campbell's conflicts with Baptists other than Graves, see J. L. Garrett Jr., *Baptist Theology: A Four-Century Study* (Macon, GA: Mercer University Press, 2009), 249–57.

[42] E. J. Mask, *A Liberty under God: Toward a Baptist Ecclesiology* (Lanham, MD: University Press of America, 1997), 14. For an example of overplaying the Campbellite factor in explaining the rise of the Landmark movement, see the comments of Alan Lefever, director of the Texas Baptist Historical Collection, in Ken Camp, "Historians Debate Reasons for the Rise of Landmarkism in 19th Century," *Baptist Standard*, January 12, 2009, 11. Lefever bluntly stated that "Landmarkism was a reaction to the Campbellite movement. . . . If Alexander Campbell had never come along, we'd never have had Landmarkism. There never would have been a need." Lefever appears to be reducing denominational rivalry on the frontier to Baptists versus Campbellites, ignoring the fact that Graves had much to say about other competing denominations. Cf. J. Early Jr., "The Cotton Grove Resolutions," *Tennessee Baptist History* 7 (Fall 2005): 45, where he ranked Campbellites lower than Methodists and other Pedobaptists on Graves's list of enemies.

Kentucky.[43] Moreover, he forged his unique understanding of Baptist distinctiveness and superiority in part by showing how far removed his denomination was in doctrine and practice from Campbellism.

In point of fact, Graves and Campbell agreed on very little except baptism by immersion, local church autonomy, and an emphasis on local churches having the primary responsibility for doing missions.[44] Furthermore, Graves did not push aggressively on the latter issue until the late 1850s. He also usually refrained from attacks on denominational agencies beyond the local church that were engaged in specialized ministries; for example, he supported associations and mission societies that worked with Native Americans. Campbell, on the other hand, opposed whatever he could not find warrant for in the New Testament, which caused him to be linked—at least in the earlier phase of his career—to the "anti-mission" movement. For his part, Graves was more interested in protecting local church independence than in advancing the negative Scripture principle (i.e., if it's not in the Bible, don't do it).

Despite the notable discontinuities between the thinking of Graves and Campbell, Christian Church researcher Gregory Holt contends that Campbell palpably influenced Graves's ideas about restoring the primitive church of the first century and his editorial style.[45] Unfortunately, Holt's evidence is relatively scanty, including the curious letter of W. G. Cogar concerning the Landmarker's alleged sympathy for Campbellism that Graves's opponents made public in 1858. Nevertheless, Holt cited the letter as attestation that "Graves owed a debt to the Restoration Movement for providing a framework for his own brand of restitutionism."[46] Furthermore, Holt seems confused about the precise impact of the Separate Baptist tradition on Graves, as well as the possible Baptist sources for the Landmark patriarch's successionism. Finally, his discussion of how Campbell's journalistic style affected Graves ignores the historical context; many denominational editors in the mid-nineteenth century generously employed ridicule and biting sarcasm

---

[43] These last three matters are discussed in previous chapters.

[44] Cf. Douglas Weaver's remark in Camp, "Historians Debate Reasons for the Rise of Landmarkism," 11, where the Baylor historian called the Baptist-Church of Christ clash a "sibling rivalry," adding that "when someone is so much like you and you have so much in common, you tend to accentuate the differences." Weaver seems to understate some significant theological differences that Graves was quick to broach.

[45] G. S. Holt, "The Influence of Alexander Campbell on the Life and Work of J. R. Graves, the Founder of the Landmark Baptist Movement" (M.Div. thesis, Emmanuel School of Religion, 1993), 3, 21.

[46] Ibid., 21–23. Holt excerpted the Cogar letter from H. L. McBeth, ed., *A Sourcebook for Baptist Heritage* (Nashville: Broadman, 1990), 317, which omits the second Cogar letter that somewhat qualifies the first one. See discussion of this episode in the first chapter.

in their writing, especially when they quarreled with each other.[47] While Graves surely refined some of his ideas in reaction to Campbell and perhaps sought to exploit some of the Restorationist leader's positions for his own purposes, Holt ultimately failed to make a convincing case that the two editors had a student-master relationship.

Although Graves sparred some with lesser figures in the Restorationist movement in the early 1850s, the most heated exchanges that he had with Campbell occurred from 1854 to 1858. This timing—along with his early salvos against the Methodists and other Pedobaptists—challenges Holt's notion that Campbellism was Graves's first targeted adversary.[48] The Graves-Campbell feud played out chiefly in their respective newspapers. Graves provided an additional forum for Campbell by reprinting some of the latter's columns from the *Millennial Harbinger* in the *Tennessee Baptist*, as well as in a published collection of relevant materials.[49] As the journalistic debate unfolded, it became quite obvious that the two editors did not care much for each other either as gentlemen or theologians.

One of the more frivolous disputes that flared up between Graves and Campbell was whether the two men had personally met each other, with the former taking the affirmative and the latter denying it.[50] At that stage of his career, the Restorationist preacher was based in Bethany, Virginia—later to become West Virginia—yet he itinerated widely in surrounding states, including Tennessee. On one occasion, in fact, Graves exuberantly described an "unsuccessful" visit that Campbell had made to Nashville in 1854: "Mr. C. has returned to Bethany convinced of the truth of our assertions, that his pseudo reformation is defunct in the South-West. It is the corruption of Christianity, the most specious form of infidelity of this age."[51] Graves's statement comes across as self-serving; it also falls short of establishing that the two combatants had opportunity to meet in

---

[47] Holt, "The Influence of Alexander Campbell," 23–35, 36–38.

[48] Ibid., 40. On early conflicts between Graves and Campbellites, see Graves, "Ferguson, McFerrin & Co.," *Tennessee Baptist,* March 27, 1852, [2]. J. B. Ferguson was a Restorationist pastor in Nashville and editor of the *Christian Magazine*. He called Graves "reckless." See O. L. Hailey, *J. R. Graves: Life, Times and Teachings* (Nashville: by the author, 1929), 26–32, on Graves's early battles in Nashville with Campbellism and Methodism as virtually simultaneous. He also recounted how an anticipated public debate between Graves and some Restorationist preachers never took place.

[49] See Graves, *Campbell and Campbellism Exposed: A Series of Replies (to A. Campbell's Articles in the Millennial Harbinger)* (Nashville: Graves & Marks, 1855). In 1854 Campbell made an offer: "I challenge Mr. Graves to give me a hearing in his paper. I will give him line for line, and word for word in my pages." See Campbell, "A. Campbell's May 'Notice' of J. R. Graves. Number Three," *Tennessee Baptist,* June 10, 1854, [2]. Graves took him up on this.

[50] Graves, *Campbell and Campbellism Exposed*, 3, 14, 26.

[51] Graves, "Homeward Bound and Homeward Found," *Tennessee Baptist,* February 10, 1855, [2].

that context since Graves had just returned to the Tennessee capital after a five-month absence. It may be that Graves had encountered Campbell in some other setting and that Campbell had simply forgotten about it.

Graves's invocation of unflattering language such as "infidelity" in reference to Campbell's ideology testified to the prominent place of colorful invective in their literary dispute. In various instances the Baptist editor spoke of his rival's lack of orthodoxy, feeble argumentation, "mad articles," labors "with the high priests of Antichrist," and "sophistical" reasoning that resulted in "inextricable contradictions and absurdities."[52] Campbell was fully capable of responding in kind, and on more than one occasion accused Graves of spewing venom, falsehood, and slander; he likewise leveled ad hominem attacks at his antagonist by characterizing him as "a distinguished braggart" and "an ecclesiastical knight errant."[53] In what might have been Campbell's most vicious attack on his Baptist counterpart, he basically portrayed Graves as a vain and ineffective windbag: "In gasconade and blustering pretence this gentlemen has few superiors; in political and guileful trickery, he has fewer equals; in sound relevant and candid argument, he has rarely an inferior. . . . The boastful and swaggering style of his exordium may have created some high expectations."[54] As readers scrambled for copies of Webster's on their desks, they must have wondered what had happened to substantive dialogue based on real issues.

Despite the caustic rhetoric, the debate revealed Graves's abiding concern that Campbell professed dangerous theological beliefs regarding repentance, faith, and salvation. For Graves, Campbell's deviations from biblical soteriology were far more acute than the personal side of their conflict. The Landmark editor did not hesitate to draw some doctrinal boundaries:

> We regard Campbellism as the most pernicious and deadly heresy ever
> propagated under the name of christianity [*sic*]. All its fiery darts are hurled
> against the faith of the gospel—its dagger is driven towards the very vitals of

---

[52] See respectively Graves, "Mr. A. Campbell and Orthodoxy," *Tennessee Baptist,* April 8, 1854, [2]; Graves, "Reply to Mr. A. Campbell's May Notice, Number Three," and Graves, "Elder J. M. Hurt," *Tennessee Baptist,* June 10, 1854): [2]; Graves, "To Alexander Campbell. No. 4," *Tennessee Baptist,* July 15, 1854, [2]; and Graves, "Letter to Alexander Campbell—No. 7," *Tennessee Baptist,* September 9, 1854, [2].

[53] Campbell, "A. Campbell's May 'Notice' of J. R. Graves," 2; and Campbell in Graves, *Campbell and Campbellism Exposed,* 3–4.

[54] Campbell, "Mr. Graves' Silence," *Tennessee Baptist,* March 17, 1855, [2]. This was reprinted from the *Millennial Harbinger.*

the Christian Religion. The proper agency of the Holy Spirit in regeneration is denied—the spirituality of religion assailed and made a mock of, and the ungodly sinner without repentance produced by godly sorrow—and without a prayer for the mercy of an offended God, is hurried to the water to seek a new birth, a cleansing by the blood of Christ and regeneration unto life in its embrace.[55]

Here Graves alluded to the commonly held notion among Baptists that the "reformation" of Campbell essentially taught baptismal regeneration where immersion in water was viewed as a saving act; it did not require deep conviction of sin or repentance, only a verbal profession of Jesus as the Christ. In characteristic style, Graves groused that the Restorationist leader "makes the water of a brook or pond as essential as the death and blood of Christ."[56] All these considerations, of course, stood behind his stern counsel that Baptist churches not accept the validity of Restorationist immersions.

For his part, Campbell took offense at how Graves depicted his theology of baptism. Indeed, he outright denied that he taught regeneration through the baptismal waters. He emphasized that baptism was for the remission of sins (Acts 2:38) and then suggested his version of the *ordo salutis*: "The original cause is *grace*. The meritorious cause is *blood*. The instrumental causes are *faith, repentance, baptism*, all expressed in the last act."[57] Nevertheless, Campbell's apologetic still seemed to minimize the role of the Holy Spirit before baptism. Graves correctly sensed that his editorial foe understood baptism as necessary for salvation, thus undercutting the gospel of redemption rooted in the finished work of Christ's death and resurrection. As Timothy George has discerned, nineteenth-century Baptists "rejected Campbell's watered-down doctrine of the Holy Spirit and his reductionist understanding of conversion."[58] In the final analysis, Baptists and Restorationists both disallowed infant baptism and practiced immersion; however, their soteriological doctrines—as well as their concepts of the nature and meaning of baptism—were widely divergent.

The intimation of baptismal regeneration in Restorationist theology also provided Graves with an opening for connecting the Campbellite movement to Roman

---

[55] Graves, "Mr. Campbell's Last Article for 1854," *Tennessee Baptist*, March 17, 1855, [2].

[56] Graves, *Campbell and Campbellism Exposed*, 144–45. For a later, more systematic treatment of the issue, see Graves, *The Relation of Baptism to Salvation* (Memphis: Baptist Book House, 1881).

[57] Campbell in ibid., 9. Cf. pp. 188–91, where he called baptism "the consummating act of a preached and received gospel" and explicitly rejected baptismal regeneration.

[58] George, "Southern Baptist Ghosts," 20.

Catholicism, even though that appeared to be a more difficult task than he faced with Pedobaptists. The new "reformation," in fact, did not really identify with the sixteenth-century Reformation, so Graves could not argue that the rise of Campbellism in the nineteenth century involved a break with Rome. Nonetheless, Graves inferred that by its embrace of baptismal regeneration, Restorationism "hopelessly delivers man into the hands of priests, to all intents and purposes, as rigorously as does iron handed Popery."[59] Graves presupposed that an allegedly sacramental view of baptism required a priest-hood, just as in Catholicism. Since Campbellite congregations set up structures similar to those in Baptist churches—and conveyed nothing close to a priestly or authoritarian conception of the ministry—Graves's efforts to trace Campbell and his followers to Rome certainly represented the weakest aspect of his campaign against them.

In the midst of their controversies, Campbell erred in assuming that Graves was a lone wolf who did not speak for most Baptists in the mid-nineteenth century.[60] At that time, Baptists of many stripes agreed with most of Graves's criticisms of Campbell's movement. For example, in 1854 the Baptist General Association of Middle Tennessee and North Alabama passed a resolution vindicating the *Tennessee Baptist* editor and condemning the "current reformation" for "gross heresy" on matters like baptism. Moreover, the association commended Graves as "an able and valiant defender and advocate of the faith of the gospel, and faithfully devoted to the interest of the Baptist denomination."[61] Although a skeptic might point out that this association had shown a marked sympathy for Landmarkism, non-Landmark Baptists also chimed in strongly against Campbellism, including J. B. Jeter of Virginia and A. P. Williams of Missouri.[62] Graves was even able to cite a letter from Jeter in which the Richmond pastor wholly endorsed the *Tennessee Baptist* articles on Campbell.[63] In his jousting with Graves, Campbell seriously underestimated the depth of animosity that Southern Baptists felt toward his movement. Campbell's Baptist critics did not necessarily imitate Graves's abrasive tactics, but they sensed that they were fighting the same war.

---

[59] Graves, "To Alexander Campbell. No. 4," [2]. Cf. Graves, "Desire of All Nations," 16.

[60] See Campbell in Graves, *Campbell and Campbellism Exposed*, 140.

[61] Hailey, *J. R. Graves*, 29–30. Cf. Graves, *Campbell and Campbellism Exposed*, 128ff.

[62] J. B. Jeter, *Campbellism Examined* (New York: Sheldon, Lamport, & Blakeman, 1855); and A. P. Williams, *Campbellism Exposed, in an Examination of Lard's Review of Jeter* (Memphis: Graves & Mahaffy, 1866).

[63] Graves, *Campbell and Campbellism Exposed*, 214–16. The letter was dated November 17, 1854. In a later time, Jeter indicated that although he had "the highest regard for many Landmarkers, I think their views are a serious hindrance to the progress of Baptist principles." Jeter to Graves, September 17, 1879, Graves Collection, AR. 9, SBHLA, Nashville, Tennessee. At that time Jeter edited the *Religious Herald*, which was critical of Landmarkism.

Graves clearly assigned a high grade to his crusade against Campbellism, calling it "the most laudable labor of our editorial career."[64] He evidently felt that he had stood his ground against the older journalist; indeed, his columns communicated a degree of cockiness that he had Campbell on the ropes. The baptismal issue seemed to loom the largest in his anti-Campbellite polemic, because it related both to basic questions of the gospel's meaning and to his Landmarkist principles. Since Campbell's theology of baptism clashed so much with historic Baptist belief, Graves sensed an urgency to mark the proper boundaries for his denomination, even as he went up against another boundary setter who moved in an entirely different direction.

THE METHODIST IRON WHEEL

When J. R. and Lua Graves relocated to Nashville in 1845, the Methodist Episcopal Church, South was organizing itself following a schism with northern Methodists that was provoked mainly by slavery. Not only was Methodism the strongest denomination in the city, but the Tennessee capital also functioned as a strategic center for Methodist operations throughout the South. Nashville was home to the senior bishop of the new denomination, Joshua Soule, the regional *Christian Advocate*, and other publishing endeavors such as the Methodist Book Concern.[65] Methodist prosperity undoubtedly posed an impediment for Baptists and other groups as they sought to enlarge their spheres of influence in Middle Tennessee.

Baptist conflict with Methodism actually preceded Graves's arrival in Nashville. When R. B. C. Howell served either as editor of the *Baptist* or contributor to the *Baptist Banner and Western Pioneer*, he skirmished with local Methodist leaders about issues like infant baptism and Calvinism, including *Christian Advocate* editor J. B. McFerrin. The pugnacious McFerrin directly insulted Howell by calling him "[t]he inflated bird of Nashville, bigoted, presumptuous for anything; lacking only the power to become a pope." The Methodist journalist also alleged that Baptists believed

---

[64] Graves, "Mr. Campbell's Last Article for 1854," [2].

[65] J. A. Smith, *Cross and Flame: Two Centuries of United Methodism in Middle Tennessee* (Nashville: Commission on Archives and History of the Tennessee Conference, United Methodist Church, 1984), 85–100, 123–38. For the broader context, see J. H. Wigger, *Taking Heaven by Storm: Methodism and the Rise of Popular Christianity in America*, Religion in America Series (New York: Oxford University Press, 1998). In regard to Methodist success in Nashville, Graves's son-in-law wrote that "Methodism was in the saddle and rode forth with domineering and triumphant air." See Hailey, *J. R. Graves*, 51.

in infant damnation, even as he tried to connect their baptismal doctrine to Alexander Campbell.[66] Although Howell's responses to McFerrin seemed to be comparatively restrained, the two editors had thrown down the gauntlet in advance of a more heated controversy to come.

In light of both the earlier Howell-McFerrin disputes and the ensuing editorial transition at the Baptist newspaper in the late 1840s, biographer Hailey inferred that the First Baptist pastor "practically turned over" the Methodist challenge to Graves.[67] Whether or not the aspiring journalist discerned a definite commission from Howell in that regard, he plainly ramped up the rhetoric against McFerrin and the whole Methodist enterprise. His campaign unquestionably took into account the size and strength of Methodism in the Nashville area; yet those factors by themselves do not explain his ardent opposition.[68] The Methodist Episcopal Church fit both the categories of Protestant and Pedobaptist, so he could lump them in with the Presbyterians for accepting some of the same unbiblical traditions such as sprinkling babies. Likewise, he grouped them with Campbellites on baptismal regeneration, although that correlation raised more questions than it answered. Furthermore, Methodism was fundamentally a child of the Church of England, and thus a grandchild of the Roman Church.[69] Hence, Graves could utilize some of the same bullets against the Methodists that he used against other branches of Christianity, including the oft-repeated classification of Methodist bodies as societies and not churches.

One of Graves's earliest attacks on Methodism came as an indirect swipe at its doctrine. In his sermon on God's sovereignty, in which he labeled Calvinism as fatalistic, he asserted that to be an "Armenian" [*sic*] was to be a universalist.[70] Here Graves

---

[66] Hailey, *J. R. Graves*, 24, 27. Cf. L. T. Horne, "A Study of the Life and Work of R. B. C. Howell" (Th.D. diss., Southern Baptist Theological Seminary 1958), 200–04; and L. K. Harper, "The Historical Context for the Rise of Old Landmarkism" (M.A. thesis, Murray State University, 1986), 66–68. The Howell-McFerrin exchanges began as early as 1841.

[67] Hailey, *J. R. Graves*, 28.

[68] He was conscious of Methodist success, ruefully noting in 1851 that his paper had 5,000 subscribers, whereas the *Christian Advocate* boasted 14,000. See Graves, "Vol. VIII," *Tennessee Baptist,* September 6, 1851, [2].

[69] For an example of his connecting of Methodism to Catholicism, see his discussion of "Roman Catholic features" in Graves, *The Great Iron Wheel; or, Republicanism Backwards and Christianity Reversed*, 9th ed. (Nashville: Graves, Marks, and Rutland, 1855), 234–46. On baptism, see ibid., 415ff.

[70] Graves, "The Sovereignty of God: Proposition III," *Tennessee Baptist,* February 17, 1848, [2]. Cf. Graves, *Satan Dethroned*, 57, where the spelling was corrected to "Arminian."

was making a veiled reference to the theology of John Wesley, the eighteenth-century founding father of the Methodist movement. Wesley's doctrines followed closely the lead of Dutch theologian James Arminius, who challenged the dominant Calvinism of his homeland in the late sixteenth and early seventeenth centuries. Although the Wesleyan tradition emphasized free grace and a universal atonement, most nineteenth-century Methodists would have taken offense at the equating of Arminianism with universal salvation; regrettably, Graves left that point vague and undeveloped. In later years, however, he consistently challenged Methodist opponents with anti-Arminian arguments, particularly in reference to their denial of perseverance (i.e., a genuinely regenerated believer cannot lose the gift of salvation).[71] Oddly enough, he did not press that issue nearly as much in his controversies with the Arminian Alexander Campbell and his followers.

Like Howell in an earlier time, Graves carried on editorial exchanges with J. B. McFerrin, even suggesting that the Methodist journalist seemed to be intent on using "choicely assorted epithets" for whoever was editing the Baptist newspaper.[72] In the midst of this war of words, public debates between Baptist and Methodist representatives took place in western Tennessee both before and after the famed Cotton Grove meeting in June of 1851. Graves himself participated in some of these, perhaps most notably in the rural venue of Quincy in what was then Gibson County. This event, right on the heels of the Big Hatchie Association's endorsement of the Cotton Grove Resolutions, stretched out for several days and mostly involved Graves going toe-to-toe with a "Mr. Fly," the Methodist spokesman. After several rounds of discussion on issues like baptism and perseverance, the audience swelled to 2,500 on the fifth day. One anonymous Baptist eyewitness observed that "Mr. Graves was exulting in conscious triumph, and the audience dispersed, fully under the impression that he had been grossly assaulted—and

---

[71] See "Quincy Correspondence: Further News from the Debate," *Tennessee Baptist,* August 16, 1851, [2]; and Graves and Jacob Ditzler, *The Graves–Ditzler: or, Great Carrollton Debate* (Memphis: Southern Baptist Publication Society, 1876), 1117–75. In the transcript of the debate with Ditzler (p. 1126) Graves declared that the hope of perseverance "involves the very foundation of Christianity itself . . . concerning the foundation upon which this doctrine rests[,] a mistake is fatal to the soul's eternal salvation."

[72] Graves, "The Methodist Advocate Again," *Tennessee Baptist,* March 15, 1849, [2]. Cf. Graves, "Ferguson, McFerrin & Co.," *Tennessee Baptist,* March 27, 1852, [2]. Hailey gives a brief account of the Graves-McFerrin clash in *J. R. Graves* (pp. 24–25) where he claimed that "Dr. Graves was not the aggressor, but responded to the most vicious attacks."

gained a complete victory." [73] The proximity of the Cotton Grove assembly and these formal debates helps to confirm that heated conflict with Methodists was a key element in the formative stages of the Landmark movement.

Intense controversy with Methodism also appeared to spawn a libel suit against the *Tennessee Baptist* in 1852. Apparently, when Graves was in Bowling Green helping J. M. Pendleton with a revival, a letter from Elisha Collins appeared in the Baptist paper in February of that year signed by his friend, William M. Lea. [74] Collins, pastor of the First Baptist Church of Lexington, Tennessee, at the time was engaged in a personal dispute with R. B. Jones, a local Methodist minister. Jones responded to the correspondence—which accused him of lies, slander, and financial misconduct—by filing the lawsuit against Collins, Lea, and Graves. A jury in Madison County, Tennessee, ruled in favor of Jones and awarded damages of $7,500. In the meantime, Collins died, leaving all the costs to Graves; the editor, in turn, negotiated a smaller settlement. [75] Although Graves distanced himself from the publication of the offending letter, the whole matter illustrated the problems of editorial oversight that could result when he was gone from Nashville for extended periods. The legal ruckus, moreover, detracted from his attempts to gain the upper hand on a competing denomination.

In his battles with Methodism, Graves's favorite image was his description of its institutional system as a "great iron wheel." He initially used this in the last day of the Quincy debate in 1851 when he told the crowd that "this grand Methodist machine grinds into dust the *consciences* of men." [76] Less than a year later, the Landmark leader began to publish in his paper a series of lengthy letters addressed to Bishop Joshua

---

[73] "Quincy Correspondence: Further News from the Debate," [2]. For an account of previous days, see "Communications: Quincy Correspondence: News from the Debate," *Tennessee Baptist,* August 9, 1851, [2–3]. The Quincy debate lasted eight days in the period between July 31 and August 9; see "Communications: Quincy Correspondence: The Debate," *Tennessee Baptist,* August 30, 1851, [2]. A shorter debate in nearby Jackson between Graves and a Rev. I. L. Chapman followed almost immediately. See Champ C. Connor, "Communications: Jackson Correspondence: The Debate," *Tennessee Baptist,* September 6, 1851, [2–3]. Additional installments appeared in the issues of September 13, 1851, [2–3]; and October 11, 1851, [2]. Connor, a Baptist, was one of the moderators. His reports obviously lagged behind the mid-August event.

[74] Letter from William M. Lea, *Tennessee Baptist,* February 21, 1852, [3].

[75] Graves's account can be found in Graves, ed., *Little Iron Wheel: A Declaration of Christian Rights and Articles, Showing the Despotism of Episcopal Methodism* (Nashville: South-Western Publishing House; Graves, Marks & Co., 1856), 279–82. Cf. Hailey, *J. R. Graves,* 38–40. Hailey mistakenly cited the letter writer as "Dean" instead of "Lea." In Early, "The Cotton Grove Resolutions" (p. 48), the author located the lawsuit out of sequence in relation to the Cotton Grove meeting, and incorrectly stated that the "article" (letter) was published under Graves's name.

[76] "Communications: Quincy Correspondence: The Debate," 2.

Soule on matters that separated Baptists from Methodists.[77] These letters became the basis for his major work against the Methodist Episcopal Church, *The Great Iron Wheel*, which was published in 1855 and went through several editions; Graves later claimed that 50,000 copies of this volume were printed before Soule died in 1867.[78] The turning wheel motif continued in 1856 when the Baptist editor repeated some of his stock charges against Methodism and also responded to Methodist criticisms of *The Great Iron Wheel*.[79]

The Great Iron Wheel—and its subsequent iterations—treated Methodism in much the same way that Graves dealt with Protestant Pedobaptists in general, including the argument that "all the leading Protestant sects" imitated "popery" in terms of ecclesiastical organization.[80] While he never wrote at length about the Church of England, he readily connected Methodism to it by pointing out that both "societies" had a liturgy that could be traced to the Roman Church, a confession that promoted Calvinism, and a clergy that espoused Arminianism.[81] At the same time, Graves injected a few noteworthy twists that pertained specifically to Methodism. For example, he commonly employed Baptist successionism against Catholics and Protestants to uphold the notion that his denomination could boast both apostolicity and perpetuity. Hence, Baptists were older than all other groups, sects, or movements. Since institutional Methodism did not emerge until the late eighteenth century, its position was actually inferior to Catholicism and

---

[77] Graves, "The Great Iron Wheel. Number One," *Tennessee Baptist,* March 20, 1852, [1]. Editor McFerrin's assaults on Graves apparently helped to provoke these letters.

[78] Graves, *The New Great Iron Wheel: An Examination of the New M. E. Church South* (Memphis: Baptist Book House, 1884), 10. This version represented a tweaking of *The Great Iron Wheel* without substantive changes. Graves noted in the same context that the plates from the earlier book were destroyed when Nashville was occupied by the Union army during the Civil War. In addition, the published transcript of the Graves-Ditzler debate of 1876 shows that Graves did not introduce much there that was not already expressed in *The Great Iron Wheel*. See n. 71 above.

[79] Graves, ed., *The Little Iron Wheel*. He gave the earlier sections of this book over to H. B. Bascom, a minister and later a bishop in the Methodist Episcopal Church, South. Bascom had written "declaration" of Christian rights in the 1820s when he attempted to expedite structural reforms in his church. Graves saw this as support for his contention that ecclesiastical rule by bishops constituted despotism. Like so many of Graves's books, this one began as a series of articles in his newspaper. See the first installment, H. B. Bascom, "Chapter I. Summary Declaration of Rights, Explanatory of the Reasons and Principles of Government," *Tennessee Baptist,* January 19, 1856, [2]. To each Bascom piece in the series, Graves added "Notes of Explanation and Application," which constituted a major part of the book.

[80] Graves, *The Great Iron Wheel*, 259.

[81] Ibid., 500–543.

Reformation Protestantism; in other words, he sarcastically avowed that the Methodist Church was a human creation simply too young to be taken seriously.[82]

Graves's polemic against Methodism sparked an extraordinary outrage from its leaders. Perhaps the most vociferous protest outside of Nashville emanated from the pen of William G. Brownlow, the editor of the *Knoxville Whig*. Consistent with the tenor of journalistic debate in the 1850s, Brownlow aimed some of his harshest blows against Graves as a person. After dismissing the *Tennessee Baptist* as "a low, dirty, scurrilous sheet" that "intelligent" Baptists would not read, Brownlow proceeded to ridicule Graves as "a very little man" who "has been barking, neighing, bleating, braying, mewing, puffing, swaggering, strutting, and in every situation, an offensive *smell*, to gentlemen of refined tastes and Christian habits, has gone out from him."[83] Brownlow evidently borrowed some pages from Campbell's book of etiquette, again illustrating that Graves was not the sole example of rude and uncharitable denominational apologetics in the mid-nineteenth century.

At the heart of Graves's unfriendly disposition toward Methodism was its episcopalian form of church government, which allowed him to tie it to Roman Catholicism. More important, the ecclesiastical composition of the Methodist Episcopal Church, South, meant that it was inherently undemocratic and anti-republican. Perhaps more than the leadership of any other group that he attacked, the Methodist bishops came across in his diatribes against them as tyrannical absolutists who squelched individual and congregational freedom. The examination of Graves's Christian republicanism in the following chapter lays out both a crucial ingredient of his ecclesiology as well as an explanation of his enmity toward those who controlled the "great iron wheel."

---

[82] Ibid., 19–33. Oddly enough, Graves evidently borrowed a sizable chunk of his material in *The Great Iron Wheel* from Presbyterian editor Fred A. Ross. See Smith, "A Critical Analysis of the Theology of J. R. Graves," 106–8.

[83] W. G. Brownlow, *The Great Iron Wheel Examined; or, Its False Spokes Extracted, and an Exhibition of Elder Graves, Its Builder, in a Series of Chapters* (Nashville: For the Author, 1856), 20, 26. Brownlow (p. 312) also suggested that Graves as "Northern man" was opposed to slavery, a charge that—as noted in the first chapter—some of his Baptist opponents leveled. Oddly enough, Brownlow served as both Tennessee governor and senator during Reconstruction, when he embraced Radical Republican sentiments and policies. See E. M. Coulter, *William G. Brownlow: Fighting Parson of the Southern Highlands* (1937; repr., Knoxville: University of Tennessee Press, 1999), 262ff. Brownlow's attacks likely account for Graves's defense of slavery in *The Little Iron Wheel*, 10–17. In the same volume, 244ff, Graves responded to Brownlow, calling him "a convicted libeller." This required him (pp. 279–82) to explain his own libel case referred to above.

Chapter 4

Christian Republicanism and Landmarkist Ecclesiology

The Graves Synthesis, Part I

THE GEORGETOWN COLLEGE ADDRESS

In 1858 J. R. Graves addressed the Ciceronian and Tau Theta Kappa literary societies at Georgetown College in Kentucky on the subject of "Individualism." The Landmark patriarch, who had little formal education but heartily promoted Baptist institutions of higher learning, began his remarks by challenging the collegians to think for themselves. Perhaps as a reflection on his own experience in Baptist controversies, Graves openly fretted that too many people allowed others to do their thinking for them. In contrast to such an anemic or conformist attitude, he urged his audience to accept individualism as a bedrock principle for Christian faith and practice: "The whole structure of Christianity is based upon it." Furthermore, he pointed to a moral imperative by sternly warning the students that "man cannot concede the exercise of his individuality without sin against God & injury to himself, his country & his race."[1]

As the speaker proceeded, it became apparent that he regarded individualism as both a natural and inalienable right as well as a duty. Since God deals with people as individuals and the gospel is addressed to individuals, Graves inferred a divine mandate for individualism in all spheres of life, not just the religious. All legitimate government

---

[1] J. R. Graves, "Individualism" (handwritten text of address delivered at Georgetown College, Georgetown, Kentucky, on June 22 [?], 1858), 9, 13, 19, Graves Collection, AR. 9, SBHLA, Nashville, Tennessee. The date on the manuscript seems unlikely—see n4 below. For evidence of Graves's active role in Baptist higher education, see Minutes of the Board of Trustees, Southwestern Baptist [later Union] University, 1874–1906, Emma Waters Summar Library Archives, Union University, Jackson, Tennessee. These records document Graves's service as a trustee, including a stint as board president (1885–92).

in church or state, he forcefully averred, must be based on the individual. In fact, the Nashville journalist dismissed any government that was not democratic or representative as incompatible with individualism.[2]

In his intriguing discourse at Georgetown, Graves clearly intended to link individualism with freedom. Hence, he frequently employed colorful language to alert his listeners to the dangers of despotism, absolutism, and tyranny in both secular and ecclesiastical contexts. Individualism, he declared, must be cultivated and extended as a primary weapon in the defense of civil liberties and free institutions. Finally, Graves called on the American educational system to do its part to inculcate an ideology of individualism in the minds and hearts of young learners.[3]

Graves later seemed pleased with his visit to Georgetown, commenting that he spoke before a "large audience," and that some in attendance requested that he consider publishing his speech. He noted that he had inadequate time to prepare his discourse and hoped "to perfect it at a future day."[4] He also attached a notice from the *Western Recorder* in which an unnamed observer exuded his approval, remarking that the topic was one on which "every Georgetonian and every true hearted Baptist will give Bro. Graves the right hand of fellowship."[5] Indeed, Graves had sounded chords that would have resonated well throughout much of Protestant evangelicalism in the middle of the nineteenth century; individualism was a vital component of the Christian republican tradition.

HISTORIOGRAPHICAL CONSIDERATIONS

Recent interpreters of Graves, without citing his Georgetown oration, have acknowledged the Landmark leader's indebtedness to the cultural and political currents that shaped the ethos of mid-nineteenth-century America, including religious and secular individualism. For instance, Baptist historian Marty Bell's Ph.D. dissertation at Vanderbilt perceptively depicts Graves as "a collector and purveyor of popular ideas of democracy and primitiv-

---

[2] Graves, "Individualism," 18–20, 61.

[3] Ibid., 28–73.

[4] Graves, "Marks by the Way. No. 1," *Tennessee Baptist,* April 10, 1858, [3]. Apparently the speech was never published; the dispute at First Baptist of Nashville, which was heating up in 1858, may have been a distraction. The date on the handwritten copy of the address does not fit with the timing of the notice about it in Graves's newspaper, so it was probably recorded incorrectly on the manuscript.

[5] Ibid.

ism" during his era.[6] Drawing on Nathan Hatch's thesis about the "democratization" of Christianity in the United States between the Revolution and the Civil War, Bell convincingly demonstrates that Graves brewed a creative mixture of "republican" rhetoric, which had wide circulation in the nineteenth century, with a Landmark theology that was allegedly rooted in the New Testament, thus providing "a religious justification for popular sovereignty."[7] While Bell conceded that Graves energetically spread his message, the Belmont professor was obviously put off by what he characterized as "demagogy." In fact, Bell injudiciously dropped some of his scholarly caution when he branded Graves as "excessively disputatious, outrageously arrogant, extremely bigoted, and at times desperately paranoid."[8] Nonetheless, Bell's work surpasses all earlier investigations of Graves by deftly establishing the broader contexts in which the Tennessee Landmarker operated; in other words, Bell was interested in more than just denominational history.

In a similar vein, Raymond Carroll's doctoral dissertation on Southern Baptist individualism is sensitive to the ways that J. R. Graves mirrored the broader political impulses of his time. Carroll commented, for example, that Graves "coaligned religious and political democracy, envisioning an egalitarianism that had an aura of the new independent America."[9] In Carroll's analysis, Graves embraced an ideology that was imbued with individualism, motivating him to attack hierarchy, tyranny, creeds, inequalities, and anything else that threatened individual liberties.[10] Carroll's insightful treatment of Graves, however, is marred when he categorized the Landmarker's individualism as an "incipient," subordinate theme in his work.[11] In reality, individualism permeated most of what Graves wrote about both the church and the American political scene. Indeed,

---

[6] M. G. Bell, "James Robinson Graves and the Rhetoric of Demagogy: Primitivism and Democracy in Old Landmarkism" (Ph.D. diss., Vanderbilt University, 1990), 4. For the broader historical context, see the following excellent overviews: D. W. Howe, *What Hath God Wrought: The Transformation of America, 1815–1848,* Oxford History of the United States (New York: Oxford University Press, 2007); and W. A. McDougall, *Throes of Democracy: The American Civil War Era, 1829–1877* (New York: HarperCollins, 2008).

[7] Bell, "James Robinson Graves and the Rhetoric of Demagogy," 41. Cf. N. O. Hatch, *The Democratization of American Christianity* (New Haven: Yale University Press, 1989). Hatch's contribution has been recently recalled in K. Myers, "Contours of Culture," *Touchstone* 23 (July/August 2010): 10–11. Myers expressed particular concern about populism and the dangers of the church surrendering "its vocation when it allies itself with dubious cultural trends." As the remainder of this chapter illustrates, Graves was guilty of uncritically allowing the political culture of his time to infiltrate his ecclesiology.

[8] Bell, "James Robinson Graves and the Rhetoric of Demagogy," 240.

[9] R. E. Carroll, "Dimensions of Individualism in Southern Baptist Thought" (Ph.D. diss., New Orleans Baptist Theological Seminary, 1995), 52.

[10] Ibid., 53–60.

[11] Ibid., 16, 44–46.

Graves's ecclesiology cannot be fully understood apart from the radical individualism that undergirded it.

Some additional interpretive angles that help to flesh out the overall context for Graves's life and thought can be found in Mark Noll's magisterial tome, *America's God*. The Notre Dame professor incisively elucidated how evangelical Protestantism, republican political ideology, and commonsense moral reasoning came together to form a powerful synthesis in nineteenth-century America. While all three elements of this compound contributed to the thinking of J. R. Graves, Noll's discussion of republicanism holds particular relevance for the concerns of this essay. Although the term "republicanism" has lost some precision through a wide range of definitions, it almost always presupposed a connection between virtue and freedom. Noll points out, moreover, that "American republican language returned consistently to two main themes: fear of abuses from illegitimate power and a nearly messianic belief in the benefits of liberty."[12] This political ideology not only inspired many colonists at the time of the American Revolution, but it also continued to claim the allegiance of most Americans in the nineteenth century, especially as it embraced more assertive notions of inalienable, individual rights.[13] Since Graves expounded a conspicuous Christian republicanism during his long career as an editor, publisher, and preacher, Noll's analysis of pertinent political and cultural backgrounds suggests some plausible sources for Graves's ideas.

In a subsequent article, Noll expanded and clarified his discussion of these subjects by showing how nineteenth-century Protestants understood the significance of America's founding. He also carefully explained how they wove together revivalism, voluntarism, and millennialism with their republicanism to form a compelling ideology that stressed individual freedoms; at the same time, it was "hyper-alert to the corruptions of power," which was detected in institutions like the Roman Catholic Church.[14] Noll then provided a handy summary of the evangelical Protestant mindset on these matters:

---

[12] M. A. Noll, *America's God: From Jonathan Edwards to Abraham Lincoln* (New York: Oxford University Press, 2002), 56.

[13] Ibid., 211–17. For a similar analysis, see W. G. McLoughlin, *Isaac Backus and the American Pietistic Tradition* (Boston: Little, Brown and Company, 1967), 233. He stressed how Baptist doctrines of egalitarianism and individualism helped to reinforce republican ideas, also noting that after 1775 "[e]xperimental religion and Jeffersonian republicanism merged . . . to form the quintessence of the new nation. Both contained a fundamental belief in the freedom and trustworthiness of the conscience, 'the moral sense,' of the common man." Cf. the more generalized discussion in E. Sandoz, *Republicanism, Religion, and the Soul of America* (Columbia: University of Missouri Press, 2006).

[14] M. A. Noll, "America's Two Foundings," *First Things,* December 2007, 32.

The American religion that flourished so luxuriantly in the first sixty years of the nineteenth century was *republican*: It had internalized the fear of unchecked authority and the commitment to private virtue that drove the ideology of the first political founding. But it was also *Christian republican*: The virtue that the United States' energetic itinerants promoted was not classical manliness but humility in Christ. The religion that came to prevail was more *antiformal* than formal. It did not trust in ascribed authority or inherited bureaucracies but rather in achieved authority and ad hoc networking. It was *populist* or democratic, championing the ability of any white man to assume leadership in any religious assembly. And it was *biblicist*, speaking of the Scriptures as a supreme authority that trumped or even revoked all other religious authorities.[15]

Although Noll did not cite Graves in his essay, many of the Landmark founder's ideological principles match quite well with the adjectives that Noll utilized in his description of prevailing nineteenth-century thought.

The broader landscape that Bell, Carroll, and Noll depicted is absolutely essential for appreciating how Graves merged the individualism of nineteenth-century America with his construal of New Testament Christianity. The Landmark pioneer's passionate defense of his thought as biblical probably served to mask the fact that the political and cultural realities of the day exercised a profound impact on his ecclesiology. Graves himself may not have fully realized just how much he had filtered some of his ideas about the church through the contemporary ideologies of individualism and its natural corollary, republicanism. For him, the slogans and rhetoric of these philosophies meshed seamlessly with the apostolic faith as it unfolded in the New Testament documents.

GRAVES'S REPUBLICAN ECCLESIOLOGY

The Graves synthesis found its primary expression in his apologetic for a Landmarkist understanding of the church. One of his core ecclesiological convictions, over against notions of a universal, national, or provincial church, was that the New Testament

---

[15] Ibid. The relevance of these themes for another nineteenth-century leader is addressed in D. L. Alexander-Payne, "Alexander Campbell and the Dilemma of Republican Millennialism" (Ph.D. diss., Texas Christian University, 2009).

restricted *ekklēsia* to visible, local, and absolutely independent congregations of believers:

> [T]he primitive model was a single congregation, complete in itself, independent of all other bodies, civil or religious, and the highest and only source of ecclesiastical authority on earth, amenable only to Christ, whose laws alone it receives and executes. . . . This church acknowledges no body of men on earth, council, conference or assembly as its head, but Christ alone, who is invisible, as "head over all things" to it.[16]

For Graves, this primitive model was not a human creation but divine; because Christ was its architect and founder, the New Testament church was "a perfect product of infinite wisdom."[17] While he stated these ecclesiological concepts most systematically in one of his later books, they had been evident in his thinking about the church for some time.

This affirmation of the church's supernatural origin, however, did not preclude Graves from invoking less lofty matters when setting forth his ecclesiological ideas. As Raymond Carroll noted, Graves's emphasis on singular, independent, and self-sufficient congregations signified that "individualism took on institutional garb."[18] In addition, Graves repeatedly integrated the tenets of individualism and republicanism with his Landmarkism.

He apparently first began to develop this synthesis late in 1848 when he reviewed a series of lectures that had been given by E. L. Magoon (1810–86), a Baptist pastor who was born in New Hampshire and eventually served churches in Cincinnati, New York, and Philadelphia. Graves was attracted to Magoon's confident assertions that Jesus possessed a republican character, the apostolic church had a republican constitution, and Christian doctrine exercised a republican influence; moreover, the early church blissfully lacked kings, popes, bishops, priests, and aristocrats. The *Tennessee Baptist* editor seconded Magoon's major points, then employed them in a typical attack on non-Baptist denominations: "Pedo-baptist societies are Monarchies, Aristocracies & hierarchies, into which the spirit of Republicanism cannot enter. They are all great *Anti-Republics*, the practical workings and tendency of which are antagonistic to both the teachings of

---

[16] J. R. Graves, *Old Landmarkism: What Is It?* 2nd ed. (Memphis: Baptist Book House; Graves, Mahaffy & Co., 1881), 38–39.

[17] Ibid., 29.

[18] Carroll, "Dimensions of Individualism," 63.

Christ and the genius of the American Constitution."[19] The alleged absence of republican virtues among Roman Catholics and Protestant Pedobaptists served as a key marker for Graves as he distinguished his Baptist heritage from these competing traditions.

By 1850 Graves's writings clearly bore signals of Magoon's impact. In his almanac for that year, Graves reiterated many of Magoon's themes about the republicanism of Jesus and the primitive church. He likewise held out the Bible as functionally equivalent to the Declaration of Independence in that "[i]t recognizes every man the possessor of absolute liberty of conscience and the director of his own religious acts."[20] Furthermore, the (Baptist) churches of the first century were republics that Jesus had instituted; his kingdom allowed no human domination or tyranny, "but a perfect equality among his subjects."[21] The Baptist editor also emphasized that a republican church government meant that everyone enjoyed an equal right to elect officers, choose pastors, and receive and exclude members.[22] Again, Graves readily harmonized the truth and authority of Scripture with the values of American republicanism; his appeal to the Bible was mixed with language that was culturally germane to the United States of the mid-nineteenth century. What is more, he would continue to work these biblical and political motifs into his arguments against other denominations that did not extend such divinely-mandated liberties.

In addition, Graves did not hesitate to incorporate republican ideology into his preaching. In "The Watchman's Reply," which he delivered to the Mississippi Baptist

---

[19] Graves, "Mr. Magoon's Works," *Tennessee Baptist,* December 14, 1848, [3]. Magoon's lectures were published as *Republican Christianity; or, True Liberty as Exhibited in the Life, Precepts and Early Disciples of the Great Redeemer* (Boston: Gould, Kendall, and Lincoln, 1849). For Graves's response to a critic of Magoon, see Graves, "'Christianity is as Much Monarchial, as It is Republican,'" *Tennessee Baptist,* November 1, 1849, [2], where he replied negatively to an editorial from the *South Western Baptist Chronicle.* For a short discussion of Magoon's influence on Graves, see H. S. Smith, "A Critical Analysis of the Theology of J. R. Graves" (Th.D. diss., Southern Baptist Theological Seminary, 1966), 108–9, where he mistakenly put Magoon's death in 1866 instead of 1886. Smith (p. 109, n29) also noted that Graves credited his mother for implanting a love of republicanism in her son. See Graves, *The Great Iron Wheel; or Republicanism Backwards and Christianity Reversed,* 9th ed. (Nashville: Graves, Marks, and Rutland, 1855), dedication page.

[20] Graves, "The Genius of the Gospel Republican," in Graves, ed., *The Southern Baptist Almanac and Annual Register for the Year of Our Lord 1850* (Nashville: Graves & Shankland, 1850), 28. He earlier anticipated some of this discussion in "Volume Sixth," *Tennessee Baptist,* September 6, 1849, [2].

[21] Graves, "The Churches of Christ Republics," in *The Southern Baptist Almanac . . . 1850,* 32–33. This piece was also carried in *Tennessee Baptist,* March 7, 1850, [2]. From the late 1840s to the Civil War there is plentiful—and often repetitive—evidence for Graves's virtually uninterrupted interest in republicanism.

[22] Graves, "What Societies Are Republics, or Churches of Christ?," in Graves, ed., *The Southern Baptist Almanac . . . 1850,* 34. This also appeared in *Tennessee Baptist,* March 14, 1850, [2].

Education society in 1852, the Baptist journalist warned against unnamed papal and Protestant agents who were attempting to undermine republican government in the United States. On a more positive note, he once again extolled the benefits of self-government in both religious and political contexts: "The 19th century has demonstrated the truth of God's word that man is capable of and created for self-government, and that it is the only form of government that will secure for humanity, individually or nationally, in Church or State, the proper incentive to progress, the largest freedom and the greatest happiness."[23] His optimistic rhetoric, which in many ways reflected the political stump speeches of his day, neither seemed fully attuned to biblical concepts of human sinfulness nor to the Constitution's ingenious provision for checks and balances. At the same time, Graves failed to offer texts in support of his perspective on the divine design in creation.

In another sermon from the early 1850s, Graves portrayed Jesus as a revolutionary who was "the first asserter of popular rights" and enemy of tyrants, especially those in churches. Furthermore, Graves affirmed, Jesus taught a doctrine of "*individual sovereignty*" that challenged any who would oppress free moral agents.[24] In the same context, he explicitly linked republican theory with the gospel itself. Indeed, he even proposed that Christianity in part spread through the world via America's governmental institutions; this was a reasonable assumption, he averred, because the Founding Fathers "copied the glorious republican principles of Christ's teachings, and laid the foundations of our government upon the Bible."[25] Hence, Graves creatively blended patriotism and nationalism into a message based on Old Testament prophetic texts (Ezek 21:27; Hag 2:6–7), suggesting that he sensed no inherent conflict between biblical faith and American ideals. After all, the "Desire of All Nations" taught a thoroughly republican way of life, even if—in Graves's estimation—his ecclesiastical opponents failed to acknowledge that.

In a subsequent context where he was endorsing the successionist history of the British Baptist G. H. Orchard, Graves employed some noteworthy rhetoric to uphold the superiority of specifically Baptist polity over its competitors:

> Through the influence of our religious principles, and the example of our form
> of Church government, Republicanism and republican institutions have already

---

[23] Graves, "The Watchman's Reply: A Sermon" (Nashville: Graves & Shankland, 1853), 20, 51.
[24] Graves, "The Desire of All Nations: A Sermon" (Nashville: Graves & Shankland, 1853), 43–44.
[25] Ibid., 46.

been bequeathed to half the world, and are now rocking the other half to its cen-
tre, crumbling the thrones of its tyrants, and arousing and energizing oppressed
humanity, to assert its rights, and overthrow its oppressors.[26]

Here Graves did not manifestly appeal to scriptural arguments but rather to the assumed
compatibility of his ecclesiology with republicanism and individual rights. Jesus may
have designed the original pattern for the first Baptist congregation, but it was left to
later champions of the faith to work out the political implications of the New Testament
model.

For Graves, as a matter of fact, Baptists ascended over other denominational polities
and traditions in part because of their historic defense of both civil and religious liberties. In one of his customary apologetic works against Pedobaptists and Campbellites,
he faulted them for doctrines and practices that undermined human freedom. Baptists,
on the other hand, had paved the way for the inalienable rights that nineteenth-century
Americans took for granted. Graves applied successionist dogma to claim that, for 18
centuries, wherever liberty prevailed it had been "planted there by Baptist hands, and
watered by Baptist blood."[27] Moreover, the Landmark patriarch credited his denomination in America "for the *idea* of a pure Democratic form of civil government, and
then for having prepared the popular mind by the molding influence of their principles
to receive such a government, as well as for its present strength and sole hope of its
perpetuity."[28] Thus Graves audaciously carved out a monumental niche for Baptists
in the shaping of the entire American experiment in government of the people, by the
people, and for the people. Landmark ecclesiology, successionist history, and republican
theory all came together in an intriguing and provocative amalgamation.

---

[26] Graves, "Introductory Essay," in G. H. Orchard, *A Concise History of Baptists from the Time of Christ
Their Founder to the 18th Century* (Nashville: Graves & Marks, 1855; repr., Lexington, KY: Ashland Avenue
Baptist Church, 1956), xviii–xix. W. T. Lane in "A Baptist Doctrine of Ordination Studied in the Confessional
Tradition, the Works of J. R. Graves and R. B. C. Howell and Actual Practice in Kentucky" (Th.D. diss.,
Southern Baptist Theological Seminary, 1958), 64, n203, commented that Graves "identified the political
culture and spirit of his day with his ecclesiological views. To be a patriot was to be a Baptist and to be a
Baptist was to be a patriot."

[27] Graves, *Trilemma: All Human Churches without Baptism, or Death by Three Horns*, 2nd ed. (Memphis:
Graves & Mahaffy, 1881; repr., Memphis: J. R. Graves & Son, 1890), 138–39. The original edition was published in 1860 (Nashville: Graves, Marks, & Co.).

[28] Ibid., 143–44. R. B. C. Howell, Graves's onetime colleague and eventual rival, argued that Baptist pol-
ity in Virginia influenced Thomas Jefferson's republican ideas. See J. E. Hilton, "Robert Boyté Howell's
Contribution to Baptist Ecclesiology: Nineteenth-Century Baptist Ecclesiology in Controversy" (Ph.D. diss.,
Southeastern Baptist Theological Seminary, 2005), 70.

FREEDOM AND ECCLESIASTICAL STRUCTURES

Graves's version of Landmarkism incorporated an unconcealed individualistic component, in part to protect the rights of individual members of local churches. As he
avowed many times, the Christian gospel was deeply personal, demanding personal acts
like repentance, faith, and obedience. Genuine Christianity, Graves declared, could be
distinguished from counterfeits by "its intense *individuality*—that it knows no proxies,
no sponsors, no attorneyship."[29] In light of the individual nature of true faith, Graves felt
compelled to defend certain liberties, such as the right of common believers to "freely
read and interpret the Scriptures for themselves"; he went so far as to commend this as
the highest Christian duty.[30] Although the context of this discussion was a polemical
attack on infant baptism, which Graves reviled as much as any practice in the Roman
Catholic tradition, it appears that the Landmark pioneer earnestly desired to preserve the
private study and interpretation of the Bible as an essential right.

In addition, Graves sought to safeguard the prerogatives of individual congregations. In chap. 4 of *Old Landmarkism*, he catalogued the divine, inalienable, and
exclusive rights of a Christian church: (1) to preserve and preach the gospel; (2) to elect
and ordain her own officers; (3) to receive, discipline, and exclude her own members;
(4) to administer the ordinances of baptism and the Lord's Supper. These rights—and
duties—could not be surrendered to any other organization or individual leader without
compromising the biblical pattern.[31] As a matter of fact, Graves vigilantly spelled out
limitations on ministerial authority in relation to discipline and the ordinances to thwart
the concentration of power in the hands of one person; one of his greatest fears was the
emergence of a "petty pope" or "autocrat" in the local church.[32] Gospel ministers, then,
were to be the servants and not the masters of the churches. Graves left it to what he
termed "executive democracy" to dispossess "the minister of temptation to arrogance,
pride and haughtiness, and domination."[33] Of course, only Baptist congregations enjoyed
this protection against authoritarian leadership.

---

[29] Graves, *Old Landmarkism*, 243.

[30] Ibid., 240.

[31] Ibid., 43–52. Cf. Graves, *The Lord's Supper: A Church Ordinance, and So Observed by the Apostolic Churches* (1881; repr., Texarkana, AR: Baptist Sunday School Committee, 1928 and 1968), 5–15. This tract was limited to the ordinances, and Graves had moved to a tighter policy on the Lord's Supper during his years in Memphis. He restricted it to the membership of a local church.

[32] Ibid., 49, 268.

[33] Graves, "A Pre-Penticostal [*sic*] Church a Baptist Church," in Graves, ed., *Southern Baptist Almanac and Annual Register, for the Year of Our Lord 1852* (Nashville: Graves & Shankland, 1852), 33.

It is worth repeating that Graves unswervingly validated his ecclesiology as biblical. At the same time, he unmistakably feared the tyranny and oppression that he observed in Christian and secular polities, past and present. It is also evident that Graves directed his Landmarkist convictions against any kind of centralized ecclesiastical structure. In 1858 he ran a series in the *Tennessee Baptist* on "centralism." Although he did not actually write the articles, they were consistent with his concerns about centralized authority. For instance, W. C. Buck, who had previously served the Nashville-based Bible Board as secretary and wrote frequently for the *Tennessee Baptist*, warned readers that the activities of mission and benevolent societies in Baptist life could lead to "a *centralism* of ecclesiastical power, aiming to subvert the *liberty* of the churches and the inalienable *rights* of individuals, and its *hierarchical assumptions* should be frowned upon by every lover of *Church independence* and civil liberty, as a foe to both."[34] Buck thus precisely echoed what was one of J. R. Graves's fears—the tyrannical concentration of power in some body or entity beyond the local church. Whether the danger came from an association, a publishing society, or a mission board, the antidote for Graves included appeals both to Scripture and to the populist political slogans of the era. In addition, he at least indirectly drew on the Separate Baptist tradition of his native New England, with its emphases on local church autonomy and congregational freedom.

Graves's adherence to the individualistic and republican features of the American political heritage also helps to explain why he was so zealous in his opposition to competing Christian denominations and movements. To be sure, Graves fervently believed that Roman Catholics, Presbyterians, and Methodists had all established ecclesiastical systems that deviated significantly from the New Testament pattern.[35] It also is apparent that his hostility toward the Restorationism of Alexander Campbell was centered more on its alleged theory of baptismal regeneration and its concept of saving faith than on issues of church polity.[36] Nevertheless, his attacks on the former, more centralized denominational groups commonly owed as much to his cultural and political context as to his scriptural exegesis.

In particular, Graves demonstrated a special animus toward the Methodist Church. He regarded Methodism's episcopalian structure as a form of clerical "despotism,"

---

[34] W. C. Buck, "Centralism—No. 2," *Tennessee Baptist,* March 27, 1858, 4. Buck's series helped to set the stage for Graves's battle with the Southern Baptist Convention in 1859 over the role of the Foreign Mission Board.

[35] E.g., see Graves, *Old Landmarkism*, 36–40.

[36] Ibid., 242–43.

absolutism," and "hierarchism" of the worst sort.[37] He even likened the repressive characteristics of Methodist polity to what he knew about the Roman Catholic Society of Jesus: "Is not such a government as anti-American as it is despotic? Are not the people governed without the faintest voice in the election of *their* rulers or direction of their government? . . . Are not the people—the members—arrogantly denied the right to participate in the legislative councils of their Church? Is this not anti-American?"[38] Overall, Graves dismissed the Methodist system as unbiblical and as an ominous threat to liberty; he further insisted that Methodists—like Catholics—simply could not be good republicans.[39] It is not a stretch to conclude that he would have similar concerns about other denominational systems that located authority beyond the level of local congregations.

As if to reinforce his claim that Methodism was un-American, Graves quoted from the Declaration of Rights of the First Continental Congress, as well as chiding the Methodist Church for taxing its people without the right of representation, which he charged was "an oppressive form of tyranny."[40] Methodism, then, failed to measure up to the great republican principles and traditions that had marked the American experiment since the Revolution. Furthermore, the Methodists denied people their right to be "sovereign," which Graves clearly interpreted by the canons of individualism; in other words, each individual was created "a sovereign."[41] In response to the rhetoric found in *The Great Iron Wheel*, Mark Noll fittingly discerns that "Graves's attacks on the Methodists came close to being a pure application of American ideological reasoning to Christian doctrine."[42] While the level of purity might be questioned, there can be no

---

[37] Graves, *The Great Iron Wheel*, 159–60. For similar critiques of Methodism, see Graves, ed., *The Little Iron Wheel: A Declaration of Christian Rights and Articles, Showing the Despotism of Episcopal Methodism* (Nashville: South-Western Publishing House; Graves, Marks & Co., 1856), 27–76; and Graves and Jacob Ditzler, *The Graves-Ditzler; or, Great Carrollton Debate* (Memphis: Southern Baptist Publication Society, 1876), 971.

[38] Graves, *The Great Iron Wheel*, 167. The relationship of individualism and fear of tyranny is insightfully discussed in G. C. Bowden, "Piety and Property: Locke and the Development of American Protestantism," *Christian Scholar's Review* 37 (Spring 2008): 273–87. Bowden did not reference Graves but demonstrated that resistance to tyranny in church and state traced its roots to pre-Revolutionary America.

[39] Graves, "Anti-Republican Religion," *Tennessee Baptist,* October 28, 1854, [2]. In *The Little Iron Wheel*, 41, Graves declared that Methodist bishops and circuit riders who assembled in General Conference "claim the same prerogatives and exercise the same power and authority . . . that the Pope and his Cardinals do in the Vatican."

[40] Graves, *The Great Iron Wheel*, 167–68, 294.

[41] Ibid., 278.

[42] Noll, *America's God*, 245.

doubt that Graves creatively applied the criteria of a Christian republicanism to justify his Landmark Baptist ideas and to denigrate conflicting ideologies.

Graves's appeals to individualism and republicanism likewise help to illuminate classic Landmark documents like the "Cotton Grove Resolutions" of 1851. The Resolutions, which originated as a set of questions that Graves posed to his listeners at a meeting in West Tennessee, suggested that (1) religious societies not organized according to the New Testament model could not be considered true churches; (2) such societies could not be called "gospel" churches; (3) clergy of such societies could not be recognized as "gospel" ministers; (4) pulpit affiliation was not an appropriate practice; and (5) people associated with societies that were not true churches could not be addressed as "brethren."[43] Graves was convinced beyond a shadow of a doubt that the other denominations of his day plainly did not measure up to the first-century Jerusalem church. Even so, his dogmatic repudiation of other Christian movements was also informed by his conviction that the groups with hierarchical traditions posed tangible threats to both civil and ecclesiastical liberties. For the Baptist controversialist, proper boundary maintenance required him to publicize these concerns.

So for Graves, an ecclesiology rooted in free and wholly independent local churches was best suited to avert centralism and tyranny. Since his defense of Landmarkism sometimes conveyed a rigid and eccentric spirit, Graves is often perceived as a figure who was outside the mainstream of the historic Baptist tradition.[44] In his adoption of the ideologies of individualism and republicanism, however, the Landmark patriarch stood in continuity with some earlier Baptist leaders in America. For example, his ardent interest in freedom, both civil and ecclesiastical, points to some affinities with the thought of John Leland (1754–1841). As Bradley Creed has shown in his dissertation on Leland, the Separate Baptist evangelist's campaign for religious freedom and church-state separation presupposed an individualism that dreaded the prospect of religious tyranny.[45] When

---

[43] See the listing in Graves, *Old Landmarkism*, xi–xii. There is a fuller discussion above in chap. 2.

[44] E.g., H. L. Grice, "Graves, James Robinson," in *Encyclopedia of Southern Baptists* (Nashville: Broadman, 1958), 1:576–78.

[45] J. B. Creed, "John Leland, American Prophet of Religious Individualism" (Ph.D. diss., Southwestern Baptist Theological Seminary, 1986). Cf. the treatment of Leland in Hatch, *The Democratization of American Christianity*, 93–101. Hatch (p. 97) called Leland "an important bridge between the Revolutionary Era and the quest for localism and independence that confounded Baptist history throughout the Jacksonian period." Cf. B. C. Lambert, "The Rise of the Anti-Mission Baptists: Sources and Leaders, 1800–1840 (A Study in Religious Individualism)" (Ph.D. diss., University of Chicago, 1957), 116–52, where he referred to Leland as a "Jeffersonian Baptist." For the most part, Graves did not subscribe to Leland's anti-missionism except for similar suspicions about boards and agencies beyond the local church.

Leland condemned clerical hierarchy and commended Baptists for being liberated from it, he employed language that Graves surely would have cheered: "[We are] without pope or king for head—without spiritual or civil courts established by law—without a conclave of bishops, or convocation of clergy—without legalized creeds or formularies of worship—without a ministry supported by law, or any human coercion in discipline."[46] Undeniably, Leland and Graves ministered in different contexts and their agendas certainly were not identical. At the same time, both men demonstrated palpable affinities for the Separate Baptist tradition that championed a localist ecclesiology. Moreover, they found individualism and republicanism to be effective vehicles for articulating their devotion to freedom and independence in Baptist church life.

Since Graves at times exemplified a pronounced libertarian streak in his ecclesiology, recent attempts to find Landmarkist characteristics in twentieth-century Southern Baptist "fundamentalism" may prove to be ill-advised.[47] Graves's commitment to the independence and autonomy of the local church, his staunch individualism, and his republican rhetoric, which emphasized especially civil and ecclesiastical freedom, all intimate that some aspects of his ecclesiology might resonate with Southern Baptists of a more moderate or liberal stripe. Indeed, the Landmarker took great pride in "the fact that Baptists were the earliest witnesses for soul-freedom."[48] Wake Forest professor Bill Leonard is one of the few modern Baptist historians who has picked up on this thread in Graves's thought. In observing the democratic idealism of the Landmark movement, he affirmed that Graves and colleagues like J. M. Pendleton "were outspoken opponents of establishments, secular or religious, that would undermine the freedom of conscience and religious liberty."[49] Neither Graves nor Landmarkism can be easily squeezed into one-dimensional stereotypes.

---

[46] J. Leland, "Circular Letter of the Shaftsbury Association" (1793), quoted in Noll, *America's God*, 374. Additional evidence for common ground can be found in Graves's historical interest in the persecution of Baptists in colonial New England. See Graves, ed., *Trials and Sufferings for Religious Liberty in New England* (Nashville: Southwestern Publishing House; Graves, Marks and Company, 1858).

[47] See Bell, "James Robinson Graves and the Rhetoric of Demagogy," 274ff.; and J. E. Tull, *High-Church Baptists in the South: The Origin, Nature, and Influence of Landmarkism* (Macon, GA: Mercer University Press, 2000), 172.

[48] Graves, *Trilemma*, 146. In one sense, Graves foreshadowed both the "truth" (boundary staking) and "liberty" (individualism and freedom) parties that carried most of the SBC controversy from 1979 to the early 1990s. See R. A. Mohler Jr., "A Call for Baptist Evangelicals and Evangelical Baptists: Communities of Faith and a Common Quest for Identity," in *Southern Baptists and American Evangelicals: The Conversation Continues*, ed. D. S. Dockery (Nashville: B&H, 1993), 224–39.

[49] B. J. Leonard, *Baptist Ways: A History* (Valley Forge, PA: Judson Press, 2003), 184. Cf. Leonard, "*Communidades Ecclesiales de Base* and Autonomous Local Churches: Catholic Liberationists Meet Baptist

Furthermore, Graves's ecclesiological priorities appear to be out of step with the currents of "democratic authority" that church historian Gregory Wills finds among Baptists in the South from the late eighteenth to the late nineteenth centuries. In particular, the Landmark leader would have challenged the conclusion that, in the middle of the nineteenth century, "Southern Baptists understood democracy largely in terms of ecclesiastical authority."[50] Graves would have been vitally concerned about *how* ecclesiastical authority was both exercised and restrained. In his ecclesiology, churches surely had the right to order themselves and to discipline their members. At the same time, he persistently guarded against hierarchy, authoritarian ministers, or anything else that might infringe on the liberty of the local congregation and the individuals in it.

In his writings and public addresses, Graves resourcefully wove an intricate tapestry featuring a distinctive ecclesiology that was bolstered by both his understanding of the New Testament and his appropriation of key themes found in the political discourse of his time. He was probably unaware that his synthesis, particularly because of its individualistic and republican rhetoric, betrayed a culture-bound character. Additionally, his apprehensions about tyranny needed to be broadened. He seemed initially oblivious, for example, to the danger that local churches could impose a tyranny of the majority. Only after his difficult experiences at First Baptist in Nashville in the late 1850s did he become sensitive to that issue.

Even worse, Graves failed to see slavery as another form of tyranny; indeed, his support for the peculiar institution remained the most glaring inconsistency of his republican ideology. In the context of the antebellum South, of course, his defense of slavery was not especially unusual. Moreover, as a New Englander by birth and upbringing, he found it necessary to fend off accusations during the 1850s that he favored abolitionism.[51] Unfortunately, the Landmarker's defensiveness on this matter pushed him to attempt a biblical justification for human servitude. In the very book in which he attacked the Methodist Episcopal Church for its despotism, Graves argued that slavery

---

Landmarkers," in *Poverty and Ecclesiology: Nineteenth-Century Evangelicals in the Light of Liberation Theology,* ed. A. L. Dunnavant (Collegeville, MN: Liturgical Press, 1992), 68–89. For a contemporary Baptist moderate who defends the place of freedom and individualism in Baptist life, see W. B. Shurden, *The Baptist Identity: Four Fragile Freedoms* (Macon, GA: Smyth & Helwys, 1993). Shurden's interpretation of these themes would vary somewhat from that of Graves. See Shurden, *Not a Silent People: Controversies That Have Shaped Southern Baptists* (Nashville: Broadman, 1972), 68–80.

[50] G. A. Wills, *Democratic Religion: Freedom, Authority, and Church Discipline in the Baptist South, 1785–1900* (New York: Oxford University Press, 1997), 139.

[51] E.g., Graves, "Abolitionism and the S.W. Baptist," *Tennessee Baptist,* July 17, 1858, [2]. In this piece, Graves acknowledged that he was a slaveholder. Cf. the discussion above in the first chapter.

originated as part of the curse on Canaan and Ham (Gen 9:25–27).[52] After considering other texts from both the Old and New Testaments, he offered this stunning conclusion: "If slavery be a sin, so is the institution of marriage. If the latter has the sanction of the Bible, so has the former."[53]

Following the ratification of the Thirteenth Amendment to the U.S. Constitution and soon after resuming the publication of his Baptist newspaper, Graves took up the issue of Christian responsibility to the newly-freed African Americans. Due to his earlier opposition to the resettlement of Native American tribes, he seemed to be skeptical about any implausible notion of colonizing the black population. Instead, he advised that "we must teach them to read, to read the Bible, christianize [sic] them, and make them an element of safety and a blessing to us, as they would be still if christianized [sic]."[54] His somewhat clumsy steps in regard to race, however, took a turn for the worse when he aggressively defended slavery long after emancipation, even repeating some of the rationale that he had given before the Civil War.[55] Thus he never succeeded in bringing slaves, or even former slaves, under his Christian republican umbrella.

In spite of these blind spots, the Graves synthesis stands as a captivating endeavor to link ecclesiology to a broader political and cultural setting. The Baptist activist espoused individualism, republicanism, anti-Catholicism, anti-Protestantism, and Landmarkism, sometimes separately but often in a polemical package that was designed to win over fellow Baptists to his cause. The various ideological strands that guided his boundary staking all involved appeals to history, particularly to the history of his own denomination. It remains to be shown how the theory of Baptist successionism functioned in support for and vindication of his thinking about the church.

---

[52] Graves, ed., *The Little Iron Wheel*, 10. For an exposition of Graves's views on slavery, see Smith, "A Critical Analysis of the Theology of J. R. Graves," 221ff.

[53] Graves, ed., *The Little Iron Wheel*, 17. Shortly before the Civil War, Graves called for the removal of slavery's abuses so it "would be a blessing to both master and servant, and abolition fanaticism would not be fed and infuriated by Uncle Tom's Cabin." See Graves, "Way Marks—No. 2," *Tennessee Baptist*, November 19, 1859, [2].

[54] Graves, "What Shall Be Done for the Blacks," *Baptist*, May 11, 1867, 5. Almost a year later, Graves ran a five-part series in his paper under the title "The Negro: Is He Our Brute or Our Brother?" *Baptist*, February 29–March 28, 1868, all on [4].

[55] Graves, *What Is Conscience?* (Memphis: Baptist Book House; Graves & Mahaffy, 1882), 19ff. For a critical assessment of this tract, see Carroll, "Dimensions of Individualism in Southern Baptist Thought," 64: "The conjecture that Southern Baptists had not fully applied the egalitarian tenets of individualism to their habits by the closing of the nineteenth century was undergirded by this volume."

Chapter 5

History in the Service of Ecclesiology
The Graves Synthesis, Part II

THE GRAVES-CARROLL CONNECTION

At many Southern and independent Baptist churches across the United States, tract racks occupy part of the sanctuary entrance areas. In some of these settings, unsuspecting visitors who peruse the evangelistic pamphlets and missionary prayer cards might also come across a small prosaic booklet with this captivating title—*"The Trail of Blood"* . . . *Following the Christians down through the Centuries . . . or The History of Baptist Churches from the Time of Christ, Their Founder, to the Present Day.* This 56-page sprint through almost 2,000 years of church history comes equipped with a foldout timeline that is generously peppered with red dots; these marks indicate the sufferings and martyrdoms of true Christians (i.e., Baptists) through the ages, usually at the hands of "papal" Rome. On this chart, the author boldly proclaimed his purpose: "To show according to History that Baptists have an unbroken line of churches since Christ" in fulfillment of Matt 16:18.[1]

This diminutive book originated as a set of lectures that were delivered at several churches—including the Ashland Avenue Baptist Church in Lexington, Kentucky—by James Milton Carroll (1852–1931). The Texas Baptist educator and ornithologist, brother of Southwestern Baptist Seminary founder Benajah Harvey Carroll, served briefly as president of Oklahoma Baptist University when it first opened in 1910. J. M. Carroll actually died before his lectures came off the press, but his legacy lives on; more than 2.36 million copies of *The Trail of Blood* have been printed by the Ashland Avenue

---

[1] J. M. Carroll, *The Trail of Blood* (Lexington, KY: American Baptist Publishing Company, 1931), foldout attached to 56. I have used the 2005 printing by Ashland Avenue Baptist Church, which held the original copyright.

church since 1931. An additional 50,000 reprints since 1998—plus 5,000 Spanish copies and 2,000 in Ukrainian—by the independent Bryan Station Baptist Church in Lexington, Kentucky, swell the numbers even more.[2]

In essence, Carroll condensed and popularized a much longer chronicle by the British Baptist pastor, G. H. Orchard (1796–1861). In 1838 Orchard published his ambitious *A Concise History of the Baptists from the Time of Christ Their Founder to the 18th Century*, which apparently attracted little interest in England. This volume, however, quickly became a weapon in the denominational controversies on the American frontier when it was republished by J. R. Graves in 1855. Graves, who at the time was in Nashville editing the *Tennessee Baptist*, wrote a lengthy introductory essay in which he enthusiastically endorsed Orchard's successionist view of Baptist history. The Orchard text that Graves rejuvenated and then widely circulated was in turn republished in the twentieth century by Ashland Avenue Baptist; thus tens of thousands of copies of Orchard's not-so-concise history have made their way into Baptist homes and church libraries.[3]

It is doubtful that Orchard would have risen from relative obscurity or that Carroll would have even penned *The Trail of Blood* apart from the polemical, oratorical, literary, and publishing endeavors of J. R. Graves.[4] In fact, Carroll might even have derived

---

[2] On Carroll, see W. R. Estep, "Carroll, James," and S. A. Yarbrough, "Oklahoma Baptist University," in *Dictionary of Baptists in America*, ed. B. J. Leonard (Downers Grove, IL: InterVarsity, 1994), 76–77, 211. Publishing statistics for *The Trail of Blood* came in an e-mail from Michelle Manning of Ashland Avenue to the author, August 22, 2006. Bryan Station Baptist figures are from an e-mail sent to the author, August 23, 2006. This church provides, in addition to printed copies of the booklet, an online version available from http://www.bryanstation.com/trail_of_blood.htm (accessed February 24, 2009). In "The Dead End Trail: J. M. Carroll and the Trail of Blood and Its Impact upon Church Planting" (paper presented at the annual meeting of the Evangelical Theological Society, Washington, DC, November 16, 2006), Rodney Harrison, professor at Midwestern Baptist Theological Seminary, reported that over 3,100 web sites provide downloadable copies of the Carroll booklet, thus confirming that it has become fully immersed in the digital world. Harrison also demonstrated from Carroll's correspondence that the original manuscript for the lectures originated in 1918.

[3] G. H. Orchard, *A Concise History of Baptists from the Time of Christ Their Founder to the 18th Century* (Nashville: Graves & Marks, 1855; reprint, Lexington, KY: Ashland Avenue Baptist Church, 1956). On the tepid response to Orchard in his homeland, see F. H. Thomas Jr., "The Development of Denominational Consciousness in Baptist Historical Writings, 1738 to 1886" (Ph.D. diss., Southern Baptist Theological Seminary, 1975), 19. I was given my copy of Orchard about 25 years ago by a deacon at First Baptist Church, Toccoa, Georgia, who was also a trustee at Toccoa Falls College, where I was teaching at the time.

[4] Carroll spoke admiringly of Graves, who visited Texas several times, in *A History of Texas Baptists* (Dallas: Baptist Standard Publishing, 1923), 448. On the Texas connection, see J. Early Jr., "Landmarkism: Tennessee Baptists' Influence on Texas Baptists," *Tennessee Baptist History* 5 (Fall 2003): 57–66.

his title from a passage in Graves's *Trilemma*, where the Landmark patriarch placed a heavy emphasis on the history of martyrdom to help substantiate successionist claims:

> [Baptists] claim that they can trace the history of communities, essentially like themselves, back through the "wilderness" . . . by a *trail of blood*, lighted up by a thousand stake-fires, until that blood mingles with the blood of the apostles, and the Son of God, and John the Baptist. They believe that they never did, ecclesiastically, symbolize with the Papacy, but even repudiated it as Antichrist, and withdrew from it and refused to recognize its baptisms or ordinances, or its priests as the ministers of Christ.[5]

Carroll certainly gained remarkable fame among Baptists from his published lectures, but he followed the markings left on the trail by successionists who preceded him.

Indeed, in Graves's role as an amateur historian, the fiery preacher and journalist likely did more to advance this peculiar approach to Baptist history in his homeland than any other single figure. As the founder and chief architect of Landmarkism, he had become one of the best-known religious personalities in the nineteenth-century South. In Landmarkism, Baptist successionism functioned as a vital component of a distinctive ecclesiology that denied the reality of a universal church and focused on the full autonomy and freedom of local, visible congregations.

Furthermore, as discussed in the previous chapter, Graves vociferously reiterated to his constituents that other denominations were inevitably linked to the vices of ecclesiastical tyranny and centralized authority, which he did not hesitate to expose. Even in reference to Baptist life, Graves continually fretted that associations, publishing societies, mission boards, or authoritarian pastors could threaten the prerogatives of autonomous congregations. Graves's intense localism, which was pronounced among Separate Baptists in his native New England, logically led to his opposition to alien immersion and open communion. In other words, no local church could surrender its control of the

---

[5] J. R. Graves, *Trilemma: All Human Churches without Baptism, or Death by Three Horns*, 2nd ed. (Memphis: Graves & Mahaffy, 1881; repr., Memphis: J. R. Graves & Sons, 1890), 119–20. The original edition was published in 1860 (Nashville: Graves, Marks, & Co.). Graves was probably influenced to highlight the "host of martyrs" (128) by J. N. Brown, *Memorials of Baptist Martyrs: With a Preliminary Historical Essay* (Philadelphia: American Baptist Publication Society, 1854). Graves quoted at length from Brown in "An Old Landmark," in Graves, ed., *The Southern Baptist Almanac and Register, for the Year 1855* (Nashville: Graves & Marks, 1855), 32ff. The same piece was also published in *Tennessee Baptist,* November 4, 1854, [3].

ordinances to any other organization without compromising what he affirmed was the New Testament pattern.[6]

As likewise suggested in chap. 4, Graves seemed to be oblivious to the culture-bound character of his ecclesiology; without much critical reflection, he imbibed the republican rhetoric that dominated the political discourse of antebellum America. Hence, it is unlikely that he fully grasped just how his ecclesiological presuppositions influenced his approach to history. At the same time, he must have sensed an expedient linkage. As Baptist historian W. Morgan Patterson perceptively observed, "[t]he successionist view of history coincided perfectly with the Landmark ecclesiology and provided for it a certain desirable authoritativeness."[7] Thus the Tennessee Baptist polemicist utilized successionist history to buttress his ecclesiology. History functioned then as a tool to vindicate his ecclesiological position over against other denominational traditions that did not value free and autonomous congregations.

Apart from the legacy that J. R. Graves left through a busy career in which he aggressively promoted his ideas through his voluminous writings and countless public addresses, J. M. Carroll would not have been in a position to become the most important twentieth-century popularizer of the theory of Baptist successionism that the Landmark founder advanced in the previous generation. At the same time, Graves did not develop his perspective on denominational history in a vacuum. While his brand of church successionism revealed some unique features, it was also dependent on the work of other Baptist historians and leaders who set forth notions of Baptist perpetuity; in some cases, these concepts were in print well before Graves openly embraced them and utilized them in his own historical apologetics.

THE RISE OF THE BAPTIST PERPETUITY PRINCIPLE

At least one modern proponent of successionism finds evidence for the theory as early as 1652, when John Spittlehouse and John More published a document in London that

---

[6] Graves, *Old Landmarkism: What Is It?* 2nd ed. (Memphis: Baptist Book House; Graves, Mahaffy & Co., 1881), 43–52.

[7] W. M. Patterson, *Baptist Successionism: A Critical View* (Valley Forge, PA: Judson Press, 1969), 27. In a similar vein, see J. E. McGoldrick, *Baptist Successionism: A Crucial Question in Baptist History*, ATLA Monograph Series, No. 32 (Metuchen, NJ: Scarecrow Press, 1994), 4: "It appears that the successionist scheme of history is practically required by the doctrine of the church which its advocates maintain."

appeared to trace the "Anabaptists" back to the age of the apostles.[8] Whether this writing, however, actually substantiates a clear notion of Baptist successionism in the seventeenth century is debatable. First, Spittlehouse was part of the Fifth Monarchy Men, an apocalyptic organization that believed the coming of the kingdom was imminent and that it could be brought in by force of arms. Some Baptists were drawn to this extreme movement, but mainstream General and Particular Baptists both repudiated it. Second, Spittlehouse and More saw the radical German Anabaptist Thomas Müntzer as one of the heroes who brought the true church out of a 1,260-year period of hiding (Rev 12:6) when he challenged Martin Luther in the sixteenth century. Like the Fifth Monarchy Men, Müntzer justified violent measures against oppressive rulers who stood in the path of prophetic fulfillment. Third, perhaps because the pure primitive church was in a "secret and obscure condition" between the birth of Constantine and the time of Luther, it is not surprising that Spittlehouse and More evidently saw no need to track its succession through specific dissenting groups in the Middle Ages. Hence, their statement in essence lacked a trail of blood, because the true church took refuge in the wilderness, "penned up into Mountains, Dens, Deserts, and Caves of the earth."[9] The two authors manifestly affirmed believer's baptism, but their peculiar ecclesiological and eschatological speculations raise serious questions about just how representative they were of seventeenth-century English Baptist thought. Moreover, neither Orchard, Graves, nor Carroll seemed to be aware of this successionist tract, even though Graves's attitudes toward Catholics and Protestant Pedobaptists demonstrated a similar animus to that expressed by Spittlehouse and More.

In the eighteenth century, English Baptist author Thomas Crosby (1683–1751) penned a lengthy, four-volume history of Baptists in his homeland. A deacon in John Gill's Particular Baptist church in London, Crosby did not establish an unbroken chain of Baptist congregations from the New Testament era to the eighteenth century, although he sought to map out an extended line of opposition to infant baptism through church history. While he strongly implied a perpetuation of Baptist principles through the ages,

---

[8] J. R. Duvall, "The Successionism View of Baptist History," *Journal of Baptist Studies* 3 (2009): 8, accessed August 8, 2010, http://baptiststudiesonline.com/276/.

[9] J. Spittlehouse and J. More, *A Vindication of the Continued Succession of the Primitive Church of Jesus Christ (Now Scandalously Termed Anabaptists) from the Apostles unto This Present Time* (London: Printed by Gartrude Dawson, 1652), accessed August 8, 2010, http://www.reformedreader.org/history/continued succession.htm. For Spittlehouse's ties to the Fifth Monarchy Men, see P. G. Rogers, *The Fifth Monarchy Men* (London: Oxford University Press, 1966), 26–27, 30–40. On Baptist efforts to disassociate themselves from the Fifth Monarchy, see B. J. Leonard, *Baptist Ways: A History* (Valley Forge, PA: Judson Press, 2003), 33–34, 55.

he actually began his account of English Baptists in the fourteenth century with John Wycliffe. He also advocated a connection between the sixteenth-century Anabaptists and English Baptists.[10] Crosby's successionism was not as rigid or fully defined as the nineteenth-century variety; at the same time, his work provided a foundation upon which later historians would build.

Other eighteenth-century Baptist writers, while expressing sympathy with the idea of Baptist perpetuity, avoided full-blown successionism. What appeared to be a developing feature of Baptist historiography at this time was the endeavor to connect ecclesiastical dissenters in the early and medieval periods to Baptists, at least in terms of some of their doctrines and practices. In England, Robert Robinson (1735–90) followed this path with a special emphasis on how those who were accused of heresy by the Roman Catholic Church stood for liberty of conscience; this suggested a special kinship between them and Baptists.[11] Orchard later cited his work numerous times, and Graves commended Robinson for moving Baptist history "in the right direction."[12]

By the nineteenth century, notions of Baptist perpetuity or succession were not uncommon in Baptist life and thought. In particular, Orchard leaned heavily on English Baptist historian William Jones, who published a two-volume history of Christianity that Orchard became aware of in 1823. According to the advertisement that Orchard inserted at the beginning of his own history, Jones's work "gave me *the clue to the church of God*," by which he meant "a connected history" that could trace English Baptists back to the apostles. The key for Orchard was found in the history of dissent that previous

---

[10] T. Crosby, *The History of English Baptists, from the Reformation to the Beginning of the Reign of King George I*, 4 vols. (London: n.p., 1738–40). Cf. Duvall, "The Successionism View of Baptist History," 8–9; and McGoldrick, *Baptist Successionism*, 145–46.

[11] R. Robinson, *Ecclesiastical Researches* (Cambridge, UK: Francis Hodson, 1792; repr., Gallatin, TN: Church History Research and Archives, 1984), 121–23. This was published after Robinson's death by George Dyer. On Robinson as a Baptist historian, see D. A. Cureton, "The Historiography of Baptist Origins in Selected Southern Baptist Historians: William Heth Whitsitt, John Tyler Christian, and Albert Henry Newman" (Ph.D. diss., Mid-America Baptist Theological Seminary, 1998), 13–15. Andrew Fuller (1754–1815), arguably the greatest English Baptist theologian of the eighteenth century, showed considerable interest in medieval groups that had some affinities with Baptists. See his "Expository Discourses on the Apocalypse," in *The Complete Works of the Rev. Andrew Fuller with a Memoir of His Life by Andrew Gunton Fuller*, ed. Joseph Belcher (Philadelphia: American Baptist Publication Society, 1845; repr., Harrisonburg, VA: Sprinkle, 1988), 3:245–77. In America, Isaac Backus named medieval examples of opposition to tyranny, without classifying them as Baptists. See chap. 1 above, n25.

[12] E.g., Orchard, *A Concise History*, 101, 107, 233, et al. Patterson, *Baptist Successionism*, 25, n27, counted 143 references to Robinson's writings in Orchard's volume. For Graves's comment, see his "Introductory Essay" to Orchard, xi–xii.

writers had utilized. Jones had illuminated the parties and sects in a fresh way that allowed Orchard to discern the proper perspective and chronology for his own account of Baptist history.[13]

In the United States, Georgia Baptist leader Jesse Mercer (1769–1841) showed a pronounced successionist inclination earlier in the nineteenth century, which subsequently contributed to Graves's labeling of him as an "Old Landmarker."[14] Another Georgian, P. H. Mell (1814–88), who was not a Landmarker, held up the already much vaunted line of dissenters to substantiate Baptist claims to antiquity. This pastor, Mercer University professor, and early president of the Southern Baptist Convention found his denominational brethren in every age even if they did not have the Baptist name.[15] In addition, Graves's sometime rivals John L. Waller and R. B. C. Howell consistently advocated Baptist perpetuity and/or successionism. During his time in Nashville, Howell asserted that "the Baptist church has existed, in a state of comparative purity, connected with neither Papists nor Protestants, in every period since Christ, and that in this sense God has not left himself without witness."[16] Howell's sentiments about Baptist history represented the rule, not the exception, for a broad range of Southern Baptists in the nineteenth century.

While successionist theory about Baptist origins was not as widespread in the North, it did not lack supporters. In fact, the first Baptist historian in America to attempt a somewhat inclusive denominational history was the New England pastor, David Benedict (1779–1874). He initially published his *General History of the Baptist Denomination* in

---

[13] See quotation from Orchard in Graves, "Introductory Essay," *A Concise History*, xii–xiv. Cf. W. Jones, *The History of the Christian Church: From the Birth of Christ to the Eighteenth Century, Including a Very Interesting Account of the Waldenses and Albigenses*, 2 vols. (New York: Spencer H. Cone, 1824). This was originally published as *The History of the Waldenses*, 2 vols. (London: Gale and Fenner, 1812).

[14] Graves, *Old Landmarkism*, 262–64. As early as 1811, Mercer wrote a circular letter for the Georgia Baptist Association in which he argued for the perpetuity of the true church since the first century. See Duvall, "The Successionism View of Baptist History," 13. Cf. L. B. Hogue, "A Study of the Antecedents of Landmarkism" (Th.D. diss., Southwestern Baptist Theological Seminary, 1966), 255, where he referred to Mercer as a successionist.

[15] P. H. Mell, *Baptism in Its Mode and Subjects* (Charleston, SC: Southern Baptist Publication Society, 1853), 179–80.

[16] R. B. C. Howell, *The Terms of Sacramental Communion*, 2nd ed. (Philadelphia: American Baptist Publication Society, 1846), 248. Cf. Howell, *The Early Baptists of Virginia: An Address, Delivered in New York, Before the American Baptist Historical Society, May 10, 1856* (Philadelphia: American Baptist Historical Society, 1857), 28, where he contended that "Baptists are not, and never were Protestants." For John Waller's views on Baptist perpetuity, see his "Reformation," *Christian Repository* 1 (January 1852): 5–14; 1 (September 1852): 543–48; and 1 (October 1852): 631–36.

1813, a year before the creation of the Triennial Convention, and released an updated version 30 years later. While he appeared to focus more on a succession of ideas and principles rather than churches, he followed the standard pattern of nineteenth-century Baptist historiography by giving special attention to the baptistic groups of the Middle Ages and beyond who refused to conform to oppressive state churches.[17]

Benedict's successionist perspective was likewise reflected in the work of Israel Roberds (1799–1851), pastor of the First Baptist Church in New Haven, Connecticut. Following a revival in his congregation, Roberds wrote a guide to assist his new converts that was published in 1838—the same year that Orchard's *Concise History* first went to press. One of the topics that he incorporated was church history, and he provided a quick overview in which he contrasted "the true church" and "the Romish church." The former, he maintained, "has been known by the name of Baptists, Anabaptists, Wickliffites, Lollards, Hugonots [*sic*], Mennonites, Hussites, Petrobrusians, Albigenses, Waldenses, Paulicians, &c; and to oppose image worship, infant baptism, transubstantiation, and the unwarrantable power of the Pope, have ever been characteristics of this people."[18] Moreover, he championed successionism in a roundabout way with a quote from *Brown's Bible Dictionary*: "it is easy to trace a succession of witnesses for Jesus Christ against His rival at Rome." Since Brown was a Scottish Presbyterian, it is not entirely clear how this brief excerpt corroborated a distinctly *Baptist* succession.[19]

At the same time, Roberds's discipleship tool indicated just how widespread perpetuity and succession concepts had become in Baptist thinking during the first half of the nineteenth century. This confirms Alan Cureton's observation that "[n]either Graves, nor any other Landmarker, invented successionism; they simply adopted what most Baptist

---

[17] D. Benedict, *A General History of the Baptist Denomination in America: and Other Parts of the World*, 2 vols. (Boston: Lincoln & Edmands [vol. 1] and Manning and Loring [vol. 2], 1813). This was later revised and published with the same title (New York: L. Colby and Co., 1848). For the influence of successionism on Primitive and Separate Baptists—some of whom read Benedict—see respectively M. A. Dain, "The Development of the Primitive Impulse in American Baptist Life, 1707–1842" (Ph.D. diss., Southwestern Baptist Theological Seminary, 2001), 134–47; and J. O. Renault, "The Development of Separate Baptist Ecclesiology in the South, 1755–1976" (Ph.D. diss., Southern Baptist Theological Seminary, 1978), 233–36.

[18] I. Roberds, *The Convert's Guide to First Principles or Evangelical Truth Sustained by the United Testimony of Our Lord Jesus Christ, the Holy Apostles, and Our Pedobaptist Brethren* (New Haven, CT: William Storer, 1838), 79. I am indebted to Ben Stratton, a former student and now a Baptist pastor in Farmington, Kentucky, for alerting me to this text.

[19] Ibid., 97–98. On Brown, see W. Brown, ed., *The Life of John Brown, with Select Writings* (Edinburgh: Banner of Truth Trust, 2004). These memoirs were originally published in 1856.

historians of the nineteenth century espoused."[20] The multiplicity of advocates for this viewpoint of the Baptist past, of course, does not authenticate it as historically sound or reliable. Nevertheless, the theory's popularity means that neither Orchard nor Graves were especially innovative in their embrace of it; a trail of Baptists who endorsed some version of it had already been blazed for several decades.

GRAVES AND CHURCH SUCCESSION

W. Morgan Patterson proposed that Baptist successionist thought shifted from a spiritual or ideological type to a full-fledged church successionism with an unbroken chronology through the literary efforts of G. H. Orchard, enthusiastically assisted by J. R. Graves.[21] One of the Landmark Baptist's earliest references to Orchard came through the mouth of "Fidus" in the context of the controversy with John Waller over alien immersion. "Fidus" cited both Robert Robinson and Orchard in support of identifying medieval dissenters as Baptists because "they abjured all hierarchies, and superior orders of clergy. They observed but two ordinances, Baptism and the Supper. They administered baptism by immersion to *believers* only. They were *strict in their communion*."[22] Since this was a debate involving questions of proper church order, history appears to have been brought in to support specific ecclesiological positions. Pedobaptists, who did not belong to true gospel churches, were outside of the line of dissent. Hence, "Fidus" sought to undermine

---

[20] Cureton, "The Historiography of Baptist Origins," 45. G. S. Holt, "The Influence of Alexander Campbell on the Life and Work of J. R. Graves, the Founder of the Landmark Movement" (M.Div. thesis, Emmanuel School of Religion, 1993), 27, incorrectly stated that the succession principle had "its origin with Graves." In a similar vein, T. A. Patterson, "The Theology of J. R. Graves and Its Influence on Southern Baptist Life" (Th.D. diss., Southwestern Baptist Theological Seminary, 1944), 265, wrongly judged that in 1846 church succession "seems not to have been widely advocated."

[21] Patterson, *Baptist Successionism*, 24–26. J. E. Tull, "A Study of Southern Baptist Landmarkism in the Light of Historical Baptist Ecclesiology" (Ph.D. diss., Columbia University, 1960), 302, asserted that Orchard, because he did not advocate "the view that Baptist churches make up either the universal visible church or the kingdom of God" (as Graves did), did not set forth "expressly a theory of church succession, but rather a theory of Baptist perpetuity." Orchard's long subtitle to his book, however, explicitly referred to his desire to exhibit Baptist "churches with their order in various countries under different names from the establishment of Christianity to the present age." See *A Concise History*, title page.

[22] "'Fidus,'" Muscle Shoals, November 27, 1848—'Re-Baptism. No. VII,'" *Tennessee Baptist,* December 7, 1848, [1]. A. H. Lanier Jr., "The Relationship of the Ecclesiology of John Lightfoot Waller to Early Landmarkism" (Th.M. thesis, Southeastern Baptist Theological Seminary, 1963), 70, plausibly argued that Graves moved from baptismal to church successionism as a result of his conflict with Waller.

Waller's acceptance of Pedobaptist immersion through an appeal to a historical perspective for which the Kentucky editor would have sympathy.

By 1855, the year that he printed an American edition of Orchard's *Concise History*, Graves displayed a more systematic interest in the field of church history. His two-part series on the topic in the newly-minted *Southern Baptist Review and Eclectic* actually had all the appearances of an intentional plan to help promote the sale of the Orchard volume. Indeed, the first installment bore a close resemblance to the introduction that Graves had written for the British Baptist's book.[23] In his essay, Graves lamented the ignorance of church history that he found among Christians but suggested that this might be "attributable to the unfaithfulness of those who have professed to write it."[24] Graves seemed to imply that Orchard's history could be a necessary corrective to renew interest in such an instructive discipline.

In the second part of his series, Graves continued to accentuate the need for a new approach to the history of Christianity, calling for a "radical revision" that would "vindicate the antiquity and Apostolicity of our history and origin, and redeem our name, and principles and the names of the martyrs, who have honored our history from undeserved reproach, and imputations of crime."[25] Since he was marketing Orchard's book as an inexpensive text to take its place next to the Bible in the homes of faithful Baptists, perhaps he can be excused for minimizing the contributions of earlier historians who had assumed some kind of Baptist perpetuity.

What Graves (and Orchard) essentially did was to adjust the already established Baptist successionism by directly linking a consecutive chain of true churches. Graves rooted church succession in the ministry of Jesus, who came to earth to set up a visible kingdom that would stand through the centuries. For the Landmark leader, the implications of this were indisputable:

> If we believe our Savior [Matt. 16:18], we are compelled to believe that
> churches, identical with those of Jerusalem, Judea and Samaria, have existed in
> every age, from the day of the ascension until now, and that such bodies are still

---

[23] Cf. Graves, ["Church History," (I)] *Southern Baptist Review and Eclectic* 1 (January 1855): 18–31; and Graves, "Introductory Essay," in Orchard, *A Concise History*, iii–xxiv.

[24] Graves, ["Church History," (I)] 23.

[25] Graves, ["Church History," (II)] *Southern Baptist Review and Eclectic* 1 (April and May 1855): 194, 203. He enlisted J. Newton Brown as support for the notion that church history needed to be rewritten. See pp. 205–15 for a circular that Brown had prepared for the Central Union Association of Pennsylvania on this point.

extant, claiming our veneration and undivided support. And does it not pertain most intimately to the honor of our Savior, that the history of such a people shall one day be brought into clearest light? How else can we—can the world—know he has kept his promises?[26]

Thus, histories like Orchard's served to accomplish much more than simply chronicling information; they highlighted the providential purposes of God in the unfolding of his kingdom.

Orchard's historical labors also served to reinforce the Landmark patriarch's Christian republicanism. Graves's ecclesiology, which was so thoroughly infused with his republican convictions, predisposed him to see history as a titanic struggle between freedom and tyranny. One of the features of Orchard's history that appealed to Graves was the heavy emphasis on persecuted dissidents who experienced tortures inflicted by the Roman Catholic Church; this suffering, of course, was pictured in the worst possible terms. Consequently Orchard, Graves, and later Carroll came close to identifying Baptists through history not so much by their doctrines but rather by the blood that they spilled because they bucked the established church. In particular, Graves believed that the genuine history of Christianity was a largely untold story of underground movements that rejected the authority of Rome. In his introduction to the Orchard volume, Graves vividly conveyed the historical continuity of faithful witnesses to Jesus: "[S]uccessions of Baptist communities have come down to us from the apostles, all striped and scarred and blood covered—a line of martyrs slain by prisons, by fire, and by sword."[27] Graves then invoked typically passionate language to commend the superior Baptist "religious principles" and polity that ultimately allowed these victimized minorities both to challenge their enemies and hoist the banner of freedom and republican institutions around the world. According to Graves, Baptist ecclesiology was not only biblical; it likewise held important political implications that were being revealed in the revolutions of the modern world. In this context, moreover, he cited favorable comments on Baptist church government by one of America's Founding Fathers, Thomas Jefferson.[28] Once again Graves sought to demonstrate the full compatibility of Landmarkism and republicanism.

In reality, the "religious principles" to which Graves alluded were more associated with polity than doctrine. Neither he nor Orchard said much about the doctrinal

---

[26] Ibid., 196.

[27] Graves, "Introductory Essay," in Orchard, *A Concise History*, xviii.

[28] Ibid., xviii–xix.

beliefs of the nonconformist groups that constituted their version of Baptist history. As a result, Orchard and Graves uncritically interchanged "Baptists" with a host of disparate dissenting groups including Montanists, Novationists, Paulicians, Bogomils, Albigensians, Waldensians, Lollards, Hussites, and Anabaptists. Apparently it was not imperative for these movements to have held Baptist doctrinal distinctives; indeed, some of them held theological views that most modern Baptists would categorize as heretical. The lack of tangible evidence for baptismal immersion by many of these parties, moreover, did not seem to be an obstacle for their admission to the Baptist ranks. Graves probably sensed that successionists worked outside normal historical canons; echoing Orchard, the Tennessee Landmarker stressed that most church history until the nineteenth century had been written by faithless "Paedobaptists" who suppressed or destroyed the information that would conclusively validate Baptist continuity. Historical accounts by Baptists, he averred, rested on a different foundation of facts than those supplied by Catholics or Protestants.[29] Since he lacked the documentary evidence to prove conclusively that Baptists enjoyed an unbroken history, he ended up staking more stringent boundaries for the Baptists of his own day than for the baptistic groups and movements that he included in the historical succession.

For Graves, logic seemed to eclipse supportive data when it came to maintaining a long chain of Baptist churches through the ages. While introducing Orchard, Graves underscored the promises Jesus made to his disciples that the gates of hell would not prevail against the true church (Matt 16:18) and that he would be with them until the end of the age (Matt 28:20). These assurances, he reasoned, helped to establish a successionist interpretation of Baptist history: "[They] certainly secure the integrity and perpetuity of churches of Christ in and through all subsequent ages, even to the end of this dispensation."[30] In other words, Graves understood the Baptist trail as necessary to sustain the truthfulness of the words of Jesus. Yale historian Sydney Ahlstrom pertinently discerned that, in essence, Graves substituted a syllogism for credible historical research: "the Kingdom has prevailed; the Kingdom must always have included true churches; Baptist churches are the only true churches; therefore, Baptist churches have always

---

[29] Ibid., vii–xiv. Graves did not view Baptists as Protestants; Baptists had a long, independent existence and never had to come out of the Roman Catholic Church. See "Editorial Telegrams," *Tennessee Baptist,* June 26, 1858, [2], which reported on lectures that Graves was delivering on the theme that Baptists were not Protestants. Cf. the follow up, "Rev. J. R. Graves," *Tennessee Baptist,* July 24, 1858, [2], which reprinted a letter from A. T. Holmes to the *Christian Index* of Georgia that gave an account of Graves's lectures at First Baptist Church, Atlanta, which included "Baptists Not Protestants."

[30] Graves, "Introductory Essay," in Orchard, *A Concise History,* iv.

existed."[31] Hence a particular take on defending the fidelity of Scripture as well as ecclesiology virtually demanded that Graves embrace successionism. As Harold Smith put it, Graves basically used history as a tool; it was important to him for "its ability to answer questions regarding the nature, practices, and identity of genuine gospel churches."[32] In essence, Graves brought an agenda to the study of history, which adversely affected the breadth of his research and his readiness to learn from it.

The successionist impulse also shaped Graves's positions on particular chronological and interpretive issues. For instance, he jumped into the debate over which congregation in colonial Rhode Island was the oldest Baptist church in the New World by editing and republishing S. Adlam's *The First Baptist Church in America.*[33] Adlam, the pastor at First Baptist, Newport, from 1849 to 1864, argued that his church could be traced back earlier than First Baptist, Providence, which for many years had claimed precedence. The dating controversy also involved attitudes toward the two most significant personalities in seventeenth-century Rhode Island, Roger Williams and John Clarke. Williams was considered a founder of the Providence church, although he soon broke fellowship with it; Clarke was identified as a key player in the establishment of the Newport congregation. Adlam and Graves clearly preferred Clarke as the superior prototype of Baptist virtue in early America.

Graves chimed into the discussion primarily through his introduction, editorial comments, and appendix in the Adlam volume. Prior to his resounding endorsement of Adlam's history, Graves had visited Newport in 1854–55, met with Adlam, and engaged in some historical research of his own. While the Tennessee journalist admitted that written records for the early histories of the two churches were not plentiful, he satisfied himself that Adlam's conclusions were sound. Graves consequently dated the founding

---

[31] S. E. Ahlstrom, *A Religious History of the American People* (New Haven, CT: Yale University Press, 1972), 723. What Ahlstrom noticed inevitably raises issues of historical method, which successionists usually chose not to address. For insightful criticisms of their historiography, including a questionable use of sources and logical fallacies, see Patterson, *Baptist Successionism,* 30–62.

[32] H. S. Smith, "A Critical Analysis of the Theology of J. R. Graves" (Th.D. diss., Southern Baptist Theological Seminary, 1966), 150.

[33] S. Adlam, *The First Baptist Church in America,* 2nd ed., ed. J. R. Graves (1887; repr., Texarkana, AR: Baptist Sunday School Committee, 1939). This was originally published as *The First Baptist Church in Providence Not the Oldest Baptist Church in America* and included in Graves, ed., *Trials and Sufferings for Religious Liberty in New England* (Nashville: Graves, Marks & Co., 1857). Adlam's book was serialized in the *Tennessee Baptist* beginning October 9, 1852, [1]. Graves's edited volume on New England began as a series in *Tennessee Baptist,* September 12, 1857, [1]. Because Graves did not clearly communicate that he was the *editor* of these materials, he was accused of plagiarism. See Graves, "Who Wrote the Historical Sketch Entitled 'Trials and Sufferings for Religious Liberty'?" *Tennessee Baptist,* May 1, 1858, [2].

of the Newport church to 1638, citing an imprecise statement on Clarke's tombstone about the gathering of a congregation. He contended, moreover, that the Providence church lacked both valid baptisms and a continuous history, whereas Newport seemingly boasted both (at least in Adlam's estimation).[34]

The successionist trail most likely drove Graves to choose Newport as the original Baptist church in the colonies. His examination of the Roger Williams legacy evidently convinced the Landmark pioneer to keep his distance. Williams affiliated with Rhode Island Baptists for only a few months and then became a "Seeker." In addition, the Massachusetts émigré later questioned the baptisms at Providence, including his own. Furthermore, he absolutely repudiated any notion of baptismal succession by insisting that new apostles with a direct commission from Christ would have to appear to reestablish the true church; its original foundation, he surmised, had been lost in the Middle Ages. He likewise questioned both the immersion baptisms that Baptists began to employ in the 1640s, as well as the authority by which they performed them.[35] Williams's actions and his subsequent reflections on the Baptist tradition together threatened successionism. If there was a historical chain, he was surely not one of the links.

Perhaps most telling was Graves's complaint that, in public debates, his Pedobaptist and Campbellite opponents attacked Baptists for not possessing "baptism, ordinances, or even a *history* that entitles them to be considered churches of Christ." The primary ground for this indictment was that Baptists emerged in recent times, having been founded by Williams on the basis of an illegitimate baptism that he allegedly passed on "to all succeeding Baptist Churches in America."[36] Therefore, Graves's role as denominational apologist virtually required that he weed Williams out of the historic Baptist line. Church successionism allowed Graves to trace Baptist origins back many centuries before Williams and thus counter the arguments of his non-Baptist foes.

Overall, Williams's role in early New England Baptist life made Graves extremely uncomfortable. In his conclusions to Adlam's defense of the Newport church's priority,

---

[34] Graves, "Introduction," in Adlam, *The First Baptist Church*, 12–29. The founding of the church in Providence is usually dated in 1638. This date is used on a brochure that I received when touring the church November 20, 2008. The current building was constructed in 1774–75. J. M. Carroll followed Graves in dating Newport as the earlier church. See *The Trail of Blood*, 47–48. I. Roberds, *The Convert's Guide*, 78, accepted Providence as the earliest church in America, as did David Benedict. Graves commented on Benedict's view in Adlam, *The First Baptist Church*, 21.

[35] Adlam, *The First Baptist Church*, 155–57. Williams expressed his reservations about the Baptist practices of his day in a letter to John Winthrop Jr. in 1649. See E. S. Gaustad, ed., *Baptist Piety: The Last Will and Testimony of Obadiah Holmes* (Tuscaloosa: University of Alabama Press, 2005), 17.

[36] Graves, "Introduction," in Adlam, *The First Baptist Church*, 11.

Graves practically dismissed Williams as a champion of religious liberty and then basically drummed him out of the Baptist fellowship: "He has no claim to be acknowledged as a Baptist, and better would it be for his memory if his short and abortive religious Baptistical life was obliterated from the pages of history, and the memory of men."[37] In short, Roger Williams failed to serve successionist purposes. John Clarke, on the other hand, represented the true Baptist line to such a degree that Graves in another context branded him an "Old Landmarker."[38] The Newport congregation, therefore, had to be the first Baptist church in America and part of the Baptist succession through the ages; the Providence assembly did not even qualify as a legitimate Baptist church.

Graves's handling of this historical issue was a microcosm of his entire approach to the past. He ignored the inconvenient facts that: (1) little was known about Clarke's baptism or roots as a Baptist; (2) there is no evidence to show that Clarke's Newport congregation was singularly Baptist until the mid-1640s; and (3) immersion was probably not adopted by the Newport church until 1644.[39] This information makes things untidy for successionist claims. For Graves, however, ecclesiology constantly trumped sound methods of inquiry. History then took on a decidedly partisan edge as it was shaped to accommodate Landmark perspectives.

THE SUCCESSIONIST TRAIL ON TRIAL

In time, Graves found resistance to his successionist history in some Southern Baptist circles, as well as among the non-Baptist denominations that emerged as villains in the account of church history put forth in Orchard's *Concise History*. In 1870, after Graves had moved to Memphis, the *Biblical Recorder* of North Carolina ran an article citing *Religious Herald* editor J. B. Jeter's challenge to church successionism in which he apparently compared it to the Roman Church's claims to the apostolic succession of its bishops and popes. Ever sensitive to what appeared in other Baptist state papers, Graves replied that Baptist successionism did not require a doctrine of apostolic succession,

---

[37] Graves, "Appendix," in Adlam, *The First Baptist Church*, 182. One of the earliest indications of his rejection of Williams as a Baptist can be found in Graves, "True History of Roger Williams," in Graves, ed., *The Southern Baptist Almanac and Annual Register, for the Year of Our Lord 1849* (Nashville: Graves & Shankland, 1849), 22–24. Cf. Graves, *Trilemma*, 120–21.

[38] Graves, *Old Landmarkism*, 212.

[39] Gaustad, *Baptist Piety*, 17–22, 140, n1.

which he called a "pestilent dogma." [40] Graves's Landmark ecclesiology, of course, stressed that the ordinances belonged to the local church, not to its ministers.

Graves also sensed that the faculty at Southern Baptist Theological Seminary, which was launched in 1859 and remained in Greenville, South Carolina, until 1877, failed to uphold successionism. In particular, he openly fretted about William Williams (1821–77), one of the original four professors who at times taught church history courses. Williams also was suspect because his stance on alien immersions deviated from Landmark orthodoxy. [41] Graves even suggested in 1873 that Williams was a latitudinarian because of his stance on Baptist history. Moreover, the *Baptist* editor felt compelled in the same context to deal with the problem of the historical gaps in successionist theory, maintaining that meager evidence did not wipe out the trail of blood:

> That every link in the chain has been discovered we do not claim, but enough to show that there is a chain. That a part of her history is hidden is but a fulfillment of prophecy, which declares the woman was driven into the wilderness by her persecutors. The day is coming, we believe, when she will be able to vindicate her history—when she will be seen coming out of the wilderness (her obscurity), fair as the moon, clear as the sun. We believe that the documents would establish every year of her existence since the days of Catholic persecution are now locked up in the archives of inquisitions and the Vatican, and the day may not be distant when these will be open to all. [42]

Graves no doubt felt some heat from Williams and others on one of successionism's key blemishes; in reaction, he constructed what was essentially an argument from the

---

[40] Graves, "Church Authority," *Baptist,* April 2, 1870, [4]. See the background to this article in Graves, "The Succession Question in North Carolina," *Baptist,* February 19, 1870, [4]. Decades later church historian W. W. Barnes explained that "[t]he difference between Roman and Baptist succession is just this: The Roman succession of bishops assures the continuity of the body; the Baptist succession of the body assures a continuity of pastors (bishops in the New Testament sense)." See Barnes, *The Southern Baptist Convention: A Study in the Development of Ecclesiology* (Fort Worth: By the author, 1934), 61.

[41] Graves, "Succession," *Baptist,* August 10, 1872, [4]. On Williams, see G. A. Wills, *Southern Baptist Theological Seminary, 1859–2009* (New York: Oxford University Press, 2009), 102, 161–63. For the broader context of the alien immersion issue at Southern Seminary, see Wills, 98–103.

[42] Graves, "Able Latitudinarians," *Baptist,* June 7, 1873, [4]. The woman in the wilderness theme echoed the *Vindication* of Spittlehouse and More; a key difference was the timing of the end of the true church's obscurity.

absence—or perhaps, more accurately, the currently concealed nature—of the supporting data.

In 1876 Graves returned to Jeter's persistent assaults on church successionism. This time, he focused on the *Religious Herald* editor's endeavor to associate the Zwickau prophets and the radical, violent Anabaptists of the Münster uprising with the successionist trail, conceding that the deliberate confusion of "the historical Baptists of Europe with the Anabaptists of the sixteenth century is the most popular and effective argument that our enemies are wont to bring against us." [43] Unlike Spittlehouse and More, who saw the rise of the more extreme Anabaptists as a sign that the true church had come out of hiding, Graves clearly sought to eliminate the more radical links from the Baptist chain.

To make matters worse on the anti-successionist front, the *Religious Herald* ran articles in 1875 and 1876 by the pseudonymous "Pike," who some observers thought might be affiliated with Southern Seminary—perhaps ecclesiastical historian William H. Whitsitt (1841–1911). "Pike" posed some probing historical questions about when the baptismal practice of immersion was introduced or recovered; he also leveled harsh attacks on Landmarkist ecclesiology, including its position on alien immersion. Whether or not "Pike" was actually Whitsitt, his colorful thrusts at both baptismal and church successionism certainly were congruent with the Southern Seminary educator's later published writings.[44]

Around the time of the "Pike" articles, Graves also found himself responding to a scathing critique of successionism that Methodist Jacob Ditzler threw at him in their extended public debate in Carrollton, Missouri. Ditzler evidently kept up with the controversy in Baptist circles about historical questions:

---

[43] Graves, "The Religious Herald—Anabaptists and Landmarkism," *Baptist,* January 29, 1876, 148. This issue led to a series by Graves. See "The Anabaptists of the Sixteenth Century—Were They Baptists or Anarantists? No. 2," *Baptist,* February 5, 1876, 164; "The Anabaptists of the Sixteenth Century—Were They Baptists or Anarantists? No. 3," *Baptist,* February 12, 1876, 181; and "Historical. No. 4," *Baptist,* February 26, 1876, 213.

[44] "Pike's" literary contributions were summarized in Tull, "A Study of Southern Baptist Landmarkism in the Light of Historical Baptist Ecclesiology," 545–50. Cf. Tull, 580ff., on the probability that "Pike" was indeed Whitsitt. James H. Slatton, who had access to Whitsitt's diaries and personal papers, omits any discussion of "Pike." For the period 1875–76 of Whitsitt's life, see Slatton, *W. H. Whitsitt: The Man and the Controversy* (Macon, GA: Mercer University Press, 2009), 58ff. At one point, Graves asked "Who Is 'Pike'?" *Baptist,* November 4, 1876, 758. He reported President James P. Boyce's denial that "Pike" was anyone from Southern Seminary (Graves had suspected Williams).

[A]ll the best historians among them know that all this parade about succession, that old woman they have hid in the wilderness, not the pure one of Scripture, is a bastard, a fiction, a myth, without one word of reason, Scripture, history, truth, or fact in its favor—gotten up by such pernicious and vicious writers as Orchard, who falsifies all history, misquotes all records and facts as wholes, distorts, and makes all history a huge burlesque, to impose on the ignorant.[45]

In the face of this challenge, Graves primarily repeated his oft-utilized argument from Scripture (Matt 16:18): "If Christ's words be true, His church has had a continuous existence from His day until our own, and if His words are not true He is not the Christ of God, and we have no Savior."[46] Since history could not always provide what was needed to validate successionist dogma, Graves turned to his trusted biblical hermeneutic to defend his cause.

By the time Graves wrote his most definitive book on Landmark ideology, he had already endured several anti-successionist stings. If his pride had been wounded, he did not show it outwardly. In fact, he vigorously reaffirmed his long-held convictions. As he interwove his church successionism with his unusual theory on how the kingdom related to the church, he continued to claim that all this was quite different from apostolic succession:

[M]y position is that Christ, in the very "days of John the Baptist," did establish a visible kingdom on earth and that this *kingdom* has never yet been "broken in pieces," or given to another class of subjects—has never for a day "been moved," or ceased from the earth, and never will until Christ returns personally to reign over it; that the organization he first set up, which John called "the Bride," and which Christ called his church, constituted that visible kingdom, and to-day all his true churches on earth constitute it; and, therefore, if his *kingdom* has stood unchanged, and will to the end, he must always have had true and uncorrupted churches, since his kingdom can not exist without true churches.[47]

---

[45] Graves and J. Ditzler, *The Graves-Ditzler Debate: or, Great Carrollton Debate* (Memphis: Southern Baptist Publication Society, 1876), 912.
[46] Ibid., 1050. Graves did not help his cause in the matter of historical accuracy. E.g., he linked Thomas Müntzer to the Münster rebellion, even though Müntzer was killed in the Peasants' War almost a decade before the Münster uprising. See ibid., 892.
[47] Graves, *Old Landmarkism*, 122–23. For other defenses of successionism in the last few decades of the nineteenth century, see D. B. Ray, *Baptist Succession: A Handbook of Baptist History* (Cincinnati: G. E. Stevens & Co., 1870); and W. A. Jarrel, *Baptist Church Perpetuity: or, the Continuous Existence of Baptist Churches*

While this understanding of Baptist perpetuity was not as widely endorsed as it had been three decades earlier, it remained a vital trademark that was indelibly stamped on Graves's ecclesiology.

In *Old Landmarkism*, Graves also appeared to raise the standards for who actually qualified to be a branch on the Baptist family tree. Indeed, the embattled propagandist set forth the proposition that the real Baptists of the past were in fact "Old Landmarkers." He accordingly found Landmark Baptists from the first through the nineteenth centuries, and in geographical regions as far east as Russia and as far west as North America. For instance, William Kiffin of Particular Baptist fame in seventeenth-century England and Philadelphia Association Baptists of the early eighteenth century were Old Landmarkers. So it was not enough just to be a Baptist—the true bride during earlier eras and Graves's own "Laodicean" age consisted of the "faithful and zealous few" who practiced a strict Landmark ecclesiology.[48] Graves's inclination to project nineteenth-century issues and controversies back into the past exposed a markedly anachronistic approach to history, which suggests a major flaw in his thinking—and, for that matter, in successionism as a whole. History became easily abused as it was subordinated to ideological agendas.

HISTORY IS MESSY

In James McGoldrick's critique of successionist historiography, he remarked that Baptists have more difficulties tracing their historical origins than have other major traditions, suggesting that this predicament has generated a denominational "identity crisis."[49] In many respects, J. R. Graves's ventures into the historical arena epitomized an intrepid attempt to discover or establish a Baptist identity. After all, identity is partly built on memory and memory has inevitable links to the past. So Graves was compelled to search aggressively for an extended line of Baptist forebears. During the heated denominational rivalries of the mid-nineteenth century, Graves undoubtedly longed to

---

from the Apostolic to the Present Day Demonstrated by the Bible and by History (Dallas: By the author, 1894). Jarrel dedicated his book to three men, one of whom was J. R. Graves, who had died the previous year.

[48] Graves, *Old Landmarkism*, 211–14, 236, 264–65. Graves accepted a dispensational view of history, which reinforced his propensity to focus on persecuted minorities that persevered against beastly tyranny. On his dispensationalism, see Graves, *The Work of Christ in the Covenant of Redemption; Developed in Seven Dispensations* (1883; repr., Texarkana, AR: Baptist Sunday School Committee, 1928 and 1963). His eschatology receives more attention in chap. 7 below.

[49] McGoldrick, *Baptist Successionism*, 1.

give fellow Baptists a sure identity with deep historical roots. His ecclesiology, moreover, demanded a long trail of Baptist testimonies to the fulfilled promises of Jesus about the survival of true—and local—churches.

Successionism might have appealed to Graves in part because it helped to unify the various ideological threads of his thought. Theologian James Tull observed that this view of Baptist origins and history "is a compact summary of the Landmark faith, holding all its elements in one concept. The successionist theory gave the movement a sharp cutting edge, and added greatly to its dynamism. Its simplicity was part of its strength."[50] At the same time, successionist history could not live up to its unrealistic expectations; it imposed some very tight requirements in order to keep the historical chain intact, which turned out to be an impossible task. Tull concluded that ultimately "the Landmarkers placed an intolerable strain upon their own ecclesiology." [51]

What J. R. Graves failed to comprehend is that history is messy. He seemed to be oblivious to the immense scope and thorny intricacies of Christian history in general and Baptist history in particular. While he rightly valued the necessity of a denominational memory rooted in the past, he refused to admit that history could be easily distorted when it was used to legitimize a set of ecclesiological convictions. What former *First Things* editor Joseph Bottum has warned about employing memory for autobiographical purposes applies equally well to larger projects: "Memory may be our best tool for self-understanding, but only if we remember how weak a tool it really is: prone to warping under the narrative drive of storytelling, vulnerable to self-interest, susceptible to outside influence." [52] Through a highly selective approach to the past, Graves allowed historical memory to be held captive to ideology; in turn, this thoroughly reworked the contours of Baptist history, which resulted in a blurred and thus confused denominational identity.

Faulty historical memory also caused the Landmark patriarch to oversimplify Baptist history. He seems to have assumed a relatively unswerving historical track of Baptist life and thought that the data plainly did not support. Baptist historian Bill Leonard warned against narratives that overlook the sometimes tangled roots and complications of denominational history: "Baptists should not succumb to the fallacy of origins, that noble but naïve belief that there exists a pristine, systematic, and unified source of Baptist identity in the beginning that only need be discovered and installed. In fact, there are multiple Baptist traditions—theological, regional, and institutional—from

---

[50] Tull, "A Study of Southern Baptist Landmarkism in the Light of Historical Baptist Ecclesiology," 189.
[51] Ibid., 321.
[52] J. Bottum, "The Judgment of Memory," *First Things,* March 2008, 30.

which churches may choose." [53] Graves might have done a better job of setting denomi-national boundaries if he had cultivated a deeper appreciation for the rich complexity of the Baptist heritage.

Sadly, Graves's uncritical embrace of G. H. Orchard's mythical cloud of witnesses ended up doing an arrant disservice to several generations of Baptists. The identity that he popularized as "Baptist" intermingled Baptists with a potpourri of heretics, ecclesiastical misfits, and valiant reformers who challenged the established church but did not necessarily articulate Baptist doctrines. Moreover, it seems that he did not grasp the reality that dissent in the history of the church was not infrequently linked to deviation from Christian orthodoxy. Hence, his use and abuse of history taught many independent and Southern Baptists a fictitious past.

Graves additionally passed on a legacy of intense anti-Catholicism, as well as a fundamental indifference toward the Protestant Reformation; after all, if Baptists could be traced back to the apostolic age, they predated the Reformation and were by definition not Protestants. Graves's version of church history in many ways trivialized the Reformation; he seems to have accepted several of the central doctrines that the Reformers taught, but he simultaneously dismissed their movements with pejorative epithets. His erection of hefty ecclesiastical barriers did not effectively discriminate between Catholics and Protestants—they all were enemies who could not be trusted, in part because of their prior crusades against the Baptist bride. As church historian Timothy George asserted, Landmarkism helps to account for the anti-ecumenical "isolation and separatism" that has characterized significant sectors of Baptist life since the middle of the nineteenth century.[54]

One of the consequences of Graves's myopic outlook on non-Baptist traditions is that it stamped the Landmark movement with a spirit of triumphalism.[55] The Baptist editor contributed to a heightened sense of denominational pride in part because he did not do justice to the ambiguities of history. In his recounting of history, the preserved remnant through the centuries seemingly avoided the corruptions and apostasies that afflicted Catholicism and Protestantism. He invoked the alleged purity of the historic

---

[53] B. J. Leonard, "Whose Story, Which Story? Memory and Identity among Baptists in the South," in *History and the Christian Historian*, ed. R. A. Wells (Grand Rapids: Eerdmans, 1998), 135.

[54] T. George, "Southern Baptist Ghosts," *First Things,* May 1999, 21.

[55] See R. T. Hughes and C. L. Allen, *Illusions of Innocence: Protestant Primitivism in America, 1630–1875* (Chicago: University of Chicago, 1988), 98. They relate Graves's triumphalism to both his primitivism and millennialism. Cf. J. C. Fletcher, "Shapers of the Southern Baptist Spirit," *Baptist History and Heritage* 30 (July 1995): 8, where he linked successionism to triumphalism.

Baptist witness to help set it apart from the tainted records of other movements and denominations. In the process, gospel humility took a back seat.

As time went on, Graves spawned further efforts to perpetuate a bogus denominational identity, which only intensified a mistaken understanding of the relationship of faith and history among some Baptists. A few years after Graves's death, a muddled conception of Baptist history and identity contributed to the severe reaction that greeted William Whitsitt when he endeavored to apply earnest historical scholarship to the issue of Baptist origins.[56] Successionist apologetics reached a nadir with *The Trail of Blood*, but there were others like New Orleans professor John T. Christian (1854–1925) who offered a somewhat more sophisticated version.[57] Ultimately, Graves's subordination of history to ecclesiology dealt a troublesome setback to the Baptist historical enterprise. After carefully assessing the successionist legacy, Baptists who are serious about history might well wonder whether they have been victims of identity theft.

---

[56] W. H. Whitsitt, *A Question in Baptist History: Whether the Anabaptists in England Practiced Immersion before the Year 1641?* (Louisville, KY: C. T. Dearing, 1896). On the Whitsitt dispute, see R. Beck, "The Whitsitt Controversy: A Denomination in Crisis" (Ph.D. diss., Baylor University, 1984); and Wills, *Southern Baptist Theological Seminary,* 189–229. Whitsitt, who was elected president of Southern Seminary in 1895, had not been in office for long when conflict erupted over his rejection of successionism. As a result, he stepped down in 1899 and moved to a teaching position at Richmond College (now the University of Richmond) in 1901. Ironically, Whitsitt had significant exposure to Landmark influences in his youth, and Graves preached at his ordination. See Slatton, *W. H. Whitsitt,* 15–22. Slatton devoted a significant portion of his book to the embattled Whitsitt presidency.

[57] J. T. Christian, *A History of the Baptists Together with Some Account of Their Principles and Practices,* 2 vols. (Nashville: Broadman, 1922). Christian apparently obtained some of Graves's library. See J. M. King, "John Tyler Christian: A Study of His Life and Work" (Th.D. diss., New Orleans Baptist Theological Seminary, 1953), 85–86.

Chapter 6

Denominational Boundaries and Growing Pains

The Nashville Years (1845–62), Part III

A lmost as soon as J. R. Graves accepted editorial responsibilities with the *Tennessee Baptist* in the late 1840s, he demonstrated an unequivocal penchant for stirring up religious controversy. In numerous articles and columns, he sparred repeatedly with fellow Baptists like John Waller, former Baptists like Alexander Campbell, or Pedobaptists like J. B. McFerrin. In retrospect, his earlier journalistic polemics served to prime Graves for a head-on clash with the man who had assisted him in several ways during his initial transition to Nashville.

A hectic period that commenced in 1857 with the return of R. B. C. Howell to the pulpit of First Baptist Church in Nashville framed the setting for the most intense and bruising mêlée of Graves's career. Since the Landmark patriarch was a member of the congregation that called Howell to a second tour of duty, the contentious disputes of the late 1850s brought Graves into a direct and tragic confrontation with his own pastor. While Graves had already earned a reputation as an enthusiastic combatant in religious warfare, Howell had been away from Nashville for seven years and his more restrained confrontational style had become a dim memory to most observers. Even so, the heated altercations between these two prominent personalities in Southern Baptist life revealed some palpable flaws in both men. By the end of the decade, neither one could rightfully lay claim to holding the higher moral ground.

The conflict between Graves and Howell, which might have begun to fester in a low-key way as early as 1847, defies any simple analysis.[1] Since it became increasingly

---

[1] For the most noteworthy scholarship on the Graves-Howell confrontation, see J. E. Hilton, "Robert Boyté Howell's Contribution to Baptist Ecclesiology: Nineteenth-Century Baptist Ecclesiology in Controversy" (Ph.D. diss., Southeastern Baptist Theological Seminary, 2005), 139–219; L. T. Horne, "A Study of the Life and Work of R. B. C. Howell" (Th.D. diss., Southern Baptist Theological Seminary, 1958), 326–88; and K. V. Weatherford, "The Graves-Howell Controversy" (Ph.D. diss., Baylor University, 1991).

apparent that neither man liked the other very much, their feud plainly had a personal side. Their social, cultural, and educational backgrounds, after all, were very different. In addition, retrospective views suggest that their earlier working relationship at the *Tennessee Baptist* was not exactly cozy or even "cordial." [2] As their dispute unfolded, neither of them may have fully appreciated its emotionally-charged character. While that ingredient is the most difficult for the historian to measure, it surely contributed to the *ad hominem* barbs that emanated from each adversary. The harsh and nasty tones of their exchanges suggest that at times both of them pushed the boundaries of propriety.

Second, their squabble possessed a sometimes understated ideological component that was linked to Graves's Landmarkist agenda. In particular, Howell occasionally protested that his opposition to Graves in the Nashville arena was unrelated to the latter's ecclesiological views.[3] On one hand, Howell's endorsement of Baptist perpetuity through the ages positioned him in reasonable proximity to the successionism of the Landmarkers. At the same time, Howell never expressed much sympathy for the tenets of Graves's theology of the church that had wrought discord among Baptists in the mid-South. The First Baptist pastor, moreover, never entirely separated his personal dislike for Graves from his aversion to many of the Landmark patriarch's ideas. Furthermore, Howell undoubtedly realized that Graves's promotion of his distinctive ecclesiology had profound repercussions for denominational life well beyond the confines of Nashville.

At a third level, the row between Graves and Howell can be understood as a battle for turf. Even before deciding to return to the Tennessee capital, Howell discovered just how large a network of support that Graves had built up in less than a decade as editor of the *Tennessee Baptist*. Although he had made his share of enemies, the Landmark leader nonetheless enjoyed a significant following in several southern states. Harold Smith acknowledged this in his synopsis of what can best be categorized as a test of two strong-willed religious activists jockeying to enhance their respective strengths: "Howell was no longer the leader in Tennessee. Graves's success with the paper far exceeded anything

---

[2] E.g., R. B. C. Howell, "Charges against Rev. J. R. Graves," Robert Boyté Howell Collection, AR. 595, Vol. 1:[2], SBHLA, Nashville, Tennessee. Hilton, "Robert Boyté Howell's Contribution," 142, offered a puzzling description of the Howell-Graves relationship before 1858 as "cordial." Howell's son claimed much later that Graves was responsible for making the controversy with his father personal. See M. B. Howell to T. T. Eaton, April 6, 1900, T. T. Eaton Papers, box 1, folder 33, James P. Boyce Centennial Library Archives, Southern Baptist Theological Seminary, Louisville, Kentucky.

[3] Howell, "Charges against Rev. J. R. Graves," Howell Collection, 1:[3].

Howell had accomplished. Howell's jealousy was balanced by Graves's judgment that Howell had been recalled to Nashville to displace him and his theological viewpoint." [4]

While Smith likewise recognized the personal and doctrinal dimensions of the Graves-Howell conflict, he clearly perceived that the two antagonists were engaged in campaigns to exercise power and influence in several realms of ecclesiastical life, including First Baptist Church of Nashville, regional associations, and ultimately the Southern Baptist Convention. The SBC, in fact, found itself at a pivotal stage in its early history; in that setting, Graves and Howell represented competing visions of denominational identity and direction. In this formative period, rival parties set the stakes high, producing what some researchers have dubbed "the greatest controversy" to afflict Southern Baptists before 1979. [5]

The boundaries that Graves laid out to fend off non-Landmark Baptists were manifestly different from the ones that he employed against Pedobaptists and the followers of Campbell. Nevertheless, they cemented his reputation as a feisty controversialist who rarely backed away from a good fight. In the case of his dispute with Howell, Graves aggressively fenced himself off from an ostensible colleague and very close "neighbor." Howell promptly reciprocated and a major fracas ensued.

Prelude: Graves and First Baptist Church of Nashville before 1857

As described in chap. 2, J. R. Graves's formal affiliation with First Baptist Church in Nashville began almost immediately after he and his first wife settled in the city during the summer of 1845. Howell, who had already served as the congregation's pastor for more than a decade, facilitated his younger member's transition into a pastoral role at Second Baptist Church, where Graves ministered for about four years. The two clerics also worked together on the editorial staff of the *Baptist*, which was renamed the *Tennessee Baptist* in 1847.

---

[4] H. S. Smith, "A Critical Analysis of the Theology of J. R. Graves" (Th.D. diss., Southern Baptist Theological Seminary, 1966), 23.

[5] J. E. Tull, *High-Church Baptists in the South: The Origin, Nature, and Influence of Landmarkism*, ed. M. Ashcraft (Macon, GA: Mercer University Press, 2000), 85. Tull echoed a similar conclusion written two decades prior to the more recent SBC conflict. See H. L. Grice and R. P. Caudill, "Graves-Howell Controversy (1857–1862)," in *Encyclopedia of Southern Baptists* (Nashville: Broadman, 1958), 1:585.

Outwardly Graves and Howell seemed to benefit from an amicable relationship, although the situation with the denominational paper undoubtedly caused some strains. Perhaps issues relating to changes at the *Baptist* partly explain Howell's blunt reaction to their later hostilities and the subsequent trial at First Baptist, when he expressed some bitterness about the paper and also dismissed the labors of Graves at Second Baptist as "unsuccessful." [6] In that retrospective mood, Howell even suggested that Graves exploited the good will of the folks at First Baptist for evil purposes. After noting that the young editor lacked polish as a speaker, Pastor Howell claimed that his congregation nonetheless "received him cordially as a teacher, and as a minister to give him character and influence. Thus was the church betrayed into the support of a man whose depravity has seldom been equaled in this or any other country." [7] At the same time, any tensions between the two men in the period from 1845 to 1850 remained tacit rather than overt. Howell plainly used his experiences beginning in 1857 as a prism by which to reevaluate his earlier relationship with Graves.

When Graves resigned his position at Second Baptist in 1849 to focus on the *Tennessee Baptist* and other publishing ventures, he and his wife Lua rejoined First Baptist. For the next several years, he apparently played an active role in the life of the Nashville congregation. When Howell left the church in 1850 to become pastor of Second Baptist Church in Richmond, Virginia, First Baptist voted unanimously for Graves to fill the pulpit until a new pastor was called.[8] In addition, Graves chaired committees, represented the church at associational and convention meetings, moderated business sessions, sat on ordaining councils, and assisted in planting new churches.[9] Although he was frequently away from Nashville, Graves still managed to be strategically involved in the life of his church.

Graves's preaching at First Baptist attracted the attention of a correspondent from Kentucky—probably J. M. Pendleton of Bowling Green—who reported in the *Baptist Banner* of Louisville that the Nashville congregation had responded favorably to it:

---

[6] Howell, "Charges against Rev. J. R. Graves," Howell Collection, 1:[2]. In Howell, *A Memorial of the First Baptist Church, Nashville, Tennessee: From 1820 to 1863* (Nashville: First Baptist Church, 1863), 1:214, he asserted that Graves and his successors at Second Baptist "accomplished nothing." The *Memorial* has been preserved in a typescript version of Howell's original longhand.

[7] Howell, *A Memorial*, 1:328.

[8] J. R. Graves, "A Recall," *Tennessee Baptist,* April 18, 1850, [2]. On Howell's departure, see "Resignation," *Tennessee Baptist,* March 14, 1850, [2]; and "The Farewell," *Tennessee Baptist,* April 18, 1850, [2].

[9] Smith, "A Critical Analysis of the Theology of J. R. Graves," 21, n65.

[Graves] is a young man of splendid order of mind, and has preached most acceptably to the church and congregation. As a minister of the gospel, he has few superiors anywhere. He is already one of the most useful men in Tennessee, and the area of his influence is extending. He does not pander to the capricious fancies of the multitude; and, notwithstanding he is very popular, he is what he is—fearless, unflinching, and always earnestly contending for what he conceives to be truth and duty.[10]

In commending the 26-year-old supply preacher, "P." evidently failed to anticipate that in a half decade Graves's popularity at First Baptist would diminish, in part because his brash style of contending for a Landmark version of Baptist faith and order ended up alienating a sizable portion of the congregation. In broad strokes, moreover, the Kentucky correspondent's assessment ironically bore a vague resemblance to what Howell wrote about Graves and First Baptist in his *Memorial* several years later. Howell's *Memorial*, however, offered an intentionally negative retrospect of Graves's membership at First Baptist in the 1850s, whereas "P." conveyed a more glowing, premature testimony that did not foresee how the Landmark patriarch's approach might ultimately be considered offensive.

For his part, Howell constantly pointed out signals that Graves was a troublesome presence at First Baptist. For example, Howell alleged that Graves "undermined" Samuel Baker's pastorate (1850–53) and inflicted "unceasing vexations" on Baker himself.[11] Furthermore, Howell recounted that a "whirlpool of Landmarkism" gained strength during the pastorate of William H. Bayless (1854–56); those who resisted it, including the new pastor, faced "perpetual agitations and heart-burnings." [12] In Howell's judgment, which he apparently drew based on communications that he had with individuals in Nashville while he was in Richmond, the potential for a serious breach between Graves and the church existed well before Howell returned as pastor in 1857.

In fact, Graves engaged in a scuffle with a fellow church member, medical doctor William P. Jones (1819–97), during Bayless's tenure at First Baptist. Deacon Jones, who served as a correspondent for the *Western Recorder* of Kentucky and also edited the *Parlor Visitor*, reportedly sued Graves for libel over some unflattering attacks that

---

[10] P., "Tennessee Correspondence," *Baptist Banner*, May 18, 1850, quoted in *Tennessee Baptist*, June 29, 1850, [2]. At the time of "P's" comments, Graves had been preaching at First Baptist for only a short period, perhaps less than a month.

[11] Howell, *A Memorial*, 1:327, 332.

[12] Ibid., 2:2.

had appeared in the *Tennessee Baptist* after Jones raised questions about the Tennessee Baptist Publication Society's imprint on some of Graves's published works. In 1855 B. F. King of Windsor, North Carolina, made inquiry about the dispute, which prompted First Baptist to appoint a committee to investigate. One of the committee's conclusions acknowledged the controversial side of Graves's personality: "Brother Graves does not stand well with some members of the First Baptist Church of the city of Nashville, of which he is a member, nor would it be agreeable to those members for him to occupy the pulpit, whilst on the other hand he has many warm friends in the church, and has never been denied the occupancy of the pulpit."[13] After the internal committee failed to bring about a meaningful reconciliation between the two men, the church resorted to an outside group to assist with mediation efforts. Five participants, including James B. Taylor, secretary of the Foreign Mission Board of the SBC, and Joseph H. Eaton, president of Union University in nearby Murfreesboro, helped to affect at least a partial resolution of the conflict. Church historian Lynn May later hinted that this kind of turmoil may have influenced Bayless's decision to leave in 1856, when he accepted a call to the First Baptist Church of Waco, Texas.[14]

In spite of this, Graves tendered a more optimistic spin on the whole affair by suggesting that a satisfactory settlement between himself and Jones had been reached. This came in the context of his response in 1856 to this question: "Have you ever been tried in the First Church on the charge of unministerial or unchristian conduct?" The embattled Landmarker then produced an 1855 letter from Bayless in which the pastor declared, "No charge or charges have been performed against you on the records of the 1st Church, since I have been its pastor."[15] Furthermore, when he reported that he had filled the First Baptist pulpit twice in the past two weeks, he also affirmed his "love and respect" for those in the congregation who did not share his Landmarkism.[16] While Graves seemed

---

[13] Ibid., 1:331.

[14] L. E. May Jr., *The First Baptist Church of Nashville, Tennessee, 1820–1970* (Nashville: First Baptist Church, 1970), 80–81. For other brief accounts of this incident, see Grice and Caudill, "Graves-Howell Controversy," 580; Smith, "A Critical Analysis of the Theology of J. R. Graves," 22; and A. W. Wardin Jr., *Tennessee Baptists: A Comprehensive History, 1779–1999* (Brentwood, TN: Executive Board of the Tennessee Baptist Convention, 1999), 185. None of these summaries refer to Jones's libel suit that Howell recounted in *A Memorial*, 1:330. Horne, "A Study of the Life and Work of R. B. C. Howell," 339, cited the legal suit and described the Jones-Graves reconciliation as partial.

[15] See Graves, ed., *The Little Iron Wheel: A Declaration of Christian Rights and Articles, Showing the Despotism of Episcopal Methodism* (Nashville: South-Western Publishing House; Graves, Marks & Co., 1856), 275–76.

[16] Ibid., 277–78.

to underplay the magnitude of his clash with Jones, the very fact that he answered such a question so soon afterward stands as an uncanny foreshadowing of the later difficulties that he would experience at the church. A year before Howell's homecoming, moreover, Graves perhaps did not suspect that steps had already been taken to persuade the Richmond pastor that his presence was needed in Nashville—in part to stem the influence of the *Tennessee Baptist* editor and his Landmark ideology.

POSITIONING FOR THE INEVITABLE SHOWDOWN: HOWELL'S RETURN TO FIRST BAPTIST

Although R. B. C. Howell did not accept an invitation to his second pastorate at First Baptist Church until July of 1857, evidence indicates that the Nashville congregation initially sought to bring him back both before and after William Bayless's stint in the pulpit. Eventually the church issued a unanimous call in March of 1857, with the transparent implication that Howell was the one leader who could rescue this beleaguered assembly from the onslaught of Landmarkism in its midst. At first delaying his response, he visited Nashville after the SBC meeting in Louisville. Evidently convinced that the tensions in the congregation could largely be traced to Graves and his ecclesiological views, Howell soon confirmed the call to return as pastor and resigned his position in Richmond.[17] While the Graves-Howell controversy ultimately proved to be deep and complicated, First Baptist's apprehensions about Landmarkism—and the divisions that it was causing—played a major role in the church's pleas for him to come back and help restore harmony.[18]

For his part, Graves in 1857 was commanding the Landmark tide to its probable high watermark of influence in the mid-South. Since the formal adoption of the Cotton Grove Resolutions in 1851, the founder of Landmarkism continued to refine and publicize his ideology. He had already begun to insert into the *Tennessee Baptist* a summary of Baptist doctrines, facts, principles, corollaries, and axioms that became a regular feature of the newspaper. Some of the items that he listed would have gained widespread endorsement in Baptist circles, including baptism of believers by immersion, the compatibility of Baptist polity with republicanism, and the supreme authority of the Bible for

---

[17] Hilton, "Robert Boyté Howell's Contribution to Baptist Ecclesiology," 65, 143; and Horne, "A Study of the Life and Work of R. B. C. Howell," 323–25.

[18] Howell, *A Memorial*, 2:2.

shaping Baptist faith and practice. At the same time, the editor used this posting to reiter-
ate the spirit of Cotton Grove, particularly in its dismissal of Pedobaptist denominations
as merely "religious societies" and not authentic churches; a suitable warning against
pulpit affiliation was likewise included. In repudiating "popery," the new section of the
paper also rejected the notion that Baptists were Protestants. Overall, the list conveyed
the uncompromising nature of Landmarkism with its refusal to distinguish between
"essentials and non-essentials" in the drawing of boundaries between Baptists and other
movements or groups.[19]

In light of all that transpired during his dispute with Howell, Graves likely came
to regret two topics that he included in the Baptist paper's standing column. First, the
Landmark patriarch demonstrated in his fifth and sixth "corollaries" how the Separate
Baptist localism of New England had shaped Landmark ecclesiology:

> That a body of immersed believers is the highest ecclesiastical authority in the
> world, and the only tribunal for the trial of cases of discipline; that the acts of
> the church are of superior binding force over those of an association, conven-
> tion, council, or presbytery—and no association or convention can impose a
> moral obligation upon the constituent parts composing them. . . . That no asso-
> ciation or convention has the right to demand support for any project or scheme
> which they have originated, but may only recommend, advise, and urge the per-
> formance of duty in subservience to the great Christian voluntary principle.[20]

As it turned out, his expulsion from First Baptist of Nashville in 1858 prompted Graves
to back away from a strict insistence on local church autonomy in cases involving the discipline of members. In fact, this ecclesiological shift would place him in a diametrically
opposite position from that of Howell on the rights and privileges of local congregations.

Second, the Baptist editor affirmed that it was a Baptist policy "[t]o employ all the
energy of the denomination for the conversion of the world, through the most effectual

---

[19] E.g., Graves, "Keep before the People," *Tennessee Baptist,* January 31, 1857, [3]. The same article from the
October 3, 1857 issue has been reprinted in O. L. Hailey, *J. R. Graves: Life, Times and Teachings* (Nashville:
By the author, 1929), 53–56; and H. L. McBeth, ed., *A Sourcebook for Baptist Heritage* (Nashville:
Broadman, 1990), 318–20. Both Hailey and McBeth gave the wrong issue date of October 6. See appendix for
the full text from the February 1, 1867, issue of the *Baptist,* which Graves modified in light of his expulsion
from First Baptist, Nashville.

[20] Graves, "Keep before the People," [3]. He expressed similar sentiments in *The Great Iron Wheel; or,
Republicanism Backwards and Christianity Reversed,* 17th ed. (Nashville: Graves, Marks & Rutland, 1856),
311, 559.

means and agencies, as our missionary organization, Bible and publication societies, theological seminaries, male and female colleges, and Sunday schools, prayer meetings, and regular periodicals."[21] While the editorial stances of the *Tennessee Baptist*—as well as Graves's denominational activities up to this point in his career—were generally consistent with this statement, he nevertheless adopted a much more negative attitude toward the SBC's "missionary organization" in the aftermath of the actions taken against him at First Baptist Church. As the convention's president for several terms in the 1850s, Howell naturally defended the function and inherent value of the Foreign Mission Board. On this issue, Graves and Howell assumed different perspectives on the relationship of cooperative missions to local church independence. Latent ecclesiological contradictions that emerged may have been partly connected to the personal aspects of their conflict.[22]

At the same time, the two antagonists held disparate visions for denominational life. While Howell was sufficiently engaged with Southern Baptist institutions to be considered part of the "establishment," Graves was more of a lone ranger who devoted the bulk of his energies to his own publishing empire. In addition, the Baptist journalist's style frequently irritated those who exercised leadership in official SBC circles. To put it another way, many in the SBC recognized Howell as a denominational statesman, whereas Graves was perceived more as the leader of a distinct party movement that was attempting to steer Baptist agencies and institutions in a narrow ideological direction. In reality, Howell staked out Baptist parameters as heartily as Graves, but he did so with more nuance, a larger concern for denominational consensus, and a greater stress on the merits of unified endeavor beyond the level of the local church. As James Hilton has aptly explained it, "Howell envisioned a Baptist identity that was centered on Scripture, defined by believer's baptism and communion, a church governed by the executive power of its members, and individual, autonomous churches cooperating together for missions."[23] For Graves, those ingredients had undeniable value but were hardly sufficient for mapping out distinctive denominational boundaries in the mid-nineteenth century when the SBC had not even reached adolescence.

Along with their manifest disagreements on a wide range of issues, neither Graves nor Howell trusted each other. After their conflict at First Baptist had pretty

---

[21] Graves, "Keep before the People," [3].

[22] Baptist historian Albert Wardin adds a sociological side to their clash, pointing out that "Howell reflected the ethos of the East, particularly Virginia. . . . Graves reflected the ethos of the West and identified with the West." See Wardin, *Tennessee Baptists*, 184. Their different educational attainments also likely factored into this cultural gap.

[23] Hilton, "Robert Boyté Howell's Contribution to Baptist Ecclesiology," 232.

much played out, the *Tennessee Baptist* editor claimed that his pastor arrived from Richmond with a premeditated strategy to undermine his younger adversary and weaken the Landmark faction at the church: "That it was the understanding between Elder H. [Howell] and this Kentucky party in the Church, that Elder H. was to use his influence to put down the editor of the *Tennessee Baptist*, his paper and the South-Western Publishing House, crush out the Old Landmark principles and influences, and restore these men to influence in the denomination."[24] While Graves did not name the individuals who allegedly conspired with Howell, the Landmarker seemed convinced that deep-seated tensions between the two men stood behind the momentous happenings at First Baptist in 1858.

When Howell later penned his *Memorial*, his patent bitterness toward Graves in point of fact lent credence to the latter's conjectures about the former's sinister designs. The First Baptist minister, for example, dismissed Landmarkism as an "absurd theory"; at the same time, he characterized Union University in Murfreesboro—where Graves was a trustee—as "the fountain of his new doctrine." Furthermore, Howell employed acerbic language in tarring his by then ex-parishioner as belligerent, arrogant, and "a most consummate demagogue."[25] Given this emotionally-charged rhetoric, it is difficult to imagine how "Elder H." was able to separate Graves's ecclesiological beliefs from the behavioral issues that constituted the substance of the official indictments that were brought against the well-known editor at First Baptist in 1858.

Although it is reasonable to surmise that part of Howell's motivation in returning to Nashville in the summer of 1857 was to deal with Graves and his sizable influence, the Baptist cleric nonetheless cannot be directly implicated in an apparent campaign—which was initially launched during that same time frame—by editors of some other Baptist newspapers to discredit the *Tennessee Baptist* journalist. Graves, of course, had a history of tangling with other denominational editors, going back to his lively exchanges with John L. Waller in the late 1840s that are discussed in chap. 2. In the mid-1850s Landmarkism's foremost advocate used his editorial columns to sustain controversies with his counterparts at papers like the *New Orleans Weekly Baptist Chronicle* and the

---

[24] Graves, "External History," *Tennessee Baptist*, March 12, 1859, [4].

[25] Howell, *A Memorial*, 1:331–32. A few months after his return to Nashville, Howell complained in a letter that "Landmarkism has done a destructive work throughout this whole region . . . in drying up all spirituality in the churches and in the ministry, and in closing the ears of the people against our preaching." Howell to J. A. Broadus, October 11, 1857, John Albert Broadus Collection, box 1, folder 29, James P. Boyce Centennial Library Archives, Southern Baptist Theological Seminary, Louisville, Kentucky.

Western Recorder of Kentucky, even while his battle with Alexander Campbell reached its peak of ferocity.[26]

By the late spring of 1857, Graves found it necessary to respond to both the *Religious Herald* of Richmond, Virginia, and the *Southern Baptist* of Charleston, South Carolina, over their advocacy of practices that he and other Landmarkers opposed like open communion and pulpit affiliation.[27] His dispute with the *Southern Baptist* editor, J. B. Tustin, soon took on the character of a personal feud that went well beyond ecclesiological differences. Tustin, for instance, even blamed Graves's contentious manner on his Vermont roots; a year later, this kind of *ad hominem* allegation would carry with it the strong hint that someone who hailed from the North likely was an abolitionist.[28]

A more important—albeit underlying—facet of Graves's conflict with Tustin centered on the complicated status of publication agencies in Southern Baptist life during the 1850s. Graves himself was heavily involved in publishing efforts in Nashville through both the Tennessee Baptist Publication Society and South-Western Publishing House. In fact, he reorganized the corporate base for the latter early in 1857; at the same time, he reassured the readers of the *Tennessee Baptist* that South-Western would never publish what "is not true to the *true* principles and policy of our denomination." [29] In addition, the Landmark founder showed special attention to the Bible Board in Nashville, which was organized in 1851 as a Southern Baptist Convention entity. In 1854 his compatriot A. C. Dayton became the board's second secretary, and the two men sought to infuse the organization's materials with Landmark ideology. Furthermore, they desired to have the Bible Board produce Sunday school literature; even though that was not really part of its original mission, the SBC allowed this by 1856.[30] Graves undoubtedly sensed strategic opportunities to help shape the emerging denominational ethos through a variety of print media.

---

[26] Grice and Caudill, "Graves-Howell Controversy," 580.

[27] See Graves, "The Religious Herald and Orchard," *Tennessee Baptist,* May 30, 1857, [2]; and Graves, "This Paper and the Southern Baptist; or Ourself [*sic*] and J. B. Tustin," *Tennessee Baptist,* June 13, 1857, [2].

[28] "Bro Tustin's Mild (?) Reply.—The Tennessee Baptist," *Tennessee Baptist,* June 13, 1857, [4]. On Graves versus Tustin, see Samuel H. Ford, "Life, Times and Teachings of J. R. Graves," *Ford's Christian Repository and Home Circle,* March 1900, 162–63; and Grice and Caudill, "Graves-Howell Controversy," 580.

[29] Senior Publishers, "A New Firm," *Tennessee Baptist,* March 21, 1857, [2]. Cf. Grice, "Graves (James Robinson) Publication Organizations," *Encyclopedia of Southern Baptists,* 1:578–79.

[30] Grice and Caudill, "Graves-Howell Controversy," 580; Grice, "Bible Board, Southern Baptist Convention," *Encyclopedia of Southern Baptists,* 1:163; and H. L. McBeth, *The Baptist Heritage: Four Centuries of Baptist Witness* (Nashville: Broadman, 1987), 434–35. The Bible Board's first secretary was W. C. Buck, a Landmark sympathizer who regularly contributed articles to the *Tennessee Baptist.*

Tustin, however, represented one of the obstacles to Graves's ambitious quest for publishing dominance in Southern Baptist life. The South Carolinian's newspaper was a primary organ of the Southern Baptist Publication Society, which Tustin also served as secretary. Founded in 1847, this agency was not institutionally related to the SBC. Nevertheless, the SBPS was regarded by many Southern Baptists as a replacement for the northern-based American Baptist Publication Society, which significantly reduced its presence in the South in the decade and a half leading up to the Civil War. Even before his scrap with Tustin, Graves had been critical of the SBPS's relatively modest achievements in publishing pamphlets, books, and Sunday school materials.[31] Graves plainly viewed the Charleston organization as competition for his own entrepreneurial interests.

In reality, the discernible friction between rival publishing ventures in Southern Baptist life helped to precipitate Howell's open conflict with Graves. The active pastor-theologian not only assisted in the launching of the Southern Baptist Publication Society during his first Nashville pastorate; he also authored several of its printed materials, including the first book that the society released.[32] As SBC president for much of the 1850s, moreover, Howell exercised some oversight for the Bible Board since it was an official denominational agency. Therefore, it was hardly surprising that after arriving back in Nashville in 1857, Howell displayed a much more urgent interest in the operations of the Bible Board. In particular, he sought to reverse the Dayton agenda that had been encouraged and promoted by Graves. The fact that Howell, Dayton, Graves, and all the members of the Bible Board worshipped in the same church held ominous implications.

Not a Sunday School Picnic

In the fall of 1857 Howell responded to escalating criticisms of Dayton by some Bible Board members, including Graves's nemesis W. P. Jones. The newly installed First Baptist pastor appointed a committee, which functioned for several months, to investigate Dayton's management of the agency and determine whether it conformed with

---

[31] Grice, "Graves (James Robinson) Publication Organizations," 578; and Grice, "Southern Baptist Publication Society (Charleston, SC, 1847–63)," *Encyclopedia of Southern Baptists*, 2:1266–67. In the latter article, Grice noted that Tustin eventually was ordained as an Episcopal priest, a move that did not help the cause of the struggling agency. Cf. Ford, "Life, Times and Teachings of J. R. Graves," 162–63, who also remarked that Tustin moved to the North.

[32] Howell, *The Way of Salvation* (Charleston, SC: Southern Baptist Publication Society, 1849). For the same publisher, he also wrote *The Evils of Infant Baptism* (1852), *The Cross* (1854), and *The Covenants* (1855).

stated SBC policies. The Landmark secretary apparently sensed early in the process that the majority of the committee would not come to favorable conclusions about his leadership and was not an especially cooperative member.[33]

In the meantime, Howell had offered a resolution in support of Sunday school work at the August meeting of the Concord Baptist Association, which primarily included churches east of Nashville. He proposed that there be a special convention devoted to the Sabbath school to be convened just before the annual meeting of the Baptist General Association of Tennessee and North Alabama in October.[34] While Howell certainly had a track record of support for Christian education as both a pastor and denominational leader, he also might have entertained hopes of countering the publishing efforts of the Landmarkers and strengthening the position of the Southern Baptist Publication Society.

As it turned out, the Nashville cleric failed to anticipate the composition of the convention. Although this gathering was open to all Southern Baptists, the majority of attendees were from Tennessee and many were Landmarkers. In fact, A. C. Dayton boldly introduced a constitution for a new agency to be known as the Southern Baptist Sunday School Union. As he envisioned it, the SBSSU would publish and recommend materials for Sunday school programs throughout the SBC. Provisions for book printing contracts appeared to allow for Graves's publishing enterprise in Nashville to play a major role. After much debate, Dayton's recommendation was approved, and he was named to be president of the board for the new endeavor. Graves became recording secretary, and several other Landmarkers were elected as managers. There was simply no ambiguity about the ideological orientation that the SBSSU would assume. About the only concession that Howell was able to gain was an agreement that the new organization would have a provisional character until there could be a more representative meeting in 1858. That event never occurred, and the SBSSU was formally organized at a Landmark-dominated gathering in Memphis late in 1858. Although not an official SBC entity, the agency operated in Nashville between 1859 and 1862; the Civil War inflicted serious damage on the SBSSU from which it would not recover.[35]

---

[33] See Howell to Rev. J. E. Dawson, May 11, 1858, Howell Collection, 1:[2–5]; "Impeachment of James R. Graves," Howell Collection, 1:5; Howell, *A Memorial*, 2:18–19; and May, *The First Baptist Church*, 86.

[34] Grice and Caudill, "Graves-Howell Controversy," 580–81; and Wardin, *Tennessee Baptists*, 185.

[35] Grice, "Southern Baptist Sunday School Union," *Encyclopedia of Southern Baptists*, 2:1267–68; and Wardin, *Tennessee Baptists*, 185. For a factually muddled account of the Sunday school convention, see F. Rolater, "The Local Origins of Landmarkism: First Baptist, Nashville; Concord Baptist Association; and Union University and the Definitive Controversy among Southern Baptists," *Tennessee Baptist History* 12 (Fall 2010): 85.

For his part, Howell obviously understood that the SBSSU would be thoroughly Landmarkist, so he vigorously opposed it at the special meeting in 1857 and in other venues. His most calculated protest came in the form of a letter published early in 1858 in the *Christian Index* of Georgia, which was reprinted in some other Baptist papers like the *Southern Baptist.* In his epistle, the SBC president vented about the situation with the new Sunday school agency, declaring that "this whole thing is repugnant." In particular, he fretted about the potential impact on the Southern Baptist Publication Society, which he claimed was charged with the responsibility for publishing Sunday school literature. Furthermore, he urged that Dayton should send books that he was preparing for the SBSSU to the SBPS. While Howell claimed that ecclesiological issues were not germane to this current dispute, he nonetheless managed to take a few swipes at the movement that he had come to loathe: "Nor do I refer especially to the 'Landmark' doctrine, known to be 'a hobby' among them; which, by the way, they do not understand, since they have never yet learned the teaching of the Bible, nor the opinions of our brethren in the South, regarding it." He then proceeded to deride the premillennialism of the Landmarkers, suggesting that it was "practically much more injurious" than their views about the church.[36] Such pointed, public criticism leads to the reasonable conclusion that Howell's motivations in attacking the SBSSU project were both institutional and theological.

Although the Howell-Graves relationship seemed to be fraying even before the *Christian Index* letter, the publication and circulation of the document signaled that the two men had reached an impasse. Early in 1858 Graves evidently decided that any reconciliation with his pastor was hopeless. In the very issue of the *Tennessee Baptist* where he ran Howell's infamous letter, the Landmark editor sought to vindicate the SBSSU and its role in denominational life. He especially spurned Howell's arguments that the new board would threaten the SBPS: "The Union will do its work without interfering with, or the least expense to the society in Charleston, and when books enough have been produced, and Baptists of the South say the Union is no longer needed it will dissolve and give up its work." [37] At this point, Graves moved to a defense of the embattled

---

[36] Howell to Brother Walker, December 21, 1857, published as "Letter from Dr. Howell," *Christian Index,* January 6, 1858, reprinted in *Tennessee Baptist,* February 20, 1858, [2]. In *A Memorial,* 2:21, Howell charged that the actions of the 1857 Sunday school convention constituted an attempt to "overthrow" the SBPS by "transferring its patronage" to Graves's publishing house in Nashville. On Howell's postmillennialism, see C. M. Wren Jr., "R. B. C. Howell and the Theological Foundation for Baptist Participation in the Benevolent Empire" (Ph.D. diss., Southern Baptist Theological Seminary, 2007), chap. 6.

[37] Graves, "Review. Was Brother Howell Deceived or Duped?" *Tennessee Baptist,* February 20, 1858, [2].

Dayton and his position with the Bible Board. Graves's tone became more strident with a personal attack on Howell:

> If it is a sin against morals or the Holy Spirit for the Secretary of a Board to write a book or tract, while so connected, is it not as heinous a sin for the pastor of a church who *sells* all his time for a stipulated sum? Establish this law, and our Bro. Howell is the most guilty man known to me, unless Bro. Everts of Louisville . . .
>
> Those who live in glass *houses* ought not to throw stones into their neighbor's *windows*.[38]

Graves's noticeable resentment revealed that he regarded his pastor as a major obstacle to the Landmarkist agenda that he had in mind for the Bible Board and the SBSSU, just as Howell saw the Baptist editor as a threat to the continuing viability of the SBPS. Their calamitous warfare had begun in earnest.

As the Bible Board committee neared the closing stages of its inquiry into Dayton's leadership, Graves combined his case for the SBSSU proposal with a spirited defense of Dayton, his Landmark colleague and fellow author. Graves repeatedly alleged that there was "a manifestly systematic attempt to cripple down the Secretary of the Bible Board on the part of Anti-Landmark *men* and editors," citing publications such as the *Baptist Watchman*, the *South Western Baptist*, and Jones's *Parlor Visitor*.[39] In a later reflection on Dayton's difficulties with several members of the Bible Board, the Landmark patriarch tagged Howell as the primary culprit behind the campaign against the board secretary, insisting that "Elder Howell used his influence to destroy Elder Dayton." [40]

---

[38] Ibid., [2–3]. Graves apparently was alluding to the practice of earning some income on the side for work beyond that pertaining to a salaried position. Howell and his allies on the Bible Board complained that Dayton spent too much time writing books (e.g., *Theodosia Ernest*), thus distracting him from his official duties as board secretary. See "Bible Board (of SBC) Meeting—Paper Read by J. C. Darden [chairman]," Howell Collection, 1:[21]. Graves's insinuation that Howell preached and engaged in various ministries for money served as a primary basis for the charges of slander and libel when the Landmark editor was tried by First Baptist of Nashville later in 1858.

[39] Graves, "Systematic Opposition," *Tennessee Baptist,* March 13, 1858, [2]. Cf. Graves, "The Secretary of the Bible Board," *Tennessee Baptist,* March 6, 1858, [2–3], where the editor credited Dayton with erecting "an impregnable fortress for Old Landmarkism." In the second installment of March 13, 1858, [2], Graves listed and responded to the "petty attacks" that had been leveled at Dayton.

[40] Graves, "External History," *Tennessee Baptist,* March 12, 1859, [2].

For Graves, the success of the SBSSU, Dayton's professional career, and the future of Landmarkism were all at stake; hence, he drew the battle lines as starkly as possible.

By early April of 1858 the Bible Board committee arrived at some decisions that did not bode well for Dayton. In particular, the committee report included resolutions that chastised the secretary for circulating books other than "Bibles, Testaments, and the publications of our societies," as well as ignoring the board's wishes that he "devote himself wholly to the duties assigned him." In addition, the committee regretted that Dayton showed "disrespect" toward the Bible Board, most notably in his own report to the committee: "Your committee must say that they cannot approve either the tone, or language of this report of the Secretary, nor do they concur in his interpretation of the instructions of the Convention in the premises."[41] Reading between the lines, the committee members went beyond simply rebuking Dayton for his operational policies and practices; they also judged that his "duties" did not include promoting the SBSSU or writing for Graves's publishing house. In light of the strong committee sentiment against him, Dayton resigned his position with the board on April 8, 1858.[42]

Graves soon expressed his intense displeasure with the Bible Board's treatment of his Landmark compatriot. In the same issue of the *Tennessee Baptist* in which he announced that Dayton and J. M. Pendleton had been added as associate editors, Graves predicted—wrongly as it turned out—that the recent changes at the Bible Board would lead to its relocation to Charleston and merger with the Southern Baptist Publication Society. Moreover, he blamed Dayton's resignation on "an anti-Landmark combination that had its head in this city, and a mouthpiece in Knoxville, Tuskegee and Charleston."[43] This represented a thinly veiled assault on Howell, as well as editors of other Southern Baptist newspapers like Matthew Hillsman (*Baptist Watchman*), Samuel Henderson (*South Western Baptist*), and J. B. Tustin (*Southern Baptist*) who all opposed Graves, Landmarkism, and the SBSSU.[44]

The attack mode that Graves had regularly employed against leaders of non-Baptist denominations was being utilized once again to counteract those in the SBC whom the Landmark patriarch deemed as ideological enemies. While his strikes against his own denominational brethren had earlier precedents, their partisan nature seemed to inten-

[41] Howell to Rev. J. E. Dawson, May 11, 1858, Howell Collection, 1:[14–26].

[42] "Bible Board (of SBC) Meeting," Howell Collection, 1:[14].

[43] Graves, "A Prophecy," *Tennessee Baptist*, May 15, 1858, [2]. On the appointment of associate editors, see "Announcement" in same issue, 3.

[44] Specific links to Graves's vague allusions are provided in Grice and Caudill, "Graves-Howell Controversy," 581.

sify noticeably in the context of the overlapping SBSSU and Dayton controversies. The Landmark editor found it difficult to refrain from highly charged rhetoric, especially when he believed that vital causes were threatened. His primary target, R. B. C. Howell, peevishly evaluated Graves's journalistic tactics in 1863, by which time most of the dust had settled on the frenzied episodes of 1858. In his judgment, the *Tennessee Baptist* under Graves's editorial direction had served no useful cause:

> If it had been swallowed up in the depths of the sea five years ago, its destruction would have been a blessing to our whole country. . . . It has inflamed their [Baptist] passions, engendered distrust, put them in fierce conflict with each other, substituted sectarian cancer for the love of Christ, and wherever it has had influence, well nigh driven all spirituality from the heart.[45]

In short, Graves shunned the role of diplomat; he saw himself and fellow Landmarkers engaged in a righteous battle for essential Baptist distinctives. The very manner in which he defined his mission basically precluded compromise.

At the same time, Graves found himself locked in mortal combat with other Baptist editors like Hillsman, Henderson, and Tustin who jumped into the fray to stand with Howell. Graves, of course, had skirmished with the SBPS's Tustin in 1857 even before the contentious efforts to organize the SBSSU, which Tustin understandably opposed. Soon after Dayton's resignation from the Bible Board post in the spring of 1858, Graves guardedly sought a truce in the conflict over the SBSSU that was being waged in Baptist papers; he even offered columns in the *Tennessee Baptist* for Howell to explain his public letter to the *Christian Index*.[46] Then, following issues of his newspaper in which he voiced belligerent comments concerning the Dayton case, Graves professed that he was "willing to discuss any item of doctrine or polity we have advocated in this paper in a kind and Christian spirit, and when convinced to confess it openly." [47] Since his conciliatory attempts to soften the acrimony in Nashville and beyond seemed so out of character, they were largely ignored.

Howell, in fact, must have choked on some of the language in Graves's ceasefire proposals. By that time, the Nashville pastor had ceased attempting to visit Graves because of "misrepresentations and perversions" of their private conversations that had appeared

---

[45] Howell, *A Memorial*, 2:52.

[46] Graves, "A Proposition to Settle the Present Controversy—to All Who Are Concerned in It," *Tennessee Baptist,* April 10, 1858, [2].

[47] Graves, "Peace Once More Proposed," *Tennessee Baptist,* June 12, 1858, [2].

in the *Tennessee Baptist*. Howell even wrote his son in May of 1858 that he shut down virtually all communication with Graves, including written correspondence: "When he has written me notes, I have sent them back unopened." [48] Indeed, the prospects appeared extremely dim for any kind of reconciliation between Graves and his pastor.

It is not clear just how much contact Howell had with editors who championed him in his struggles with Graves. During the summer of 1858, the *Tennessee Baptist* editor spilled much ink fighting off charges discussed in chap. 1 above that he could be linked to Campbellism, abolitionism, and plagiarism. These accusations especially emanated from Samuel Henderson's *South Western Baptist* in Alabama, forcing Graves to review and explain some of his prior experiences in Vermont and Kentucky, as well as to vindicate his literary style as author and editor.[49]

It seems possible that Howell may well have provided ammunition to Graves's opponents in other states that helps to account for the commonly repeated refrain that the Landmark leader opposed slavery. In *A Memorial*, Howell persistently labeled Graves as a northerner who harbored abolitionist sentiments, at the same time that he dismissed some of the SBSSU advocates as "northern men." He went so far as to characterize the Graves faction at First Baptist of Nashville as an "abolition element . . . nearly all from the North." [50] It is not clear how such sectional animosity and prejudice could be sustained as late as 1863, by which time Graves had been an outspoken defender of both slavery and the Confederacy.[51] Nevertheless, the antislavery caricature points to likely collaboration between Howell and Henderson in their alliance against Graves, reinforc-

---

[48] Howell to M. Howell, May 5, 1858, Morton B. Howell Collection, Tennessee State Library and Archives, Nashville, Tennessee, quoted in Wardin, *Tennessee Baptists*, 186. Cf. "Charges against Rev. J. R. Graves," Howell Collection, 1:[5]. These sources do not mesh well with Howell's later claim that he harbored "no enmity" toward Graves and was willing to reconcile. See Howell, *A Memorial*, 2:52.

[49] See W. T. Martin, "Samuel Henderson and His Responses to J. R. Graves and Landmarkism through South Western Baptist, 1857–1859" (M.A. thesis, Samford University, 1977). Various issues of the *Tennessee Baptist* from May to October of 1858, some of which are cited in chap. 1, contain Graves's often prolonged responses to Henderson and other Baptist editors.

[50] Howell, *A Memorial*, 1:244, 327–29; 2:22, 422. As noted in chap. 3 above, Methodist polemicist William G. Brownlow, editor of the *Knoxville Whig*, referred to Graves in 1856 as "a Northern man . . . he is *anti-slavery* at heart." See *The Great Iron Wheel Examined; or, Its False Spokes Extracted, and an Exhibition of Elder Graves, Its Builder, in a Series of Chapters* (Nashville: published for the author, 1856), 312. There is no paper trail to establish that Howell, Henderson et al. directly pulled this censure from Brownlow.

[51] Graves, "Abolitionism and the S.W. Baptist," *Tennessee Baptist*, July 17, 1858, [2], where he acknowledged himself as a slaveholder; and Graves, "Our Country," *Tennessee Baptist*, November 24, 1860, [2], which was one of the earliest clues of his sentiment favoring Southern secession.

ing the perception that personal vendettas and *ad hominem* innuendos could be found on both sides.

If the editorial combat in Southern Baptist life indicated profound divisions between Landmarkers and their foes, the situation was even more severe at First Baptist of Nashville. In light of all that had transpired since Howell's return to the pulpit in 1857, it seemed unworkable for the pastor and Graves to remain part of the same congregation. While fending off broadsides from other Baptist papers during the summer of 1858, Graves seemed resigned to an inevitable rupture where he might lose his ecclesiastical standing.[52] His premonition of looming dark days proved to be correct.

CHURCH TRIAL AT FIRST BAPTIST, NASHVILLE

Since Graves's journalistic barrage against his pastor was so public—even while Howell's negative ruminations about the editor were more private—few were surprised when First Baptist brought formal charges against the Landmark patriarch in September of 1858. Graves evidently was not in Nashville when the indictment against him was initially presented. After some delay, the actual trial ran October 12–18 of the same year and centered on five specific allegations, all of which came under the umbrella of what church documents labeled "grossly immoral and unchristian conduct." [53] In particular, the church cited Graves for: (1) seeking to bring "reproach and injury" upon his pastor through "false and malicious representations" in the *Tennessee Baptist*, thus forcing a "collision" between Howell and A. C. Dayton; (2) distracting and dividing First Baptist by stirring conflict through "inflammatory articles" in his newspaper; (3) publishing "foul and atrocious libels" in his paper against Howell; (4) attacking and slandering

---

[52] Grice and Caudill, "Graves-Howell Controversy," 581–82.

[53] "Impeachment Charges," Howell Collection, 1:[1ff.], which stated and documented the charges against Graves. An earlier draft was sent by Howell to Samuel Henderson of the *South Western Baptist*, further intimating direct contact between the Nashville pastor and one of Graves's adversaries. See "Impeachment Charges vs. Graves sent to Sam Henderson of Tuskegee, Ala., for Review," Howell Collection, 1:[1–15]. The papers in the Howell Collection mainly give his and the church's perspective, although they include statements and letters from Graves. See also Howell's *A Memorial*, 2:25ff. For a document that primarily represented Graves's defense against the charges, see Graves, ed., *Both Sides: A Full Investigation of the Charges Preferred against Elder J. R. Graves by R. B. C. Howell and Others* (Nashville: South-Western Publishing House; Graves, Marks & Co., 1859). Some of this volume incorporated material from the *Tennessee Baptist*, which naturally looked after Graves's interests during and after the trial. In response, some members at First Baptist launched the *Baptist Standard* less than a month after the trial, with church member L. B. Woolfork serving as editor. It survived about two years. See Grice and Caudill, "Howell-Graves Controversy," 582.

other Baptist ministers and leaders in his paper; (5) uttering and publishing "willful and deliberate falsehoods." [54] In substance, the counts that the church cataloged against a controversial member were at best indirectly connected to Landmarkism. Graves was actually being investigated primarily for alleged ethical and behavioral breaches relating to his work as a religious journalist. At the same time, Landmarkism remained as the elephant in the room; the most prominent Landmarker of the time faced a tribunal where his anti-Landmark enemies outnumbered his pro-Landmark friends.

Even though it involved some issues that stretched well beyond the life of one local church, the case against Graves moved forward when the congregation gathered on October 12, 1858. The session continued after midnight, and by vote of 91 to 48, the members present agreed to continue with the trial. Graves, who was accompanied by a large group of apparently noisy followers, avowed that the proceedings violated the guidelines of Matt 18:15–17 for resolving disputes among believers in the church. When it became clear that he would lose his argument, he and 23 followers exited the meeting, reconvened in another location, and declared themselves to be the "true" First Baptist Church of Nashville. In the absence of Graves and his supporters, Howell's church conducted five more trial sittings with the result that Graves was found guilty on all five charges. On October 18, the church voted overwhelmingly—with one dissenting vote on one of the counts—to expel the *Tennessee Baptist* editor from its membership. [55]

In the end, both sides claimed their causes were righteous and their motives pure. First Baptist felt compelled to act and believed that it did so "deliberately, prayerfully, scripturally, intelligently, firmly, unmoved by the fear of man, or the apprehension of consequences. Duty is ours. We leave consequences to God." [56] As for Graves, by the end of 1858 he assumed the stance of a holy martyr who had suffered unjustly: "We have been called to pass through a fiery trial. . . . We were charged, yea, under plea and cover of Church authority, openly defamed and libeled mightily before the public, and the specifications slanderously withheld from us." [57] As is often the situation in fervent conflict, both parties appeared to be blinded to their own foibles and missteps.

For example, Howell's own comments in the archival papers indicate that he suffered singular grief over Graves's handling of a piece of personal correspondence. On April 3, 1858, the First Baptist pastor sent Graves a note about the editor's "prominent"

---

[54] "Impeachment Charges," Howell Collection, 1:[1ff.].

[55] "The Graves Trial," Howell Collection," 1:[1–31]. Cf. "Proceedings of the First Baptist Church at the Meeting on the Night of the 12th of Oct. 1858," *Tennessee Baptist*, October 23, 1858, [2–3].

[56] "The Graves Trial," Howell Collection, 1:[31].

[57] Graves, "The Year and Its Close," *Tennessee Baptist*, December 25, 1858, [3].

participation in a church prayer meeting when Howell was absent. Although Howell marked the letter "strictly private," Graves apparently showed it to other church members and then printed it several months later "with false glosses in his paper." [58] Hence Howell's hurt over a betrayal of confidentiality compounded his annoyance, which had been brewing for many months, over Graves's public crusade against him.

While Graves's standards of journalistic decorum certainly fell well short of what might be expected from an ordained minister, let alone a committed Christian, Howell's spin on the entire controversy misleadingly portrays him as the utterly innocent party. The official charges against Graves, which the First Baptist pastor surely approved in advance of the trial, blamed the Landmark editor for the feud between Dayton and Howell. Yet in *A Memorial*, Howell later wrote dismissingly of Dayton, calling the one-time Bible Board secretary an "agent of Mr. Graves." Howell also judged Dayton as an example of the reality that "talents and Christian morals are not always associated." [59] In short, Graves's editorial columns were not absolutely essential ingredients in the Graves-Dayton rift. Howell did not like either Dayton or Graves because they were Landmarkers and northerners. More important, the SBC president easily sustained his controversy with the author of *Theodosia Ernest* on personal, ideological, and institutional grounds. Graves might have aggravated the strained relationship between Howell and Dayton, but he did not cause it. It may well be that in the broader framework of the Graves-Howell quarrel, Dayton became an unwitting pawn who was used in different ways by each side.

At the same time, Graves probably went too far when he contended five months after his trial that his then former pastor "used his influence to destroy Elder Dayton." In that same context, the Landmark founder bitterly claimed that his exclusion from First Baptist "was maliciously determined upon and avowed before the prosecutor left Richmond. . . . The course he pursued, from the day of his arrival, to effect my disgrace, when *professing friendship* to my face, you have seen." [60] Graves evidently had not learned much from what transpired in 1858; it was precisely this kind of unrestrained and accusatory rhetoric that had contributed to his ecclesiastical troubles in the first place. The tragedy of the discord at First Baptist is that the two major antagonists were

---

[58] "The Graves Trial," Howell Collection, 1:[11–14]. Cf. Graves, "That Correspondence," *Tennessee Baptist*, October 9, 1858, [2]. In the latter piece, Graves reported that he had sent a letter to Howell on April 5, 1858, requesting a private meeting. The letter was unopened, and other correspondence during the summer of 1858 reveals that further attempts to resolve the Graves-Howell conflict in a nonpublic manner came to naught. Cf. "The Graves Trial," [15–26].

[59] Howell, *A Memorial*, 2:18–19.

[60] Graves, "External History," *Tennessee Baptist*, March 12, 1859, [2].

both stubborn men whose egos bruised too readily. Neither Graves nor Howell seemed disposed to settling their differences in constructive ways; reconciliation might undermine the pursuit of goals for which they were both willing to contend. Indeed, both leaders may have sensed that in this local congregational upheaval some broader questions about Baptist polity and identity would inevitably surface. Unfortunately, their courses of action sometimes seemed to imply that the end justified the means.

LANDMARK VICTORIES IN TWO ASSOCIATIONS

Despite his setback at First Baptist, J. R. Graves knew that he still enjoyed significant backing in Middle Tennessee and other areas. Just five days after Graves was disciplined by his former church, the Baptist General Association of Tennessee and North Alabama met in Lebanon, a smaller town east of Nashville. The assembly elected Dayton as moderator to replace Graves, who had held the position at the three previous annual sessions. This association also accepted the Graves faction as the legitimate First Baptist Church of Nashville, refusing to sit delegates from the historic congregation because it had violated New Testament procedures and could no longer be considered a genuine Baptist church.[61] Just as anti-Landmarkers had excluded Graves from a local church, his Landmarkist allies promptly barred the original First Baptist Church from a relatively large association that actually functioned like a state convention. Howell found this deeply disturbing, depicting the General Association as a missionary organization that lacked the ecclesiastical authority to take such action. Moreover, he proclaimed that Baptist principles were at stake: "This case will test the polity of our churches. It will either destroy or establish it." [62] From this point on, Howell relentlessly warned against Landmarkist threats to the rights and privileges of autonomous Baptist churches.

In February of 1859 First Baptist of Nashville responded to the actions of the General Association by formally expelling Dayton and other supporters of Graves, including employees of both the South-Western Publishing House and the *Tennessee Baptist*. By that time, the Graves group had elected the *Tennessee Baptist* editor as pastor and was worshipping in a rented fireman's hall; it named itself the Spring Street

---

[61] "Address of Howell to Committee of Baptist State Convention of Mississippi, Aug. 1860," Howell Collection, 2:[50]; "Proceedings of the General Association in Regard to the First Baptist Church of Nashville," *Tennessee Baptist,* October 30, 1858 and November 6, 1858, both [2]; and A. C. Dayton, "Can We Have Peace Now?" *Tennessee Baptist,* November 13, 1858, [3].

[62] Howell, *A Memorial,* 2:68–69, 85.

Baptist Church upon learning that it could not legally use the First Baptist moniker. In addition, the Spring Street congregation derisively referred to its former church as "the Howell society." In light of these steps of overt separation, traditional First Baptist primarily invoked charges of schism against Dayton, W. P. Marks, A. B. Shankland, and other Graves associates. By the end of February, a total of 23 members of FBC had been excluded "as persons who have banded themselves against the church, as persons who refuse to hear the church, as defamers of its character, as conspiring to break down its discipline, and as having placed themselves without the pale of Christian fellowship."[63] The fact that the rupture was officially spread out over several months likely compounded its agony and emotional intensity.

Early in March of the same year, 20 churches from the Concord Baptist Association—at the request of Graves's new congregation—conducted a council at the Odd Fellow's Hall in Nashville at which Graves himself spoke for a total of 16 hours over three days to answer the charges that had been the grounds of his dismissal from First Baptist. No one from Howell's church was invited or in attendance at this gathering. The Landmark patriarch reiterated many of the arguments he had already set forth, particularly the claim that his former church had not followed Matthew 18 and, therefore, its actions against him were null and void and it could not be regarded as a true church. Although its ecclesiastical status was debatable, the council absolved Graves of all counts of wrongdoing and also condemned First Baptist for its proceedings against the Baptist editor. Graves's colleague J. M. Pendleton wrote that "[t]he decision of the Council was a triumphant acquittal of Brother G. from the absurd charges brought against him." [64]

As a follow-up in August, the Concord Association ratified with only one negative vote the decisions made at both the General Association meeting in the fall of 1858 and the February 1859 special council. It likewise called upon First Baptist "to correct the disorder into which it has fallen, so that peace may be restored to our Zion." [65] In effect, First Baptist had now lost its standing in two key cooperative organizations, even as the Spring Street congregation gained recognition. At least at regional and state levels, FBC

---

[63] "Report from Committee to 'labor with' Graves's Followers," *Howell Collection*, 1:[7]. For a helpful summary of the expulsion process, see Grice and Caudill, "Graves-Howell Controversy," 582, which reported that the number of exclusions reached 47 by April of 1860. Cf. Howell, *A Memorial*, 2:75–83.

[64] See J. M. Pendleton, "The Council," *Tennessee Baptist,* March 12, 1859, [2]. Reports on the examining council continued to run in the newspaper through the issue of May 14, 1859. Much of the material from the council and the articles in the *Tennessee Baptist* ended up in Graves, ed., *Both Sides.* Cf. Howell, *A Memorial*, 1:244; 2:93–95.

[65] "Report of the Committee," *Tennessee Baptist,* August 13, 1859, [2]. As chair of the committee, Pendleton was one of the Concord report's signatories.

came to experience what James Tull aptly described as "the progressive isolation" from its own denomination.[66]

Given Landmarkism's preoccupation with the nature and practices of the church, a note of irony surfaced when Pastor Howell raised ecclesiological issues in his rejoinder to what had transpired at the associational sessions. In his comments on one of the addresses in which Graves defended himself against the FBC indictment, Howell averred that the Landmarker now

> denies that the disciplinary decisions of a *church* are final, since a council, or an association, may revise, annul, or reverse them. Thus he repudiates the whole doctrine of church independance [*sic*] and sovereignty. . . . It is therefore an unquestionable fact that Mr. Graves is not now a Baptist in principle. . . . To our minds it is clear that *Mr. Graves intends to organise, and that he is now engaged in organising a new sect of his own.*[67]

Furthermore, Howell sounded off in tones reminiscent of Graves's republican rhetoric when he characterized as "ecclesiastical despotism" and "tyranny" the recently discernible trend of associations disrespecting the disciplinary actions of a local church. Moreover, the Nashville pastor repudiated *ex parte* councils like the one held by the Concord churches: "[They] are unscriptural, unbaptistic, and their decisions are of no force, or authority whatever." [68] In the aftermath of the fracas in his own congregation, Howell ultimately emerged as the more aggressive champion of local church autonomy than his Landmark opponents.

On the other hand, Graves divulged soon after his ecclesiastical trial that he allowed for limitations on the independence of a single church in some circumstances. He commenced to emphasize the rights of minorities, especially if they were trampled on by an oppressive congregation or its pastor. Indeed, the Landmark founder sought to lace his arguments with the same republican language that he had used earlier to caution against the unchecked power of agencies or institutions beyond the local church. In one of his most definitive statements on the matter, he disparaged the "unscriptural and unscrupulous action" of First Baptist Church, declaring that it was not binding on other churches.

---

[66] J. E. Tull, "A Study of Southern Baptist Landmarkism in the Light of Historical Baptist Ecclesiology" (Ph.D. diss., Columbia University, 1960), 414.

[67] "Graves's Speech before the Tenn. Convention [?], March 1859," Howell Collection, 1:[23, 33–34]. The emphases are in the original.

[68] Howell, *A Memorial*, 2:66, 102.

For Graves, the majority at his former church represented an unbiblical and intolerable tyranny. He thus posed some rhetorical questions about majority rule: "Is it popery full grown? . . . Will they [Baptists] enthrone the papacy in every Church and crown their pastors popes? Will they not rebuke this impious assumption of Church and ecclesiastical power on the part of a few ministers and their partisans who seem determined to uphold them, if it cost the ruin of the denomination?" The editor concluded with a ringing avowal of the inalienable rights of an unjustly expelled church member—like himself—to appeal his case to another church or group of churches: "No individual, however humble, can be long unrighteously oppressed by the tyranny of the pastor, or the malice of the dominant party in the Church. His just rights, if denied him in one Church, can be restored to him in another. It is like this in our glorious Republic." [69] It was from these considerations that Graves built his rationale for authorizing associations to serve as courts of appeal, that is, to review and even reverse the internal verdicts of local congregations, especially those involving church discipline.

It was precisely this notion of associational power that unnerved Howell. He roundly accused the Landmarkers of compromising their principles of church polity, quoting passages from Graves's *The Great Iron Wheel* and Dayton's *Theodosia Ernest* to show that they strongly upheld local church autonomy before the conflicts of 1857–58.[70] The SBC president sniffed out a potential hierarchy that would accompany these appellate tribunals. Moreover, he eventually dressed down the Graves party for both its inconsistency and expediency:

At present the danger threatens to come, and quite naturally, from that very quarter in our ranks, which is most vociferous in its denunciations of the power and tyranny alleged to be exercised in the government of other denominations. With these men, power it would seem, is only deprecated, when it is against them, and church sovereignty only maintained when it can be made to subserve

[69] All the citations in this paragraph are from Graves, "The Rights of a Church, and the Rights of Church Members," *Tennessee Baptist,* May 21, 1859, [2].
[70] "Address of Howell to Committee of Baptist State Convention of Mississippi," Howell Collection, 2:[48–49]. Cf. n20 above. As far back as 1848, however, "Veritas" complained that "Fidus" "sets up the association as a kind of court of appeal, where the action of churches may be negatived and overruled." See "Letter from 'Veritas,'" *Tennessee Baptist,* June 22, 1848, [2]. If "Fidus" and Graves were indeed one and the same, this comment might have been an early hint about a latent Landmark discrepancy in reference to the autonomy of the local church.

their purpose. Power in their own hands, legal, or illegal, is exercised and defended to the last extremity.[71]

While perhaps exaggerating the ulterior motives of his rivals, Howell nonetheless scored some debating points by suggesting that Landmark ecclesiology had been adjusted in reaction to what had occurred at First Baptist Church.

As James Hilton astutely observed, the Graves-Howell dispute provoked discussions of significant polity issues in Baptist life. In his assessment, the standoff of 1857–59 "perhaps more than any other controversy in Baptist history, examined the competency of a local congregation to deal with its own affairs and also questioned the authority an association, convention, or special council has in recognizing the autonomy of a local church." [72] In the context of formative denominational expansion by Baptists in the South, both Graves and Howell alerted their constituencies to fundamental questions about the authority and structure of various ecclesiastical bodies. For the most part, Hilton's theological analysis probes the implications of the debate in the late 1850s for Baptist views of local church autonomy and independence; the marks of a true church; the exercise of church discipline; the relationship of discipline to church comity (i.e., how an act of exclusion in one congregation influences other churches); and the role and authority of associations, especially pertaining to councils and tribunals that might be set up to examine specific cases of discipline in local churches. Hilton measured the strengths and weaknesses of the competing ecclesiologies, concluding that Howell was more protective of individual church autonomy than his Landmarker foe. At the same time, Graves seemed more sensitive to the rights of minorities, as well as to the independence and sovereignty of all other churches—particularly those that might be part of an association or convention.[73]

Since the ecclesiological aspect of the controversy between Graves and Howell encompassed basic matters of a young denomination's identity, it was inevitable that dissonance between these two leaders would escalate beyond Middle Tennessee and

---

[71] Howell, *A Memorial*, 2:66. Ironically, Graves complained in the late summer of 1859 that he had faced intense opposition—presumably during his controversy with Howell—because "we have opposed and exposed the errors in the doctrines and practices of other denominations." See Graves, "Volume XVI," *Tennessee Baptist,* September 3, 1859, [2]. Howell surely would have been quick to dispel that notion. For a more recent critique of Landmark inconsistency, see Tull, "A Study of Southern Baptist Landmarkism," 418–26.

[72] Hilton, "Robert Boyté Howell's Contribution to Baptist Ecclesiology," 141.

[73] See ibid., 156–214, for Hilton's extended discussion of ecclesiological issues.

come to occupy the attention of the Southern Baptist Convention as a whole. After all, Howell served as SBC president during the time that he was battling Graves. In addition, Graves's newspaper had circulated in other regions of the South for many years. They were probably two of the best known personalities in denominational life. Consequently, no one was really shocked when Howell's former stomping ground of Richmond, Virginia, provided the venue for the next phase of his clash with Graves and the Landmarkers.

THE SBC MEETING OF 1859

Although J. R. Graves was not as heavily involved as R. B. C. Howell in the institutional side of his denomination, the Landmark founder had demonstrated a generally favorable attitude to the SBC since its founding in 1845. In addition to reporting regularly on denominational life in the *Tennessee Baptist*, he was active in associational life, as well as in some educational and mission agencies that boasted at least an indirect affiliation with the SBC. His accounts of what were then biennial convention meetings sometimes testified to his own participation. For example, he was a "delegate" to the 1851 SBC gathering in Nashville over which Howell presided; he also made an unsuccessful run for the office of corresponding secretary, losing on the fourth ballot.[74] At the same time, the Baptist editor never hesitated to criticize denominational organizations—local, state, or national—when he felt that they were not operating at full effectiveness.[75]

By the time that the Richmond assembly of the SBC convened in early May of 1859, several developments over the previous two years provided much fodder for contentious floor sessions: (1) A. C. Dayton's resignation from the denomination's Bible Board; (2) the launching of the independent Southern Baptist Sunday School Union with Dayton as its head; (3) Graves's expulsion from a church pastored by the convention president serving his fourth consecutive term; (4) the Spring Street church's affirmation by the Baptist General Association of Tennessee and North Alabama; (5) the full vindication

---

[74] "Southern Baptist Convention," *Tennessee Baptist,* May 17, 1851, [2–3]; and May 24, 1851, [2–3]. The 1851 convention occurred not too long before the famous Cotton Grove meeting.

[75] E.g., Graves, "Address to the Baptist [*sic*] of Tennessee—Number 2. Home Mission Boards—Defects in Their Missionary Polity and Operations—Suggestions," *Tennessee Baptist,* May 24, 1849, [2]; and Graves, "Address to the Baptist [*sic*] of Tennessee. Number 3. Defects in the Appropriations and Instruction by Our Executive Boards—Tract Distribution—Pastors Work—Policy of Our Executive Boards," *Tennessee Baptist,* July 12, 1849, [3].

of Graves by a special council of the Concord Association; and (6) the stripping of Howell's church in Nashville of all its denominational ties except the SBC. The gathering in Richmond certainly had the potential to splinter the young SBC. In reality, the organization faced its first momentous crisis since it had been established 14 years earlier.

On top of the issues that had caused the messy schism at First Baptist of Nashville, Graves hammered away at a separate polity question in the months leading up to the Richmond meeting. Drawing once again on his roots in the Separate Baptist tradition, the Landmark editor critically targeted the suitability and ecclesiological integrity of denominational mission entities. It was in that setting that he enlisted the help of independent-minded New Englander Francis Wayland, the pastor and college president who staunchly defended the prerogatives of local churches over against the "centralizing machinery" of missionary agencies (e.g., the American Baptist Missionary Union) that might undermine them. Early in 1859 Graves ran Wayland's opinions in a three-part series in the *Tennessee Baptist.* One of Wayland's proposals, in fact, gave an inkling of what Graves had in mind for Southern Baptist missions. The distinguished Baptist educator called on individual churches or groups of churches to appoint and support missionaries: "The mission or missionary thus supported by a Church, would look to this Church, or combination of Churches, for support, and would be responsible to them and them only." [76]

Way land's direct missions approach, which promised to eliminate bureaucratic structures in the missionary enterprise, attracted the attention of N. M. Crawford, the president of Mercer University in Georgia. Crawford then sounded similar notes for Baptists in the South, providing Graves with another respected voice to cite in support of efforts to streamline missions.[77] At the same time, it was not entirely clear in the weeks before the 1859 convention that Graves intended to seek the imminent eradication of the

[76] Francis Wayland, "Missions. Thoughts on the Missionary Organizations of the Baptist Denomination, Number I," *Tennessee Baptist,* February 12, 1859, [3]. The other two articles appeared in the February 19 and 26, 1859, issues of the same newspaper. Cf. the discussion of Wayland in the first chapter above. For the broader context of Graves's interest in Wayland's ideas about mission agencies, see M. G. Bell, "James Robinson Graves and the Rhetoric of Demagogy: Primitivism and Democracy in Old Landmarkism" (Ph.D. diss., Vanderbilt University, 1990), 180–230; A. Lamkin Jr., "The Gospel Mission Movement within the Southern Baptist Convention" (Ph.D. diss., Southern Baptist Theological Seminary, 1980), 31–40; D. L. Saunders, "The Relation of Landmarkism to Mission Methods," *Quarterly Review* 26 (April–May–June 1966): 43–57; and Tull, "A Study of Southern Baptist Landmarkism," 430–51.

[77] N. M. Crawford, "The Gospel System of Missions," *Tennessee Baptist,* September 4, 1858, [1]; Graves, "Missionary Boards, & c," *Tennessee Baptist,* April 16, 1859, [2]; and Crawford, letter to the *Christian Index,* April 8, 1859, reprinted in *Tennessee Baptist,* May 14, 1859, [1].

SBC's most visible missionary agency. In March of 1859 he indicated that such a move would require extensive groundwork: "The Foreign Mission Board, with some modifications of its powers, is doubtless a necessity now, and will be for years to come. It ought not to be abolished until a better one can be devised to take its place, and the new one well understood and cheerfully acquiesced in by the churches or the larger portion of them." [78] Nevertheless, Southern Baptists had cause to worry that yet more tinder might stoke the fires of discord that threatened to spread from Middle Tennessee.

The Richmond meeting turned out not to be nearly as cataclysmic as many anticipated. There were 580 messengers in attendance, which was a remarkable increase from the 184 at the 1857 biennial in Louisville. In a compromise, messengers from both Spring Street and First Baptist churches in Nashville were seated. Despite the best efforts of Graves, Dayton, Pendleton, and other Landmarkers against him, Howell was reelected as convention president on the first ballot. Perhaps sensing that this might not be in the best interests of Southern Baptist harmony, the Nashville pastor "respectfully declined" to serve; Richard Fuller of Baltimore, Maryland, was then chosen after four ballots to replace Howell. Attempts by Landmarkers to abolish the Bible Board—which they had been attacking since Dayton's resignation as secretary—or relocate it to Macon, Georgia, were similarly rebuffed.[79] Thus through the first few days of the convention, Landmarkers had failed to make significant progress on their goals.

On the matter of missions and missionary organizations, the convention struck a workable compromise. A special committee of inquiry was assigned the task of determining whether any changes were needed in the home and foreign boards to improve their efficiency. Graves was no doubt pleased that N. M. Crawford and J. M. Pendleton were among the 15 appointed to this group. On the last day of the 1859 gathering, committee chair W. P. Chilton presented the report in which the convention was reassured that no major changes in "the existing plans of missionary operation" were being contemplated. At the same time, a concession was granted to Graves and his supporters with the resolution that

---

[78] Graves, "Remarks," *Tennessee Baptist*, March 19, 1859, [2]. This item was in response to a column in the *Mississippi Baptist* that had speculated on the possible effects of the Graves-Howell controversy on the upcoming SBC gathering. Graves pledged to work for peace, which might explain the conciliatory tone of his comments.

[79] *Proceedings of the Southern Baptist Convention at Its Seventh Biennial Session, Held in the First Baptist Church, Richmond, VA, May 6th, 7th, 8th, 9th and 10th, 1859* (Richmond, VA: H. K. Ellyson, Printer, 1859), 13–24. On the messenger count, see J. C. Fletcher, *The Southern Baptist Convention: A Sesquicentennial History* (Nashville: B&H, 1994), 395. The count was twice as much as any previous SBC biennial.

in case any churches, associations, or other bodies entitled to representation in this Convention, should prefer to appoint their own missionaries and to assume the responsibility of defraying their salaries and entire expenses, that the respective Boards are authorized, under our present organization and fundamental rules, to become the disbursing agents of the bodies so appointing missionaries and appropriating funds, whether such contributions be intended for the civilization or the evangelization of the heathen; provided that such expenses of forwarding the money, as have to be specially incurred, be borne by the contributors.[80]

Following a floor discussion, which included an address by Graves, the committee report was adopted unanimously.[81]

Although the Richmond convention of 1859 represented at least a partial setback for the Landmark forces, Graves nevertheless put a positive face on what transpired. In the weeks after the meeting, he commented favorably on the "two plans" now available to churches for the appointing and sending of missionaries, and hence announced his intention to support SBC missionary endeavor with trust and enthusiasm: "We shall co-operate with the Foreign Mission Board with great pleasure, so far as it is in our power. A better Board, or one more worthy of confidence, cannot be found, in our opinion." [82] Rather than divide the SBC in a bitter response to his protracted warfare with Howell, Graves chose instead to affirm the missions consensus that had been central to the denomination's ethos since it had been organized in 1845. In fact, his loyalty to the SBC remained basically intact for the rest of his life.

The Landmark patriarch likewise took some steps to bury the hatchet with Howell and First Baptist of Nashville. Pendleton recounted that Graves utilized the mediatorial

---

[80] *Proceedings* (1859), Appendix L, 95–96.

[81] See ibid., 24–27, for the work of the committee on missions. Some of Graves's concerns about the FMB apparently focused on rumors that the SBC agency was assuming ecclesiastical authority in its examination of missionary candidates, perhaps even functioning somewhat as an ordination council. After receiving assurances about the board's operations in this regard, Graves's disposition became much more cooperative. See Ford, "Life, Times and Teachings of J. R. Graves," *Ford's Christian Repository and Home Circle*, March 1900, 164ff. In one of his few criticisms of Graves, Ford remarked that the Landmark founder sometimes accepted "exaggerated rumors without investigation." See also "Southern Baptist Convention," *Tennessee Baptist*, June 25, 1859, [4].

[82] Graves, "Inside and Outside Marks.—No. 3," *Tennessee Baptist*, June 25, 1859, [2]. Cf. Graves, "Way Marks. No. II," *Tennessee Baptist*, June 18, 1859, [2]. Additional Landmark support for the FMB was evident in J. M. Pendleton, "Southern Baptist Convention," *Tennessee Baptist*, May 21, 1859, [2].

services of N. M. Crawford in an attempt to confer with Howell at the Richmond meeting. Howell reacted to this approach with an ultimatum that Graves "should go to H's. Church and make confession, & c.," which effectively dashed any hopes for the two adversaries coming together.[83] Furthermore, the aforementioned action of the Concord Association in Middle Tennessee against First Baptist during the summer of 1859 put a virtually insurmountable distance between Howell's church and the Landmarkers.

The Aftermath of the Richmond Biennial

Nevertheless, Graves began 1860 with a pledge to avoid "[a]ll unnecessary controversies, personalities, and severity of language." [84] By the summer of that year the Baptist editor apparently sent a letter to his former church in which he confessed that "in his defence [*sic*] of the truth" as preacher and journalist he may "have erred as to some of my supposed facts, and possibly may have stated others too strongly, and without sufficient care as to the effect which they might produce on the feelings of my brethren." Moreover, he expressed manifest regret for possible offense given to Howell and even offered to "withdraw any thing and everything that may justly be construed into an intended insult, or injury to any of the parties concerned." [85] Graves's overture, which was made in advance of an unsuccessful bid by a committee from the Baptist State Convention of Mississippi to help reconcile the Landmarker with Howell and First Baptist, was spurned by the church.[86] Sadly, Howell died in 1868, without ever seeking a meaningful resolution to his rift with the Landmark founder. At that point, a somewhat chastened Graves noted his preference "to think of those pleasant years before alienation ensued that resulted in the disruption of our social and church relations." [87]

---

[83] Pendleton, "The Interview Sought and Avoided," *Tennessee Baptist,* June 4, 1859, [2].

[84] Graves, "The Tennessee Baptist for 1860," *Tennessee Baptist,* January 7, 1860, [2].

[85] "Report Prepared for Committee Appointed to Conduct on Behalf of the Church Negotiations with the Comm. of the Baptist State Convention of Mississippi, but Which Was Not Adopted," Howell Collection, 2:10.

[86] On the Mississippi Baptist mediation efforts, see Howell Collection, vol. 2, and Howell, *A Memorial,* 2:169–213.

[87] Graves, "Death of Eld. R. B. C. Howell," *Baptist,* April 11, 1868, [4]. In Wardin, *Tennessee Baptists,* 187, the dean of Tennessee Baptist historians interprets the Graves-Howell feud as a struggle for power with tragic results: "The episode injured the Baptist witness in Nashville, caused a serious church split, threatened to divide the SBC, forced Howell to forego another term as SBC president, and unfortunately left Howell, now nearing the end of an outstanding career, embittered against the Landmark leadership, an embitterment he carried with him to the grave." Bitterness is evident in ample abundance in Howell's *A Memorial.*

At times throughout 1860 Graves displayed a distinct edginess that detracted from his professed yearning for peace. Even as he continued to stress the rights of ecclesiastical minorities and otherwise to promote his Landmark agenda, he also uttered what appeared to be in blatant contradiction to his earlier statements: "I repudiate Associations and Councils as 'Courts of Appeal,' or as possessing authority over the church." [88] The Landmark spokesman, who was undoubtedly becoming weary of conflict, may have sensed that his revised ecclesiological principles now faced renewed challenges. Georgia Baptist leader P. H. Mell (1814–88), who would preside over the SBC for seven terms between 1863 and 1871, essentially sided with Howell and First Baptist of Nashville on the right of a local congregation to impose discipline on a member, which would be binding on all other churches who might otherwise be tempted to receive the excluded individual.[89] By the end of 1860, a weakened Landmark movement, despite an unending stream of *Tennessee Baptist* columns from Graves's pen, seemed incapable of mounting either a coherent or compelling campaign to match the efforts of the more promising years before 1859.

In point of fact, Graves ultimately lost the war with his former pastor and church, even though Howell incurred some collateral damage to both his emotional ballast and reputation as a statesman. In the matter of where to draw denominational boundaries, Howell's version of Baptist ecclesiological principles gained more adherents in the SBC than did Graves's. While both leaders contributed to compromises that salvaged denominational unity in 1859, Howell's views on local church governance and cooperative missionary strategies still held sway.[90] As the clouds of war darkened the horizon at the close of 1860, Southern Baptists turned to other priorities that were deemed to be more importunate than prolonging intramural struggles that worked against a still fragile denominational unity.

---

[88] Graves, "The Revised Iron Wheel. No. 1," *Tennessee Baptist,* July 21, 1860, [2].

[89] See P. H. Mell, *Corrective Church Discipline* (Charleston, SC: Southern Baptist Publication Society, 1860); and Graves, "The Revised Iron Wheel. No. 2. Which Polity Will Baptists Undertake to Defend: The Mell Polity or the Old Scriptural One?" *Tennessee Baptist,* July 28, 1860, [2]. Graves's ally, A. S. Worrell, a professor of Greek and Hebrew at Union University in Murfreesboro, wrote *Review of Corrective Church Discipline* (Nashville: South-Western Publishing House, 1860), as a counter to Mell.

[90]Weatherford, "The Graves-Howell Controversy," 259–64.

Chapter 7

Challenging Transitions and New Boundaries

The Memphis Years (1867–93)

BACKGROUND: THE CIVIL WAR YEARS

As the Graves-Howell controversy gradually ebbed, the *Tennessee Baptist* editor faced a significant crisis of a much different sort in the early 1860s. During his final years in Nashville, Graves directed a sizable portion of his editorial columns to the ever-growing likelihood of war between the North and South. While not abandoning the ecclesiological themes and denominational interests on which he had built his journalistic career, Graves clearly revealed his anxiety about the future of the United States. In light of the election of Abraham Lincoln to the presidency in November of 1860, the Landmark leader openly wondered whether a unified nation could continue to exist in any meaningful way. Graves professed to disavow party politics, but at the same time indicated that his newspaper would not ignore the divisive issues of the day. Moreover, the former Vermonter plainly expressed his opinions as a Tennessean who hoped that the national predicament could be resolved without violating the freedom of the section in which he had resided for two decades: "Our honor, personal interests, our property, our rights, our family and hearthstone are as much affected by its solution as those of any man upon whom a Southern sun shines." He ended his editorial with a prayer that the Union could somehow be preserved: "May Almighty God, save the fairest, and the most prosperous and happiest nation the sun ever looked down upon." [1] If his support for Southern secession was a bit muffled in November of 1860, a month later he boldly declared that

---

[1] J. R. Graves, "Our Country," *Tennessee Baptist,* November 24, 1860, [2].

if Tennessee did not join with South Carolina and potentially other Southern states in forming a separate government, *"we shall move South."* [2]

From late 1860 on Graves consistently wrote in favor of secession and the Confederacy, seeking to rally support in his own state as he alluded to the presence of Federal troops in the South: "What remains for us to do but to make common cause with our sister Southern States, and under a common flag manfully resist this invasion or perish in the ruins of our country." [3] His militant rhetoric paralleled what he sometimes used in other polemical contexts, showing that he could draw the boundaries of a divided nation as sharply as he previously set ecclesiastical and denominational borders. Just as he vigorously battled for genuine Baptist distinctives, he now entered the lists for the cause of sectional identity and honor. J. R. Graves was not one to back away from a fight that he deemed to be righteous.

What Graves may not have bargained for, however, was the relatively immediate toll that the war levied on the *Tennessee Baptist.* By the middle of 1861, he was forced to note a change in the paper's format that reduced it to its 1847 size; unpaid subscriptions had wreaked havoc with the periodical's finances.[4] Furthermore, his Landmark alliances began to unravel under wartime pressures. J. M. Pendleton, for example, stepped down as associate editor of the *Tennessee Baptist* in 1861 and moved to Ohio the following year. Pendleton's support for the gradual abolition of slavery and opposition to Southern secession put him at odds with his Landmark colleague—as well as making it unsafe for him and his family to remain in Murfreesboro.[5] Whereas Graves's publication ventures had generally prospered throughout the 1850s, he presently discovered that normal business routines often succumbed to the harsh realities of war.

---

[2] Graves, "A North and a South Preparing in the South," *Tennessee Baptist,* December 22, 1860, [2].

[3] Graves, "Our Danger and Our Duty," *Tennessee Baptist,* April 27, 1861, [2]. This was just after the Confederate bombardment of Fort Sumter in Charleston, South Carolina, and Lincoln's imposition of a blockade on the southern coast. Tennessee voted to secede on June 8, 1861, the last state to join the Confederacy. See Graves, "Duties Past and Present," *Tennessee Baptist,* June 22, 1861, [2].

[4] Graves, "Retrenchment," *Tennessee Baptist,* June 29, 1861, [2]. There was a brief restoration of the bigger format with the issue of October 19, 1861. Graves's *Southern Baptist Review* also permanently ceased publication in the summer of 1861 as part of the "retrenchment."

[5] Graves, "Our Associate," *Tennessee Baptist,* July 13, 1861, [2]. Cf. Graves, "Professor Pendleton," *Tennessee Baptist,* January 11, 1862, [2], where the editor claimed that Pendleton had shared his disappointment with Lincoln's government, although such sentiment does not mesh well with the latter's exit from the South several months later. On his relocation, see J. M. Pendleton, *Reminiscences of a Long Life* (Louisville: Baptist Book Concern, 1891), 129–34.

Undeterred, Graves valiantly attempted to keep the printing presses running. In August of 1861 he announced that his publishing house in Nashville was issuing a new series of Sunday school books.[6] He likewise solicited funds to print and provide Bibles and Testaments for Confederate soldiers. In fact, Jefferson Davis's secretary of war, L. P. Walker, soon authorized Graves to visit military camps and hospitals in Virginia to distribute copies of the Scriptures.[7] Graves's activism and support for the Confederacy, however, did not prevent the steady decline of its military situation in Middle Tennessee.

By early 1862, in fact, Nashville faced imminent danger in the form of advancing Union troops. Graves enlisted in the Confederate army and urged all who could handle a gun to mobilize for the defense of the Tennessee capital.[8] The February 15, 1862, issue of his paper proved to be the last one for five years, as the Baptist editor fled the city with his family upon hearing the news while in the pulpit of his church that Fort Donelson on the Cumberland River had fallen to the Federals. The city of Nashville was subsequently captured on February 24. In the meantime, the Graves clan headed to Huntsville, Alabama, on their way to Magnolia, Mississippi, where his father-in-law, George Snider, had set up residence since moving the previous year from Jackson, Tennessee.[9] A late March 1862 issue of the *Florence* (Alabama) *Gazette* posted a letter from Graves in which he explained to his readers that he had been forced to suspend publication of the *Tennessee Baptist*; his abrupt departure from Nashville prevented him from removing any of the equipment that would be necessary to keep his newspaper in circulation. He then painted a grim picture of his status, though at the same time he indicated his readiness for military action:

My business destroyed, my home in the possession of the enemy, and myself a refugee, I feel it my duty to offer my services to my country in this hour of her imminent peril. I have been urged by several prominent citizens of my own

---

[6] Graves, "The Grand March of Southern Independence," *Tennessee Baptist*, August 3, 1861, [2].
[7] Graves, "Way-Marks from the Potomac," *Tennessee Baptist*, October 12, 1861, [2]. Follow-up "Way-Marks" appeared in the issues of October 19 and 26, 1861. Cf. Graves, "Present Duties. No. 4," *Tennessee Baptist*, July 20, 1861, [2]; Graves, "Bibles and Testaments for the Soldiers of Our Confederate Army—A Great Southern Movement," *Tennessee Baptist*, August 10, 1861, [2]; and Graves's letter of August 29, 1861, "To the Baptists of the Southern Confederacy," *Tennessee Baptist*, September 7, 1861, [1].
[8] Graves, "Editorial Telegrams: The War at Our Doors," *Tennessee Baptist*, February 15, 1862, [2].
[9] On Snider's relocation, see "Dr. Graves in Mississippi—Dedication at Summit," *Tennessee Baptist*, April 13, 1861, [2], which was a reprint from the *Mississippi Baptist*. Unlike Graves, R. B. C. Howell decided to stay in Nashville and was arrested and imprisoned in 1862 when he refused to take a loyalty oath to the Union. See Howell, *A Memorial of the First Baptist Church, Nashville, Tennessee: From 1820 to 1863* (Nashville: First Baptist Church, 1863), 2:379–419.

State to raise a regiment, battalion or legion of true and tried men willing to bear a pike to thrust the vandal foe from our hearth-stones. Believing it to be a most formidable weapon in the hands of men determined to be free, I am willing by both word and deed to encourage our people to seize it with promptness and rush to the conflict.[10]

While Graves would eventually return to his primary calling as a Baptist journalist, the chaos of war marked the end of a long relationship with Nashville and a shorter one with the Spring Street Baptist Church in that city.

Graves's activities and transitions during the Civil War—including gainful employment—are decidedly difficult to track. He apparently was not in any one particular locale for any considerable length of time; rather, he moved around on a regular basis and served in various capacities: military chaplain, commander of a regiment of pike men, colporteur for the Virginia Baptist Sunday School and Publication Board, salt miner and pastor in Louisiana, revival preacher, and minister to the sick as well as supporter of an orphanage in Mississippi.[11] Presumably his family was based in Mississippi during most of the war, which allowed him to travel extensively. In 1863 he wrote to former colleague A. C. Dayton—who by then was in Georgia pastoring a church and editing the *Baptist Banner*—that he had journeyed almost 800 miles on horseback in the past year, in part because he was ministering to soldiers who were constantly on the march.[12] According to biographer O. L. Hailey, Graves accompanied Confederate troops at the battle of

---

[10] Graves, "To the Patrons of the Tennessee Baptist," *Florence Gazette,* March 26, 1862, available at http://freepages.genealogy.rootsweb.ancestry.com/~henle/Baptist/GravesLetter.htm (accessed November 19, 2010). The web site identifies the original date of the letter as February 12, 1862, although this would make it earlier than the last issue of the *Tennessee Baptist.* At Graves's request, his epistle was published in other periodicals. For example, see *Biblical Recorder,* April 16, 1862: 1. See O. L. Hailey, *J. R. Graves: Life, Times and Teachings* (Nashville: By the author), 78–79, on Graves's escape from Nashville, which is essentially borrowed from S. H. Ford, "Life, Times and Teachings of J. R. Graves," *Ford's Christian Repository and Home Circle,* March 1900, 166ff.

[11] For the best and most complete account of Graves's life during this period, see H. S. Smith, "A Critical Analysis of the Theology of J. R. Graves" (Th.D. diss., Southern Baptist Theological Seminary, 1966), 26–37. Smith engaged in an extraordinary search for information on Graves during the war years, when there was much less to go by from the Landmarker's own pen. For a broader context, see J. Early Jr., "Tennessee Baptists and the Civil War," *Tennessee Baptist History* 8 (Fall 2006): 7–24.

[12] Graves to A. C. Dayton, October 20, 1863, printed in *Baptist Banner,* November 28, 1863, 3, cited in Smith, "A Critical Analysis of the Theology of J. R. Graves," 35, n105. On Dayton's later years, see J. Burch, "A Tennessee Baptist Returns to Georgia: The Latter Life of A. C. Dayton," *Tennessee Baptist History* 7 (Fall 2005): 19–28.

Shiloh, Tennessee, in April of 1862. The Baptist chaplain allegedly assisted the mortally wounded General Albert Sydney Johnston "into a safe refuge beneath a sheltering tree," even though one eyewitness account does not confirm that incident.[13]

Although precise details are often missing for Graves's wartime experiences, he certainly was forced to cope with abundant discontinuity from his antebellum career. He enjoyed few opportunities to write, and his publishing endeavors remained suspended for the duration of the conflict. Family time appeared to be even more limited than it had been during the eventful period of the 1850s. While he probably welcomed a respite from the ecclesiastical controversy that preoccupied him before the war, normal church life proved to be elusive once hostilities commenced in 1861. In short, J. R. Graves likely yearned for more peaceful times and the prospect of resuming the pursuits that he had cherished during his years in Nashville.

Relocation to Memphis

After discovering that barely anything from his publishing business in Nashville had survived the war, Graves and his family relocated from Mississippi to Memphis, Tennessee, in early 1867.[14] The growing city on the bluffs above the Mississippi River, which was formally laid out in 1819, boasted over 22,000 inhabitants on the eve of the Civil War; this figure made it the sixth largest city in the South and the most populous in Tennessee. Despite the ensuing wartime conditions, growth remained steady in the 1860s, with the population almost doubling to 40,000.

Since its founding, Memphis gained economic strength largely through trade in slaves and cotton. In addition, its strategic location on the banks of a main river spurred the development of a major transportation network, first undergirded by flatboats and steamboats and later reinforced with an expanding railroad infrastructure. Location and transportation facilities combined to make Memphis a gateway to the West; indeed, its modern status as a distribution center actually has a long history. After an 1852

---

[13] Hailey, *J. R. Graves*, 80. Cf. Smith, "A Critical Analysis of the Theology of J. R. Graves," 31–32. I. T. Tichenor, another prominent Southern Baptist leader, was also present at Shiloh as a chaplain who actually moved to the front combat lines and engaged Union forces. See M. E. Williams Sr., *Isaac Taylor Tichenor: The Creation of the Baptist New South* (Tuscaloosa: University of Alabama Press, 2005), 33–37. Tichenor later served for a year (1871–72) as pastor of First Baptist Church of Memphis, where Graves was a member, and in 1882 became secretary of the SBC's Home Mission Board. See Williams, 68, 97ff.

[14] Hailey, *J. R. Graves*, 80; and Smith, "A Critical Analysis of the Theology of J. R. Graves," 37.

preaching appointment in the Bluff City, Graves himself sensed its remarkable potential: "This city is still growing rapidly, and is destined to become the commercial emporium of the South-West." [15]

The religious history of Memphis shared some parallels with that of Nashville. In both places an abundant number of camp meetings preceded structured congregational life. Likewise, Methodists and Baptists achieved early positions of denominational strength in both locations. For his part, Graves always enjoyed itinerating in West Tennessee and regarded the Baptists of the region as having at least some inclination toward Landmark principles. After all, he launched his movement in a rural part of Madison County, which was only about 75 miles from Memphis. Furthermore, C. R. Hendrickson, pastor of First Baptist Church in Memphis from 1852 to 1856, on occasion welcomed the *Tennessee Baptist* editor to his pulpit and also at times wrote for Graves's paper.[16] Memphis arguably lagged behind Nashville culturally, but the spiritual and ecclesiastical environment would not have appeared alien or unusual to Graves either as a visitor before the war or a permanent resident after it.

When the Graves family arrived in 1867, they found a city that had endured the Civil War with less overt damage and disruption than Nashville, even though Memphis had submitted to Union control as early as June of 1862. At the same time, the postwar situation signaled some acute medical, political, and social problems that threatened to impede the city's progress and cloud its future direction. Historian Gerald Capers colorfully described the unattractive urban landscape: ". . . in the late sixties the seamy side of Memphis with its mud, filth, political corruption, municipal debt, disease, and crime stood out in bolder relief than ever before." [17]

---

[15] Graves, "Our Note Book," *Tennessee Baptist,* July 24, 1852, [2]. For general historical information on Memphis, see G. M. Capers Jr., *The Biography of a River Town—Memphis: Its Heroic Age,* 2nd ed. (New Orleans: By the author, 1966); C. W. Crawford, *Yesterday's Memphis* (Miami: E. A. Seemann Pub., 1976); and W. Rushing, *Memphis and the Paradox of Place: Globalization in the American South* (Chapel Hill: University of North Carolina Press, 2009).

[16] See Graves, "Our Note Book," [2]; C. R. Hendrickson, "Will the World Be Converted before the Second Advent of Christ?" *Tennessee Baptist,* September 9, 1854, [3]; and "Brother Graves in Memphis," *Tennessee Baptist,* February 2, 1856, [2], which referred to "Pedobaptists" in attendance at Graves's sermons. On early religious life in Memphis and the 1839 founding of First Baptist, see R. P. Caudill, *Intertwined: A History of First Baptist Church, Memphis, Tennessee as Intertwined with the City of Memphis and Shelby County and the Baptists of the World* (Memphis: Riverside Press, 1989), 2–7. Graves and his wife affiliated with this church. He served as interim pastor for six months in 1868, as well as filling the pulpit on many other occasions. See Graves, "First Church," *Baptist,* July 25, 1868, [4]; and Caudill, *Intertwined,* 18.

[17] Capers, *Biography of a River Town,* 180.

In particular, two urgent matters caught the attention of J. R. Graves, albeit in different ways. First, a large influx of African Americans into Memphis during the war touched off a trend where they would constitute half of the city's population before the end of the nineteenth century. Most immediately, the demographic shift contributed to urban race riots and the shadowy presence of the Ku Klux Klan, at least in the more rural areas of Shelby County. Moreover, Radical Republican political dominance in Tennessee during the early part of Reconstruction only complicated the already strained relationships between blacks and whites.[18] Graves's columns in his newspaper, which he began publishing once again early in 1867 under the title the *Baptist*, demonstrated that he was well aware of the racial dilemma. Despite his earlier advocacy of slavery, he now sought to find more constructive solutions to the challenges of educating, employing, and evangelizing black citizens.[19] Of course, racial tension has persisted to this day as an intractable issue for Memphians.

Second, Memphis continued to suffer periodic outbreaks of infectious diseases due mainly to the poor sanitation to which Capers alluded. In the year that Graves and his family arrived, the city was hit with a cholera attack as well as the third yellow fever epidemic of its not quite half-century history.[20] Tragedy soon struck their household, as the editor's beloved mother Lois—a longtime widow who was 78 and had lived with Graves and his family for two decades—fell victim to the "yellow jack" in late October of 1867. Before Graves could work through the grief of losing his mother, his second wife Louise, whom he married in 1856, died of the same cause less than a week later. The Baptist editor, who occasionally composed poetry for his paper, expressed his profound sadness in "Alone," written in honor of his late wife. The last stanza is especially poignant:

> Lonely, lonely!
> Circled by her darkness only.
> While the flickering firelight fades,
> And the night-winds mournful sighing
> Seems to my sad heart replying

---

[18] Ibid., 163–79.

[19] Graves, "What Shall Be Done for the Blacks?" *Baptist,* May 11, 1867, 4. Cf. Smith, "A Critical Analysis of the Theology of J. R. Graves," 37–38.

[20] Capers, *Biography of a River Town*, 182–83. For the broader context of yellow fever, see M. C. Crosby, *The American Plague: The Untold Story of Yellow Fever, the Epidemic That Shaped Our History* (New York: Berkley Publishing Group, 2007).

With its ever wailing tone,

All alone, all alone! [21]

Since Graves was normally very reticent to share the inmost feelings about his personal life, the poem represents a rare moment of transparency.

Although Graves received many words of comfort and support from friends and colleagues, including J. M. Pendleton, the untimely deaths of his mother and wife meant essential adjustments for the family and disruptions to the *Baptist's* publishing schedule. Daughter Nora, who later married biographer Hailey, recovered from yellow fever; arrangements had to be made for her care as well as that of the other four children, since Graves still maintained a busy itinerary of preaching and other activities that often required extensive travel. In fact, Louise was commended after her passing for how she had made it possible for her husband to fulfill his many out-of-town appointments. [22] In order to find homes for his children—and recovery for his own mind and body from "what they have endured this past month"—Graves took a leave of absence and temporarily suspended publication of the paper for the remainder of 1867. [23] Ultimately, with the

---

[21] Graves, "Alone," *Baptist,* November 16, 1867, 4. For the death notices in Graves's newspaper, see "T." (J. Tovell), "Death of Mrs. Lois Graves," *Baptist,* November 2, 1867, 4; Graves, "The Shadow of Death," *Baptist,* November 16, 1867, 4; and "T.," "Another Death in the Editor's Family," *Baptist,* November 16, 1867, 4. Hailey, *J. R. Graves,* 101, incorrectly dated the deaths to 1868. S. H. Ford, who preached at both funerals, provided some of the information for Hailey, including the wrong date. See Ford, "Life, Times and Teachings of J. R. Graves," *Ford's Christian Repository and Home Circle,* April 1900, 231–33; and May 1900, 287. For Ford's participation in the funerals, see "T.," "The Funeral Service," and "Dr. Ford's Funeral Oration," *Baptist,* November 2, 1867, 4; and "Dr. Ford's Oration at the First Baptist Church," *Baptist,* November 16, 1867, 4. These articles confirm that Ford was off a year in his account, even though he was editing his journal in Memphis at the time.

[22] "T.," "Another Death in the Editor's Family," 4. On Nora, see Hailey, *J. R. Graves,* 102. On Pendleton's condolences, expressed in a letter of November 7, 1867, see "Sympathy," *Baptist,* November 23, 1867, 4. By early 1868 Pendleton was listed in the paper as an "Editorial Contributor." See Graves, "Our New Contributors," *Baptist,* January 1868, 4.

[23] Graves, "To Our Patrons," *Baptist,* November 23, 1867, 4. Cf. Graves, "Lights in the Darkness," *Baptist,* November 16, 1867, 4. The worst yellow fever epidemics in Memphis actually occurred in 1873 and 1878–79, when sometimes more than half the population evacuated. See Capers, *The Biography of a River Town,* 187–209. Graves was in Mississippi when the plague broke out in 1873, and his house in the suburbs was plundered. See Graves, "The Shadow of Death Passed," *Baptist,* November 22, 1873, [4]. The medical crisis in 1878 caused another hiatus in the publication of his newspaper. See "Resumption," *Baptist,* November 16, 1878, 596. He was away from Memphis for six months in 1878–79, which was not uncommon among the Protestant clergy during the intense outbreak of disease at that time. See Graves, "Home and Work," *Baptist,* March 15, 1879, 52–53. Cf. his somewhat defensive piece, "The Duties of Ministers in Epidemics," *Baptist,* March 22, 1879, 69. On ministerial evacuations, see Capers, *The Biography of A River Town,* 195.

encouragement of S. H. Ford, Graves decided that family stability would be enhanced by remarriage. In early 1869, about a year and three months after Louisa's death, he tied the knot with her youngest sister, Georgia Snider; they enjoyed what proved to be the longest of his three marriages, ending with the Landmark leader's death in 1893.[24]

In his reactions, first to the bruising conflict at First Baptist of Nashville in the late 1850s, and then to the subsequent dislocations of the war years, Graves had already pledged more than once to refrain from needless controversies, soften his rhetoric, and avoid *ad hominem* assaults on those with whom he disagreed.[25] The family calamities of the last several weeks of 1867 almost certainly inclined Graves to stick to these resolutions. He continued to stake out generally unmovable ecclesiological positions during the Memphis years, just as he had as a younger man. At the same time, he conveyed a gentler and more charitable tone in his publications.[26] In an earlier era, Graves was sometimes downright nasty; his literary demeanor became noticeably more tranquil after the Civil War, which seemed to make the *Baptist* both a less provocative and more pedestrian journal.[27]

Deadly yellow fever outbreaks and interrupted production of his paper were not the only setbacks that Graves encountered during his early years in Memphis. In fact, his difficulties in sustaining the *Baptist's* momentum on a scale like he had grown accustomed to in prewar Nashville were tied to more than just mosquito-spread infestations in swampy Memphis. Graves quickly discovered that running a publishing business in the economically-depressed South was a tricky proposition. Soon after settling in the Bluff City the Landmark entrepreneur attempted to revive his ruined Nashville firm under the label "Graves, Jones and Co." Due to inadequate private funding, he established the Southwestern Publishing Company late in 1868 as a joint-stock corporation. This venture failed in 1871, bringing substantial loss to those who had invested in it. In addition,

---

[24] See Ford, "Life, Times and Teachings of J. R. Graves," *Ford's Christian Repository and Home Circle,* June 1900, 354–55. Ford wrote of the renewed "family felicity" that Graves experienced after the 1869 wedding. Hailey, *J. R. Graves,* 3, dedicated his book to Georgia Graves and spoke of her long widowhood—she was still living when the volume was released in 1929.

[25] Graves, "The Tennessee Baptist for 1860," *Tennessee Baptist,* January 7, 1860, [2]; and Graves, "Half–Volume," *Baptist,* October 5, 1867, 4.

[26] In "Graves, James Robinson," *Encyclopedia of Southern Baptists* (Nashville: Broadman, 1958), 1:577, Homer Grice noted Graves's mellower disposition, although he saw it first evident in 1877. See also J. E. Tull, "A Study of Southern Baptist Landmarkism in the Light of Historical Baptist Ecclesiology" (Ph.D. diss., Columbia University, 1960), 498–99.

[27] C. W. Sumerlin, "A History of Southern Baptist State Newspapers" (Ph.D. diss., 1968), 350, characterizes the *Baptist* in Memphis as "mediocre" compared to the *Tennessee Baptist* in Nashville.

Graves's fundraising trips on behalf of the company not only were unsuccessful but also distracted him from his editorial responsibilities at the *Baptist*.[28]

Furthermore, the collapse of Southwestern contributed to the demise of the Southern Baptist Sunday School Union, which had been formally launched in Memphis in 1858 but had faltered during the Civil War. Graves sought to revive it, proposing in 1867 that the Southern Baptist Convention transfer its first Sunday School Board—which was set up in 1863—from Greenville, South Carolina, to Memphis and merge it with the SBSSU. Although the SBC approved this ill-fated step in 1868, it did not bode well for either organization. Southwestern procured a publishing contract with the SSB but, with the failures of both the publishing company and the SBSSU, the SBC consolidated the Sunday School Board with the Domestic and Indian Mission Board in 1873; a permanent Sunday School Board finally emerged in 1891.[29]

In the meantime, Graves desperately hatched one more publishing endeavor when he undertook to organize a new Southern Baptist Publication Society. Initially proposed in 1870, the agency began printing religious literature in 1873. The Landmarker based his ambitious plans on the belief that Memphis constituted a denominational center for the Baptists of the South and Southwest, which he documented with a railroad map supplied by the local Chamber of Commerce.[30] Graves's efforts, however, came in the context of a troubled decade marked by disease, widespread crop failures, and the lingering effects of the 1873 market panic. Moreover, it turned out that many of the SBPS's pledged bonds were never paid, leading to an extremely precarious financial situation. Questionable business decisions culminated with the Landmark champion's expensive desire to publish the full account of his debate in Carrollton, Missouri, with Methodist spokesman Jacob Ditzler. While this book project represented Graves's ongoing desire

---

[28] See Graves, "Absence," *Baptist*, May 2, 1868, [4]; "A.C.C." (A. C. Caperton), "'The Baptist' and Southwestern Publishing House," *Baptist*, May 2, 1868, [5]; Graves, "The Southwestern Publishing Company," *Baptist*, December 5, 1868, [4]; Graves, "Volume III," *Baptist*, July 10, 1869, [4]; and Graves, "'The Great West' and the S.W. Publishing House," *Baptist*, March 19, 1870. For a useful summary of publishing matters, see Grice, "Graves, James Robinson," 1:576–77.

[29] See Graves, "Sabbath-School Board," *Baptist*, June 4, 1870, [4]; and Grice, "Southern Baptist Sunday School Union," *Encyclopedia of Southern Baptists*, 2:1268.

[30] Graves, "Memphis As the Denominational Center of the Southern States," *Baptist*, June 6, 1874, [4]. For typical comments by the editor on the SBPS, see "Graves, "1871," *Baptist*, January 7, 1871, [4]; and Graves, "Volume Seven," *Baptist*, September 6, 1873, [4]. Coverage of the new SPBS in secondary sources includes Grice, "Graves, James Robinson," 577; Hailey, *J. R. Graves*, 99; Ford, "Life, Times and Teachings of J. R. Graves," *Ford's Christian Repository and Home Circle*, April 1900, 229–31; and Smith, "A Critical Analysis of the Theology of J. R. Graves," 45–48.

to highlight the borders between Baptists and other denominations, the over 1,100-page volume basically broke the bank.[31]

A disappointed Graves announced the liquidation of the SBPS in 1878. Its debt had been settled, but it lacked the financial resources to stay in business. The Baptist editor put up a brave front, writing that the society "will suspend further operations until the present hard times pass over, and confidence can be restored." [32] The SBPS, however, was never revived; instead, Graves assisted first his son and subsequently J. S. Mahaffy in the establishment of the Baptist Book House in Memphis, which published the books that he penned in the 1880s.[33] Through all the tribulations with his publishing business, his newspaper ultimately suffered as a constantly fluctuating subscriber base and his extended absences from Memphis took their toll, causing him to plead regularly with his readers for financial assistance.[34] Since Graves had always taken great pride in his journalistic achievements, the declining fortunes of the *Baptist* during most of the Memphis period undoubtedly grieved him. The overall frail condition of his postwar publishing enterprise confirms the judgment that the transition to Memphis was demanding, and that Graves's most successful years were in Nashville during the 1850s.

BOUNDARIES WITH CULTIC MOVEMENTS

The Graves-Ditzler tome demonstrated the continuity of Graves's longstanding proclivity to engage representatives of other denominations in heated debate. During his years in Memphis, he enlarged his passion for marking boundaries by taking on some

---

[31] J. R. Graves and J. Ditzler, *The Graves-Ditzler: or, Great Carrollton Debate* (Memphis: Southern Baptist Publication Society, 1876). See earlier references to this debate in chaps. 3, 4, and 5 above. The high cost of this book is noted in Ford, "Life, Times and Teachings of J. R. Graves," *Ford's Christian Repository and Home Circle*, April 1900, 229–30. For Graves's perspective, see his "Returned," *Baptist*, December 11, 1875, 52–53; and "Closed," *Baptist*, May 20, 1876, 405. The Landmark founder was aware of the society's shaky economic status even before planning to publish his debate with Ditzler. See Graves, "The S.B.P. Society," *Baptist*, January 16, 1875, [2].

[32] Graves, "Southern Baptist Publication Society," *Baptist*, March 16, 1878, 245. See his later postmortem in Graves, "Memphis and Its Papers, Etc.," *Baptist*, May 13, 1882, 756.

[33] Graves, "Southern Baptist Publication Society," 245; and Graves, "A New Firm," *Baptist*, April 17, 1880, 692. The *Baptist* editor had no direct financial interest in this publishing agency.

[34] See the following appeals by Graves: "Help Just Now," *Baptist*, December 6, 1873, [4]; "A Word with Our Patrons," *Baptist*, January 24, 1874, [4]; "Shall We Intermit Our Issues?," *Baptist*, June 20, 1874, [4]; and "Our Paper," *Baptist*, March 6, 1875, [2].

movements that can best be described as "new thought" or "harmonial" in nature.[35] In particular, the Landmark leader took on spiritism, the belief found in Swedenborgianism and other nineteenth-century religious groups that the dead exist in a spirit realm and communicate with those on earth through a medium.[36] Biographer Hailey, who seemed quite intrigued with the topic, wrote that his father-in-law took on the cult in the 1870s. The *Baptist*, however, published outlines of a lecture series on spiritism that Graves delivered in 1868 at First Baptist of Memphis in which he dismissed the ideology of the movement as a combination of Hinduism, Islam, and universalism.[37]

In the early 1870s the *Baptist* editor engaged Methodist Samuel Watson—a presiding elder in his denomination who endorsed spiritism—in a debate at the Greenlaw Opera House in Memphis. Hailey, waxing to the extreme limits of hagiography, judged that Graves had inflicted a death blow to spiritism in the region:

> Dr. Graves was in his prime, and what a man. Physically, without a blemish, and as graceful as Apollo. Intellectually, a combination of Aristotle and Paul the Apostle. Oratorically, a Cicero and a Chalmers combined. He was a philosopher, a theologian, and a "veritable walking encyclopedia," and a speaker with a voice upon which he could play as an organ. . . . He was a perfect master of himself, and of his subject, and soon was easily the master of his audience. He grasped the situation and dominated it and compelled the popular verdict.[38]

While the Landmark patriarch surely held his own, without Watson's testimony it cannot be ascertained whether it was, as Hailey asserted, a performance for the ages.

As a follow up to his encounter with Graves, Watson invited his sparring partner to a séance in early 1873 hosted by Charles Foster, the much-heralded "Chief of

---

[35] For the use of these terms, see S. E. Ahlstrom, *A Religious History of the American People* (New Haven, CT: Yale University Press, 1972), 1019–29.

[36] On the "Swedenborgian impulse" and spiritualism, see ibid., 483–90.

[37] Cf. Hailey, *J. R. Graves*, 85; and Graves, "Spiritism," *Baptist*, April 4, 1868, [4–5]; April 11, 1868, [4]; April 18, 1868, [4]; April 25, 1868, [4]; and July 4, 1868, [5–7]. Cf. Graves, *Spiritism. A Lecture* (Memphis: Southwestern Publishing Company, 1869). Later Graves dialogued critically with universalist John C. Burress. See Graves and Burress, *A Discussion on the Doctrine of Endless Punishment between Rev. J. R. Graves and Rev. John C. Burress* (Atlanta: J. O. Perkins & Co., 1880); and *Restorationism Refuted: The Last Letters of the Written Discussion between J. C. Burress and J. R. Graves* (Memphis: Baptist Book House, 1880). The Burress-Graves exchange began as a series in the *Baptist*, January 5, 1878, 82–84.

[38] Hailey, *J. R. Graves*, 87. He did not draw this effusive language from Ford. Cf. Graves, "The Clock Struck One, and Christian Spiritualist, Etc.," *Baptist*, July 27, 1872, [4]. Watson had written a book, *The Clock Struck One, and Christian Spiritualist* (New York: Samuel R. Wells, 1872).

Spiritualistic Mediums." The *Baptist* editor wrote at length in one of his columns about this weird incident, and Hailey incorporated it into his biography. Graves essentially played mind games with Foster that ended up embarrassing the spiritist in front of his other guests. For his part, Graves rejected the possibility of communicating with dead spirits and was surely convinced that none of *his* departed friends had been in contact with Foster. He also suggested that when some in attendance appeared satisfied that their host communicated with the dead, it was the result of mesmerism, animal magnetism, or clairvoyance.[39]

It may be problematic that Graves even agreed to attend the séance, although he seemed to take pleasure in setting Foster up for a fall. At any rate, the prolific Landmark writer utilized his encounters with Watson and Foster in a short study of the "middle life," or the intermediate state of souls before the resurrection and final judgment. In addition to attacking spiritism, Graves put forth a doctrine—in what he thought was his greatest book—that put him at variance with Baptist pastor-theologians like T. T. Eaton and J. M. Pendleton. The Baptist journalist drew a sharp distinction between paradise and heaven, arguing that the spirits of departed believers went to the former, which was part of *Hades*, while awaiting the ultimate paradise on earth after being reunited with their bodies. Conversely, the souls of the lost who died went to *Sheol*; they did not go to hell until after the final judgment. Where heaven fit into this scheme was not entirely clear, although Graves seemed to suggest that the bride of Christ would go there at the end of the millennial age.[40]

It is difficult to ascertain whether Graves's theology of the intermediate life predisposed him to become interested in refuting spiritism, or whether his combat with Watson and Foster motivated him to think through more systematically his understanding of the future state. There is no evidence that these issues interested him before his move to Memphis. Moreover, his growing interest in dispensational eschatology, which is discussed later in this chapter, possibly provoked his discussion of the relationship of paradise to the millennium. Whatever the reasons might have been, Graves manifested

---

[39] Graves, "Our 'Séance' with Foster, the Noted Test Spiritist of New York," *Baptist*, January 18, 1873, [4]; and Hailey, *J. R. Graves*, 87–96.

[40] Graves, *The Bible Doctrine of the Middle Life as Opposed to Swedenborgianism and Spiritism* (Memphis: Southern Baptist Publication Society, 1873), 22, 29–30, 53–78, 105. For the comment on this as his greatest book, see Graves, "Exegetical," *Baptist*, October 28, 1876, 740. For his differences with Eaton and Pendleton respectively, see Graves, "Paradise—Intermediate State," *Baptist*, January 24, 1874, [4]; and Graves, "Where is Paradise?" *Tennessee Baptist*, February 13, 1886, 6–7. His paper reverted to the *Tennessee Baptist* title with the issue of September 2, 1882.

a continuing fascination with the powers of the human mind, as well as a concern to set biblical Christianity apart from heretical deviations.[41] Indeed, his studies of these subjects in due course affected the assessment of postwar revivalism that he had previously begun.

PROPER BOUNDARIES IN REVIVALS

Throughout most of his career, J. R. Graves itinerated widely, filling many pulpits and conducting numerous revival meetings during which he developed some concerns about how his own power and eloquence as a speaker might unduly sway an audience.[42] After the Civil War, he commenced a meticulous scrutiny of the revival techniques of his day. Like Jonathan Edwards of an earlier epoch, Graves upheld the need for and value of genuine revival; at the same time, he shared the colonial New Englander's alertness to the dangers of counterfeit religion.[43] His eagerness for maintaining boundaries of propriety in revivalism almost equaled his zeal for preserving Baptist distinctives versus other groups.

Hence, between 1867 and 1883 the Landmark founder wrote several critical pieces about methods and exercises that typified much of nineteenth-century revivalism. He began by examining the popular tradition of holding revival meetings for prolonged periods of several days or more. While he had participated in protracted services and

---

[41] E.g., he launched a series in his paper that probed deeper into the problems with spiritualism and Swedenborgianism. It began with Graves, "The Science of Presentiments—Revelations to the Mind. No. 1," *Tennessee Baptist,* February 3, 1883, 6–7. It concluded with his "Mentigraphy—Mind Communicating Direct with Mind. No. VI," *Tennessee Baptist,* March 10, 1883, 6. Toward the end of his career, he wrote critically of the rising new thought religion known as Christian Science. His series began with Graves, "Christian Science Reviewed and Shown to Be Both Anti-Christian and Unscientific and Absurd," *Baptist and Reflector,* August 22, 1889, 7–8. It ended with his "Christian Science, No. IV; or, the Mediatorship of Christ," *Baptist and Reflector,* September 12, 1889, 7. In 1887 the *Tennessee Baptist* merged with the *Baptist Gleaner* to become the *Baptist,* effective with the issue of July 9, 1887. The new *Baptist* then consolidated with the *Baptist Reflector* of Chattanooga and began publishing in Nashville as the *Baptist and Reflector* with the August 22, 1889 issue. These developments were covered in the cited issues. Cf. Sumerlin, "A History of Southern Baptist State Newspapers," 360–61.

[42] See Hailey, "Dr. Graves as a Revivalist," *J. R. Graves,* 70–72. Ford, "The Life, Times and Teachings of J. R. Graves," *Ford's Christian Repository and Home Circle,* December 1899, 741–42, was not so explicit regarding Graves's fears about his personal magnetism as a preacher.

[43] See J. Edwards, *The Great Awakening,* ed. C. C. Goen, The Works of Jonathan Edwards, vol. 4 (New Haven, CT: Yale University Press, 1972).

did not object to them in principle, he feared that they were prone to certain abuses, including "boisterous preaching," as well as shouts and other noises for which he mostly blamed the Methodists.[44] The fact that he frequently targeted Methodism in his negative reviews of revivals indicates that he saw the opportunity to kill two birds with one stone: the boundaries he drew for revivalism likewise reinforced the ones he set against non-Baptist denominations. In later columns, he faulted Methodists for the "altar and bodily exercises" that filled their camp meetings, as well as their emotional abuse of the mourning bench where those under conviction went to pray and seek the prayers of others.[45]

After the publication of his article on protracted meetings, Graves found himself in a new row with the followers of Alexander Campbell. The Campbell movement as a rule took a more rational approach to the religious life that normally left minimal room for emotional outbreaks. Thus some Restorationists used Graves's warnings about protracted revivals as evidence that the Landmarker was opposed to "experimental religion." Of course, Graves expressed caveats about emotionalism for different reasons than did the Campbellites. In his response to them, he took yet another swipe at an issue that separated them from Baptists: "We assure our brethren when we embrace Mr. Campbell's views of baptism, we shall join the Catholic Church." [46] Perhaps he was subtly alluding to Campbell's belief that that there was no regenerating work of the Holy Spirit—which Graves knew might be accompanied by emotional manifestations—prior to baptism.

Nevertheless, Graves shared with Restorationists an uneasiness about revivals that centered excessively on religious experience. If anything, his concerns deepened in the aftermath of his exchanges with spiritists. In fact, the *Baptist* editor's hypothesis that mesmerism—a type of hypnotism—was lurking behind Charles Foster's séance apparently made him even more skeptical about the experimental aspects of some revivals. For example, later in the same year as the Foster episode, Graves penned a two-part series for his paper on the place of "feelings" in the Christian life. On the more negative side, he remarked that feeling was not a dependable base for assurance about salvation. More positively, he listed several signs of a truly regenerate person that carefully balanced the

---

[44] Graves, "Protracted Meetings," *Baptist*, September 7, 1867, 4.

[45] Graves, "Altar and Bodily Exercises," *Baptist*, August 8, 1868, [4]; and Graves, "Experience and the Mourners' Bench," *Baptist*, May 4, 1878, 357. His reactions to Methodist practices help to explain his opposition to "union" meetings where churches of different denominations came together to support revival. See Graves, "Revival," *Baptist*, April 24, 1875, 37; and "The Revival Period," *Baptist*, August 19, 1876, 581.

[46] Graves, "Altar and Bodily Exercises," 4. At the end of this column, he reprinted "Protracted Meetings."

emotional and volitional aspects of a believer's walk. Overall, he emphasized the transient nature of religious feelings.[47]

By the following year, Graves reflected specifically on "animal mesmerism" and its link to revival excitements. After a more general column on mesmerism and its relationship to dancing, he authored two articles in which he questioned emotional preaching that was directed to "animal sympathies," along with the hypnotic effects of altar calls and mourners' seats. He also identified manifestations of mesmerism in revivals such as the "happy laugh," jerking, and visions of angels. All such "overwrought excitement was the result of purely *mesmeric* influences" that needed to be divorced from revivals.[48]

Graves's crusade against revivalistic excess, while partly spurred by his propensity to stake out religious boundaries at several levels, nonetheless represents one of his more profound contributions to Baptist life in the second half of his career. Although the revival tradition has played a significant role in the shaping of both American Protestantism in general and Baptist culture in the South more specifically, it has not been an unmixed blessing. That a part-time itinerant evangelist emerged as an insightful critic of revivalism's more suspect practices is in itself an intriguing story.[49]

OLD LANDMARKISM AND A CLOSED TABLE

During his years in Memphis J. R. Graves continued to press his reading public on the issues of Baptist identity, particularly as they related to the doctrine of the church. For the most part, however, the Landmark patriarch seemed content to rehash the themes and arguments that had made him a widely-known controversialist before the Civil War. In the last quarter-century of his life, he failed to achieve a level of creativity that had sometimes characterized his work in Nashville. While his more restrained temperament was certainly welcomed in denominational circles, it appeared to have taken some of the verve out of his literary efforts.

---

[47] Graves, "Feeling in Religion. Feeling as an Evidence of Acceptance with God," *Baptist*, September 6, 1873; and "Feelings in Religion: No. 2. Evidences of Salvation," *Baptist,* September 13, 1873, [4].

[48] See Graves, "Mesmerism in Revivals," *Baptist,* September 26, 1874, [4]; and "Mesmerism in Religion," *Baptist,* October 10, 1874, [4]. His more general piece was "Facts in Mesmerism," *Baptist,* September 12, 1874, [4].

[49] One of Graves's last columns on revival was "Thoughts on a Revival," *Tennessee Baptist,* August 25, 1883, 6, where he declared that "the conviction and conversion of sinners is the inseparable fruit of a revival."

A dearth of freshness was evident in Graves's attempt in 1880 to set forth a definitive statement of his ecclesiology in *Old Landmarkism: What Is It?* As he reflected on a campaign that began early during his time in Nashville, he claimed a resounding vindication in the Baptist newspapers and associations throughout the South for his opposition to the practices of alien immersion and pulpit affiliation.[50] He likewise reiterated his longstanding hostility toward Pedobaptists and Campbellites, as well as his rejection of any notion of a universal church. Furthermore, he voiced fervent support for Baptist successionism, believers' baptism by immersion, the inalienable rights of autonomous local churches, and other cardinal features of a rigorous congregational church polity.[51] This manifesto of Landmark ideology incorporated very little that Graves had not expounded on many times in previous newspaper columns and books.

In his treatment of the Lord's Supper in *Old Landmarkism*, however, the Baptist editor's by now settled opinions disguised the reality that both his thought and practice on this subject had evolved over the years. When he discussed the distinguishing marks of an authentic church, his seventh point centered on the memorial meal as "a local church ordinance . . . never expressive of personal fellowship, or of courtesy for others." [52] The implications of this became clear in the next two chapters in which Graves vigorously attacked the practice of "intercommunion" or "denominational communion" where visiting Baptists were granted the privilege of receiving the elements in a Baptist church of which they were not members.[53]

In other words, the Lord's Supper was a local church ordinance exclusively for its members and no one else. As it turns out, Graves had shifted over a period of time to this stricter position of *closed* communion from an earlier acceptance of *close* communion, which allowed for intercommunion between Baptist churches. There is no evidence that he ever accepted *open* communion, where some Baptist congregations granted all believers in Christ—regardless of denominational affiliation—access to the communion table.[54]

---

[50] Graves, *Old Landmarkism: What Is It?* 2nd ed. (Memphis: Baptist Book House; Graves, Mahaffy & Company, 1881), xv. The first edition was in 1880.

[51] Ibid., passim. In light of his trial and expulsion from First Baptist Church in Nashville, it is interesting that Graves, 48, wrote: "A church is alone authorized to receive, to discipline, and to exclude her own members."

[52] Ibid., 80. In the same context (pp. 87–92), Graves maintained that the Lord's Supper should be celebrated with one loaf of unleavened bread and one cup of fermented wine.

[53] Ibid., 105–20.

[54] For a helpful clarification of the three terms used in this paragraph, see T. Wax, "The Case for Open Communion," Kingdom People, accessed January 11, 2011, http://trevinwax.com/2007/10/11/the-case-for-open-communion.

It is difficult to pinpoint exactly when the Landmark leader tightened his definition of "intercommunion." Graves himself asserted in 1881 that he had not written much about the Lord's Supper in his paper for 34 years, although this was a typical understatement on his part.[55] Evidence points to the Baptist editor participating in and even administering communion at the associational level not long after he started his career with the *Tennessee Baptist*. In addition, in 1856 he presided over the Lord's Supper at his home church in Vermont, and in 1860 permitted Baptists from other churches to receive the elements at his Spring Street church in Nashville.[56] Moreover, his earliest published comments on the Lord's Supper tended to favor close or denominational communion. In 1848, when he still accepted associational communion, he wrote of the Supper that "Baptists restrict it to immersed believers."[57] Total consistency, however, did not mark his perspective on communion practice during his years in Nashville. In response to a question put to him in 1854, he emphasized the vital connection between the Lord's Supper and local church discipline: "Let it be considered an axiom, that *each church must have the Disciplinary power over all she is warranted to invite to partake of the*

---

[55] Graves, *Intercommunion Inconsistent, Unscriptural, and Productive of Evil* (Memphis: Baptist Book House; Graves, Mahaffy & Company, 1881), 14. J. E. Taulman, "Baptism and the Lord's Supper as Viewed by J. M. Pendleton, A. C. Dayton, and J. R. Graves," *Quarterly Review* 35 (April–May–June 1975): 68, suggested a shorter span: "Graves displayed little interest in the Lord's Supper prior to 1855. His main concern was with baptism." He also imprecisely dated Graves's move to closed communion as some time before 1880. In a similar vein, Tull observed in "A Study of Southern Baptist Landmarkism," 501–2, that Graves in his later years "gave more and more attention to the strict local communion theory than he had ever done before." Cf. J. L. Garrett, *Baptist Theology: A Four-Century Study* (Macon, GA: Mercer University Press, 2009), 225, n58, where he judged that Graves fully embraced closed communion around 1875.

[56] Smith, "J. R. Graves," in *Baptist Theologians*, ed. T. George and D. S. Dockery (Nashville: Broadman, 1990), 241; and Tull, "A Study of Southern Baptist Landmarkism," 226–29. They both give an 1847 date for Graves's initial support for communion at the Concord Association in Middle Tennessee, whereas Ford and Hailey supplied the impossible date of 1867, when Graves was in Memphis. Cf. Ford, "The Life, Times and Teachings of J. R. Graves," *Ford's Christian Repository and Home Circle,* October 1899, 678–79; and Hailey, *J. R. Graves,* 50–51. This is symptomatic of the latter two's brief, chronologically confusing account of Graves's changed thinking about the Lord's Supper. Ford actually has the 1847 date in "Intercommunion between Churches," *Tennessee Baptist*, June 16, 1883, 4. Graves followed this article with his "Remarks," 4–5, explaining that he had taken part in associational communion because he "knew no better." On officiating in Vermont, see Graves, "Reaction of Injury," *Tennessee Baptist,* July 10, 1858, [2].

[57] Graves, "The Lord's Supper," in *The Southern Baptist Almanac and Annual Register for the Year of Our Lord 1848* (Nashville: Graves & Shankland, for the Tennessee Baptist Publication Society, 1848), 31. Cf. Graves, "Communion: On the Distinction between Christian, and Church Fellowship," in *The Southern Baptist Almanac and Annual Register, for the Year of Our Lord 1851* (Nashville: Graves & Shankland, for the Tennessee Publication Society, 1851), 4ff., where he labeled Baptists as "close communionists." At the same time, he emphasized the Supper as a church act or ordinance.

Supper." [58] While this seemed to preclude all but restricted local church communion, his standing list of "fundamental doctrines" at least left the door cracked for close communion: "The members of one church (though of the same faith and order) can come to the communion of another [church] only by an act of courtesy and not by *right*, for each church is independent, being made the guardian of the purity of the sacred feast, is invested with the authority to discipline those whose relationship ordinarily gives them the right."[59] Through the Civil War and early Reconstruction, therefore, Graves avoided an unconditional insistence on a strict closed communion policy.

After resuming the publication of his paper, in fact, the Baptist editor initially ran some columns on communion that did not explicitly espouse a more restrictive position.[60] In 1868, moreover, he spoke against permitting Pedobaptists to the table in Baptist churches but did not endorse a fully closed Supper.[61] Early in the following year, however, he pronounced that "the Lord's Supper is purely a church ordinance, to be observed by the members of each local church, according to Divine directions." [62] From that point on, Graves—for all practical purposes—championed closed communion. Indeed, by 1875 he even advised against taking the Lord's Supper to sick members who were unable to attend church; it was only to be celebrated when the entire local congregation could gather at the table.[63]

Graves's most definitive statement on the need for restricted communion was published in 1881 and spelled out in more detail what he had included the year before in *Old Landmarkism*. He brought together his major objections to close communion, including

[58] Graves, "Querist," *Tennessee Baptist*, August 12, 1854, [2]. His conviction here is reflected in "Keep before the People," *Tennessee Baptist*, January 31, 1857, [3]: "[O]nly those churches can participate in this ordinance that agree in faith and practice. But the members of no one church have a right to come to the table spread in another church, though 'of the same faith and order'; for each church is independent, and is invested with the authority to discipline those whom she invites to the sacred feast." This point did not demand restricted or closed communion but left it up to each local church whether Baptists from other congregations could participate. Tull truncated this statement and wrongly concluded that it showed Graves's support for "strict local church communion" in the 1850s. See "A Study of Southern Baptist Landmarkism," 228.

[59] Graves, "Baptist Doctrines, Principles and Facts," *Baptist*, February 1, 1867, 1. This indicates a likely clarification of the 1857 statement in "Keep before the People" cited in the previous footnote.

[60] For example, see "The Pulpit. The Lord's Supper," *Baptist*, July 20, 1867, 2. This was a notice of a sermon that Graves delivered at First Baptist Church, Memphis, entitled "The Relative Position of the Lord's Supper to Baptism and the Church." He pronounced that Baptist intercommunion was acceptable "whenever such are present and their standing in their own church is known, and their faith and walk such as is fellowshipped by the inviting church."

[61] Graves, "Communion," *Baptist*, April 11, 1868, [1].

[62] Graves, "The Apostolic Commission," *Baptist*, January 23, 1869, [4].

[63] Graves, "Things Misapprehended by Baptists," *Baptist*, April 3, 1875, [2].

the complete independence of local churches, their sole authority and guardianship over the ordinances, and their exclusive disciplinary rights.[64] He likewise expressed his utter rejection of a social gesture that he had accepted in an earlier era when he remarked that the Supper was not "appointed to be used as a mark or expression of 'courtesy' and 'comity,' or good feeling for, our brethren of other churches, or Christian friends." [65] As in so many areas of his thought, he allowed precious little room for compromise when it came to the proper boundaries of Baptist life and practice.

So Graves's "old" Landmarkism had come full swing by the early 1880s. His relentless logic pushed him to tie together pulpit affiliation, alien immersion, as well as both open and denominational communion as enemies to both local congregational autonomy and Baptist identity.[66] As he liked to put it, true Baptists need to guard against the corrupting influences of non-Baptists by closing the pulpit to them, protecting the integrity of the baptistery, and fencing the Lord's table.[67] He refrained, however, from pushing his radical localism to the point of requiring new members of a Southern Baptist church to be rebaptized if they had been previously immersed within the denomination, although that would seem to have been a logical corollary of his strict views on the Lord's Supper. Nevertheless, Graves wrapped a pretty tight ecclesiological package using the ropes of his Landmarkist principles. At the same time, it was not entirely clear whether he could successfully merge his long-cherished Landmark Baptist beliefs with the dispensational theology that he heartily adopted in the post-Civil War era.

[64] Graves, *Intercommunion*, 161–84, 183, 312–16. This long volume overlapped material also found in Graves, *The Lord's Supper: A Church Ordinance, and So Observed by the Apostolic Churches* (1881; repr., Texarkana, AR: Baptist Sunday School Committee, 1928 and 1968); Graves, *What Is It to Eat and Drink Unworthily? The Symbolism of the Lord's Supper* (Memphis: Baptist Book House, 1881); and Graves, "The Lord's Supper," *Baptist,* February 7, 1880, 533, where he insisted that "[t]here is no consistent middle ground between church communion and unrestricted communion." In 1880 he also attacked the editorial position of a Baptist newspaper that would later in the decade merge with his. See Graves, "The Reflector and Communion," *Baptist,* December 18, 1880, 437.

[65] Graves, *Intercommunion*, 234.

[66] Friend and supporter Ford, who nonetheless rejected a rigid closed communion, noted Graves's "mental habit of running out every doctrine or proposition to its logical extremity." See Ford, "The Life, Times and Teachings of J. R. Graves," *Ford's Christian Repository and Home Circle,* August 1900, 492–93. In 1881 Graves reiterated long-sustained beliefs about baptism in *The Act of Baptism* (Memphis: Baptist Book House, 1881); *Christian Baptism: The Profession of the Faith of the Gospel* (1881; repr., Texarkana, AR: Baptist Sunday School Committee, 1928 and 1968); and *The Relation of Baptism to Salvation* (Memphis: Baptist Book House, 1881). The year 1881 was indeed an active year of publication for him.

[67] See Graves, "Outlook for 1874," *Baptist,* January 3, 1874, [4]; and "A Clear Statement on the Communion Issue," *Baptist,* October 9, 1875, 388–89. Graves directed both of these columns against Baptists who loosened the standards on these issues.

A Curious Mixture of Landmark Ecclesiology and Dispensational Eschatology

In his classic study of American fundamentalism, Ernest Sandeen described the apocalyptic mood that characterized nineteenth-century Protestantism in the United States: "America in the early nineteenth century was drunk on the millennium. Whether in support of optimism or pessimism, radicalism or conservatism, Americans seemed unable to avoid—seemed bound to utilize—the vocabulary of Christian eschatology." [68] In the revival waves of the Second Great Awakening, surging millennial interests captured the imaginations of many preachers and converts, including some who pushed beyond the boundaries of evangelical orthodoxy. In the northeastern states, which included J. R. Graves's native Vermont, Adventists, Latter Day Saints, and Shakers all promoted eschatological zeal, often with unconventional prophetic schemes. For instance, William Miller—who started out as a Baptist—challenged the prevailing postmillennialism of his day with a speculative premillennialism that boldly set dates for the Second Coming of Christ. Graves, who possibly heard Miller give lectures in 1837, later fretted that "[t]he madness and folly of the Millerites, the wildness and absurdity of some prophetic expositors, has brought discredit on the whole subject of prophetic study." [69]

Despite his recognition that the study of eschatology could be abused through fanciful interpretations, Graves nevertheless cultivated an intense fascination in it beginning with his years in Nashville. How or exactly when he first took up the study of prophecy is not entirely clear. Danny Howe, who has provided the most thorough and insightful study of Graves's eschatology and its possible sources, traced the start of the Baptist editor's attraction to premillennialism to 1855–56 when he penned articles on chiliasm for

---

[68] E. R. Sandeen, *The Roots of Fundamentalism: British and American Millenarianism, 1800–1930* (1970; repr., Grand Rapids: Baker, 1978), 42.

[69] Graves, editorial introduction to Mr. Faber, "Napoleon III—The Man of Prophecy," *Southern Baptist Review* 7 (March 1861): 24–25. In a similar vein, he commented later that same year in "Prophetical Studies, or the Old Landmarks of Prophecy. The Call to Prophetic Study. Chapter 1," *Tennessee Baptist*, August 3, 1861, [1]: "It is certainly to be deplored that error and fanaticism have been so often mingled with prophetic studies." In this context, he was paraphrasing Horatius Bonar without acknowledging his source (see note 78 below), so he might not have had Miller specifically in mind. For the general setting of American millenarianism in the first half of the nineteenth century, see Sandeen, *The Roots of Fundamentalism*, 42–58. He observed (p. 58) that Miller's failed prophecies "disillusioned most of his followers and marked the whole millenarian cause, rightly or wrongly, with the stigma of fanaticism and quackery." On the early Southern Baptist postmillennial "consensus," see J. Spivey, "The Millennium," in *Has Our Theology Changed? Southern Baptist Thought since 1845*, ed. P. A. Basden (Nashville: B&H, 1994), 234–39.

his *Southern Baptist Review and Eclectic.*[70] Graves, however, at least as early as 1852 seemed to assume a premillennial scenario without actually employing the specific term. In an editorial discussion about the spread of republicanism in Europe, he spoke hopefully of its prophetic implications: "The curtain is rising to exhibit the last great act upon the theater of earth, previous to the fall of the 'Beast,' and the 'coming of the Son of Man in his brightness.'" [71] The following year, the Landmark patriarch again utilized prophetic language as he amplified the role of a weakened papacy as a prelude to the "drying up of the River Euphrates," which pointed to the fulfillment of Rev 16:12 by no later than 1866 and hence the soon arrival of the "last days." [72]

Thus, even before his journal articles of 1855 and 1856, Graves demonstrated a striking interest in prophetic themes, usually in the context of an expressed concern about how the believers of his day were interpreting the Bible. At the end of 1853 he complained about a figurative hermeneutic that was being commonly used in reference to the return of the Jews to the Holy Land and the reign of Christ upon the earth. Graves classified such "spiritual" interpretation as "gross infidelity." [73] By 1854 he explicitly drew on premillennial terminology as he argued that the Jews would be restored to their homeland and Christ would return to earth before the millennium, although he stretched the limits of his literalism on one point when he affirmed that Christ would reign with his

---

[70] D. E. Howe, "An Analysis of Dispensationalism and Its Implications for the Theologies of James Robinson Graves, John Franklyn Norris, and Wallie Amos Criswell" (Ph.D. diss., Southwestern Baptist Theological Seminary, 1988), 78, 80, 137–38. See Graves, "Chiliasm: The Orthodoxy of the Primitive and the Heterodoxy of the Present Christian Church," *Southern Baptist Review and Eclectic* 1 (October–December 1855): 635–71; and "Chiliasm in the 19th Century," *Southern Baptist Review and Eclectic* 2 (May–June 1856): 241–72. Howe did not point out that in the 1856 article (p. 241) Graves referred to the millennium as "a new and glorious dispensation," although he did not seem to be using the term in any explicit connection to dispensational theology.

[71] Graves, "January 1, 1852," *Tennessee Baptist,* January 3, 1852, [2]. See chap. 3 above for his identification of the "Beast" with papal Rome.

[72] Graves, "The Drying Up of the River Euphrates," *Tennessee Baptist,* October 1, 1853, [2]. Graves mistakenly gave the reference as Rev 5:12. He also dealt with the Euphrates prophecy in "The Scriptures—No. 1. The Sinful Neglect of the Scriptures," *Tennessee Baptist,* September 3, 1853, [2]. Harold Smith, without specifically citing Graves, asserted that the Landmarker saw the Euphrates as a symbol for Turkey, whose downfall would allow a return of the Jews to Palestine. See "A Critical Analysis of the Theology of J. R. Graves," 301–2. This, however, was not Graves's interpretation in the 1850s.

[73] Graves, "The Scriptures, No. 4. Virtual Infidelity Advocated by Modern Christians, by Interpreting Literal Language Figuratively—and Figurative or Symbolical Language Literally," *Tennessee Baptist,* December 17, 1853, [2]. His series on the Scriptures clearly anticipated the literal hermeneutic that would characterize his more overt dispensationalism after the Civil War.

saints on earth "during the great Sabbath of 1000 *prophetic*, or 360,000 literal years." [74] Howe's 1855–56 time frame then needs to be pushed back to 1853–54 to account for a considerable amount of material that flowed from Graves's pen on prophetic matters.

Consequently, Graves's contributions to the *Southern Baptist Review* only advanced some ideas that he had already expounded in his newspaper. It appeared, in fact, that he used the more reflective journal to fill in supporting details for the positions that he espoused in the *Tennessee Baptist*. This was especially true of his lengthy forays into Christian history as he attempted to prove that the early church fathers were premillennialists.[75] By 1858 he had become somewhat defensive about those in his own denominational ranks who regarded premillennialism as "a pernicious heresy": "Can they be ignorant of the fact that it was held by all orthodox Christians in the purest ages of Christianity—that it has ever been the distinguishing doctrine of Baptists?" [76] Ever the boundary setter, the Landmark leader now applied his Baptist successionist method to the history of eschatology.

Indeed, in the early Civil War period Graves launched a new series in which he proposed "to re-set the old Landmarks of the fathers," particularly as they related to prophecy. In this context, some of his sources became more visible; he specifically named writers like D. T. Taylor, David Nevins Lord, and especially Horatius Bonar. In fact, he acknowledged his liberal dependence on them, averring that "we prefer to be considered in these days merely as the editor and collator rather than as an original author." [77] This confession, as Harold Smith documented, merely hinted at what could be classified as a case of plagiarism. In reality, Graves's series on biblical prophecy leaned heavily on

---

[74] Graves, "The Scriptures, No. 13. What Saith the Scriptures?—Will the Jews Be Restored to Palestine?" *Tennessee Baptist,* March 11, 1854, [2]. As in his later *Southern Baptist Review and Eclectic* article (1856) referred to in note 70, Graves here invoked the term "dispensation" in an apparently non-technical sense. For additional pieces on the restoration of the Jews, see Graves, "The Scriptures, No. 14. What Saith the Scriptures?—Will the Jews Return to Palestine?" *Tennessee Baptist,* March 18, 1854, [2]; and "The Scriptures, No. 15. What Saith the Scriptures?—Will the Jews Return to Palestine?" *Tennessee Baptist,* March 25, 1854, [2]. There is a reference to "subsequent dispensations" in Graves, "The Design of Christ's Second Coming, Number 5," *Tennessee Baptist,* July 8, 1854, [2].

[75] E.g., Graves, "Chiliasm: The Orthodoxy of the Primitive and the Heterodoxy of the Present Christian Church," 644ff.

[76] Graves, review of *Lectures on the Apocalypse,* by R. Ryland, *Southern Baptist Review* 4 (December 1858): 629.

[77] Graves, "Prophetical Studies, or the Old Landmarks of Prophecy. Introductory Remarks—No. 1," *Tennessee Baptist,* July 27, 1861, [2]. The last installment in the series was heavily indebted to Bonar. See Graves, "The Old Landmarks of Prophecy. The Interval. Chapter 7," *Tennessee Baptist,* February 15, 1862, [1]. This was in the last issue of his paper until 1867.

Horatius Bonar's (1808–89) *Prophetical Landmarks*; more than half of the series came verbatim, without direct attribution, from the Scottish Presbyterian's book.[78]

Since Graves began this series during the early months of a bloody national struggle, his obvious apocalyptic flair was perhaps fitting. Furthermore, his first article—which seemed to be the least dependent on Bonar—revealed what can best be described as an incipient dispensational posture, even though the scholarly consensus classifies him as a historic premillennialist before the war who did not openly embrace dispensationalism until he resumed the publication of his newspaper in 1867.[79] The Baptist journalist introduced his "end times" calendar by painting a gloomy picture of a period of severe tribulation that would precede the return of Christ: "[W]e are living in the afternoon of the 'last times.' The sun of this dispensation is rapidly descending to its setting in clouds and darkness, and a horrible tempest of unconceived calamaties [*sic*] and earthly woes never borne or ever conceived of before, to give way to the rising of the Sun of righteousness with healing in his wings."[80] While this sounded like standard historic premillenial fare, Graves then raised for consideration what appeared to be for him a new concept, the pretribulational rapture of the faithful. He intimated that there would be some Christians who would be "caught away from the evils to come and the tribulations of the last hour." Moreover, citing the parable of the 10 virgins, Graves proposed that only those who truly believed in Christ's second advent would be candidates for the rapture, while the fate of others would not be so promising: "[T]hose Christians who disbelieve in his second coming, and consequently are not ready for it, will be left to pass through these awful scenes and be saved *yet so as by fire*."[81] Here the Landmark editor palpably understood the pretribulational rapture as a partial catching away of the truly committed, a theme that he would return to in his book-length study of the parables of Jesus.[82]

---

[78] Smith, "A Critical Analysis of the Theology of J. R. Graves," 115. His broader discussion points to how Graves's careless use and identification of sources led to allegations of plagiarism. The Bonar work in question was *Prophetical Landmarks: Containing Data for Helping to Determine the Question of Christ's Pre-Millennial Advent*, 2nd ed. (London: James Nisbet and Company, 1848).

[79] See Garrett, *Baptist Theology*, 562. He follows Howe, "An Analysis of Dispensationalism," 85, 138. Smith, "A Critical Analysis of the Theology of J. R. Graves," 113, concluded that by 1870 Graves "was organizing his thoughts into a dispensational framework," but he overlooked some earlier materials that Howe cited.

[80] Graves, "Prophetical Studies, . . . No. 1," [2].

[81] Ibid.

[82] See Graves, *The Dispensational Expositions of the Parables and Prophecies of Christ* (Memphis: Graves & Mahaffy, 1887), 12, 244–71. His 1861 article indicated some tentativeness on the partial rapture idea when he wrote in anticipation of more study: "This will be an interesting future inquiry."

Although Graves assuredly shared much common ground with historic premillennialism, including a keen sense of urgency about the fulfillment of biblical prophecies, his division of the return of Christ into two distinct events separated by the tribulation exposes his eschatology as a work in progress. As early as 1862, he seemed to be gravitating toward a dispensational perspective that would eventually become more overt after the Civil War. Overall, his eschatology showed more continuity than is conveyed in labeling him a "historic premillennialist" in the antebellum period and a "dispensationalist" following the war.[83] The fluidity of some of his categories, in fact, warns against projecting distinctions back on him that were not as precise in his day as they ultimately became in a later generation.

At the same time, dispensational threads ran more noticeably through Graves's written works beginning in 1867. In the *Baptist* he demonstrated a continuing interest in the restoration of the Jews to Palestine. While many historic premillennialists likewise gave attention to this issue, Graves would increasingly spin it in a dispensational direction as he looked for a literal fulfillment of the Abrahamic covenant.[84] Moreover, he maintained his prewar notion of a partial, pretribulational rapture, although he would temporarily back away from this in *The Work of Christ in the Covenant of Redemption*, where he advocated a more typical dispensational view.[85]

Perhaps the most prominent signal that Graves had plainly taken up residence in the dispensationalist camp came in 1870 when he initiated a new series in the *Baptist* with the title "The Seven Dispensations." He embarked again on a similar series in 1876—which he told his readers was "in our estimation, the most valuable writing of our life"—

---

[83] Howe tended to stress the discontinuity of Graves's transition. See his "An Analysis of Dispensationalism," 137–38. Cf. Spivey, "The Millennium," 240.

[84] In the spring of 1867, Graves launched a long series that probed recent developments in the Middle East and how they bore on the return of the Jews. See "The Eastern Question. War Prospects—The Jews—No.1," *Baptist*, May 25, 1867, 4. Here he anticipated a major role for Russia in prophetic fulfillment. In "Signs of the Times," *Baptist*, July 24, 1869, [4], Graves declared that the Jews would "be nationalized upon the mountains of Israel . . . as a sign to all the world that Christ is at the very door." His gaze eastward is also evident in "The Suez Canal," December 25, 1869, [4], where he envisioned a weakened Turkey and now connected this to the "drying up of the Euphrates." At the same time, he kept an eye on events that he claimed had damaged the papacy. See his "The Pope's Doings," *Baptist*, November 14, 1868, [4]. Cf. Graves, "Query—The Seven Horned Beast," *Baptist*, April 8, 1871, [5]; and "Exegetical. The Scarlet Colored Beast—The Re-Nationalized Papacy. No. 2," *Baptist*, January 9, 1875, [2].

[85] Graves, "The Great Tribulation," *Baptist*, September 14, 1867, 10. Cf. Graves, *The Work of Christ in the Covenant of Redemption; Developed in Seven Dispensations* (1883; repr., Texarkana, AR: Baptist Sunday School Committee, 1928 and 1963), 392–411. As discussed in n82 above, he returned to the partial rapture theory in *The Dispensational Expositions* (1887).

and once more in 1882.[86] The contents of these series, as well as one that he began late in 1877 on "The Parables of Christ," became the basis for his two primary elucidations of dispensational theology, *The Work of Christ* and *The Dispensational Expositions.*[87]

Graves's postwar writings included several dispensational hallmarks that echoed the theology of John Nelson Darby (1800–1882), the Irish futurist and prototypical dispensationalist who made seven visits to the United States to promulgate his ideas between 1862 and 1877.[88] Graves, however, never quoted Darby or otherwise indicated any dependence on his writings or lectures, leading to much speculation about the sources of Graves's dispensationalism. S. H. Ford, for instance, proposed in 1900 that his Landmark friend might have been influenced by the work of Robert Breckenridge, a Presbyterian theologian from Kentucky who divided redemptive history into seven "grand epochs" that had some affinity with Graves's—and Darby's—dispensations.[89] Nonetheless, Danny Howe has shown conclusively in his dissertation that Breckenridge, although a premillennialist, was not a Darbyite and "never espoused the hermeneutic of Darby or developed any of its tenets." [90] Instead, he argued that Graves largely imbibed Darby's theories indirectly; they were mediated to the Landmark founder by other dispensationalist writers, including some like Baptist pastors C. R. Hendrickson and A. J. Frost who contributed articles to his newspaper.[91] Howe especially targets Joseph A. Seiss (1823–1904), a

---

[86] Graves, "The Seven Dispensations," *Baptist,* September 3, 1870, [4]; and November 18, 1876, 789; and the *Tennessee Baptist,* November 18, 1882, 1–2.

[87] Graves, "The Parables of Christ, No. 1," *Baptist,* November 24, 1877, 6. Graves began serializing *The Work of Christ* in the *Baptist,* February 3, 1877, 130–31. Another dispensational volume is Graves, *John's Baptism: Was It from Moses or Christ? Jewish or Christian: Objections to Its Christian Character Answered* (Memphis: Southern Baptist Book House, 1891), which is discussed in chap. 3 above—it is not as pertinent to his eschatology as the other two books.

[88] Sandeen, *The Roots of Fundamentalism,* 59–80.

[89] Ford, "The Life, Times and Teachings of J. R. Graves," *Ford's Christian Repository and Home Circle,* August 1900, 491. Cf. R. J. Breckenridge, *The Knowledge of God Objectively Considered* (New York: Robert Carter & Brothers, 1858). T. A. Patterson, "The Theology of J. R. Graves and Its Influence on Southern Baptist Life" (Th.D. diss., Southwestern Baptist Theological Seminary, 1944), 9, gave credence to Breckenridge as a source for Graves. Harold Smith also seemed open to Breckenridge's possible impact on the Baptist editor. See "A Critical Analysis of the Theology of J. R. Graves," 113–14.

[90] Howe, "An Analysis of Dispensationalism," 138.

[91] Ibid., 85–87, 93–96. Graves preached in Hendrickson's church in Memphis in the 1850s and in Frost's church in California on a trip in 1878–79. See "Dr. Graves in California," *Baptist,* November 23, 1878, 613; and "Dr. Graves in San Francisco," *Baptist,* February 22, 1879, 5. For examples of their work, see C. R. Hendrickson, "Destiny of Israel," *Baptist,* November 22, 1873, [2]; and A. J. Frost, "How to Study the Bible," *Tennessee Baptist,* January 10, 1885, 6. Hendrickson, whom Graves knew as early as the 1850s, was probably the source of the Landmark patriarch's restricted understanding of the apostolic commission to evangelize

Lutheran pastor from Philadelphia who edited the monthly *Prophetic Times*, as "the most pivotal influence" on Graves's dispensationalism.[92] The Lutheran editor, according to Howe, not only embraced a literal method of biblical interpretation similar to that advanced by historic premillennialists like David Lord; Seiss also adopted Darby's "ecclesiological hermeneutic" that posed a radical disjunction between God's plan for Israel and his purposes for the church. In other words, redemptive history unfolds on the basis of God's twofold program; Darby, Seiss, and Graves all accepted this assumption as foundational for eschatology.[93]

It is ironic that Graves's dispensationalism was explicitly shaped by the Lutheran Seiss and indirectly influenced by Darby, who moved from the Church of Ireland (Anglican) to the Plymouth Brethren. Furthermore, the Landmark editor expressed enthusiasm about the interdenominational prophetic conferences—which had a strong Presbyterian presence—that dotted the American Protestant scene in the late nineteenth century. Graves, in fact, was scheduled to speak on "Palestine Restored and Repeopled" at an 1886 conference in Chicago, but ill health probably prevented him from attending.[94] Even though he normally leveled withering assaults on other denominations and warned against "union" meetings or causes, he apparently loosened his otherwise rigid Baptist boundaries when it came to biblical prophecy. He seemed disposed to associate with non-Baptist dispensationalists, even if they belonged to religious "societies" and not genuine churches.

---

the world. Graves published Hendrickson's letter, "Will the World Be Converted before the Second Advent of Christ?" *Tennessee Baptist,* July 15, 1854, [3], in which Hendrickson answered in the negative. The very next year, Graves wrote: "Let us no longer preach and teach that the heathen world is to be converted to God through our operations, but the Gospel simply to be preached for a witness among all nations, and then for the end to come, and a new dispensation ushered in." This provoked a concerned response from J. B. Taylor of the Foreign Mission Board. See A. W. Wardin Jr., *Tennessee Baptists: A Comprehensive History* (Brentwood, TN: Tennessee Baptist Convention, 1999), 188. Graves, however, persisted in this way of thinking and later incorporated it as a premillennial distinctive in *The Dispensational Expositions,* 28, 35, 71–72, 241; and *The Work of Christ,* 293.

[92] Howe, "An Analysis of Dispensationalism," 138.

[93] Ibid., 53–56, 99–101. See J. A. Seiss, *The Last Times and the Great Consummation; An Earnest Discussion of Momentous Themes* (Philadelphia: Smith, English, and Co., 1870), 196–98. In Graves, *The Work of Christ,* 325, he quoted directly from Seiss. Cf. Graves, "The Seven Dispensations," *Tennessee Baptist,* December 2, 1882, 1–3. On Lord's significance for Graves, see Howe, "An Analysis of Dispensationalism," 103–4. Lord's influential work for Graves's method of biblical interpretation was *The Characteristic and Laws of Figurative Language* (New York: Franklin Knight, 1854).

[94] Howe, "An Analysis of Dispensationalism," 93. For an overview of the conference movement, see Sandeen, *The Roots of Fundamentalism,* 132–61. See Graves, "Report of the Prophetic Conference," *Baptist,* January 4, 1879, 694, for his positive review of the 1878 conference in New York, although he was not present.

As Howe sets forth in his detailed expositions of Graves's *Work of Christ* and *Dispensational Expositions*, the Landmarker held much in common with J. N. Darby. Both were dispensationalists who: (1) assumed a literal hermeneutic for interpreting Scripture; (2) divided history into seven distinct ages using different names but implying virtually the same concepts (Graves, however, rejected the notion that God changed his methods of dealing with humanity from one age to another); (3) employed an "ecclesiological hermeneutic" to distinguish God's plan for Israel from his design for the church; (4) read Revelation 2–3 *symbolically* as a foreshadowing of seven consecutive eras of church history; (5) separated the return of Christ into two stages by affirming a premillennial, pretribulational secret rapture (although Graves eventually settled on a partial catching away of truly-prepared saints); and (6) displayed comparable understandings of the great tribulation, the millennium, final judgment, and consummation.[95] While Graves's specific dependence on Darby cannot be absolutely confirmed, Howe's linking of the two is surely warranted.

Despite several shared ideas and their mutual application of an ecclesiological hermeneutic, it was in their doctrines of the church where Graves and Darby diverged most significantly. On one hand, Darbyite dispensationalism stressed the apostate nature of virtually all of Christendom, a sharp distinction between the kingdom and the church, and the ultimately spiritual nature of the true church. The late Baptist historian Robert Torbet aptly summed up the limitations of standard dispensationalist ecclesiology where the church functioned as "a temporary expedient" to evangelize the Gentiles before the postponed kingdom of Israel was fully reestablished in the millennial reign of Christ:

> Through this system of Bible interpretation the concept of the church was narrowed and the existence of the church was limited to a parenthesis between the old kingdom of Israel and the kingdom of Israel which is yet to be restored. The church, being strictly spiritual, is not to be identified with any of the existing denominational structures. The kingdom, by contrast, is to be earthly and political.[96]

---

[95] Howe, "An Analysis of Dispensationalism," 106–39. Although he did not seem interested in the Graves-Darby connection, Smith overviewed the Baptist editor's eschatology in "A Critical Analysis of the Theology of J. R. Graves," 144–46, 301–8. For a helpful summary of Darby's doctrines, see Garrett, *Baptist Theology*, 561.

[96] R. G. Torbet, "Dispensationalist Ecclesiology," in *Baptist Concepts of the Church: A Survey of the Historical and Theological Issues Which Have Produced Changes in Church Order*, ed. Winthrop S. Hudson

Indeed, well over a century after the initial enthrallment with dispensationalism in Britain and America, commentators continue to note its embryonic doctrine of the church.[97]

On the other hand, Graves's Landmarkism and Baptist successionism led him to a major emphasis on the church as a local, observable institution. Unlike most dispensationalists, Graves conceived of the church and the kingdom as essentially one and the same, while also emphasizing its visibility:

> This kingdom, then, could not have been the **ideal conceptual** invisible kingdom of Christ of some, consisting of all the saved of all nations and in all ages, known in the Scriptures as "the family of God" (Eph. iii.15); for this family is nowhere called a kingdom. It was never set up or organized. It has no organization, and therefore is not an **institution**, and can not properly be called a kingdom, which implies organization, and can not be or exist without it.[98]

Furthermore, the true churches persisted through the ages as concrete realities that survived the very real threats and persecutions visited upon them by apostate and false churches. Graves's interpretation of the two witnesses in Revelation 11 attempted to bring together successionist history and dispensational eschatology:

> The teaching of this prophecy, then, is that Christ has had, and will preserve, a succession of true churches and of faithful ministers, through all the ages, to bear witness to his truth and denounce God's fierce judgments upon all who turn away from and corrupt it; and that these will suffer during all the ages for

---

(Philadelphia: Judson Press, 1959), 222–23. For an argument that ecclesiological concerns motivated Darby and that he included tangible, local assemblies in his definition of the "church," see J. M. Utzinger, *Yet Saints Their Watch Are Keeping: Fundamentalists, Modernists, and the Development of Evangelical Ecclesiology, 1887–1937* (Macon, GA: Mercer University Press, 2006), 114–18. At the same time, Torbet was correct to assert that dispensational theology tends to relegate the church to a secondary role in God's redemptive plan.

[97] E.g., see M. D. Williams, "Where's the Church? The Church as the Unfinished Business of Dispensational Theology," *Grace Theological Journal* 10 (Fall 1989): 165–82.

[98] Graves, *The Dispensational Expositions*, 142 (bold face in original). He made the church-kingdom link explicit on p. 144: "Then it follows that the aggregate of Christ's true churches constitute His kingdom." This was a long-held belief here given eschatological significance. Cf. Graves, *The Work of Christ*, 263. In response to Graves's virtual neglect of the spiritual dimension of the church, Harold Smith characterized the Landmark founder's ecclesiology as "mechanical and institutional." See "A Critical Analysis of the Theology of J. R. Graves," 325.

their faithfulness at the hands of **apostates**, and that this Dispensation will be closed by their universal slaughter within the territory of the Wild Beast.[99]

For Graves, then, the true church had a real historical existence through the unbroken succession of Baptist congregations. After all, it would be hard to draw distinct denominational boundaries around an amorphous, invisible entity.

In addition, the Landmarker's revision of the classical dispensational concept of a secret rapture may have played into his boundary setting. As Graves intimated in *The Dispensational Expositions*, only the "pure and chaste" will be taken out of the world to escape the great tribulation. From his perspective, this select group would be made up of those believers who had preserved the ancient ecclesiological "landmarks." [100] He seemed to infer that the foolish virgins left behind might be Pedobaptists and other Baptists who were not part of the "true bride" because of their failure to follow the groom's instructions on the proper ordering of their churches. Moreover, he may have seen his boundary staking as one way to help prepare the true and uncorrupted churches for the apocalyptic events that were about to unfold. These considerations fortify Howe's conclusion that Graves "utilized some of his Dispensational tenets in order to reinforce his own ecclesiological views." [101] At the same time, the Baptist editor's conviction about the imminency of the end times probably supplied him with a fresh urgency to finish the work that he was doing.

THE FINAL YEARS

During the 1870s Graves continued to edit the *Baptist*, write books, preach widely, and oversee his publishing interests in Memphis. He remained a faithful supporter and promoter of Southern Baptist schools; in particular, he boasted that "[t]he great educational awakening in the Southwest, and especially with respect to female education, is largely attributable to the 'Cotton Grove Mass Meeting.'" [102] While the connection that he drew was not exactly an obvious one, the Landmark founder deeply appreciated the value of a

---

[99] Graves, *The Work of Christ*, 359 (bold face in original). The "Wild Beast" was understood as a confederation of 10 European nations. It is not entirely clear how the slaughter of the two witnesses meshes with Graves's statement on 361 that they will be raptured.

[100] Graves, *The Dispensational Expositions*, 252–54.

[101] Howe, "An Analysis of Dispensationalism," 269.

[102] Graves, "Our Schools," *Baptist,* June 25, 1870, [4].

good education, probably because he had not enjoyed the benefits of much formal training. Since he had been a trustee at Union University in Murfreesboro, which officially closed in 1873 as a result of the ravages of war, it is not surprising that in 1874 he began a similar stint of service to a Baptist collegiate endeavor in Jackson, Tennessee. In that year the newly reorganized Tennessee Baptist Convention authorized the opening of Southwestern Baptist University, which—for all practical purposes—emerged as a successor school to Union in Murfreesboro and West Tennessee College in Jackson. Graves was appointed by the convention as a trustee and served in that capacity until 1892. He was joined on the first Jackson board by his old friend C. R. Hendrickson, the chair of the initial trustee executive committee and pastor of the local First Baptist Church.[103]

Minutes of trustee meetings between 1874 and 1892 reveal that Graves assumed an active role on the board. For example, he was chosen in 1877 to be a member of a group that selected new trustees and also to serve on a committee charged with assisting in the reorganization of the faculty. Furthermore, after he was honored with the naming of the J. R. Graves Society for Religious Inquiry in 1875, he paid in 1879 to furnish a room on campus for use by this group. In the same year, he donated a gift of geological rocks to the university. Then, in 1885, the Baptist editor was elected president of the Board of Trustees and remained in that leadership position until 1892.[104]

While serving as trustee chair in 1889, Graves made a motion to admit women to the university. This step reflected a career-long interest of his in support of female education. Indeed, he noted his commitment to this cause just six years prior to his proposal: "We have been for forty years the earnest advocate of the higher education of our daughters—the women of the South. The Mary Sharp is the substantial monument of this fact." [105] Here he was referring to Mary Sharpe College, a Baptist women's institution in Winchester, Tennessee, which his brother Zuinglius led as president from 1850

---

[103] On the demise of Union in Murfreesboro and the initial launching of Southwestern Baptist, see J. A. Baggett, *So Great a Cloud of Witnesses: Union University, 1823–2000* (Jackson, TN: Union University Press, 2000), 47–56; J. H. Davis, "Union University: Over 175 Years of Christian Education: Part 1," *Tennessee Baptist History* 4 (Fall 2002): 55–56; and Davis, "Union University: Over 175 Years of Christian Education: Part [2]," *Tennessee Baptist History* 5 (Fall 2003): 35–37.

[104] Minutes of the Board of Trustees, Southwestern Baptist [later Union] University, 1874–1906, 7–277, Emma Waters Summar Library Archives, Union University, Jackson, TN. One wonders if the rocks represented a different twist on the ancient "landmarks"! During his trustee service, the Landmark editor often appealed for support of the school through his newspaper. See Graves, "The Future of Southwestern Baptist University," *Baptist,* February 13, 1875, [2]; and "The Southwestern Baptist University," *Baptist,* March 6, 1880, 597.

[105] Graves, "The Higher Education of Our Daughters," *Tennessee Baptist,* August 4, 1883, 7. For the motion, see Minutes of the Board, 237–38.

to 1889. J. R., in fact, included in his motion a proviso that his brother open a "Female Annex" at Southwestern. The female department never materialized, and only a handful of women gained admission in the 1890s. Nevertheless, Graves helped to bring the matter to the table, and the number of female students increased markedly in the early twentieth century.[106]

In 1891 son-in-law O. L. Hailey took leadership of efforts to raise funds for a professorial chair at Southwestern to be named in Graves's honor. In his absence, the board voted the following June to establish the J. R. Graves Chair of Logic and Moral Philosophy. Although the chair was not fully funded, George M. Savage was approved in 1908—by the board of what was now the newly-renamed *Union* University—as the first professor to hold it.[107] Graves himself was deeply moved by the initiative to establish the chair in his honor but did not get his wish to see a professor installed before he died.[108]

In 1884, during his tenure on the Southwestern Board of Trustees, Graves ignored medical advice to rest after getting soaked as he traveled from Nashville in a heavy rainstorm; instead, he accepted an invitation to preach at First Baptist Church in Memphis a week later. While in the pulpit, the editor, now age 64, suffered a serious stroke that primarily affected his left side. At first, he remained confined to his room in a paralytic condition for several months, a portion of which he spent under the influence of narcotics. In time, he recovered his speech but was still unable to write, so he dictated his words to his daughter Nora. After more than a year, he began to limp around with the help of a stick, regained his capacity to write, and eventually resumed a limited travel schedule. In fact, he became known for the "chair talks" on the church and salvation that he delivered on his trips. After hearing a series, Southern Seminary head James P. Boyce commented to S. H. Ford on its merits: "It was really a feast. He is doing more real good

---

[106] See Baggett, *So Great a Cloud*, 62–63; and Davis, "Part [2]," 39, where he quoted Graves: "Educate your sons and they marry uneducated women and sink to their levels. Educate your daughters and then the elevation of the whole family will follow." Z. C. Graves evidently was elected again to the presidency of Mary Sharpe after his brother's death. See Z. C. Graves, "A Statement," *Baptist and Reflector*, July 6, 1893, 4.

[107] See Minutes of the Board, 274; Davis, "Part [2]," 49; O. L. Hailey, "The J. R. Graves Chair," *Baptist and Reflector*, August 6, 1891, 7; Hailey, "The J. R. Graves Professorship," *Baptist and Reflector*, February 18, 1892, 7; and Hailey, "The J. R. Graves Chair," *Baptist and Reflector*, March 3, 1892, 7. On the name change to Union and Savage, who served as the institution's president for three separate terms, see Baggett, *So Great a Cloud*, 66–67, 83, 85.

[108] Graves, "The New Chair," *Baptist and Reflector*, June 2, 1892, 7. Although the chair eventually lapsed when Savage vacated it in 1934, it was brought back with an indirect connection to the Landmarker in 2000 as the Graves Chair of Moral Philosophy. Baptist ethicist C. Ben Mitchell is the current occupant of this chair.

now than as [*sic*] any time of his life." [109] Despite his physical handicaps, Graves maintained sufficient mental agility to carry on his work, even though in a more limited way.

Graves's weakened condition ultimately helped to spark the merger of his *Tennessee Baptist* and J. B. Moody's *Baptist Gleaner* in 1887, with the new *Baptist* based in Memphis and the two editors serving jointly.[110] Further changes came in 1889, as the Tennessee Baptist Convention worked to consolidate the state's denominational papers into one weekly publication. By August of that year the first issue of the *Baptist and Reflector* rolled off the presses, showing Graves, Moody, and Edgar Folk as editors. The Landmark patriarch, however, soon turned over all his financial interests in the newspaper to son-in-law Hailey; furthermore, as a "special editor" he reduced his literary role to an occasional column.[111]

These transitions proved to be propitious for Baptist journalism in Tennessee, because in 1890 Graves stepped in a hole in his yard in Memphis almost six years to the day after his stroke. He aggravated his left side, dislocated a hip, and endured a second stroke.[112] Although he entertained ambitious writing goals, he would never walk again. In 1891 he noted that he was the oldest Baptist editor on the continent; less than two years later he soberly anticipated that his remaining days were now numbered.[113] On June 26, 1893, he died at his home in Memphis, and the funeral service was held in the city's First Baptist Church.[114]

Graves's last nine years represented a pale imitation of his prior career. The once energetic and aggressive editor saw his journalistic contributions decline to the point

---

[109] Ford, "The Life, Times and Teachings of J. R. Graves," *Ford's Christian Repository and Home Circle,* September 1900, 559. For other information on the stroke and its aftermath, see untitled editorial by his daughter, *Tennessee Baptist,* September 13, 1884, 6; Graves, "A Chat with Our Friends," *Tennessee Baptist,* October 11, 1884, 6–7; Graves, "Personal," *Tennessee Baptist,* November 21, 1885, [6, though misnumbered as 9 in original]; Hailey, *J. R. Graves,* 106; and J. B. Moody, "Visit to Dr. Graves," *Tennessee Baptist,* December 20, 1884, 6.

[110] Graves, "A Consolidation," *Tennessee Baptist,* June 18, 1887, 6.

[111] Graves, "Consolidation Plans," *Baptist,* February 2, 1889, 8; Graves and Moody, "Important Announcement," *Baptist,* August 3, 1889, 6; "Consolidation," *Baptist and Reflector,* August 22, 1889, 7; and Graves, "Dr. Graves Gives His Blessing," *Baptist and Reflector,* October 31, 1889, 8.

[112] O. L. Hailey, "Dr. Graves' Vacation," *Baptist and Reflector,* September 11, 1890, 8; and Graves, untitled editorial, *Baptist and Reflector,* October 9, 1890, 7.

[113] Graves, "The Eldest," *Baptist and Reflector,* September 10, 1891, 7; and "April 10," *Baptist and Reflector,* April 13, 1893, 4. The date in the title of the second article cited was his seventy-third birthday. It turned out to be his last editorial column for the paper.

[114] E. E. Folk, "Recent Events," *Baptist and Reflector,* June 29, 1893, 9; and Hailey, "Under the Shadow," *Baptist and Reflector,* July 6, 1893, 7. Cf. Hailey, *J. R. Graves,* 107–11.

where he was no longer the dominant or even controversial voice of the Baptist press. He still preached with eloquence and conviction but with not nearly the frequency of the pre-stroke years. Indeed, the hectic pace of writing, traveling, and speaking that typified his life for decades may very well have set the stage for the debilitating episode of 1884. All the same, as editor, author, publishing entrepreneur, pastor, orator, and promoter of various denominational causes, he left such an indelible mark in so many areas of Southern Baptist life that he could not be quickly forgotten. To the end, he continued to challenge his fellow Baptists to stake out and defend their distinctives. His take on denominational identity triggered much opposition, even as it forced Baptists to think through what was really essential to their doctrines and practices. This winnowing process proved to be vital for his contemporaries as well as for succeeding generations.

The Graves Legacy

A Continuing Trail

I n a seminal lecture at Southeastern Baptist Theological Seminary in 1980, Baptist historian Walter "Buddy" Shurden perceptively identified four different strands of faith and practice from the eighteenth and nineteenth centuries that he believed had shaped a profound—and endangered—Southern Baptist synthesis. The fourth one that he proposed was "the Tennessee Tradition," which he summarized as follows: "J. R. Graves was the central figure. Landmarkism was the movement. And Nashville and Memphis, the respective homes of Graves, were the places." He went on to conclude that the tradition from the Volunteer State "yielded an *ecclesiological* identity resulting in a narrow sectarianism." At the same time, this tradition "gave a sense of pride to nineteenth-century Southern Baptists." [1]

This discourse would have undoubtedly seemed foreign to Graves, who bristled at the notion that there was more than one legitimate Baptist identity. Nonetheless, Shurden's historical breakdown of the diverse components in Southern Baptist life suggests a framework for understanding why the famous Landmarker comes across the pages of history as a somewhat provincial character, even though he would have rejected that appellation. As he attempted to draw lines of demarcation for the Baptists of his day, he sometimes appeared to be astounded that his boundaries were often neither appreciated nor endorsed. Even so, as Shurden inferred, the Landmark founder exemplified better than anyone else one of the major impulses that helped to mold the Southern Baptist ethos.

---

[1] W. B. Shurden, "The Southern Baptist Synthesis: Is It Cracking?" *Baptist History and Heritage* 16 (April 1981): 7–8. The emphasis is Shurden's. The other three traditions that he described were Charleston, Sandy Creek, and Georgia. H. Leon McBeth later added a fifth tradition to Shurden's list. See McBeth, "The Texas Tradition: A Study in Baptist Regionalism," *Baptist History and Heritage* 26 (January 1991): 37–57, in two parts. For an expansion of some of McBeth's analysis, see J. Early Jr., "Landmarkism: Tennessee Baptists' Influence on Texas Baptists," *Tennessee Baptist History* 5 (Fall 2003): 57–66.

Since Graves and the "Tennessee Tradition" fit somewhat awkwardly with the other SBC traditions, conflict was inevitable. Graves himself, of course, played the leading role in the storied battles of the 1850s. As new controversies began to surface during his years of declining health, however, it was left to others to contend for the ideas and principles that he had championed for so long. Nevertheless, through his writings, friendships, and overall reputation, he remained a looming presence well into the twentieth century. He and the Landmark movement generated what historian Jesse Fletcher calls a "fault line" that "runs through all three dimensions of confessional, connectional, and cooperative aspects of Southern Baptist life." [2]

In the 1880s a mêlée that involved Graves indirectly began to brew in China over Foreign Mission Board policies and practices. It was set off by Tarleton P. Crawford (1821–1902), one of the earliest graduates of Union University in Murfreesboro and an FMB missionary since 1852, first in Shanghai and then in Shandong. During his service there, he became convinced that only local churches should send out and oversee missionaries. Furthermore, Crawford believed that missionaries should strive to become self-supporting; he also sought to limit the missionary task to direct evangelism. He drew many of his ideas from his experiences with faith missions in China rather than from a distinct Landmark ideology. While he was not directly aligned with Graves, the opinions that Crawford voiced in China were consistent with the positions espoused by the Landmark leader before and during the 1859 SBC meeting. Indeed, in 1881 Graves reiterated his views about churches needing to be in the "front rank" of missions and assuming "the responsibility of selecting, and adopting and supporting the missionaries, and the Executive Boards content to be used as financial agencies of the churches." He then cited Crawford as an example of a missionary who at one time had been supported by an association in Tennessee. [3] In addition, both Crawford and Graves shared a similar antipathy toward centralization, particularly in reference to mission efforts. [4] Crawford may not have

---

[2] J. C. Fletcher, *The Southern Baptist Convention: A Sesquicentennial History* (Nashville: B&H, 1994), 375–76.

[3] Graves, "To All Who Are Interested in the Work of the Southern Baptist Convention," *Baptist*, March 26, 1881, 645. On Crawford, see A. Lamkin Jr., "The Gospel Mission Movement within the Southern Baptist Convention" (Ph.D. diss., Southern Baptist Theological Seminary, 1980). Lamkin questions any close Crawford link to Landmarkism. On Crawford's Union connection, see J. A. Baggett, *So Great a Cloud of Witnesses: Union University, 1823–2000* (Jackson, TN: Union University Press, 2000), 50. On Crawford's wife Martha, see C. A. Vaughn, "'Living in the Lives of Men': A Southern Baptist Woman's Missionary Journey from Alabama to Shandong, 1830–1909" (Ph.D. diss., Auburn University, 1998).

[4] T. P. Crawford, *Churches to the Front!* (China: By the author, 1892); and Graves, "Co-operation, and Not Centralization, Is What Is Needed in All Our State Work," *Baptist,* May 7, 1881, 741.

been a Landmarker, but his fear of a burdensome missions hierarchy and his accent on the sending churches put him in close proximity to some elements of Graves's ecclesiology.

In response to his evolving missiology, Crawford organized the Gospel Mission Association on the field in 1890. His outspoken criticisms of the FMB continued, so he, his wife, and some other missionaries officially parted ways with the board in 1892–93. The Gospel Mission could not compete with the FMB and eventually floundered after the deaths of the Crawfords. By 1910 some missionaries returned to the FMB and a remnant of Gospel Mission supporters on the home front joined with Landmarkers who had separated from the SBC.[5] Just as in 1859, the missions structure of the SBC remained intact despite aggressive opposition to it.

The Whitsitt controversy (see chap. 5) exploded to an intense level in the SBC after Graves died. The Southern Seminary educator, another Union University alumnus, had moved well beyond the "Tennessee Tradition" in which he was nurtured. His research in early English Baptist history exposed some glaring chinks in the armor of the successionist theory that Graves, G. H. Orchard, and others had widely trumpeted as a key pillar of an enduring and uniform Baptist identity through the ages. It was left to some who were not thorough-going Landmarkers to engage in damage control by laboring to drive Whitsitt from his strategic position as president of what was then the SBC's only graduate-level theological institution. In particular, the anti-Whitsitt crusade was led by T. T. Eaton (1845–1907), yet another Union graduate and Whitsitt's pastor in Louisville, and B. H. Carroll (1843–1914), then a Baptist minister in Waco, Texas, and a Southern Seminary trustee. While Landmarkers cheered on Eaton and Carroll, Whitsitt's resignation was more a victory—albeit temporary—for successionism than for Graves's entire ecclesiology. In the long run, moreover, the successionist rendition of Baptist history struggled ineffectually to gain any credibility with professionally-trained church historians, although several websites testify to its continuing appeal at a popular level.[6]

---

[5] Baggett, *So Great a Cloud*, 50; and Lamkin, "The Gospel Mission Movement," chap. 5.

[6] On the *Trail of Blood* web sites, see chap. 5, note 2 above. Of the sources cited in chap. 5, note 56, the most recent and detailed treatment of the Whitsitt episode is James H. Slatton, *W. H. Whitsitt: The Man and the Controversy* (Macon, GA: Mercer University Press, 2009). Slatton (p. 319) remarked that "it is difficult to imagine successionism or the date for the beginning of the practice of immersion having any longer the power to provoke serious division." For information on the connections of Eaton and Whitsitt to Union University in Murfreesboro, see Baggett, *So Great a Cloud*, 48, 51. Eaton's personal papers contain letters about the conflict, including some from Whitsitt. See T. T. Eaton Papers, box 1, several folders, James P. Boyce Centennial Library Archives, Southern Baptist Theological Seminary, Louisville, Kentucky. For one of Graves's few references to Whitsitt, which was well before the events of the 1890s, see Graves, "Statement in 'The Baptist' about Professors Whitsitt and Broadus," *Baptist,* July 17, 1880, 86. This concerned the Crawford Toy controversy, not Whitsitt's views on Baptist history.

Two additional clashes in the late nineteenth and early twentieth centuries indicated a willingness on the part of some Landmarkers to bolt from Southern Baptist organizations, especially at the state level. First, a heated row unfolded in Texas, where Landmarkism had made significant inroads, in part due to Graves's preaching tours in the Lone Star State. The primary combatants, as it turned out, were all successionists as well as Landmarkers of one stripe or another. The key instigator, pastor and *Texas Baptist* editor Samuel Hayden (1839–1918), attacked denominational boards and agencies as unbiblical threats to the autonomy of local congregations. Moreover, he openly assailed the leaders of what he regarded as the Texas Baptist establishment, men like B. H. Carroll, J. B. Gambrell, and J. B. Cranfill, all of whom enjoyed influence and prestige in the Baptist General Convention of Texas.

Like so many intramural religious disputes, this one showed some tangible signs of being a power struggle. After all, Cranfill had launched the *Baptist Standard* in competition with Hayden's newspaper, and Carroll represented Baptist interests in Waco, which often collided with those in Hayden's stronghold of Dallas. At the same time, a distinct ecclesiological difference separated the two sides: Hayden believed that the BGCT was made up of independent churches and derived its authority from them; his opponents viewed the convention as constituted by individuals who had been chosen by churches as messengers, but who spoke for themselves at convention meetings and not with delegated authority from their congregations. As James Tull noted in his lengthy study of Landmarkism, Gambrell feared that Hayden and other more extreme Landmarkers viewed "Baptist general bodies as combinative in structure, possessing ecclesiastical powers, in spite of an ostensible emphasis upon local church authority." [7] Graves himself, of course, had displayed a similar tendency in the aftermath of his expulsion from First Baptist Church of Nashville in 1858.

In a sense then, Hayden was clearly more of a Landmarker in the Graves tradition than Carroll and his allies. After being denied a seat at the BGCT in 1897, Hayden led his followers in 1900 to organize a new Landmark entity, the East Texas Baptist Convention, which was soon renamed as the Baptist Missionary Association of Texas. [8]

---

[7] J. E. Tull, "A Study of Southern Baptist Landmarkism in the Light of Historical Baptist Ecclesiology" (Ph.D. diss., Columbia University, 1960), 620.

[8] For a concise summary of the scholarly interpretations of the Hayden controversy, see J. L. Garrett, *Baptist Theology: A Four-Century Study* (Macon, GA: Mercer University Press, 2009), 237–39. For a fairly recent and thorough analysis of the Texas battle, see J. E. Early Jr., "The Hayden Controversy: A Detailed Examination of the First Major Internal Altercation of the Baptist General Convention of Texas" (Ph.D. diss., Southwestern Baptist Theological Seminary, 2002), which has been revised as *A Texas Power Struggle: The*

This was the first major schism in Southern Baptist life that was at least indirectly linked to some of J. R. Graves's ecclesiological ideas.

Second, the Hayden faction apparently had a sympathetic counterpart in Arkansas led by Benjamin M. Bogard (1868–1951), a Baptist pastor in Searcy. A strict Landmarker who adored Graves, Bogard and *Arkansas Baptist* editor William Allen Clark challenged the executive board of the Arkansas Baptist State Convention in 1901 on polity issues. After efforts failed to preserve unity, Bogard and his followers organized the General Association of Baptist Churches in Arkansas in 1902, which proved to be a permanent rupture. Two dissertations that were completed a year apart offer divergent interpretations of the Bogard controversy. On the one hand, J. Kristian Pratt stressed ecclesiological differences between the Bogard camp and the ABSC leadership, especially Bogard's desire to uphold a "local church protectionism" that he saw as an endangered species.[9] On the other hand, Bart Barber interpreted the Arkansas conflict as a flare up of Bogard's agrarian populism against the centralizing "New South" vision of James Philip Eagle and other ABSC luminaries; hence, he downplays the role of Landmark ideology in the quarrel.[10] As in Texas, developments in Arkansas revealed basically a family feud between cousins who divided over what constituted historic Landmarkism.[11]

Hayden Controversy (Denton: University of North Texas Press, 2005). Early stressed the Dallas-Waco power struggle as a crucial factor for explaining the conflict.

[9] J. K. Pratt, "A Landmark Baptist's Ecclesiology: Ben M. Bogard and Local Church Protectionism" (Ph.D. diss., Baylor University, 2005). On Bogard's fondness for Graves, see B. Bogard, "J. R. Graves, LL.D.," in *Pillars of Orthodoxy, or Defenders of the Faith* (Louisville, KY: Baptist Book Concern, 1900), 198–209. Bogard also had subsequent ties to early twentieth-century fundamentalism. See Pratt, "From 'Funnymentalist' to Friend: The Evolving Relationship of Ben M. Bogard and J. Frank Norris," *Baptist History & Heritage* 42 (Spring 2007): 105–13.

[10] C. B. Barber, "The Bogard Schism: An Arkansas Baptist Agrarian Revolt" (Ph.D. diss., Southwestern Baptist Theological Seminary, 2006). A letter from T. T. Eaton to Bogard in 1905 lends some indirect support for Barber's thesis. See Eaton to Bogard, February 15, 1905, Eaton Papers, box 1, folder 30, where the Louisville pastor warned Bogard about schism: "Denominational action should never be based on personal grounds." Eaton wrote a similar later earlier to S. H. Hayden, July 10, 1902, Eaton Papers, box 1, folder 29. For older, now dated studies of the Arkansas battle, see D. O. Moore, "The Landmark Baptists and Their Attack upon the Southern Baptist Convention Historically Analyzed" (Th.D. diss., Southern Baptist Theological Seminary, 1949), 48ff.; and P. R. Bryan, "An Analysis of the Ecclesiology of Associational Baptists, 1900–1950" (Ph.D. diss., Baylor University, 1973), which also has relevance for the Texas conflict.

[11] As late as 2007, the ABSC rejected an attempt to alter its articles of incorporation to eliminate the following statement: "The Baptist Faith and Message shall not be interpreted as to permit open communion and/or alien immersion." See C. Warren, "Ark. Messengers Reject Amendment," *Baptist Press*, November 9, 2007, accessed November 9, 2007. http://bpnews.net/bpnews.asp?ID=26800. Although the majority favored the change, it was not a sufficient percentage to pass, thus showing the continuing influence of Landmarkism in the SBC-related Baptist entity in the state.

Indeed, the two state controversies demonstrated an uncanny resemblance. Both involved the polemics of Baptist newspaper editors, ecclesiological differences, sociological dynamics, and divisive outcomes. Thus it should have surprised no one when in 1905 the Texas and Arkansas splinter groups met in Texarkana, following a rebuff from the SBC to a memorial—which reflected the ideology of Gospel Missionism—from the new Bogard organization. The result of the Texarkana gathering was the creation of a new national Landmark body called the Baptist General Association. By 1924 more Texas churches joined and the name was changed to the American Baptist Association. The Texas and Arkansas Landmarkers cooperated in the ABA until 1950, when an internal dispute over Bogard's authoritarian leadership and the issue of church representation at meetings precipitated a new schism, with the largely Texas-oriented North American Baptist Association separating from the ABA. The NABA became the Baptist Missionary Association of America in 1969. The ABA and the BMAA remain separate entities and together account for about 460,000 members.[12]

The denominational fractures in Texas and Arkansas a decade or so after Graves's death vividly exhibited the ongoing debates about the kinds of issues that had energized the Landmark founder, even including premillennialism, which is not a distinctively Baptist belief.[13] The fact that there were Landmarkers on each side of both controversies illustrates Stephen Stookey's helpful distinction between "Schismatic" and "Convention"

---

[12] See Garrett, *Baptist Theology*, 239–42. Garrett (p. 242) observed that the BMAA "somewhat muted" its Landmarkism in 1988, which may help explain a ministry agreement that the Baptist Missionary Association of Texas (a BMAA affiliate) recently entered into with Southern Baptists of Texas Convention for 2011. See "BMA-SBTC Ministry Agreement Proposed," *Baptist Press*, October 13, 2010, accessed October 13, 2010, http://bpnews.net/bpnews.asp?ID=33860. For statistics on the ABA (225,000) and the BMAA (235,000), see A. W. Wardin Jr., *The Twelve Baptist Tribes in the USA: A Historical and Statistical Analysis* (Atlanta: Baptist History and Heritage Society; and Nashville: Fields Publishing, 2007), 73. Several years ago I learned from a former student who tuned the piano in our house that there were independent Landmarkers like himself who belonged to unaffiliated congregations with no denominational ties. Perhaps that would be the ultimate logic of the Landmark emphasis on the complete autonomy of local churches. See Wardin, *The Twelve Baptist Tribes*, 73, for a listing of the independents, along with other small Landmark associations.

[13] On premillennial positions, see "Doctrinal Statement of the American Baptist Association," accessed January 24, 2011, http://www.abaptist.org/general.html; and "Doctrinal Statement of the BMAA," accessed January 24, 2011, http://www.discipleguide.org/pages/page.asp?page_id=40172. In the latter, premillennial conviction is not binding but expresses "the preponderance of opinion" among BMAA churches. Of course, premillennialism influenced Southern Baptists who remained in the SBC. See E. H. Cantwell, "Millennial Teachings among Southern Baptist Theologians from 1845 to 1945" (Th.M. thesis, Southwestern Baptist Theological Seminary, 1960), which includes a non-analytical chapter on Graves, 31–48; M. O. Hester, "Millennialism in Southern Baptist Thought since 1900" (Ph.D. diss., Southern Baptist Theological Seminary, 1981), who omitted Graves in his discussion of background; and D. E. Howe, "An Analysis of

Landmarkers, with the latter showing particular strength in the West but not limited to that region.[14] Since Graves himself never seriously contemplated a departure from the SBC and continued to support the work of many of its agencies, the Landmarkers who likewise stayed in the SBC might have had a stronger claim to his legacy.[15] As it turned out, the "Tennessee Tradition" remained a reasonably durable undercurrent in denominational life for some time, although at times it appeared to blend with lingering elements of an older Separate Baptist ecclesiology. For example, the original 1925 version of the Baptist Faith and Message, which followed the 1833 New Hampshire Confession at many points, defined the New Testament church in local terms only, omitting any reference to the universal church. This possible concession to Landmark sentiment, however, seemed dispensable by 1963 when the BFM revision committee added this line: "The New Testament speaks also of the church as the body of Christ which includes all the redeemed of all the ages." [16] The ensuing approval of this expanded concept of the church by the convention in Kansas City undoubtedly pointed to how much Landmarkism had waned in the denomination in the generation since the 1925 BFM.

Moreover, the development of denominational structure and programs in the SBC between 1925 and 1963 also represented a setback for Landmark ecclesiology. The inauguration of the Cooperative Program in 1925 as the primary funding mechanism for SBC agencies like the Foreign Mission Board and the Home Mission Board proved to be a devastating blow to J. R. Graves's notion—which the Gospel Mission movement embraced—that churches should appoint, send out, and fund missionaries. The centralizing character of the Cooperative Program meant that the convention system that had been established in 1845 now had a corresponding financial format; no longer did each board or agency have to fend for itself in raising money, an approach that was more

---

Dispensationalism and Its Implications for the Theologies of James Robinson Graves, John Franklyn Norris, and Wallie Amos Criswell" (Ph.D. diss., Southwestern Baptist Theological Seminary, 1988).

[14] S. M. Stookey, "The Impact of Landmarkism upon Southern Baptist Western Geographical Expansion" (Ph.D. diss., Southwestern Baptist Theological Seminary, 1994), 92.

[15] For an example of Graves's interest in and commitment to the SBC late in his life, see Graves, "The Convention," *Baptist and Reflector,* June 5, 1890, 7. This concerned the meeting that year in Fort Worth, Texas, which he apparently attended. See his "Way Marks" in Texas in the same issue and same page. His serious fall came a few months later.

[16] For the two statements in regard to the church, see "The Baptist Faith and Message," *A Sourcebook for Baptist Heritage*, ed. H. L. McBeth (Nashville: Broadman, 1990), 511. For an analysis of the ecclesiological shift that transpired between the two documents, see J. A. Durden, "A Selected Issue in Southern Baptist Ecclesiology: The Nature of the Church as Reflected in the Baptist Faith and Messages of 1925 and 1963" (Th.D. diss., Mid-America Baptist Theological Seminary, 1993).

typical of the society method that dominated Baptist life in America before 1845.[17] Graves surely would have viewed all this as a "consolidating scheme" that would ultimately weaken local church sovereignty and independence.

In the meantime, steps taken by the SBC in the early 1930s regarding representation at annual meetings heightened the convention features of the denomination. After 1931 messengers could only come from cooperating churches that gave a stipulated amount to SBC causes, presumably through the Cooperative Program. James Tull maintained that this adjustment of the financial basis or representation actually turned the SBC into "an aggregate of churches"; in other words, he saw the Landmark idea of a general visible church providing the rationale for a centralized organizational structure.[18] Robert Baker, however, later suggested that the changes in the 1930s did not constitute a Landmark triumph. He also offered a useful comparison of Landmark and non-Landmark perspectives:

> A clear distinction should be made between the Landmark position of *delegated* church representation and the position of many non-Landmarkers which might be termed a *designated* church representation. The Landmarkers viewed the Convention as a body composed of autonomous and scripturally authoritative local churches officially represented through their delegates. . . . The other view . . . denied both the necessity and the advantage of projecting the authority of local churches into general bodies. . . . It conceived of general bodies as mass meetings of representative Baptists composed of messengers *designated* by the churches, but who did not officially represent their churches, nor possess any delegated authority from the churches, nor corporately exercise any authority over the churches. According to this view, the authority of the Convention stemmed from fraternal and widespread denominational consensus, not from the authority of the churches.[19]

---

[17] On the Cooperative Program, see C. Brand and D. Hankins, *One Sacred Effort: The Cooperative Program of Southern Baptists* (Nashville: B&H, 2006).

[18] Tull, "A Study of Southern Baptist Landmarkism," 632–33. Denominational historian W. W. Barnes sounded a similar concern in *The Southern Baptist Convention: A Study in the Development of Ecclesiology* (Fort Worth: By the author, 1934), 78–79.

[19] R. A. Baker, *The Southern Baptist Convention and Its People, 1607–1972* (Nashville: Broadman, 1974), 315–16.

If Landmarkers felt any vindication in 1931, it certainly did not give any boost to their status in the denomination over the next several decades. In reality, the ecclesiology of R. B. C. Howell gained ascendency over that of J. R. Graves in the minds and hearts of most Southern Baptists.

The Graves legacy steadily declined in the post-World War II era, especially in areas like Nashville, Richmond, and Atlanta where key denominational agencies were based. Moreover, Landmarkism was generally snubbed in the Cooperative Program seminaries, although it had a following among some faculty and students at the independent Mid-America Baptist Theological Seminary in the Memphis area.[20] Regional pockets of Landmark influence and practice persisted, to be sure, but they were difficult to pick up on the radar at the national level or in most state conventions.

As a result of the conservative resurgence, which began in 1979 and dramatically changed the direction of the SBC and its agencies, it was inevitable that moderate or liberal historians would find vestiges of Graves and Landmarkism in what they classified as a "fundamentalist takeover" of the denomination. When James Tull penned his massive dissertation in 1960, he essentially dismissed any relationship between Landmarkism and fundamentalism in the 1920s and 1930s. First, he noted that the limited fundamentalist agitation in the SBC at that time had no significant connection to the Landmark movement. Second, he perceptively remarked that extreme fundamentalists in the convention could not remain consistent Landmarkers: "The non-denominational nature of fundamentalism has led the fundamentalists into a kind of ecumenical movement of their own—a movement which in the Southern Baptist Convention has tended to ignore and to disrupt denominational lines." [21]

By the late 1980s, however, Tull significantly adjusted his assessment of possible links between Landmarkism and fundamentalism. At the end of his teaching career at Southeastern Baptist Theological Seminary, he found himself on the losing side of the conservative-moderate clash that had raged for the previous decade. In fact, this controversy clearly eclipsed the earlier Landmark disputes both in scope and denominational impact; as an embattled seminary professor, he did not welcome the outcome. Since he died in 1989, what he wrote in *High-Church Baptists in the South*—a revised and shortened version of his dissertation—likely reflected his reaction to the decisive period of conservative-moderate discord. In that context, Tull sought to unveil "Landmark

[20] I base this on my 10-year (1989–99) teaching stint there, during which I wrote *To All the World: A History of Mid-America Baptist Theological Seminary, 1972–1997* (Memphis: Disciple Press, 1997).
[21] Tull, "A Study of Southern Baptist Landmarkism," 678–79. He made a similar comment about premillennial fellowships that reached across denominational lines.

characteristics" in the SBC "fundamentalist" victory. After acknowledging that SBC "fundamentalists" focused primarily on biblical inerrancy, which was not an issue in the Landmark debates, he then mapped out the most likely common ground between the two movements:

> The present movement has exhibited the same belligerent attitude of older fundamentalism, and is exclusive in that it has no kind words for other Protestant denominations, that is, the antiaffiliationism of the Landmarkists. The leaders of this current fundamentalist movement come from the heart of the Landmark Belt. The present fundamentalist control of the Southern Baptist Convention is not a Landmark movement, yet it claims to go back to a universally held Baptist position, similar to the "Old Landmarks" of Landmarkism, and calls up earlier Baptist leaders to buttress these claims, and reinterprets history to support the claims, as did the Landmarkers.[22]

Thus Tull saw a revivification of the spirit and strategies of the Landmarkers in the arrogance, exclusivism, and intimidation tactics of the SBC "fundamentalists." Perhaps the movement that had previously been defeated in the SBC had returned with a vengeance; or, as Tull regretfully put it, the mean disposition of the Landmarkers toward non-Baptists "has been assimilated in general Southern Baptist life until it is not specifically a 'Landmark' characteristic any longer."[23]

In a similar vein, other Baptist historians have attempted to link Landmarkism and fundamentalism. For example, Belmont University professor Marty Bell found parallels between Graves and late twentieth-century "fundamentalists," although he concentrated

---

[22] Tull, *High-Church Baptists in the South: The Origin, Nature and Influence of Landmarkism*, ed. Morris Ashcraft (Macon, GA: Mercer University Press, 2000), 172. There is a wide body of literature on the post-1979 developments in the SBC. For a non-conservative perspective, see D. T. Morgan, *The New Crusades, the New Holy Land: Conflict in the Southern Baptist Convention, 1969–1991* (Tuscaloosa: University of Alabama Press, 1996). For an account by a recognized SBC conservative, see J. Sutton, *The Baptist Reformation: The Conservative Resurgence in the Southern Baptist Convention* (Nashville: B&H, 2000). Furman professor Helen Lee Turner's interpretation of the more recent controversy stresses the role of dispensational premillennialism, although she focuses on J. Frank Norris, R. G. Lee, and W. A. Criswell—not J. R. Graves—as the most prominent sources of influence. See her "Fundamentalism in the Southern Baptist Convention: The Crystallization of a Millennialist Vision" (Ph.D. diss., University of Virginia, 1990). For all its fancy sociological jargon, this perspective overlooks the diversity of millennial views among SBC conservatives. See D. Roach, "END TIMES: Scholars Differ on What Bible Says about Subject," *Baptist Press* (December 30, 2009), accessed January 1, 2010, http://www.bpnews.net/bpnews.asp?ID=31963.
[23] Tull, *High-Church Baptists*, 173.

more on common attitudes than on specific ideas or beliefs.[24] In addition, William Brackney made a tantalizing statement in a *festschrift* for Leon McBeth that Landmarkism "laid the groundwork for later fundamentalism" but provided no explanation of what that signifies.[25]

The basic problem with this historiographical approach is that it tends to ignore the contexts of two very different battles in SBC life. Graves and the Landmarkers gave special attention to ecclesiology and a successionist view of Baptist history, which were conspicuous by their almost complete absence in the conservative-moderate showdown.[26] Furthermore, the thesis that Landmarkism somehow anticipated or paved the way for contemporary SBC "fundamentalism" neglects another important difference in the two movements. Except for Graves's dalliance with non-Baptist dispensationalists, Landmarkers diligently shunned ecumenical relationships. Indeed, James Leo Garrett posed the possibility that "lingering Landmark influence" contributed to mid-twentieth-century decisions by the SBC not to join the World Council of Churches or the National Council of Churches of Christ in the USA.[27] Both during and after the conservative-moderate conflict, however, an interesting phenomenon unfolded, what Beeson Divinity School dean Timothy George referred to as "the evangelicalizing" of the SBC.[28] In other words, SBC conservatives reached out to evangelical Protestants on a wide variety of fronts, and formed alliances to defend biblical inerrancy, oppose abortion, and reach a lost world with the gospel. The latter cause, in particular, has brought new coalitions and fresh questions about the possible limits of cooperative efforts that cross denominational lines.[29]

---

[24] M. G. Bell, "James Robinson Graves and the Rhetoric of Demagogy: Primitivism and Democracy in Old Landmarkism" (Ph.D. diss., Vanderbilt University, 1990), 240, 274ff.

[25] W. H. Brackney, "A Turn toward a Doctrinal Christianity: Baptist Theology, a Work in Progress," in *Turning Points in Baptist History: A Festschrift in Honor of Harry Leon McBeth*, ed. M. E. Williams and W. B. Shurden (Macon, GA: Mercer University Press, 2008), 81.

[26] In their emphasis on Baptist freedom, moderates did sound some alarms about the new SBC threatening the autonomy of local churches. For typical expositions, see C. W. Deweese, *Freedom: The Key to Baptist Genius* (Brentwood, TN: Baptist History and Heritage Society, 2006); and W. M. Pinson Jr., *Issues Testing Baptist Polity* (Brentwood, TN: Baptist History and Heritage Society, 2003), 25–34.

[27] Garrett, *Baptist Theology*, 247.

[28] T. George, "Southern Baptist Ghosts," *First Things*, May 1999, 21. George provided a listing of the evidence (p. 22), where he also astutely observed that Southern Baptist-evangelical cooperation can lead to "the diminution of Baptist identity and a sense of uprootedness from a particular tradition."

[29] See N. Finn, "With Whom Can My Church Cooperate?" *Between the Times* (January 22, 2010), accessed January 25, 2010, http://betweenthetimes.com/2010/01/22/with-whom-can-my-church-cooperate/; M. Kelly, "New Era of Cooperation Anticipated Following Historic Meetings in Germany," *Baptist Press*, June 26, 2008, accessed June 26, 2008, http://www.bpnews.net/bpnews.asp?ID=28371; and W. Lee, "Rankin Seeks Global Insights at Lausanne," *Baptist Press*, October 21, 2010, accessed October 21, 2010, http://www.bpnews.net/bpnews.asp?ID=33917.

At the same time, these trends have provoked some reaction from other conservatives in the SBC who might best be described as espousing—in Southeastern Baptist Theological Seminary historian Nathan Finn's term—not Landmarkism but "Baptocentrism."[30] Professor Malcolm Yarnell of Southwestern Baptist Theological Seminary, for example, engaged in a heated exchange with Oklahoma pastor Wade Burleson over what should be considered indispensable Baptist distinctives. The debate in part was rooted in Burleson's controversial tenure as a trustee of the International Mission Board from 2005 to 2008. Not long after he joined the board, trustees adopted policies prohibiting missionary candidates from speaking in tongues and also requiring them to have been baptized in churches that (1) exclusively practice believer's baptism by immersion; (2) teach the security of the believer; and (3) do not understand baptism as contributory to salvation. For candidates whose baptisms fell short of these standards, a request for baptism in a Southern Baptist church was expected. The IMB trustees made minor adjustments to these policies in 2007, although the changes did not satisfy Burleson. In the meantime, he began to blog critically about board members, policies, and methods. Eventually he was censured by the board, resigned in 2008, and released a book in 2009 through a moderate Baptist publisher in which he recounted his experiences.[31]

Since Burleson alleged that the IMB trustees who initiated the new policies took their clues from Southwestern Seminary President Paige Patterson, it is not surprising that he consequently entered the lists with one of the seminary's faculty members. It became clear in various blog posts that Burleson viewed the policies on tongues and alien immersion as symptomatic of a "Baptist Identity" movement's attempt to draw tight boundaries of fellowship for the SBC around a narrow understanding of Baptist principles, or "bedrock convictions." [32] For his part, Malcolm Yarnell used Peter Lumpkins's blog site to

---

[30] D. Baker, "Interview with Between the Times, Part III," Insight podcast downloaded from accessed September 19, 2008, http://www.ncbaptist.org.

[31] The sequence of events is covered in D. Alford, "Tongues Tied: Southern Baptists Bar New Missions Candidates from Glossolalia," *Christianity Today* (February 2006): 21; E. Bridges, "IMB Holds to Baptism, Prayer Guidelines," *Baptist Press*, May 10, 2007, accessed May 11, 2007, http://www.bpnews.net/bpnews. asp?ID=25616; K. Walker, "Critic Censured: Trustee Suspended from Mission Board for Airing Closed-Door Activities," *Christianity Today*, January 2008, 18–19; and "Burleson Resigns as IMB Trustee," *Baptist & Reflector,* February 6, 2008, 2. Burleson told his side of the story in *Hardball Religion: Feeling the Fury of Fundamentalism* (Macon, GA: Smyth & Helwys, 2009). Nathan Finn, a church history professor at Southeastern Seminary, drew some intriguing parallels between J. R. Graves's dissent from FMB policies in 1858–59 and Burleson's more recent criticisms of the IMB. See Finn, "The IMB Imbroglio and Historical Irony," *Author Blog*, March 26, 2007, accessed March 26, 2007, https://nathanfinn.wordpress.com.

[32] E.g., Burleson, "Baptist Identity and Ad Hominem Variants," *Grace and Truth to You* (April 29, 2008), accessed June 5, 2008, http://kerussocharis.blogspot.com/2008/04/baptist-identity-and-conversational.html.

identify himself as a "traditional Baptist" who feared that some cooperative relationships with non-Baptist evangelicals and doctrinal indifference could end up compromising Baptist identity.[33] The hard-edged nature of the Burleson-Yarnell debate echoed some nineteenth-century disputations, just as it once again revealed noteworthy fissures in the landscape of a denomination that was supposedly more unified than it had been in 1979.

"Baptocentric" chords continued to resound from Fort Worth, and some of the notes incorporated at least a low-key Landmark ring. In January of 2009 Paige Patterson proclaimed a "Radical Reformation Day" at Southwestern as an annual commemoration of the Anabaptist tradition's importance for modern Baptists.[34] While this celebratory event does not imply a full endorsement of Baptist successionism, Graves and Orchard viewed the Anabaptists as vital links in the unbroken chain of true Baptist congregations. Furthermore, some Southwestern professors have contributed to recent discussions regarding the Lord's Supper. Although not advocating a rigidly restricted communion like Graves did in his later years, they nonetheless expressed a clear inclination to "fence" the table.[35] Although this emerging "Southwestern school" should not be

---

[33] E.g., M. Yarnell, "Baptist Identity or Evangelical Anonymity? Part II," *Peter Lumpkins's Blog*, April 27, 2008, accessed June 5, 2008, http://peterlumpkins.typepad.com/peter_lumpkins/2008/04/Baptist-ident-1.html. For an overview of his ecclesiology, which is not particularly Landmarkist, see M. B. Yarnell III, "The Church," in *The Baptist Faith and Message 2000: Critical Issues in America's Largest Protestant Denomination*, ed. D. K. Blount and J. D. Wooddell (Lanham, MD: Rowman & Littlefield, 2007), 55–70.

[34] "Education Briefs: Southwestern Seminary Marks 'Radical Reformation Day,'" *Baptist Press*, January 22, 2009, accessed January 22, 2009, http://www.bpnews.net/bpnews.asp?ID=29714. Patterson set forth his appreciation for the Reformation radicals in "Learning from the Anabaptists," in *Southern Baptist Identity: An Evangelical Denomination Faces the Future*, ed. D. S. Dockery (Wheaton, IL: Crossway Books, 2009), 123–37. Southwestern has a long tradition of interest in the Radical Reformation. See the work of the late church history professor, W. R. Estep, *The Anabaptist Story*, rev. ed. (Grand Rapids: Eerdmans, 1975). The fascination with the Anabaptists tends to overlook the troublesome beliefs and practices of the Radical Reformers such as their weak soteriology. See J. E. McGoldrick, *Baptist Successionism: A Crucial Question in Baptist History*, ATLA Monograph Series, No. 32 (Metuchen, NJ: Scarecrow Press, 1994), 86–122.

[35] See T. White, "A Baptist's Theology of the Lord's Supper," in *Restoring Integrity in Baptist Churches*, ed. T. White, J. G. Duesing, and M. B. Yarnell III (Grand Rapids: Kregel, 2008), 137–61; and E. F. Caner, "Fencing the Table: The Lord's Supper, Its Participants, and Its Relationship to Church Discipline," *Restoring Integrity*, 163–78. Caner has since left The College at Southwestern and is now president of Truett-McConnell College in Georgia. These essays contrast markedly with Trevin Wax, "The Case for Open Communion," *Kingdom People* (October 11, 2007), accessed January 11, 2011, http://trevinwax.com/2007/10/11/the-case-for-open-communion/. For a mediating position that restricts the Supper to immersed believers, see N. Finn, "Baptism as a Prerequisite to the Lord's Supper," Center for Theological Research, Southwestern Baptist Theological Seminary, available at http://www.baptisttheology.org. For more evidence of renewed thinking about the Lord's Supper, see T. R. Schreiner and M. R. Crawford, eds., *The Lord's Supper: Remembering and Proclaiming Christ until He Comes*, NAC Studies in Bible and Theology Series, no. 10 (Nashville: B&H Academic, 2010).

understood as resurgent Landmarkism, it does share with J. R. Graves distinct concerns about Baptist roots and identity.

Paige Patterson signed on—with caveats—to a recent initiative in the SBC known as the Great Commission Resurgence, which was approved by messengers at the 2010 meeting in Orlando. Patterson's initial hesitation to endorse this endeavor might have been reflected in Southeastern Seminary President and GCR spokesman Danny Akin's response to one of the "myths" circulated by GCR opponents that it would dilute "our Baptist identity and distinctives so that we begin to look more like the American Evangelical Convention than the Southern Baptist Convention."[36] An overt rupture between the GCR and Baptist Identity movements never materialized, perhaps in part because GCR included a strong commitment to biblically vigorous local churches, especially in reference to missions and evangelism: "Mission is not a ministry of the church, but is at the heart of the church's identity and essence. We must encourage our churches to see themselves as the missionary bodies that they are."[37] This emphasis meshed well with a broader recognition of and support for increased engagement by local congregations in the SBC missionary enterprise.[38] While J. R. Graves operated in a much different historical context and ultimately wanted to dismantle the SBC's mission boards, he surely would have welcomed any venture to mobilize local congregations for both home and international missions. He might have been myopic about the advantages of cooperative undertakings through boards and agencies, but his appreciation for the local church as a catalyst for and facilitator of direct mission efforts may have been one of his most significant legacies.

---

[36] Daniel Akin, "Myth #7," Between the Times, available at http://betweenthetimes.com archives (accessed October 26, 2009). On Patterson's qualified support for GCR, see T. Brister, "The Backstory to the Great Commission Resurgence," Provocations and Pantings (June 17, 2009), accessed June 17, 2009, http://timmy brister.com/2009/06/17/the-back-story-to-the-great-commission-resurgence/. On the gap between GCR and the Baptist Identity movement, see Tom Ascol, "What Will We Be in the SBC?" *Founders Ministries Blog* (February 19, 2009), accessed February 20, 2009, http://www.founders.org/blog/2009/02/what-will-we-be -in-sbc.html.

[37] "Toward a Great Commission Resurgence," GCR site, February 10, 2009, accessed April 27, 2009, http:// www.greatcommissionresurgence.com.

[38] See V. Brown, "IMB Retooling to Focus Agency on Local-Church Mission Work," Associated Baptist Press (September 23, 2008, accessed on that date), at http://www.abpnews.com/content/view/3535/53; and J. Rankin, "Giving Churches Ownership," *Author Blog* (April 8, 2010), accessed April 14, 2010, http://rank-inconnecting.com/2010/04/giving-churches-ownership/. For an important article that bridges local church involvement and denominational missions, see E. Stetzer, "Life in Those Old Bones: If You are Interested in Doing Mission, There Could Hardly Be a Better Tool Than Denominations," *Christianity Today,* June 2010, 24–29. Stetzer did research and missiology for the SBC's LifeWay Christian Resources.

In a post-denominational age marked by the steady blurring of boundary lines between various Christian groups, it is not shocking that discussions among Baptists during the last several years point to a fresh interest in the subject of denominational identity.[39] As J. R. Graves understood, Baptist identity requires the drawing of boundaries informed by a knowledge of the past. What he failed to comprehend was that both Baptist identity and history were far more complicated than he suspected. Indeed, he never conceded that there was more than one genuine denominational identity.[40] As a result, his understandable sense of pride as a Baptist crossed over into a distasteful arrogance and triumphalism. As the grand patriarch of the "Tennessee Tradition," he staked out meticulous boundaries as a way to preserve the besieged "Old Landmarks." The problem was not that he set borders for Baptist faith and practice, for that legitimate enterprise has been an ongoing one since the early seventeenth century. Graves's shortcoming was that he ultimately skewed some of those boundaries because he relied on flawed historical markers. That proved to be a major weakness in the story of one of the most pivotal and influential voices from the Baptist past.

---

[39] See the essays, for example, in D. S. Dockery, *Southern Baptist Identity*. This volume includes papers presented at Baptist identity conferences held at Union University, Jackson, Tennessee, in 2004 and 2006. Cf. R. S. Norman, *More Than Just a Name: Preserving Our Baptist Identity* (Nashville: B&H, 2001). Some recent conversations have focused on ecclesiology. See J. G. Duesing, T. White, and M. B. Yarnell III, eds., *Upon This Rock: The Baptist Understanding of the Church* (Nashville: B&H Academic, 2010). Moderate and liberal Baptists, many of whom have exited from the SBC, have likewise shown concern for issues of identity. Some have proposed a more "catholic" perspective to counteract some of the more negative side effects of an obsessive focus on freedom and individualism. See S. R. Harmon, *Towards Baptist Catholicity: Essays on Tradition and the Baptist Vision*, Studies in Baptist History and Thought, vol. 27 (Milton Keynes, UK: Paternoster, 2006); and B. Ross Jr., "Challenging Individualism: N.C. Proposal Raises Age-Old Questions of Baptist Identity," *Christianity Today*, November 2010, 16. For a critical response by those committed to the value of individualism, see "Baptist Historians Affirm Individual Conscience," Associated Baptist Press (September 28, 2010), accessed September 28, 2010, http://www.abpnews.com/content/view/5738/53.

[40] The plural "identities" fits the historical and contemporary evidence better than the singular. See Nathan Finn, "Baptist Identities and the Current State of the SBC," *Author Blog* (September 21, 2007), accessed September 21, 2007, http://nathanfinn.wordpress.com. Finn saw at least seven distinct takes on Baptist identity.

Appendix

Note: J. R Graves ran standing columns similar to the two below in his newspaper for many years. This version, which reflects some changes particularly related to his difficulties in the First Baptist Church of Nashville in the late 1850s, appeared in the *Baptist*, July 20, 1867, on the first two pages. He had recently moved to Memphis, Tennessee, and resumed publication of his paper earlier that year after a five-year hiatus. Italics are in the original.

BAPTIST DOCTRINES, PRINCIPLES AND FACTS

Six Important Doctrines

1. One Lord, one Faith, one Immersion, Eph. xi [*sic*]: 5. That an immersion is the profession of that *one* faith in the *burial* and *resurrection* of that *one* Lord. See Rom. vi: 4–6; Col. ii: 12; 1 Cor. xv: 29; 1 Peter iii: 21.
2. The Grace of God, the only foundation of Hope and Faith *in* Christ, the only medium of Justification.
3. The Word of God the Instrument, and the Spirit of God the Agent in the regeneration of adults.
4. Each visible Church of Christ is a company of scripturally immersed believers only, (not of believers and their *unconverted children* and *seekers* on probation.) associated by voluntary covenant to obey and execute all the commandments of Christ, having the same organization, doctrines, officers, and ordinances of the Church at Jerusalem, and independent of all others, acknowledging no lawgiver in Zion but Christ, and submitting to no law he has not enacted. Read Rom. i: 7; 1 Cor. i: 2; Eph. i: 1; Col i: 1–5; Acts ii: 41, 42; Matt. xviii: 20–23–28 [*sic*]; 2 Cor. vii: 6–19; Rev. ii: 23; Phillip. [*sic*] xxvi: 27; 1 Cor. v: 12, 13.
5. The "Lord's Supper" is a positive and commemorative ordinance to be observed only by a Church of Christ, *as such*, (that is, in church capacity), not as a test of *Christian fellowship* or personal feeling of one communicant toward another, as Pedobaptists erroneously teach, but only to show forth Christ's *death* till he comes

205

again; and being a *Church* act, it becomes, incidentally, a symbol of *Church relationship*; consequently, only those churches can participate in this ordinance that agree in faith and practice. The members of one church (though of the same faith and order) can come to the communion of another only by an act of courtesy and not by *right*, for each church is independent, being made the guardian of the purity of the sacred feast, is invested with the authority to discipline those whose relationship ordinarily gives the right. [Note: Graves later tightened his position to a fully restricted or closed communion, as discussed above in chap. 7.]

6. Christian baptism is the immersion of a believer in water by a qualified administrator, in the name of the Trinity, in *representation* of the burial and resurrection of Christ, and profession of a death to sin, union with Christ, and consecration to his service. *One* mode only, therefore, can answer this design, and the profession of baptism cannot be made by *children* except *"the children of God by Faith."* Matt. iii: 16 and xxviii: 17; Mark xvi: 16; John iii: 2, 3 [*sic*]; Acts viii: to the close; Rom. vi: 4, 5; Col. ii: 12; Gal. iii: 26, 27.

Burying in water of one dead in sin is the only action; since the burial of a dead man is the only "likeness" or representation of death in the world, for it is called *the* likeness of death.

Six Important Principles

1. The *Bible* and the *Bible* alone, unalloyed with human devices or tradition, is, and ever has been, the religion of Baptists.
2. *Positive* laws (as baptism and the subjects of baptism, etc.) are not left to be *inferred*, but *in all cases* require *positive* and plain commands, or *examples*.
3. To divide the positive requirements of Christ into *essential* and *non-essentials*, is to decide how far Christ is to be obeyed, and in what points we may safely disobey him. But to refuse to obey one of the least of his positive requirements or teach others so, involves one in the guilt of violating all.
4. Every positive law, ordinance, or practice in the Church, *not expressly commanded* or exampled, is *positively forbidden, since the specification of one thing is the prohibition of every other.* These are all human inventions and traditions, as infant baptism, sprinkling, pouring, etc., now practiced for religious rites, for which no scriptural warrant can be found, and *are, therefore, sinful.*
5. Christ gave no men, society or church the authority to *traffic* with the ordinance or organization of his Church or Kingdom, as to make or change his laws, and substi-

tute one thing for another. To surrender what he has established, is *treachery*—to change them, treason.

6. Principles can neither be *conceded* nor *compromised*.

Six Important Facts

1. *All scholars, critics and lexicographers*, of any note, *unanimously* declare that the *primary* (that is, first) and *leading* signification of "Baptizo," is to dip or *immerse*, while some of the best scholars of any age affirm that it *has no other meanings*— [Liddell and Scott, Carson, Anthony &c].

2. Standard historians *unanimously agree* that *primitive* and *apostolic* baptism was administered by the *immersion of believers in water*, in the name of the Trinity.— [Stuart, Robinson and Wall].

3. *Nearly all standard Pedobaptist* commentators admit that the Bible does not furnish one *plain command for*, or *example of infant baptism*, and there is the utmost disagreement and *contradiction* among them on what grounds or for what purpose it is to be administered.

4. All standard historians unanimously affirm that the *government* of the apostolic churches was *purely democratic*, (that is, vested in the people or membership) and *all the churches independent republics*. All religious *societies* have *legislative powers* and *clerical* or *aristocratical* governments, (that is, in the hands of the clergy or a few as a session) are *anti-scriptural* and *anti-republican* tyrannies which no Christian can lawfully countenance, or *republican freemen* ought to support; consequently, all the acts and ordinances of such irregular bodies are *illegal*, and ought not to be received by us; nor should such societies be, in any way, recognized as scriptural churches, or their preachers as official ministers of the gospel. The Baptist Church is the parent of democratic and republican government.

5. No society, organized upon *principles* differing from those of the *apostolic churches*, having *different subjects, ordinances, orders* in the *ministry* can justly be called a *gospel church*, or *church of Christ*, or a branch of the *church of Christ*, for "things equal to the same thing are equal to each other."

6. Protestant historians frankly admit that Baptist churches are the only religious communities that have stood since the apostles, and as Christian societies, which have preserved pure the doctrine of the gospel through the ages.—[See Trilemma, p. 36].

BAPTIST COROLLARIES

1. There is no church but a body of immersed believers who have been immersed by a duly appointed officer of a Scriptural Church.

2. There are no Scriptural ministers but those who have been duly authorized by a Scriptural Church.

3. Since nothing is more evident than the fact that we teach more effectually by example than by precept—therefore, so long as we appropriate our pulpits for the official preaching of the gospel by those whom we consider duly baptized and ordained to the ministerial office, it is equally evident that it is improper for us to invite those teachers to occupy them when we know they are neither baptized nor ordained, and especially since they claim to be, and construe the act on our part into a recognition of their claims, and thus confirm their followers in error.

4. Nothing can be more inconsistent than to admit those preachers into our pulpits who hold and teach doctrines, on account of which, we would exclude both from our pulpits and churches, any minister of our denomination.

    This, we claim, is one of the old landmarks of the Baptist Church.

5. That a body of immersed believers is the highest ecclesiastical authority in the world, and the only tribunal for the trial of cases of discipline; that the acts of a church are of superior binding force over those of an association, convention, council, or presbytery—and no association or convention can impose a moral obligation upon the constituent parts composing them.

6. That since each church of Christ is an independent body, no one church can expect any other to indorse [*sic*] its acts, only so far as they are in strict accordance with the laws of Christ.

    If she excludes a member unjustly, any other church can restore him, if she sees fit.

7. Whenever any church acts in violation of the directions of her only lawgiver, as found in the New Testament, she becomes rebellious—her acts *null* and *void*; and all other churches, and associations of churches and conventions, should withdraw their fellowship from her until she repents and rectifies her order; or they become the partakers of her sins.

8. That no association or convention, or council, is a "court of appeal," or has any authority over the churches, but is simply an advisory council; therefore it has no right to dictate to the churches, or to demand support for any project or scheme

which they have originated, but may only recommend, advise, and urge to performance of duty in subservience to the great Christian voluntary principle.

9. When any church departs from the *faith*, or violates the *order* of the gospel, in the judgment of the association, it can and should withdraw its fellowship from her, and leave her to herself until she repents. This is no interference with her internal regulation.

10. Baptist are not Protestants. Since they never had any ecclesiastical connection with the Papacy, they are now, and have been the repudiators of the principles and practices of Papacy, whether found in Rome or in the Protestant sects that came out of her.

11. We regard Protestantism, as well as the Reformation of 1827, as based on the assumption that the prophecies and declarations of Christ touching His church are false, thus making Christ an imposter, and the reformers and not Christ, the saviors and preservers of the church.

Axioms

1. The unimmersed bodies of Christians are not churches, nor are any privileged companies of *the Church*; hence all Pedobaptist denominations are only religious societies.

2. That baptism and an official relation to a church are prerequisite to a regular gospel ministry; hence, all ordinances administered by an unbaptized and unordained, although immersed ministry, are null and void.

3. No church has a right to hear a case brought before it in violation of the law of Christ. The specification of the order to be observed, is the prohibition of any other order.

4. No member should submit to an arraignment or trial brought and conducted in violation of the laws of Christ. Each member is individually responsible to Christ for the faithful observance of his laws.

5. Since *right* only, not *might*, is right, a constitutional minority is in all cases the Scriptural church.

6. An unconstitutional or disorderly majority cannot exclude a member of an acknowledged constitutional church.

7. No church should receive letters of, or the members baptized by, a *disorderly* church. Nor should it admit to its communion the members of such a church, or in

any way countenance or uphold its disorder; it should keep no company with it that it may be ashamed.

Baptist Policy

1. To be in all things consistent with our principles, whether we gain or lose numbers or popularity.
2. To fulfill our peculiar mission—which is to be the Witnesses of Christ's truth against every system of error, and those who originate or advocate them; and above all by no act to countenance, recognize, aid or abet those who teach error, or to confirm those who are in error.
3. To employ all the energies of the denomination for the conversion of sinners and the upbuilding of Christ's Kingdom, through the most effectual means and agencies, such as Missionary efforts, Bible and Publication Societies, Theological Seminaries, Male and Female Colleges, Prayer-meetings, and Religious periodicals.
4. To occupy every village and city in the world with a suitable qualified, faithful, energetic and devoted minister.
5. To furnish a pastor to every church, and missionaries of the cross for every destitute region and land, at home and abroad, under the whole heaven, and to sustain them.
6. The commission to evangelize the nations having been given to the church through the Apostles, *she can not delegate her authority or her responsibility to a body, as a Board, outside of her.* The churches should select, send for and sustain the Missionaries of the Cross.

For the steadfast and uncompromising advocacy of these principles and this policy, this paper is especially devoted.

Archival Collections and Papers

James Robinson Graves Collection, AR. 9, Southern Baptist Historical Library and Archives, Nashville, TN.

John Albert Broadus Collection, James P. Boyce Centennial Library Archives, Southern Baptist Theological Seminary, Louisville, KY.

Robert Boyté Howell Collection, AR. 595, SBHLA, Nashville, TN.

T. T. Eaton Papers, James P. Boyce Centennial Library Archives, Southern Baptist Theological Seminary, Louisville, KY.

Institutional Minutes and Proceedings

Minutes of the Board of Trustees, 1874–1906, Southwest Baptist University, Emma Waters Summar Library Archives, Union University, Jackson, TN.

Minutes of Mount Freedom Baptist Church, Wilmore, KY, in Church Records, 1832–1961, Microfilm, SBHLA, Nashville, TN.

Proceedings of the Southern Baptist Convention at Its Seventh Biennial Session, Held in the First Church, Richmond, Va., May 6th, 7th, 8th, 9th and 10th, 1859. Richmond: H. K. Ellyson, Printer, 1859.

Nineteenth-Century Baptist Periodicals and State Papers

Baptist and Reflector, 1889–93.

Biblical Recorder, 1862.

Christian Repository and Literary Review, 1852–55. Also known as *Christian Repository*.

Southern Baptist Almanac and Annual Register, 1848–55.

Southern Baptist Review and Eclectic, 1855–61. Also known as *Southern Baptist Review*.

Tennessee Baptist, 1845–89. Also known as *Baptist*.
Western Baptist Review, 1848.
Western Recorder, 1855.

BOOKS BY J. R. GRAVES

The Act of Baptism. Memphis: Baptist Book House, 1881.

The Bible Doctrine of the Middle Life as Opposed to Swedenborgianism and Spiritism. Memphis: Southern Baptist Publication Society, 1873.

Editor. *Both Sides: A Full Investigation of the Charges Preferred against Elder J. R. Graves by R. B. C. Howell and Others*. Nashville: Southwestern Publishing House, 1859.

Campbell and Campbellism Exposed: A Series of Replies (to A. Campbell's Articles in the Millennial Harbinger). Nashville: Graves & Marks, 1855.

Christian Baptism: The Profession of the Faith of the Gospel. 1891. Reprint, Texarkana, AR: Baptist Sunday School Committee, 1928 and 1968.

Denominational Tracts. Memphis: Baptist Book House, 1881.

The Dispensational Expositions of the Parables and Prophecies of Christ. Memphis: Graves & Mahaffy, 1887.

The Great Iron Wheel: Or, Republicanism Backwards and Christianity Reversed. 9th ed. Nashville: Graves, Marks, and Rutland, 1855.

Intercommunion Inconsistent, Unscriptural, and Productive of Evil. Memphis: Baptist Book House; Graves & Mahaffy, 1881.

John's Baptism—Was It from Moses or Christ? Jewish or Christian? Objections to Its Christian Character Answered. Memphis: Southern Baptist Book House, 1891.

Editor. *The Little Iron Wheel: A Declaration of Christian Rights and Articles, Showing the Despotism of Episcopal Methodism*. Nashville: South-Western Publishing House; Graves, Marks and Company, 1856.

The Lord's Supper: A Church Ordinance, and So Observed by the Apostolic Churches. 1881. Reprint, Texarkana, AR: Baptist Sunday School Committee, 1928 and 1968.

Editor. *The New Baptist Psalmist and Tune Book: For Churches and Sunday-Schools*. Memphis: Memphis Book and Stationery Company, 1873.

The New Great Iron Wheel: An Examination of the New M. E. Church South. Memphis: Baptist Book House, 1884.

Old Landmarkism: What Is It? 2nd ed. Memphis: Baptist Book House; Graves, Mahaffy & Company, 1881.

The Relation of Baptism to Salvation. Memphis: Baptist Book House, 1881.

Editor. *Trials and Sufferings for Religious Liberty in New England.* Nashville: Southwestern Publishing House, 1857.

Trilemma: All Human Churches without Baptism, or Death by Three Horns. 1860. 2nd ed. Memphis: Graves, Mahaffy and Co., 1881. Reprint, Memphis: J. R. Graves & Son, 1890.

What Is It to Eat and Drink Unworthily? The Symbolism of the Lord's Supper. Memphis: Baptist Book House, 1881.

The Work of Christ in the Covenant of Redemption; Developed in Seven Dispensations. 1883. Reprint, Texarkana, AR: Baptist Sunday School Committee, 1928 and 1963.

With John C. Burress. *A Discussion on the Doctrine of Endless Punishment between Rev. J. R. Graves and Rev. John C. Burress.* Atlanta: J. O. Perkins, 1880.

———. *Restorationism Refuted: The Last Letters of the Written Discussion between J. C. Burress and J. R. Graves.* Memphis: Baptist Book House, 1880.

With Jacob Ditzler. *The Graves-Ditzler: or, Great Carrollton Debate.* Memphis: Southern Baptist Publication Society, 1876.

Editor with J. M. Pendleton. *The Southern Psalmist.* Nashville: South-Western Publishing House; Graves, Marks & Company, 1859.

PUBLISHED ADDRESSES AND SERMONS BY GRAVES

The Desire of All Nations. Nashville: Tennessee Publication Society; Graves & Shankland, 1853.

Satan Dethroned and Other Sermons. Edited by Orren L. Hailey. New York: Fleming H. Revell, 1929.

Spiritism: A Lecture. Memphis: Southwestern Publishing Company, 1869.

The Watchman's Reply. Nashville: Tennessee Publication Society; Graves & Shankland, 1853.

OTHER BOOKS

Adlam, Samuel. *The First Baptist Church in America.* 2nd ed. Edited by J. R. Graves. 1887. Reprint, Texarkana, AR: Baptist Sunday School Committee, 1939.

Ahlstrom, Sydney E. *A Religious History of the American People.* New Haven, CT: Yale University Press, 1972.

Allen, William Fletcher. *Telling the Truth in Love: A Brief History of the "Baptist and Reflector" from 1835.* Edited by Lonnie Wilkey. Nashville: Fields Publishing, 2005.

Backus, Isaac. *A Discourse, Concerning the Materials, the Manner of Building, and Power of Organizing the Church of Christ.* Boston: John Boyles, 1773.

————. *A History of New England with Particular Reference to the Denomination of Christians Called Baptists*. 2 vols. 2nd ed. Newton, MA: Backus Historical Society, 1871.

————. *The Testimony of the Two Witnesses, Explained and Improved*. 2nd ed. Boston: Samuel Hall, 1793.

Baggett, James Alex. *So Great a Cloud of Witnesses: Union University, 1823–2000*. Jackson, TN: Union University Press, 2000.

Baker, Robert A. *The Southern Baptist Convention and Its People, 1607–1972*. Nashville: Broadman Press, 1974.

Barnes, William Wright. *The Southern Baptist Convention: A Study in the Development of Ecclesiology*. Fort Worth: By the author, 1934.

————. *The Southern Baptist Convention, 1845–1953*. Nashville: Broadman Press, 1954.

Basden, Paul A., ed. *Has Our Theology Changed? Southern Baptist Thought since 1845*. Nashville: B&H, 1994.

Bauman, Zygmunt. *Thinking Sociologically*. Oxford: Basil Blackwell, 1990.

Bebbington, David W. *Baptists through the Centuries: A History of a Global People*. Waco, TX: Baylor University Press, 2010.

Benedict, David. *A General History of the Baptist Denomination in America and Other Parts of the World*. New York: Lewis Colby and Company, 1848.

Blount, Douglas K., and Joseph D. Wooddell, eds. *The Baptist Faith and Message 2000: Critical Issues in America's Largest Protestant Denomination*. Lanham, MD: Rowman & Littlefield, 2007.

Bogard, Ben M. *Pillars of Orthodoxy, or Defenders of the Faith*. Louisville: Baptist Book Concern, 1900.

Bonar, Horatius. *Prophetical Landmarks: Containing Data for Helping to Determine the Question of Christ's Pre-millennial Advent*. 2nd ed. London: James Nisbet and Company, 1848.

Borum, Joseph Henry. *Biographical Sketches of Tennessee Baptist Ministers*. Memphis: Rogers & Co., 1880.

Brackney, William H. *Historical Dictionary of the Baptists*. Lanham, MD: Scarecrow Press, 1999.

Brand, Chad, and David Hankins. *One Sacred Effort: The Cooperative Program of Southern Baptists*. Nashville: B&H, 2006.

Breckenridge, Robert. *The Knowledge of God Objectively Considered*. New York: Robert Carter & Brothers, 1858.

Broadus, John A. *Baptist Confessions, Covenants, and Catechisms*. Edited by Timothy and Denise George. Nashville: B&H, 1996.

————. *Memoir of James Petigru Boyce*. New York: A. C. Armstrong and Son, 1893.

Brown, J. Newton. *Memorials of Baptist Martyrs: With a Preliminary Historical Essay*. Philadelphia: American Baptist Publication Society, 1854.

Brown, William, ed. *The Life of John Brown, With Select Writings.* Edinburgh: Banner of Truth Trust, 2004.

Brownlow, William G. *The Great Iron Wheel Examined; or, Its False Spokes Extracted, and an Exhibition of Elder Graves, Its Builder, in a Series of Chapters.* Nashville: For the author, 1856.

Burleson, Wade. *Hardball Religion: Feeling the Fury of Fundamentalism.* Macon, GA: Smyth & Helwys, 2009.

Burnett, J. J. *Tennessee's Pioneer Baptist Preachers.* Nashville: Marshall & Bruce Company, 1919.

Burton, Joe Wright. *Road to Augusta: R. B. C. Howell and the Formation of the Southern Baptist Convention.* Nashville: Broadman Press, 1976.

Capers, Gerald M. Jr. *The Biography of a River Town: Memphis: Its Heroic Age.* 2nd ed. New Orleans: By the author, 1966.

Carroll, J. M. *A History of Texas Baptists.* Dallas: Baptist Standard Publishing, 1923.

———. *The Trail of Blood.* Lexington, KY: American Baptist Publishing Company, 1931.

Cartwright, Peter. *Autobiography.* Nashville: Abingdon Press, 1956.

Cathcart, William, ed. *The Baptist Encyclopedia.* Philadelphia: L. H. Everts, 1881.

Caudill, R. Paul. *Intertwined: A History of First Baptist Church, Memphis, Tennessee.* Memphis: Riverside Press, 1989.

Cherok, Richard J. *Debating for God: Alexander Campbell's Challenge to Skepticism in Antebellum America.* Abilene, TX: ACU Press, 2008.

Christian, John T. *A History of the Baptists Together with Some Account of Their Principles and Practices.* 2 vols. Nashville: Broadman Press, 1922.

Conkin, Paul. *Cane Ridge: America's Pentecost.* Madison: University of Wisconsin Press, 1990.

Conkwright, S. J. *History of the Churches of Boone's Creek Baptist Association of Kentucky with a Brief History of the Association.* Winchester, KY: Boone's Creek Baptist Association, 1923.

Cooke, Ronald. *The Vatican-Jesuit-Global Conspiracy.* Hollidaysburg, PA: Manahath Press, 1985.

Coulter, E. Merton. *William G. Brownlow: Fighting Parson of the Southern Highlands.* 1937. Reprint, Knoxville: University of Tennessee Press, 1999.

Crawford, Charles W. *Yesterday's Memphis.* Miami: E. A. Seemann Publishing, 1976.

Crawford, T. P. *Churches to the Front!* China: By the author, 1892.

Crismon, Leo Taylor, ed. *Baptists in Kentucky: A Bicentennial Volume.* Middletown, KY: Kentucky Baptist Convention, 1975.

Crocker, Henry. *History of the Baptists in Vermont.* Bellows Falls, VT: P. H. Gobie Press, 1913.

Crosby, Molly Caldwell. *The American Plague: The Untold Story of Yellow Fever, the Epidemic That Shaped Our History.* New York: Berkley Publishing Group, 2007.

Crosby, Thomas. *The History of English Baptists, from the Reformation to the Beginning of the Reign of King George I.* 4 vols. London: n.p., 1738–40.

Davis, David Brion, ed. *The Fear of Conspiracy: Images of Un-American Subversion from the Revolution to the Present.* Ithaca, NY: Cornell University Press, 1971.

Dayton, A. C. *Emma Livingston, the Infidel's Daughter.* Nashville: Graves & Marks, 1859.

———. *Pedobaptist and Campbellite Immersions.* Nashville: South-Western Publishing House; Graves, Marks, & Co., 1858. Reprint, Louisville: Baptist Book Concern, 1903.

———. *Theodosia Ernest: Or, The Heroine of the Faith.* Nashville: Graves & Marks, 1856.

———. *Theodosia Ernest: Ten Days' Travel in Search of the Church.* Nashville: Graves & Marks, 1857.

Deweese, Charles W. *Freedom: The Key to Baptist Genius.* Brentwood, TN: Baptist History and Heritage Society, 2006.

Dockery, David S., ed. *Southern Baptist Identity: An Evangelical Denomination Faces the Future.* Wheaton, IL: Crossway, 2009.

———, ed. *Southern Baptists and American Evangelicals: The Conversation Continues.* Nashville: B&H, 1993.

Duesing, Jason G., Thomas White, and Malcolm B. Yarnell III, eds. *Upon This Rock: The Baptist Understanding of the Church.* Nashville: B&H Academic, 2010.

Early, Joseph E., Jr. *A Texas Baptist Power Struggle: The Hayden Controversy.* Denton: University of North Texas Press, 2005.

Edwards, Jonathan. *The Great Awakening.* The Works of Jonathan Edwards, vol. 4. Edited by C. C. Goen. New Haven: Yale University Press, 1972.

Estep, William R. *The Anabaptist Story.* Rev. ed. Grand Rapids: Eerdmans, 1975.

Fletcher, Jesse C. *The Southern Baptist Convention: A Sesquicentennial History.* Nashville: B&H, 1994.

Fuller, Andrew. *The Complete Works of the Rev. Andrew Fuller with a Memoir of His Life by Andrew Gunton Fuller.* Vol. 3. Edited by Joseph Belcher. Philadelphia: American Baptist Publication Society, 1845. Reprint, Harrisonburg, VA: Sprinkle, 1988.

Garrett, James Leo. *Baptist Theology: A Four-Century Study.* Macon, GA: Mercer University Press, 2009.

Gaustad, Edwin S., ed. *Baptist Piety: The Last Will and Testimony of Obadiah Holmes.* Tuscaloosa: University of Alabama Press, 2005.

George, Timothy, and David S. Dockery, eds. *Baptist Theologians.* Nashville: Broadman Press, 1990.

Goen, C. C. *Revivalism and Separatism in New England, 1740–1800.* New Haven, CT: Yale University Press, 1962.

Goodstein, Anita Shafer. *Nashville 1780–1860: From Frontier to City.* Gainesville: University of Florida Press, 1989.

Gourley, Bruce T. *A Capsule History of Baptists*. Atlanta: Baptist History and Heritage Society, 2010.

Grenz, Stanley J. *Isaac Backus—Puritan and Baptist: His Place in History, His Thought, and Their Implications for Modern Baptist Theology*. Macon, GA: Mercer University Press, 1983.

Hailey, O. L. *J. R. Graves: Life, Times and Teachings*. Nashville: By the author, 1929.

Harmon, Steven R. *Towards Baptist Catholicity: Essays on Tradition and the Baptist Vision*. Studies in Baptist History and Thought, vol. 27. Milton Keynes, UK: Paternoster, 2006.

Hatch, Nathan O. *The Democratization of American Christianity*. New Haven, CT: Yale University Press, 1989.

Hogg, Michael A. *The Social Psychology of Group Cohesiveness: From Attraction to Social Identity*. New York: New York University Press, 1992.

Howe, Daniel Walker. *What Hath God Wrought: The Transformation of America, 1815–1848*. The Oxford History of the United States. New York: Oxford University Press, 2007.

Howell, R. B. C. *The Cross*. Charleston, SC: Southern Baptist Publication Society, 1854.

———. *The Covenants*. Charleston, SC: SBPS, 1855.

———. *The Early Baptists of Virginia: An Address, Delivered in New York, Before the American Baptist Historical Society, May 10, 1856*. Philadelphia: American Baptist Historical Society, 1857.

———. *The Evils of Infant Baptism*. Charleston, SC: SBPS, 1852.

———. *The Terms of Sacramental Communion*. 2nd ed. Philadelphia: American Baptist Publication Society, 1846.

———. *The Way of Salvation*. Charleston, SC: SBPS, 1849.

Hudson, Winthrop S., ed. *Baptist Concepts of the Church: A Survey of the Historical and Theological Issues Which Have Produced Changes in Church Order*. Philadelphia: Judson Press, 1959.

Hughes, Richard T., and C. Leonard Allen. *Illusions of Innocence: Protestant Primitivism in America, 1630–1875*. Chicago: University of Chicago Press, 1988.

Jarrel, W. A. *Baptist Church Perpetuity: or, the Continuous Existence of Baptist Churches from the Apostolic to the Present Day Demonstrated by the Bible and by History*. Dallas: By the author, 1894.

Jeter, Jeremiah B. *Campbellism Examined*. New York: Sheldon, Lamport, & Blakeman, 1855.

Johnson, Robert G. *Historical Sketch of the North Springfield Baptist Church*. Ludlow, VT: Warner & Hyde, 1880.

Jones, William. *The History of the Christian Church: From the Birth of Christ to the Eighteenth Century, Including the Very Interesting Account of the Waldenses and Albigenses*. 2 vols. New York: Spencer H. Cone, 1824.

Kahlos, Maijastina. *Debate and Dialogue: Christian and Pagan Cultures c. 360–430*. Burlington, VT: Ashgate Publishing Company, 2007.

Kendall, W. Fred. *A History of the Tennessee Baptist Convention*. Brentwood, TN: Executive Board of the Tennessee Baptist Convention, 1974.

Leland, John. *Writings of the Late Elder John Leland*. Edited by Louise F. Greene. New York: G. W. Wood, 1845.

Leonard, Bill J. *Baptist Ways: A History*. Valley Forge, PA: Judson Press, 2003.

———. *Baptists in America*. Columbia Contemporary American Religion Series. New York: Columbia University Press, 2005.

———, ed. *Dictionary of Baptists in America*. Downers Grove, IL: InterVarsity Press, 1994.

Lord, David Nevins. *The Characteristic and Laws of Figurative Language*. New York: Franklin Knight, 1854.

Lumpkin, William L. *Baptist Foundations in the South: Tracing through the Separates and the Influences of the Great Awakening, 1754–1787*. Nashville: Broadman Press, 1961.

Magoon, E. L. *Republican Christianity; or True Liberty as Exhibited in the Life, Precepts and Early Disciples of the Great Redeemer*. Boston: Gould, Kendall, and Lincoln, 1849.

Mask, E. Jeffrey. *A Liberty under God: Toward a Baptist Ecclesiology*. Lanham, MD: University Press of America, 1997.

Masters, Frank M. *A History of Baptists in Kentucky*. Louisville: Kentucky Baptist Historical Society, 1953.

May, Lynn E., Jr. *The First Baptist Church of Nashville, Tennessee, 1820–1970*. Nashville: First Baptist Church, Nashville, 1970.

McBeth, H. Leon. *The Baptist Heritage: Four Centuries of Baptist Witness*. Nashville: Broadman Press, 1987.

———. *A Sourcebook for Baptist Heritage*. Nashville: Broadman Press, 1990.

McCall, Duke K., ed./comp. *What Is the Church? A Symposium of Baptist Thought*. Nashville: Broadman Press, 1958.

McDougall, Walter A. *Throes of Democracy: The American Civil War Era, 1829–1877*. New York: HarperCollins, 2008.

McGinn, Bernard. *Antichrist: Two Thousand Years of the Human Fascination with Evil*. San Francisco: HarperSanFrancisco, 1994.

McGoldrick, James Edward. *Baptist Successionism: A Critical Question in Baptist History*. ATLA Monograph Series, No. 32. Metuchen, NJ: Scarecrow Press, 1994.

McLoughlin, William G. *Isaac Backus and the American Pietistic Tradition*. Boston: Little, Brown and Company, 1967.

———. *New England Dissent, 1630–1883: The Baptists and the Separation of Church and State*. 2 vols. Cambridge: Harvard University Press, 1971.

———. *Soul Liberty: The Baptists' Struggle in New England, 1630–1833*. Hanover, NH: University Press of New England, for Brown University Press, 1991.

Mell, Patrick Hues. *Baptism in Its Mode and Subjects.* Charleston, SC: Southern Baptist Publication Society, 1853.

———. *Corrective Church Discipline.* Charleston, SC: SBPS, 1860.

Miyakawa, T. Scott. *Protestants and Pioneers: Individualism and Conformity on the American Frontier.* Chicago: University of Chicago Press, 1964.

Morgan, David T. *The New Crusades, the New Holy Land: Conflict in the Southern Baptist Convention, 1969–1991.* Tuscaloosa: University of Alabama Press, 1996.

Noll, Mark A. *America's God: From Jonathan Edwards to Abraham Lincoln.* New York: Oxford University Press, 2002.

Norman, R. Stanton. *More Than Just a Name: Preserving Our Baptist Identity.* Nashville: B&H, 2001.

Orchard, G. H. *A Concise History of Baptists from the Time of Christ Their Founder to the 18th Century.* Nashville: Graves & Marks, 1855. Reprint, Lexington, KY: Ashland Avenue Baptist Church, 1956.

Patterson, James A. *To All the World: A History of Mid-America Baptist Theological Seminary, 1972–1997.* Memphis: Disciple Press, 1997.

Patterson, W. Morgan. *Baptist Successionism: A Critical View.* Valley Forge, PA: Judson Press, 1969.

Pendleton, J. M. *Church Manual, Designed for the Use of Baptist Churches.* Philadelphia: American Baptist Publication Society, 1867.

———. *An Old Landmark Re-set.* Nashville: Graves & Marks, 1854.

———. *Reminiscences of a Long Life.* Louisville: Baptist Book Concern, 1891.

Pinson, William M., Jr. *Issues Testing Baptist Polity.* Brentwood, TN: Baptist History and Heritage Society, 2003.

Ray, D. B. *Baptist Succession: A Handbook of Baptist History.* Cincinnati: G. E. Stevens & Co., 1870.

Robinson, Robert. *Ecclesiastical Researches.* Cambridge, UK: Francis Hodson, 1792. Reprint, Gallatin, TN: Church History Research and Archives, 1984.

Roberds, Israel. *The Convert's Guide to First Principles or Evangelical Truth Sustained by the United Testimony of Our Lord Jesus Christ, the Holy Apostles, and Our Pedobaptist Brethren.* New Haven, CT: William Storer, 1838.

Rogers, P. G. *The Fifth Monarchy Men.* London: Oxford University Press, 1966.

Ross, Bob L. *Old Landmarkism and the Baptists: An Examination of the Theories of "Church Authority" and "Church Succession."* Pasadena, TX: Pilgrim Publications, 1979.

Rowe, David L. *God's Strange Work: William Miller and the End of the World.* Grand Rapids: Eerdmans, 2008.

Rushing, Wanda. *Memphis and the Paradox of Place: Globalization in the American South.* Chapel Hill: University of North Carolina Press, 2009.

Sandeen, Ernest R. *The Roots of Fundamentalism: British and American Millenarianism, 1880–1930.* Chicago: University of Chicago Press, 1970. Reprint, Grand Rapids: Baker, 1978.

Sandoz, Ellis. *Republicanism, Religion, and the Soul of America.* Columbia: University of Missouri Press, 2006.

Schlesinger, Arthur M., Jr. *The Age of Jackson.* Boston: Little, Brown and Company, 1945.

Schreiner, Thomas R., and Matthew R. Crawford, eds. *The Lord's Supper: Remembering and Proclaiming Christ until He Comes.* NAC Studies in Bible and Theology Series, vol. 10. Nashville: B&H Academic, 2010.

Seiss, Joseph A. *The Last Times and the Great Consummation: An Earnest Discussion of Momentous Themes.* Philadelphia: Smith, English, and Co., 1870.

Shurden, Walter B. *The Baptist Identity: Four Fragile Freedoms.* Macon, GA: Smyth & Helwys, 1993.

———. *Not a Silent People: Controversies That Have Shaped Southern Baptists.* Nashville: Broadman Press, 1972.

Slatton, James H. *W. H. Whitsitt: The Man and the Controversy.* Macon, GA: Mercer University Press, 2009.

Smith, Christopher (with Michael Emerson et al.). *American Evangelicalism: Embattled and Thriving.* Chicago: University of Chicago Press, 1998.

Smith, John Abernathy. *Cross and Flame: Two Centuries of United Methodism in Middle Tennessee.* Nashville: Commission on Archives and History of the Tennessee Conference, United Methodist Church, 1984.

Spencer, John Henderson. *A History of Kentucky Baptists.* 2 vols. Cincinnati: J. R. Baumes, 1885.

Spittlehouse, John, and John More. *A Vindication of the Continued Succession of the Primitive Church of Jesus Christ (Now Scandalously Termed Anabaptists) from the Apostles unto This Present Time.* London: Printed by Gartrude Dawson, 1652.

Stone, Jon R. *On the Boundaries of American Evangelicalism: The Postwar Evangelical Coalition.* New York: St. Martin's Press, 1997.

Sutton, Jerry. *The Baptist Reformation: The Conservative Resurgence in the Southern Baptist Convention.* Nashville: B&H, 2000.

Tull, James E. *High-Church Baptists in the South: The Origin, Nature, and Influence of Landmarkism.* Rev. ed. Edited by Morris Ashcraft. Macon, GA: Mercer University Press, 2000.

———. *Shapers of Baptist Thought.* Valley Forge, PA: Judson Press, 1972.

Utzinger, J. Michael. *Yet Saints Their Watch Are Keeping: Fundamentalists, Modernists, and the Development of Evangelical Ecclesiology, 1887–1937.* Macon, GA: Mercer University Press, 2006.

Verkruyse, Peter Allan. *Prophet, Pastor, and Patriarch: The Rhetorical Leadership of Alexander Campbell.* Tuscaloosa: University of Alabama Press, 2005.

Waller, John L., and G. H. Orchard. *Baptists But the "Two Witnesses."* Nashville: South-Western Publishing House; Graves, Marks, & Co., 1857.

Wardin, Albert W., Jr. *Tennessee Baptists: A Comprehensive History, 1779–1999.* Brentwood, TN: Executive Board of the Tennessee Baptist Convention, 1999.

———. *The Twelve Baptist Tribes in the USA: A Historical and Statistical Analysis.* Atlanta: Baptist History and Heritage Society; and Nashville: Fields Publishing, 2007.

Watson, Samuel. *The Clock Struck One, and Christian Spiritualist.* New York: Samuel R. Wells, 1872.

Wayland, Francis. *Notes on the Principles and Practices of Baptist Churches.* New York: Sheldon, Blakeman, & Company; and Boston: Gould & Lincoln, 1857.

———. *Thoughts on the Missionary Organizations of the Baptist Denomination.* New York: Sheldon, Blakeman, & Company, 1859.

White, Thomas, Jason G. Duesing, and Malcolm B. Yarnell III, eds. *Restoring Integrity in Baptist Churches.* Grand Rapids: Kregel, 2008.

Whitsitt, William H. *A Question in Baptist History: Whether the Anabaptists in England Practiced Immersion before the Year 1641?* Louisville: C. T. Dearing, 1896.

Wigger, John H. *Taking Heaven by Storm: Methodism and the Rise of Popular Christianity in America.* Religion in America Series. New York: Oxford University Press, 1998.

Williams, Alvin Peter. *Campbellism Exposed, in Examination of Lard's Review of Jeter.* Memphis: Graves & Mahaffy, 1866.

Williams, Michael E., Sr. *Isaac Taylor Tichenor: The Creation of the Baptist New South.* Tuscaloosa: University of Alabama Press, 2005.

———, and Walter B. Shurden. *Turning Points in Baptist History: A Festschrift in Honor of Harry Leon McBeth.* Macon, GA: Mercer University Press, 2008.

Wills, Gregory A. *Democratic Religion: Freedom, Authority, and Church Discipline in the Baptist South, 1785–1900.* New York: Oxford University Press, 1997.

———. *Southern Baptist Theological Seminary, 1859–2009.* New York: Oxford University Press, 2009.

Woolley, Davis C., ed. *Encyclopedia of Southern Baptists.* Vols. 1–2. Nashville: Broadman Press, 1958.

Worrell, A. S. *Review of Corrective Church Discipline.* Nashville: South-Western Publishing House, 1860.

ARTICLES/CHAPTERS

Alford, Deann. "Tongues Tied: Southern Baptists Bar New Missions Candidates from Glossolalia." *Christianity Today*, February 2006, 21.

Baker, Robert A. "Factors Encouraging the Rise of Landmarkism." *Baptist History and Heritage* 10 (January 1975): 1–2, 18.

James Robinson Graves

Bottum, Joseph. "The Judgment of Memory." *First Things*, March 2008, 28–36.

Bowden, Geoffrey C. "Piety and Property: Locke and the Development of American Protestantism." *Christian Scholar's Review* 37 (Spring 2008): 273–87.

Briggs, Edward C. "Landmark Views of the Church in the Writings of J. M. Pendleton, A. C. Dayton, and J. R. Graves." *Quarterly Review* 35 (April–May–June 1975): 47–57.

Bugg, Charles B. "The Whitsitt Controversy: Implications for Southern Baptists." *Quarterly Review* 35 (April–May–June 1975): 70–77.

Burch, Jarrett. "A Tennessee Baptist Returns to Georgia: The Latter Life of A. C. Dayton." *Tennessee Baptist History* 7 (Fall 2005): 19–28.

"Burleson Resigns as IMB Trustee." *Baptist & Reflector*, February 6, 2008, 2.

Camp, Ken. "Historians Debate Reasons for the Rise of Landmarkism in 19th Century." *Baptist Standard*, January 12, 2009, 11.

Compton, Bob. "J. M. Pendleton: A Nineteenth-Century Baptist Statesman (1811–1891)." *Baptist History and Heritage* 10 (January 1975): 28–35, 56.

Davis, Jimmy H. "Union University: Over 175 Years of Christian Education," Parts I–II. *Tennessee Baptist History* 4 (Fall 2002): 45–56; and 5 (Fall 2003): 35–51.

Drinkard, Joel F., Jr. "Boundary Markers." *Biblical Illustrator* 34 (Summer 2008): 47–49.

Early, Joe, Jr. "The Cotton Grove Resolutions." *Tennessee Baptist History* 7 (Fall 2005): 41–52.

———. "Landmarkism: Tennessee Baptists' Influence on Texas Baptists." *Tennessee Baptist History* 5 (Fall 2003): 57–66.

———. "Tennessee Baptists and the Civil War." *Tennessee Baptist History* 8 (Fall 2006): 7–24.

Fletcher, Jesse C. "Shapers of the Southern Baptist Spirit." *Baptist History and Heritage* 30 (July 1995): 6–15.

Ford, Samuel H. "Life, Times and Teachings of J. R. Graves." *Ford's Christian Repository and Home Circle*, October 1899, 606–16; November 1899, 670–79; December 1899, 741–49; January 1900, 39–48; February 1900, 100–105; March 1900, 162–69; April 1900, 225–33; May 1900, 287–90; June 1900, 349–55; July 1900, 425–27; August 1900, 487–93; and September 1900, 556–59.

Garrett, James Leo, Jr. "The Distinctive Identity of Southern Baptists vis-à-vis Other Baptists." *Baptist History and Heritage* 31 (October 1996): 6–16.

George, Timothy. "Southern Baptist Ghosts." *First Things*, May 1999, 18–24.

Grice, Homer L. "Robert Boyté Crawford Howell: Denominational Statesman." *Baptist History and Heritage* 3 (July 1968): 94–98, 124. Reprint, *Tennessee Baptist History* 3 (Fall 2001): 58–62.

Hall, Chad W. "When Orphans Became Heirs: J. R. Graves and the Landmark Baptists." *Baptist History & Heritage* 38 (Winter 2002): 112–27.

Harper, Louis Keith. "Old Landmarkism: A Historiographical Appraisal." *Baptist History and Heritage* 25 (April 1990): 31–40.

Holifield, E. Brooks. "Theology as Entertainment: Oral Debate in American Religion." *Church History* 67 (September 1998): 499–520.

Horn, Sara. "Union Dedicates History Book; Traces Roots." *Baptist & Reflector*, February 21, 2001, 4.

Leonard, Bill J. "Communidades Ecclesiales de Base and Autonomous Local Churches: Catholic Liberationists Meet Baptist Landmarkers." In *Poverty and Ecclesiology: Nineteenth-Century Evangelicals in the Light of Liberation Theology.* Edited by Anthony L. Dunnavant. Collegeville, MN: Liturgical Press, 1992, 68–89.

———. "Whose Story, Which Story? Memory and Identity among Baptists in the South." In *History and the Christian Historian.* Edited by Ronald A. Wells. Grand Rapids: Eerdmans, 1998, 124–36.

McBeth, H. Leon. "Cooperation and Crisis as Shapers of Southern Baptist Identity." *Baptist History and Heritage* 30 (July 1995): 35–44.

———. "The Texas Tradition: A Study in Baptist Regionalism," Parts I–II. *Baptist History and Heritage* 26 (January 1991): 37–57.

Meigs, James Thomas. "The Whitsitt Controversy." *Quarterly Review* (January-February-March 1971): 41–61.

Moore, LeRoy. "Crazy Quilt: Southern Baptist Patterns of the Church." *Foundations* 20 (January-March 1977): 12–35.

Myers, Ken. "Contours of Culture." *Touchstone* 23 (July/August 2010): 10–11.

Noll, Mark. "America's Two Foundings." *First Things*, December 2007, 29–34.

Patterson, James A. "Changing Images of the Beast: Apocalyptic Conspiracy Theories in American History." *Journal of the Evangelical Theological Society* 31 (December 1988): 443–52.

———. "The J. R. Graves Synthesis: American Individualism and Landmarkist Ecclesiology." *Tennessee Baptist History* 7 (Fall 2005): 9–18.

———. "James Robinson Graves: History in the Service of Ecclesiology." *Baptist History & Heritage* 44 (Winter 2009): 72–83.

Patterson, W. Morgan. "The Development of the Baptist Successionist Formula." *Foundations* 5 (October 1962): 331–45.

———. "The Influence of Landmarkism among Baptists." *Baptist History and Heritage* 10 (January 1975): 44–55.

———. "The Southern Baptist Theologian as Controversialist: A Contrast." *Baptist History and Heritage* 15 (July 1980): 7–14.

Pratt, J. Kristian. "From 'Funnymentalist' to Friend: The Evolving Relationship of Ben M. Bogard and J. Frank Norris." *Baptist History & Heritage* 42 (Spring 2007): 105–13.

Rolater, Fred. "The Local Origins of Landmarkism: First Baptist, Nashville; Concord Baptist Association; and Union University and the Definitive Controversy among Southern Baptists." *Tennessee Baptist History* 12 (Fall 2010): 75–92.

Ross, Bobby, Jr. "Challenging Individualism: N.C. Proposal Raises Age-Old Questions of Baptist Identity." *Christianity Today*, November 2010, 16.

Saunders, Davis L. "The Relation of Landmarkism to Mission Methods." *Quarterly Review* 26 (April–May–June 1966): 43–57.

Shepardson, Christine. "Defining the Boundaries of Orthodoxy: Eunomius in the Anti-Jewish Polemic of His Cappadocian Opponents." *Church History: Studies in Christianity and Culture* 76 (December 2007): 699–723.

Shurden, Walter B. "The Southern Baptist Synthesis: Is It Cracking?" *Baptist History and Heritage* 16 (April 1981): 2–11.

Smith, Harold S. "The Life and Work of J. R. Graves (1820–1893)." *Baptist History and Heritage* 10 (January 1975): 19–27, 55–56.

Stetzer, Ed. "Life in These Old Bones: If You Are Interested in Doing Mission, There Could Hardly Be a Better Tool Than Denominations." *Christianity Today*, June 2010, 24–29.

Taulman, James E. "Baptism and Lord's Supper: As Viewed by J. M. Pendleton, A. C. Dayton, and J. R. Graves." *Quarterly Review* 35 (April–May–June 1975): 58–69.

———. "The Life and Writings of Amos Cooper Dayton (1813–1865)." *Baptist History and Heritage* 10 (January 1975): 36–43.

Tull, James E. "The Landmark Movement: An Historical and Theological Appraisal." *Baptist History and Heritage* 10 (January 1975): 3–18.

Walker, Ken. "Critic Censured: Trustee Suspended from Trustee Board for Airing Closed-Door Activities." *Christianity Today*, January 2008, 18–19.

Wamble, Hugh. "Landmarkism: Doctrinaire Ecclesiology among Baptists." *Church History* 33 (December 1964): 429–47.

Wardin, Albert W., Jr. "The Tie That Binds: The Struggle for Baptist Unity in Tennessee." *Tennessee Baptist History* 1 (Fall 1999): 8–12.

Williams, Michael D. "Where's the Church? The Church as the Unfinished Business of Dispensational Theology." *Grace Theological Journal* 10 (Fall 1989): 165–82.

THESES AND DISSERTATIONS

Alexander-Payne, Dawn Leslie. "Alexander Campbell and the Dilemma of Republican Millennialism." Ph.D. diss., Texas Christian University, 2009.

Balik, Shelby M. "The Religious Frontier: Church, State, and Settlement in Northern New England, 1780–1830." Ph.D. diss., University of Wisconsin, 2006.

Barber, Christopher Bart. "The Bogard Schism: An Arkansas Agrarian Revolt." Ph.D. diss., Southwestern Baptist Theological Seminary, 2006.

Beck, Rosalie. "The Whitsitt Controversy: A Denomination in Crisis." Ph.D. diss., Baylor University, 1984.

Bell, Marty G. "James Robinson Graves and the Rhetoric of Demagogy: Primitivism and Democracy in Old Landmarkism." Ph.D. diss., Vanderbilt University, 1990.

Bodiford, Carl Wayne. "The Process of Denominational Cohesion within the Southern Baptist Convention, 1845–1927." Ph.D. diss., Texas Christian University, 1998.

Bone, Michael Henry. "A Study of the Writings of J. R. Graves (1820–1893) as an Example of the Nature and Function of Absolutes in Religious Symbol Systems." Ph.D. diss., Boston University, 2001.

Boyles, Daniel Jay. "Isaac Backus and His Ecclesial Thought." Ph.D. diss., Southwestern Baptist Theological Seminary, 2002.

Bryan, Philip R. "An Analysis of the Ecclesiology of Associational Baptists, 1900–1950." Ph.D. diss., Baylor University, 1973.

Bugg, Charles Basil. "The Whitsitt Controversy: A Study in Denominational Conflict." Th.D. diss., Southern Baptist Theological Seminary, 1972.

Cantwell, Emmett H. "Millennial Teachings among Major Southern Baptist Theologians from 1845 to 1945." Th.M. thesis, Southwestern Baptist Theological Seminary, 1960.

Carroll, Raymond Evans. "Dimensions of Individualism in Southern Baptist Thought." Th.D. diss., New Orleans Baptist Theological Seminary, 1995.

Creed, John Bradley. "John Leland, American Prophet of Religious Individualism." Ph.D. diss., Southwestern Baptist Theological Seminary, 1986.

Crook, Roger H. "The Ethical Emphases of the Editors of Baptist Journals Published in the Southeastern Region of the United States up to 1865." Th.D. diss., Southern Baptist Theological Seminary, 1947.

Cureton, Donald Alan. "The Historiography of Baptist Origins in Selected Southern Baptist Historians: William Heth Whitsitt, John Tyler Christian, and Albert Henry Newman." Ph.D. diss., Mid-America Baptist Theological Seminary, 1998.

Dain, Michael Andrew. "The Development of the Primitive Impulse in American Baptist Life, 1707–1842." Ph.D. diss., Southwestern Baptist Theological Seminary, 2001.

Dobbins, Gaines S. "Southern Baptist Journalism." Th.D. diss., Southern Baptist Theological Seminary, 1914.

Durden, John Allen. "A Selected Issue in Southern Baptist Ecclesiology: The Nature of the Church as Reflected in the Baptist Faith and Messages of 1925 and 1963." Th.D. diss., Mid-America Baptist Theological Seminary, 1993.

Early, Joseph E., Jr. "The Hayden Controversy: A Detailed Examination of the First Major Internal Altercation of the Baptist General Convention of Texas." Ph.D. diss., Southwestern Baptist Theological Seminary, 2002.

English, Carl D. "The Ethical Emphases of the Editors of Baptist Journals in the Southeastern Region of the United States from 1865–1915." Th.D. diss., Southern Baptist Theological Seminary, 1948.

Fry, Russell Raymond. "Theological Principles of Isaac Backus and the Move from Congregationalism to Baptist Leadership in New England." Ph.D. diss., Drew University, 1988.

Halbrooks, Guy Thomas. "Francis Wayland: Contributor to Baptist Concepts of Church Order." Ph.D. diss., Emory University, 1971.

Harper, Louis Keith. "The Historical Context for the Rise of Old Landmarkism." M.A. thesis, Murray State University, 1986.

Heidelberg, Roger. "Landmarkism and Southern Baptists." B.L.S. thesis, Memphis State University, 1986.

Hester, Malcolm O. "Millennialism in Southern Baptist Thought since 1900." Ph.D. diss., Southern Baptist Theological Seminary, 1981.

Hill, James Emmett. "James Madison Pendleton's Theology of Baptism." Th.M. thesis, Southern Baptist Theological Seminary, 1958.

Hilton, James Esmond. "Robert Boyté Crawford Howell's Contribution to Baptist Ecclesiology: Nineteenth-Century Ecclesiology in Controversy." Ph.D. diss., Southeastern Baptist Theological Seminary, 2005.

Hogue, LeRoy Benjamin. "A Study of the Antecedents of Landmarkism." Th.D. diss., Southwestern Baptist Theological Seminary, 1966.

Holt, Gregory Steven. "The Influence of Alexander Campbell on the Life and Work of J. R. Graves, the Founder of the Landmark Baptist Movement." M.Div. thesis, Emmanuel School of Religion, 1993.

Horne, Linwood Tyler. "A Study of the Life and Work of R. B. C. Howell." Th.D. diss., Southern Baptist Theological Seminary, 1958.

Houghton, Myron James. "The Place of Baptism in the Theology of James Robinson Graves." Th.D. diss., Dallas Theological Seminary, 1971.

Howe, Danny Eugene. "An Analysis of Dispensationalism and Its Implications for the Theologies of James Robinson Graves, John Franklyn Norris, and Wallie Amos Criswell." Ph.D. diss., Southwestern Baptist Theological Seminary, 1988.

Huddleston, William C. "James Madison Pendleton: A Critical Biography." Th.M. thesis, Southern Baptist Theological Seminary, 1962.

Jones, Barry William. "James R. Graves, Baptist Newspaper Editor: Catalyst for Religious Controversy, 1846–1893." Ph.D. diss., Ohio University, 1994.

King, Joe Madison. "John Tyler Christian: A Study of His Life and Work." Th.D. diss., New Orleans Baptist Theological Seminary, 1953.

Lambert, Byron Cecil. "The Rise of the Anti-mission Baptists: Sources and Leaders, 1800–1840 (A Study in Religious Individualism)." Ph.D. diss., University of Chicago, 1957.

Lamkin, Adrian, Jr. "The Gospel Mission Movement within the Southern Baptist Convention." Ph.D. diss., Southern Baptist Theological Seminary, 1980.

Lane, William Thomas. "A Baptist Doctrine of Ordination Studied in the Confessional Tradition, the Works of J. R. Graves and R. B. C. Howell and Actual Practice in Kentucky." Th.D. diss., Southern Baptist Theological Seminary, 1958.

Lanier, Andrew Herman, Jr. "The Relationship of the Ecclesiology of John Lightfoot Waller to Early Landmarkism." Th.M. thesis, Southeastern Baptist Theological Seminary, 1963.

Martin, William Terry. "Samuel Henderson and His Responses to J. R. Graves and Landmarkism through South Western Baptist, 1857–1859." M.A. thesis, Samford University, 1977.

Mays, Livingston T. "A History of Old Landmarkism." Th.D. diss., Southern Baptist Theological Seminary, 1900.

Moore, David O. "The Landmark Baptists and Their Attack upon the Southern Baptist Convention Historically Analyzed." Th.D. diss., Southern Baptist Theological Seminary, 1949.

Moore, Eugene Tillman. "The Background of the Landmark Movement." Th.M. thesis, Southwestern Baptist Theological Seminary, 1947.

Patterson, Thomas Armour. "The Theology of J. R. Graves and Its Influence on Southern Baptist Life." Th.D. diss., Southwestern Baptist Theological Seminary, 1944.

Pratt, J. Kristian. "A Landmark Baptist's Ecclesiology: Ben Bogard and Local Church Protectionism." Ph.D. diss., Baylor University, 2005.

Renault, James O. "The Development of Separate Baptist Ecclesiology in the South, 1755–1976." Ph.D. diss., Southern Baptist Theological Seminary, 1978.

Smith, Harold Stewart. "A Critical Analysis of the Theology of J. R. Graves." Th.D. diss., Southern Baptist Theological Seminary, 1966.

Smith, Larry Douglas. "The Historiography of the Origins of Anti-Missionism Examined in Light of Kentucky Baptist History." Ph.D. diss., Southern Baptist Theological Seminary, 1982.

Spain, Rufus Bain. "R. B. C. Howell, Tennessee Baptist (1801–1868)." M.A. thesis, Vanderbilt University, 1948.

Stookey, Stephen Martin. "The Impact of Landmarkism upon Southern Baptist Western Geographical Expansion." Ph.D. diss., Southwestern Baptist Theological Seminary, 1994.

Stripling, Paul W. "Attitudes Reflected in the Editorials of J. R. Graves, 1848–1851." Th.M. thesis, Southwestern Baptist Theological Seminary, 1965.

Sumerlin, Claude W. "A History of Southern Baptist State Newspapers." Ph.D. diss., University of Missouri, 1968.

Taulman, James E. "Amos Cooper Dayton: A Critical Biography." Th.M. thesis, Southern Baptist Theological Seminary, 1965.

Thomas, Frank Hopkins, Jr. "The Development of Denominational Consciousness in Baptist Historical Writings, 1738 to 1886." Ph.D. diss., Southern Baptist Theological Seminary, 1975.

Tull, James E. "A Study of Southern Baptist Landmarkism in the Light of Historical Baptist Ecclesiology." Ph.D. diss., Columbia University, 1960.

Turner, Helen Lee. "Fundamentalism in the Southern Baptist Convention: The Crystallization of a Millennialist Vision." Ph.D. diss., University of Virginia, 1990.

Vaughn, Carol Ann. "'Living in the Lives of Men': A Southern Baptist Woman's Missionary Journey from Alabama to Shandong, 1830–1909." Ph.D. diss., Auburn University, 1998.

Weatherford, Kenneth Vaughn. "The Graves-Howell Controversy." Ph.D. diss., Baylor University, 1991.

White, Thomas. "James Madison Pendleton and His Contributions to Baptist Ecclesiology." Ph.D. diss., Southeastern Baptist Theological Seminary, 2005.

Wren, Charles Michael, Jr. "R. B. C. Howell and the Theological Foundation for Baptist Participation in the Benevolent Empire." Ph.D. diss., Southern Baptist Theological Seminary, 2007.

MISCELLANEOUS UNPUBLISHED SOURCES

Harrison, Rodney. "The Dead End Trail: J. M. Carroll and the Trail of Blood and Its Impact upon Church Planting." Paper presented at the annual meeting of the Evangelical Theological Society, Washington, D.C., November 16, 2006.

Howell, R. B. C. *A Memorial of the First Baptist Church, Nashville, Tennessee: From 1820 to 1863.* 2 vols. Nashville: First Baptist Church, 1863 (typescript from original longhand).

Inman, W. G. *Planting and Progress of the Baptist Cause in Tennessee.* Edited by Orren L. Hailey. Includes Hailey's *History of the Baptists of Tennessee*, a revision of Inman's work. Unpublished manuscript at the Southern Baptist Historical Library and Archives, Nashville, TN.

ELECTRONIC SOURCES

Akin, Danny. "Myth #7." *Between the Times*, accessed October 26, 2009, http://betweenthetimes .com archives.

Ascol, Tom. "What Will We Be in the SBC?" *Founders' Ministries Blog*, February 19, 2009, accessed February 20, 2009, http://www.founders.org/blog/2009/02/what-will-we-be-in-sbc .html.

Baker, Doug. "Interview with Between the Times, Part III." Insight podcast downloaded from http://www.ncbaptist.org (accessed September 19, 2008).

"Baptist Historians Affirm Individual Conscience." Associated Baptist Press, September 28, 2010, accessed September 28, 2010, http://www.abpnews.com/content/view/5738/53.

"Beating the Bounds," accessed April 14, 2008, http://www.bbc.co.uk/dna/h2g2/A805871.

"Beating the Cholesbury Bounds," accessed April 14, 2008, http://www.cholesbury.com/beat bounds.htm.

"BMA-SBTC Ministry Agreement Proposed," accessed October 13, 2010, *Baptist Press*, October 13, 2010. http://bpnews.net/bpnews.asp?ID=33860.

"Boundary Maintenance!" accessed June 3, 2008, http://modwestoutreach.org/ blogs/72/boundary-maintenance.

Bridges, Erich. "IMB Holds to Baptism, Prayer Guidelines." *Baptist Press*, May 10, 2007, accessed May 11, 2007, http://bpnews.net/bpnews.asp?ID=25616.

Brister, Timmy. "The Backstory to the Great Commission Resurgence." *Provocations and Pantings*, June 17, 2009, accessed June 17, 2009, http://timmybrister.com/2009/06/17/the-back-story -to-the-great-commission-resurgence.

Brown, Vicki. "IMB Retooling to Focus Agency on Local-Church Mission Work." Associated Baptist Press, September 23, 2008, accessed September 23, 2008, http://www.abpnews.com /content/view/3535/53.

Bryan Station Baptist Church, Lexington, KY. Email to author, August 23, 2006.

Burleson, Wade. "Baptist Identity and Ad Hominem Variants." Grace and Truth to You, April 29, 2008, accessed June 5, 2008, http://kerussocharis.blogspot.com/2008/04/baptist-identity -and-conservational.html.

"Doctrinal Statement of the American Baptist Association," accessed January 24, 2011, http:// www.abaptist.org/general.html.

"Doctrinal Statement of the BMAA," accessed January 24, 2011, http://www.discipleguide.org /pages/page.asp?page_id=40172.

Duvall, James R. "The Successionism View of Baptist History." *Journal of Baptist Studies* 3 (2009): 3–15, accessed August 8, 2010, http://baptiststudiesonline.com/276/.

"Education Briefs: Southwestern Seminary Marks 'Radical Reformation Day.'" *Baptist Press*, January 22, 2009, accessed January 22, 2009, http://www.bpnews.net/bpnews.asp?ID=29714.

Finn, Nathan. "Baptism as a Prerequisite to the Lord's Supper." Center for Theological Research, Southwestern Baptist Theological Seminary. http://www.baptisttheology.org.

———. "Baptist Identities and the Current State of the SBC." *Author Blog*, September 21, 2007, accessed September 21, 2007, http://nathanafinn.wordpress.com.

———. "The IMB Imbroglio and Historical Irony." *Author Blog*, March 26, 2007, accessed March 26, 2007, https://nathanafinn.wordpress.com.

———. "With Whom Can My Church Cooperate?" *Between the Times*, January 22, 2010, accessed January 25, 2010, http://betweenthetimes.com//2010/01/22/with-whom-can-my -church-cooperate.

Graves, J. R. "To the Patrons of the Tennessee Baptist." *Florence Gazette*, March 26, 1862, accessed November 19, 2010, http://freepages.genealogy.rootsweb.ancestry.com/~henle/Baptist /GravesLetter.htm.

"History of Chester," accessed March 18, 2008, http://www.chester.govoffice.com.

Hoge, Dean. "Who Is a Good Catholic? Boundaries of Catholicism." First draft of paper, accessed February 4, 2008, http://hirr.hartsem.edu/bookshelf/CathHartford.doc.

———. Email to author, March 24, 2008.

Kelly, Mark. "New Era of Cooperation Anticipated Following Historic Meetings in Germany." *Baptist Press*, June 26, 2008, accessed June 26, 2008, http://www.bpnews.net/bpnews .asp?ID=28371.

Lee, Wendy. "Rankin Seeks Global Insights at Lausanne." *Baptist Press*, October 21, 2010, accessed October 21, 2010, http://www.bpnews.net/bpnews.asp?ID=33917.

Manning, Michelle (of Ashland Avenue Baptist Church, Lexington, Kentucky). Email to author, August 22, 2006.

"Parish Maps: The Parish Boundary," accessed April 14, 2008, http://www.england-in-particular .info/parishmaps/m-boundary.html.

Rankin, Jerry. "Giving Churches Ownership." *Author Blog*, April 8, 2010, accessed April 14, 2010, http://rankinconnecting.com/2010/04/giving-churches-ownership.

Roach, David. "END TIMES: Scholars Differ on What Bible Says about Subject." *Baptist Press*, December 30, 2009, accessed January 1, 2010, http://www.bpnews.net/bpnews.asp?ID=31963.

"Toward a Great Commission Resurgence." GCR Site, February 10, 2009, accessed April 27, 2009, http://www.greatcommissionresurgence.com.

Warren, Charlie. "Ark. Messengers Reject Amendment." *Baptist Press*, November 9, 2007, accessed November 9, 2007, http://bpnews.net/bpnews.asp?ID=26800.

Wax, Trevin. "The Case for Open Communion." *Kingdom People*, October 11, 2007, accessed January 11, 2011, http://trevinwax.com/2007/10/11/the-case-for-open-communion.

Yarnell, Malcolm. "Baptist Identity or Evangelical Anonymity? Part II." *Peter Lumpkins's Blog*, April 27, 2008, accessed June 5, 2008, http://peterlumpkins.typepad.com/peter_lumpkins /2008/04/Baptist-ident-1.html.

Name Index

Subject Index

A

alien immersion 26, 29, 37, 38, 45–49, 53–55, 57–58, 77, 103, 109, 116–17, 171, 174, 193, 200
American Baptist Association 194
American Baptist Missionary Union 150
American Baptist Publication Society 17–19, 103, 106–7, 134, 214, 216–17, 219
Anabaptist(s) 15, 50, 105–6, 108, 112, 117, 122, 201
anti-Catholicism 15, 60–61, 64, 100, 121
anti-missionism 17, 24, 36, 74, 97
Arkansas Baptist State Convention ix, 193
Arminianism 13, 24, 80–81, 83

B

baptism 10, 17–18, 24–25, 38, 47–49, 52, 54, 57, 63, 66, 68–71, 77, 79–80, 94, 103, 109, 131, 169, 171–72, 174, 206–7, 209
baptismal regeneration 24, 77–78, 80, 95
baptisms 71
Baptist Book House 165
Baptist Faith and Message (1925) 18, 195
Baptist Faith and Message (1963) 18, 195
Baptist General Association of Middle Tennessee and North Alabama 78
Baptist General Association of Tennessee 39, 135, 144, 149
Baptist General Association of Tennessee and North Alabama 135, 144–45, 149
Baptist General Convention of Texas ix, 192, 225
Baptist identity 3–5, 15, 20–21, 28–29, 34, 40, 48, 52, 57–58, 73, 119–22, 125, 131, 148, 170, 174, 188–89, 191, 199, 201–3
Baptist Missionary Association of America ix, 194
Baptist Missionary Association of Texas 192, 194

Baptists identity 13
Baptist State Convention of Mississippi 144, 147, 153
Belmont University xiv, 5, 87, 198
Bible Board 56, 133–34, 137–39, 143, 149, 151
boundary, boundaries iv, vii, 1–5, 15, 21, 25–27, 34, 37, 44–45, 48, 51, 53, 55, 58–59, 69, 76, 79, 97–98, 100, 112, 121, 123–25, 130–31, 154–56, 165, 168–70, 174–75, 177, 181, 184, 189, 200, 203

C

Calvinism 9, 11, 14, 24, 66–68, 79–81, 83
Campbellism, Campbellites 24–26, 28–29, 34, 36, 49, 54, 57, 59–60, 68, 70, 72–80, 93, 114, 125, 140, 169, 171, 212, 216–17
Carroll, B. H. 191–92
centralism 17, 20–21, 95, 97, 103, 150, 190, 193, 195–96
Christian Science 168
Civil War 12, 34, 42, 53, 56, 58, 61, 83, 87, 91, 100, 134–35, 155, 158–60, 163–64, 168, 170, 173–74, 176–79
Clarke, John 13, 113, 115
close communion, intercommunion 171–74
closed communion 15, 171–74, 201, 206
Concord Baptist Association 135, 145, 150, 153, 172
Confederacy 56, 140, 156–57
Congregational, Congregationalism 9–10, 13–16, 59, 66
Congregationalist(s) 9, 11, 13, 16, 37, 59–60
Cooperative Program 195–97, 214
Cotton Grove Resolutions 49, 51–53, 68, 73, 81–82, 97, 129

D

Darby, John Nelson 180–82
direct missions 20, 74, 150, 152, 190–91, 195, 202, 210

235

dispensationalism 5, 64, 67, 70, 119, 167, 174, 176, 178–84, 198–99

E

Eaton, T. T. 191
evangelicalism 3, 14, 62, 86, 88, 175, 199, 201–2

F

First Baptist Church, Memphis 159–60, 166, 186–87
First Baptist Church, Memphis, 160, 173
First Baptist Church, Nashville 9, 28, 33–39, 44, 86, 99, 123–32, 134, 137, 140–44, 146, 148, 150–54, 157, 163, 171, 192, 205
First Baptist Church, Newport 113–15
First Baptist Church, Providence 113–15
Foreign Mission Board ix, 20, 95, 128, 131, 151–52, 181, 190–91, 195, 200
fundamentalism 98, 175, 193, 197–99

G

General Baptist(s) 13
Georgetown College 85–86
Gospel Mission Association 191, 194–95
Graves, Georgia 163
Graves in Kentucky 22, 24–29, 34–36, 60, 73–74, 140
Graves in Ohio 22, 24, 27–29, 35
Graves, Lois 9–10, 37, 161–62
Graves, Louise 41, 161–62
Graves, Lua 28, 31, 34–35, 38, 41, 50, 79, 126
Graves, Luella 41
Graves, Z. C. 7, 9–10, 22, 28, 38, 185–86
Great Commission Resurgence ix, 202

H

Hailey, Nora Graves 162, 186
Hayden, Samuel 192
high church 65, 68–69
Home Mission Board ix, 159, 195

I

immersion 9–10, 15, 17, 24, 26, 28–29, 37–38, 45–49, 53–55, 57–58, 68, 72–74, 77, 103, 109, 112, 114–17, 129, 171, 174, 191, 193, 200–201, 205–8
individualism 17, 20–21, 85–90, 92–100, 203

infant baptism 9, 13, 37, 48, 60, 62, 70, 72, 77, 79, 94, 105, 108, 206–7
International Mission Board ix, 200
invisible church 68

J

Jackson, Andrew 31–32
J. R. Graves Chair of Logic and Moral Philosophy 186
J. R. Graves Society for Religious Inquiry xii, 185

L

Landmarkism vii, xi–xiii, 3–5, 8–9, 12, 14–15, 17–22, 25–26, 29, 33, 36–38, 40, 42–43, 45, 48–49, 51–53, 55–58, 60, 62, 65–74, 76, 78–80, 82, 85–87, 89–90, 93–95, 97–100, 102–4, 107–12, 114–25, 127–30, 132–33, 135–56, 158, 160, 163–78, 180–87, 189–203, 208
Leland, Aaron 11, 15–16
local church, localism 13–22, 24, 26, 28, 34, 36, 38, 46, 48, 74, 90, 94–99, 103–4, 116, 120, 130–31, 142, 144, 146–48, 150, 154, 171–74, 183, 190, 192–94, 196, 199, 202, 206, 208
Lord's Supper, communion 11–12, 15, 17–18, 25, 28, 37, 45–46, 52, 55–57, 62, 94, 103, 109, 131, 133, 171–74, 193, 201, 205–6, 209

M

Memphis 4, 64, 135, 159–61, 163–67, 170, 180, 184, 187, 189, 197, 205
mesmerism 167, 169–70
Methodist(s) 8, 15, 32, 33–34, 38, 50, 52, 54, 59–60, 66–68, 73, 75, 79–84, 95–96, 99, 117, 128, 140, 160, 164, 166, 169
Mid-America Baptist Theological Seminary xi, xii, 106, 195, 197
middle life 167
Midwestern Baptist Theological Seminary ii, 102
millennialism 88, 121, 175
Mount Freedom Baptist Church 23–26

N

Nashville xiv–xv, 26, 29, 31–32, 34–35, 39–40, 44, 54, 56, 58–59, 64, 66–67, 73,